BIG CATS
LOOSE IN BRITAIN

MARCUS MATTHEWS

Edited by Jonathan Downes and Graham Inglis
Typeset by Jonathan Downes, Mark North, and Corinna James
Cover and internal layout by Mark North for CFZ Communications
Using Microsoft Word 2000, Microsoft , Publisher 2000, Adobe Photoshop.

First edition published 2007 CFZ Press

CFZ PRESS
Myrtle Cottage
Woolfardisworthy
Bideford
North Devon
EX39 5QR

ISBN: 978-1-905723-12-6

Dedicated to:
My Mother,
with love.

CONTENTS

PART ONE

ACKNOWLEDGEMENTS

My special thanks are due to all the witnesses, farmers, and officials of zoos and wildlife parks who have written to me, giving much useful information on Big cats. Thanks are due particularly to the people of North Devon and the Surrey/Hampshire general public, who have sent me so many letters. There are many whom I wish to thank individually, but unfortunately the space at my disposal is limited.

However, special mention and thanks must go to the following:

Mr. Trevor Beer, for his generosity in help and encouragement on the Exmoor Beasts.
Mr. Nigel Brierly, for an abundance of help on the Exmoor Beasts.
Mr. George E. Frampton, for photocopying much material from his book on Big cats.
Mr. Paul Sieveking, for help with obtaining copies of the *Fortean Times*.
Mr. Chris Hall, for help on the `Surrey Puma`.
Dr Karl Shuker, for information on the Kellas cats.
Di Francis, for pioneering the way for British Big cat hunting.

For quotations from books and newspapers, I wish to acknowledge the following:

· Mr. Paul Screeton of *Folklore Frontiers*, for some quotations from that magazine.
· Mr. Michael Williams, for quotations from three Bossiney Books: *Folklore and Superstitions, Devon Mysteries* and Westcountry *Mysteries*.
· The *South Wales Evening Post* for help in obtaining articles, and for allowing me to quote from them.
· The *Fortean Times* for permitting me to use material on mystery cats in my book.
· The *Glamorgan Gazette*, for allowing me to quote from articles in that paper, written by Joan Isacs.
· The 'News' Group in Surrey and Hampshire, for permitting me to quote from articles in their papers.
· The *West Somerset Free Press*, for allowing me to quote articles from their paper.
· *The Isle of Wight County Press* for permission to use facts in their articles on the Isle of Wight big cat.
· The *North Devon Journal/Herald* for letting me quote from their articles on the Exmoor Beasts.
· Janet and Colin Bord for permission to quote from their excellent book '*Alien Animals'*, and for being so kind as to provide me with the 1966 picture of the `Surrey Puma`.
· The *Surrey Advertiser* for giving me permission to quote from articles on the `Surrey Puma`.
· *Nottingham Evening Post* for the use of articles.
· The *Western Morning News* for article quotes.
· The magazine *Northern Earth Mysteries* for quotations from a 1983 article called 'Wild in the Countryside' by Mr Paul Screeton.
· Many thanks to Rupert Bray, who gave up a week of his time to go and photograph one of the Exmoor Beasts, and also to take illustrations for this book.

There are undoubtedly plenty of people whom I have not mentioned here, but where witnesses have given permission for me to use their sightings, I have mentioned their names (unless otherwise stated). Many thanks to everybody who made this book possible by their efforts. Finally, on a lighter note, may the big cat survive for many more years, and provide us with more speculation and tracking.

EDITOR'S NOTE:

This book was originally written between 1987 and 1990, and has acquired a semi-legendary reputation. There are several contextual problems in the book; in the cases where we know that a person mentioned in the text has died - such as in the case of Joan Amos - we have said so, and where we felt it appropriate, have added footnotes. Otherwise we have left the text as it was. So, if you read that - for example - "Mr John Smith is the Publicity Director for such and such", you can take it as read that he was so in 1990, but that we offer no guarantees as to whether he is still there now, or even if he is still alive! It would have been more accurate to place all such statements into a past tense, but we felt that doing so - whilst undoubtedly correct - would destroy the conceptual integrity of what is - after all - a remarkable book. It is remarkable, not just because it provides the best collection yet of big cat sightings in the UK from historical times up to about 1990, but because most of it was written when the author was still at school. For, while his contemporaries were obsessing about Sonic the Hedgehog, or enduring the sulky pains of teenage angst, Marcus and his mother were tramping the highways and byways of our sceptered isle in search of the truth behind the stories of big cats loose in Britain.

On a personal level, this book was a joy to work with, because of the author's innocent and infectious enthusiasm, and also - possibly more importantly - because it provides a unique snapshot of a period of British cryptozoology which is otherwise uncovered in print. It was a time before many of the animosities which have so plagued British big cat research in recent years came to a head, and it was also a time when I - and the other main members of the CFZ Permanent Directorate - were much younger than we are now, and did what we did purely for fun. They were good days, and reading Marcus's book helped me relive them.

CFZ Press would like to thank Marcus and his family, Corinna James and Mark North for their hard work on this volume.

INTRODUCTION

The primary aim of this book is to provide the reader with as much data as possible on mystery cats existing in the British Isles. Its second aim is to provide a portrait of any other species which can be confused with big cat presence.

It is left to the reader to decide whether the cats loose in each region are escapees from zoos or menageries, exotic ex-pets, wildcat crossbreeds, or indigenous cats. Maybe some readers will even find the U.F.O. connection to be acceptable.
The evidence can be broken down into four main types:

1) Sightings
2) Photographic evidence
3) Historical evidence
4) Tracks and kills evidence

The fourth type includes remains of the cats' excrement, claw-marks on trees, etc. Taken in order of bulk, the largest amount of evidence comes from sightings, with historical and tracking evidence coming a joint second, and photographic evidence being placed last.

The first four chapters of this book deal with the actual speculation and theories behind the cat phenomenon, while providing the reader with a study of the behaviour of the already-known large mammals of Britain. If anyone should see or hear anything concerning big cats loose in Britain, the author would be grateful if they would write to him at Horseshoe Cottage, Crockerton, Warminster, Wiltshire. He will reply, refunding postage and any other costs.

Marcus J. G. Matthews
Wiltshire.

- Chapter One -
THE ORIGINS OF
BIG CATS LOOSE IN BRITAIN

The following pages outline the various theories regarding these big cats. Some of the theories are bizarre; others are more orthodox. You must choose for yourself which theory you prefer.

My Own Theory

I accept that in all probability there is some truth in all the theories, and that no single assumption can account for all the incidents related. However, I have my own views as to why some big cats have been seen in one particular area for so long.

I believe that when the Romans invaded Britain they brought with them black panthers and lions, and maybe even lynxes and tigers. As the Romans built cities, it is probable that each had its own circus, such as the *Circus Maximus*. Many early civilizations, the Babylonians, the Persians, the Egyptians and the Greeks, had kept big cats, either as exotic pets or as savage beasts. Possibly the Romans deliberately introduced big cats into Britain to frighten the British; using the animals as a means of dominating the natives and gaining another country for their massive empire. Alternatively, the circus cats could have been turned loose to harass the Britons when the Roman army withdrew in order to defend Rome, circa A.D. 410.

However, if in those days there were already indigenous big cats in Britain, it is plausible to imagine that some hybridisation took place, although this can only be guesswork. Anyway, if the cats were introduced by the Romans, maybe they survived through the Dark and Middle Ages, right up to the present day, while over the generations more modern exotic escapees might have added to the colonies, so that now we are left with an unusually large, tough breed of big cat loose in our somewhat suburban islands. To amplify the theory that the Romans introduced black panthers, one only has to look at the exploits of the black dogs, which haunt many lanes and woods up and down the countryside. Confusion over the identification of some big cats has occurred. For example, lionesses have been mistaken for pumas, or mountain lions and pumas for lionesses. It is interesting to note that the solitary, shy nature of the cats has led farmers sometimes into thinking that these sheep-killers are of supernatural origin.

Evidence to support the supposition that cats have been living here for a long time can be found in the first few pages of each chapter. In addition, travelling menageries have also let their big cats loose during the past four centuries, and these have contributed to the sightings. The 1976 Dangerous Animals Act has also added to the roaming colonies, for people turned their pets free in the past decade or so, for fear of being fined £400 or more through keeping an unlicensed big cat.

I am also sure that there may still be native lynxes in this country, as officially these animals were here up to about 25,000 years ago. The lynx has been in captivity in Britain since 1540. The ranges of sizes and colours suggest that more than one species is involved in the sightings. I believe that the following species could be in this country:

Tiger *(Panthera tigris)*
Lion *(P. leo)*
Panther (Black Leopard) *(P. pardus)*
Lynx *(Lynx lynx)*
Iberian lynx *(L. pardinus)*
Canadian Lynx *(L. canadensis)*
Bobcat *(L. rufus)*
Cheetah *(Acinonyx jubatus)*
British Indigenous Lynx (spp. unknown)
Caracal *(Caracal caracal)*
Puma *(Puma concolor)*
Feral domestic cat *(Felis catus)*
Scottish (Native) wildcat *(F. sylvestris grampia)*
Feral domestic cat/wildcat hybrid
Kellas cat

And also the Genet *(Genetta tigrina)* which is - of course – a viverrid, not a felid.

The British Big Cat Theory

Diana Francis, the well-known artist, author, journalist and naturalist, has the opinion that there may be an indigenous species of cat in Britain. In 1983 she produced the controversial book '*Cat Country - The Quest for the British Big Cat'*, in which she recounted many incidents and many speculations. Diana Francis is the pioneer of this most advanced theory, which proved too much for some learned scientists. She has proof that the cat species exists, through numerous plaster-casts and five photographs, as well as kills and many sightings.

She explains that the 'black dog' legends are the result of many sightings of black British big cats, and relates various cases from past years to explain that the species is native and unique to Britain. She believes it has a puma-like head, leopard-like body, and hand-like paws. Miss Francis had by 1987 spent about seven years camping out on Dartmoor, visiting Wales, as well as the Surrey-Hampshire border area, and going to the Isle of Wight at least three times, all with the intention of trailing these big cats.

According to Miss Francis, there are two types of British big cat: the Kellas cat, and the larger type, which can be black, striped, tawny, spotted or greyish in colour. The Kellas cats, which are long-legged, slim-built beasts and have been recorded mostly in Morayshire in Scotland, were first thought to be cubs of the British big cat, but later it was suggested that they belong to a totally different race, probably unknown to science. However, more recent evidence suggests a third theory; that they are complex introgressive hybrids of the domestic cat *(F. catus)* and the Scottish wildcat *(F. sylvestris grampia)*. Needless to say, the proponents of each theory disagree wildly, and the matter is no nearer to being proved than it was when the first specimen was obtained in 1984.

The existence of the British big cat has not yet been totally proven, as more evidence in the form of a captured specimen is needed. The existence of the British indigenous lynx could be proved, as in January 1987, three lynxes were shot dead in Inverness-shire, although at the present time I am still trying to obtain details concerning them.

The Extraterrestrial Theory

Janet and Colin Bord, Brinsley Le Poer Trench, Loren Coleman and other 'mystery cat' investigators have all suggested that U.F.Os might be transporting the cats from one place to another. There are three variations of this particular theory.

Firstly, the opinion of the late Brinsley Le Poer Trench, (1911-1995) in his 1974 book '*The Secret of the Ages*', is that the 'Infonauts' come from the inner earth, and that they bring a programmed puma from their own world to this, the upper surface, and let it out under cover of darkness; then they return to collect it again, under similar conditions. Men can already program dolphins, so maybe 'they' program pumas, using their advanced ideas; or perhaps they speak the pumas' language.

Secondly, a highly favoured theory, which has been suggested by Andy Roberts and also Janet and Colin Bord, is that the big cats, or pumas, are transported to Britain from, say, America, by such creatures as those that travel on board U.F.Os. Mystery cats often appear at the same time, and in a similar area, as U.F.Os are observed. Two examples of this are at Rossendale in Lancashire, and in 1964 at Crondahl in Hampshire. However, these two examples are isolated, and far from proved, so it would seem that this theory is 'on the shelf' for the time being. Since U.F.Os might come from other planets, they might bring their own fauna with them and let them out here, either to go on some sort of mission, or as a curiosity to make men believe in 'out-of-place' cats and then in the Ufonauts themselves. Another theory, suggested at the height of the Cold War was that Russians were manning U.F.Os and using big cats as part of their experiments. However, this has always seemed one of the most unlikely scenarios *ever* suggested, in a fortean community which is prone to suggesting such things.

The truth is that all these theories are very controversial and far-fetched, so they are unlikely to be believed. These theories depend on the definite probability that U.F.Os exist as physical objects. I am certain that they *do*, yet just what they may be I can only hazard a guess. Could they have some extra-terrestrial force behind them, or are they merely stealth aircraft? I do know that in Arthur Shuttlewood's excellent book *The Warminster Mystery* (1967), U.F.Os were claimed to be the cause of all the sightings of mysterious flying craft. Mr Shuttlewood particularly believed that sheep and cattle disappearances and reappearances, safe and sound, in the same field a few days later, were connected with the U.F.Os. These few incidents took place near Cley Hill, a National Trust-owned hill near to Warminster, and a hill well-known for its connection with ley lines. If 'Ufonauts' abducted livestock and people for short periods, maybe they also abducted big cats for their own use.

The late Mrs. Joan Amos was another person convinced that the cats are connected with U.F.Os. She lived in South Devon and was the coordinator of the Plymouth U.F.O. group. Fifteen ponies had been killed through an unknown agency on Dartmoor, in 1977. It has been suggested that U.F.Os could also be behind some of the savage killings, which we connect with mystery cats. big cats are very sensitive animals; always alert, and they would make a most useful tool for the use of a more intelligent source. Perhaps cats are most effective killers, but why would somebody or something want to use them to kill sheep and cattle? That, once again, is pure speculation. We must simply keep this theory 'up our sleeves', as it may explain some of the bizarre incidents involving mystery cats.

Giant Feral Cats

Mr Nigel Brierly, a retired biologist of Bishop's Nympton in North Devon, once believed that the Exmoor beasts were large feral domestic cats. He had some hairs analysed by a world expert on cats, and they turned out to belong to the domestic cat. These hairs were found in the carcass of an 'Exmoor Beast' victim, a sheep. Could a domestic cat have scavenged from the carcass? Since working for five years on the 'Exmoor Beasts', Mr Brierly has come to the conclusion that the ones around South Molton are a lynx and a puma running together, presumably ex-exotic pets or escapees.

Mr Brierly believed that very large domestic cats, black, black-and-white and tawny in colour, were responsible for all the sightings and kills. He suggested that they had evolved into their own race of cats with certain characteristics. As for some reason or other, people have sometimes confused panthers and pumas with large domestic cats, is it any wonder that large feral cats constitute another possible theory behind the 'mystery cat' saga?

Dr Maurice Burton, a distinguished naturalist and formerly in the Mammal Society, and author of many wildlife books, investigated the 'Surrey Puma' legend for two years, between 1964 and 1966. Dr Burton came to the conclusion that the big cats were merely large feral cats, dogs and other animals.

Feral cats are known to weigh up to thirty-three pounds, which comes to within about ten pounds of a small female puma. The possibility that feral cats have gained in size and weight may lie in the possibility that they hybridise with the ex-exotic pets and escaped pumas. Dr Karl Shuker, of whom we shall hear later, thinks this is rather unlikely, genetically. However, domestic and feral cats definitely *do* hybridise with Scottish wildcats.

Escapees or Abandoned Pets

Many of the cat researchers believe that the cat phenomenon has been caused by escaped felines from wild-life parks and through private owners letting their pets loose. In 1976 the Dangerous Animals Act was passed, forbidding people to keep big cats without a licence from their local council. Many people knew that they would not qualify for this licence, so they had three choices:

1)   to put their pet down
2)   to try to sell it to a licensed owner (probably a zoo)
3)   to keep the pet and attempt to hide it. For this, the owners could be fined up to £400

A fourth option was to release their pet and allow it to run wild in whatever part of the country they had left it. Mr Trevor Beer is sure that the 'Exmoor Beasts' are escapees of this nature, as well as abandoned exotic pets; he believes also that there are escapees from zoos. Most zoo or wildlife park escapees are normally caught within a few hours and reported to the police and the local people.
The following two stories are illustrative of the exotic pet culture prevalent before the Act was passed.

Sometime in the 1970s a London householder lost some of his valuables to a burglar and decided, as a preventive measure, to buy a tame pet lion. One day a man collecting for charity found a massive bulk hurtling towards him as he opened the garden gate, whereupon he ran off to the local police station. As a result, several policemen captured the animal and took it off to London Zoo.

The second story came from a famous hotel - the 'Dorchester' in Park Lane, London, and was told to me by Mrs. Brookes, a former flower-seller there. In the 1970s she often observed the actress, Miss Elizabeth Taylor, who had a luxury suite at the hotel and kept an ocelot. It was a beautiful spotted cat from South America, and much valued for its fur.

One day Miss Taylor and her then husband, actor Richard Burton, went on a cruising holiday for two weeks, leaving their adopted daughter in the suite. The staff was very anxious lest the ocelot should attack the girl during Miss Taylor's absence. However, they fed the animal on tinned red salmon, which kept it happy and contented, so nobody was hurt.

There are other theories about the mystery wild cats in addition to those already mentioned, but these will be dealt with in subsequent chapters.

Panthers or Black Leopards

The black panther is a melanistic form of leopard *(Panthera pardus)* and is often found in the same litter of cubs with normal spotted cubs. There are many black leopards in India, and only a few less in Africa. This animal was once thought to be a separate species from all other spotted leopards.

The panther is two to three feet at the shoulder, appears to have a dappled coat - black on black spots - in strong sunlight, and is up to eight feet long. It weighs anything from 80 to 220 pounds. On the whole panthers are stocky animals, with deep chests and powerful jaws. The two Persian leopards at Bristol Zoo are higher than a Great Dane dog.

Pumas

The puma *(Puma concolor)* has many names, such as cougar, mountain lion, catamount, panther, painter, deer tiger, and American lion. It can weigh anything from 35 kilograms to 100 kilograms, and be up to nine feet long. It stands at around 24 to 30 inches high. The puma is an arboreal animal, climbing trees very easily. It can leap 20 feet into the air and jump a 30-feet chasm.

Mrs. G. Armitage, a relation of mine living on an Ontario ranch in Canada, sent me some information on the Canadian puma:

> *"He is a very large pussy (about the size of an African lioness), with the same tawny-fawn colour; lovely thick, smooth fur. Lives out west at the foot of the Rocky Mountains. He can jump on a horse, cow or antelope, turn on a rocky ledge and kill. Also eats elk, mule and deer, and is hated and feared by ranchers for many years. Now protected. He is very beautiful, fierce and cunning."*

I understand that some South American ranchers have had to stop breeding horses because of the menacing puma. However, they are generally shy animals and are comparatively rare in the United States. As they have been hunted so much, the puma has had to retreat into the remoter regions of America.

Lynxes

The lynx is a medium-sized cat, found in both the old and the new world. It is a shy, elusive and fierce animal, and is nocturnal. The Canadian lynx (*Lynx Canadensis*) mainly eats snowshoe hares, while European lynxes *(Lynx lynx)* and *(Lynx pardinus)* have a more varied diet. They are still found in Northern Spain, and has been reintroduced into parts of France. There are even lynxes in parts of Northern Asia. Obviously, with such a wide distribution they differ from area to area, creating a number of sub-species.

The average lynx weighs about 50 lbs. They are around 18 inches to 2 feet high and 3 to 4 feet long. In Europe the lynx exists upon small deer, on sheep if times are hard, and also rodents and rabbits. The lynx's powerful eyesight is able to pick up moving prey from as far away as 3 kilometres, which has led to the expression 'lynx-eyed'.

The bob-cat *(Lynx rufus)* is also described by Mrs. Armitage of Canada, in a letter dated February 1987:

> *"Bob-cat - found in all provinces of Canada (in woods). About the size of a
> badger; wild, clever, fierce and beautiful. Not too many left, so now protected.
> Eats rabbits, mice, birds, hares etc. Climbs trees; most like a large pussy-cat."*

Her description sounds very like the type of cat I observed on the Mendip Hills in November 1986. The bob-cat has ear-tufts and a striped and spotted whitish face. His coat is a greyish-tawny colour, somewhat similar to the texture of an English rabbit's fur. His deep-set eyes give an impression of alertness even when he is half-asleep. Like all cats, it is very agile.

Tigers

The natural history of British cats on the loose would not be complete without mention of lions and tigers.

In appearance tigers *(P. tigris)* are the largest of all cats, attaining sizes of up to 16 feet in length, including the tail. They are yellow and golden in colour, with a set of black stripes on the back. They have light under-parts, sometimes with white gashes down their chests. Tigers are particularly savage towards their prey and to fellow felines. A tigress was recently filmed eating a leopard whom she had caught consuming her cubs. Tigresses are particularly protective towards their offspring. Tigers have also been known to swim into the middle of a river and to pull a man off a boat from which he was fishing.

The following quotation comes from the guide to an unnamed large safari park, which was sent to me by one of its staff:

> *'The tiger is the biggest of all the big cats. Those in the safari park are Bengal tigers.
> These are smaller than the Siberian, but still attain an average length of up to 3 me-
> tres. They weigh up to 225 kgs. The Bengal tiger is a fearsome predator. Its limbs*

are massive and powerful. It can reach speeds of up to 50 miles per hour over short distances. It also has retractable claws of 6.5cm and canine teeth which can be as long as 13cm. It has an acute sense of hearing, while the distinctive striped pattern of the coat provides it with excellent camouflage.

The tiger normally hunts by stealth, approaching as close as possible to the prey, unseen before striking, bringing the victim to the ground before killing it, usually by strangulation. The tiger will then drag its victim to a secluded spot before devouring it. Often the animal will make a kill only once every three or four days, but can eat up to 27 kgs of meat at one sitting. The tiger's menu is very varied. It has a preference for deer, antelope, wild boar and buffalo, but when desperate will eat anything, including carrion and reptiles. Tigers will only be found where there is a ready supply of prey, and where the surroundings afford plenty of shade and water...'

Lions

The lion *(Panthera leo)*, popularly known as 'King of the Beasts' has, like the tiger, acquired amazing notoriety as a man-eater. Lions are slightly smaller than tigers, but they have an incredible roar. Some hunt alone when they are very old, but on the whole they keep together in a 'pride' or family of up to twenty lions. The lioness tends to do most of the hunting, while the lion patrols his territory, leaving scent marks on the various posts and trees.

Lions are often seven feet six inches long, excluding tail. The males have a splendid mane, while lionesses are maneless. In their natural habitat lions hunt zebra, antelope, buffalo and many other species of game. Lion cubs are born after 3 months' gestation. The litters vary from three to six cubs. They are blind, defenceless and dependent on the lioness for as long as eighteen months. Lions live up to twenty-five years in captivity, but rarely live longer than ten to fifteen years in the wild.

The Natural History of Big Cats

It is vital to look at the natural history of the three main species of cats loose in this country.

The general diet of a large cat in Britain is varied and interesting, consisting as it does of birds, mammals, reptiles and fish. On some occasions, rabbits, hares and game-birds such as partridges and pheasants, would form part of the beast's diet. Carrion such as crows, rooks and other scavengers feed upon is unlikely to be touched, bearing in mind the fussy nature of the cat family. Nevertheless, carrion might be taken in the winter by a hungry cat; evidence suggests that some types of cat, such as leopards, will return to feed upon their kills, but only in the event that the cat cannot easily catch other prey.

Larger animals such as fallow (*Dama dama*) or roe deer (*Capreolus capreolus*) are known to be taken from time to time. Indeed, it has been suggested that one puma-like beast in the Margam Forest in Wales thrives upon a large herd of park deer. Other places such as Exmoor have been the scene of the mass slaughter of red deer, possibly by a black panther-type cat. Domestic animals have also suffered through the agency of big cats, which, as we shall see, have consumed hens, ducks and geese. On Dartmoor a number of chickens disappeared overnight, and a black panther- type beast was seen skulking nearby. Poultry has also been taken in Scotland. It is claimed that there have been many sheep killed by big cats.

How the Big Cat Catches its Prey

The manner in which the cat catches its prey depends on the type of cat and the size of the prey. For instance, leopards and panthers spend up to three-quarters of an hour in stalking, and then pounce on the victim's back. Should the animal, such as a gazelle, be in its customary group, the lone leopard has to use all its skills even to attack the prey. On the other hand, cheetahs can easily outrun and catch a wide variety of prey. It is not, however, suited for climbing trees; unlike the puma of the Americas, which can easily ascend a tree and kill a monkey. Most of the big cats we are dealing with are arboreal, one exception being the lion, which is capable of climbing only to a height of thirty feet. The tiger is also not a particularly good climber, on account of its heavy weight.

big cats sometimes eat each other. Lions are particularly fond of eating leopard cubs, and this leads to frightening scenes, where the cubs cling for safety at the top of a tree and the lion furiously loiters around at the base of it. Points worth noting about the three main species of cats loose in Britain are the ways in which they kill. The lynx sometimes jumps down on its prey, and this is usually done from a tree or rocky ledge. Pumas occasionally follow the same procedure, but leopards are said normally to attack their prey - excepting man and some other prey - from ground-level.

Age

Leopards can live up to twenty-three years in captivity; lions live longer than ten years in the wild, although they can live up to twenty years in captivity. Pumas have survived as long as twenty-five years in a Wildlife Park, although they rarely survive much longer than twelve to fifteen years. Lynx can survive up to twenty-five years, while some domestic cats have continued to have kittens at the age of thirty-five!

Colours

The colours of cats vary according to the terrain in which they live. Leopards living on the African savanna tend to be of the normal spotted variety, while leopards in Asia are often darker or melanistic panthers. Generally speaking, cats have coats that maintain their camouflage and warmth.

Sizes

The average size of an adult puma or leopard is comparable to a large Alsatian or sizeable Labrador dog. The world record for a massive black tiger in India was said to be 20 feet long, although this figure was based only on local accounts. As that particular tiger was never shot, its length could never be proved. Some animals increase in size through the intake of certain vitamins in their diet. Size, therefore, depends largely on the cat's food, and on the type of country it inhabits.

Black Panther *(P. pardus)*

Eurasian lynx *(L. lynx)*

Puma *(P. concolor)*

EDITOR'S NOTE: The puma is also known as the cougar, and the mountain lion. These names are all used in
this book, and refer to the same creature..

- Chapter Two -
CANIDS

Sheep-killing Dogs

An estimated 10,000 farm animals are being slaughtered every year by roaming dogs. The most prominent victims of these attacks are poultry and sheep, and we are particularly concerned with the latter. Dogs are turned out of their suburban homes, or disappear on an afternoon walk. Some of these vagrants return home after a few hours, while others are lost and become totally wild.

There can be no doubt that people are sometimes mistaken, thinking in the first place that the animal they saw was a dog, whereas later they realise that it was a big cat. In areas where big cats have been present, feral dogs are by no means rare. Large dogs such as Alsatians and Great Danes are highly adaptable and in groups of two or three can attack large rams. Wild dogs behave very similarly to wolves. Farmers call upon the help of police and the R.S.P.C.A. if a dog proves to be a sheep-worrier. In such a case, farmers have the right to shoot the offender.

Warning signs are on display at various farm gates and woodland path entrances, insisting that people keep their dogs under control, and a failure to do so will entail stiff penalties. It is also illegal to purposely turn a dog on livestock. The best advice is: keep your dogs under control, and if you should lose a dog, immediately report its loss to the police, the R.S.P.C.A. and, if possible, the local farmers. The dogs that 'go wild' are very often extremely cunning, and some live as long as ten years on the loose. A pack of whippets could do a great deal of damage to pheasants and smaller mammals. Take, for example, the following case of two golden retrievers that chased deer near to my home, in the mid 1980s. Two girls riding through Longleat Woods informed me that two dogs was each chasing a separate roe-deer. The dogs' owners soon came along with two collies - on leads this time. The owners questioned the girls as to where the dogs were, but they did not need to wait long, as the dogs 'gave tongue' while chasing the deer. It is to be hoped that the dogs were caught before they had done any harm.

Other 'killers', which might be confused with big cats, are poachers' dogs, such as lurchers. When lost in the field, lurchers are extremely difficult to catch and can live for years, hiding in copses by day and attacking deer, sheep and wild prey at night. Today, when a poacher can make up to £3,000 in one night, efficient killing is essential. Lurcher dogs, cross-bows and nets all make a poacher a silent shikari.

Foxes

Foxes take lambs and poultry, but only 5% of foxes are said to take the latter. These predators are able to kill similarly to dogs; attacking a lamb at the hind legs, then at the rear-end. On Dartmoor, foxes are known to hunt in packs. My relation, Mr R. Savoury, a farmer, told me:

> '... lambs born in April are often taken by packs of foxes in October or November.' These

packs normally consist of vixen and dog foxes, or sometimes vixens and cubs. The foxes on Dartmoor are also reputed to eat lambs as they are being dropped by a helpless ewe. One fox will distract the ewe at her head, while the other fox will eat the lamb'.

There is a larger type of fox to be found in Northern England, in Wales and also in parts of Scotland. It somewhat resembles the Canadian coyote or brush-wolf. Maybe the remaining eighteenth century wolves bred with foxes and dogs, which might explain the wolf-hunts at the turn of the century. We shall be looking at these hunts later.

The fox weighs anything from 12 to 20 lbs. It consumes beetles, frogs and various small rodents such as mice and rats. It is also known to feed upon carrion, and in the cities it scavenges from dust-bins and waste tips.

In the wild, a fox is generally daring in the face of man, and is an opportunist, raiding hen-houses and returning each evening to fetch his supper. It is probably the look in the fox's eyes that has led to it being considered cunning, and in turn this cunning has led to it being hunted.

Some of the supposed big cat sightings seem to have been of red foxes, which are observed by the local people or by a passing motorist for a brief moment, immediately to be dubbed a puma. It must be noted that foxes have brush tails and long, pointed snouts, which should prevent their being confused with large cats. Foxes also have narrow pad-marks, with four toes, with the front claws very close together.

Badgers

The following information is culled from a project that I did on badgers in 1986. The badger is a member of the musk-bearing carnivores called mustelids. An adult male - a boar - weighs 11.5 kg, and is about 75cm long. The body is wedge-shaped, and is supported by four short, but very strong legs. Badgers can lift a stone of 25 kg to obtain food from underneath. The female - the sow - is slightly smaller and lighter than the male. A badger's sense of hearing is acute, but its sight is poor, and the cubs are very short-sighted. Smell is the badger's most important sense. It has an oversized nasal chamber in its skull to help in this direction.

Mating can take place between January and October, but normally occurs between February and May. Badgers mainly eat earthworms, rodents, young rabbits and hedgehogs, also insects, birds and dead mammals. In addition they eat ash fruit and cereals, along with acorns and small fruits, while occasionally poultry is consumed.

Many badgers were killed each year by the use of cyanide powder (HCN) through the Ministry of Agriculture's fear that badgers might be carrying bovine tuberculosis. However, thanks to a public outcry, badgers are once more broadly protected.

Mink

Mink *(Mustela vison)* are river-dwelling, weasel-like carnivores which escaped from captivity when being used on fur-farms from 1929, through the 1930s. At a distance they could easily be mistaken for a dark-coloured feral domestic cat, or an otter. Minks are native to North America, but they are now so common in Britain that you can hardly believe that they are an introduced species. (EDITOR'S NOTE: There is a European species, *Mustela lutreols*, but they were not kept as fur-bearing animals, and, therefore - to our knowledge – they have never become established in the UK. It is interesting to note, however, that they are endangered throughout much of their former range). Mink, an unwelcome pest, are known to kill young lambs, but since all the otter hunts were turned over to mink-hunting in 1978, the mink's numbers should be kept down. Despite this, mink are still on the increase. They can be any size from 1 to 2 feet long, including the tail.

They live on fish and thus are an unwelcome guest at fish farms, where they cause considerable depredations. These animals are so vicious that some mothers were worried that their babies might be attacked in their prams by a particularly savage mink. One lady actually found a mink in her bathroom, cornered it, and let her young brother shoot it with his air-gun!

One naturalist thought the 'Harrogate panther' might have been a feral mink.

Otters

The otter is another animal whose fish-kills and possibly appearance might be confused with that of a big cat. It is a beautiful, sleek creature, with a dark brown, waterproof coat and small ears. Its tail acts as a rudder when it is in the water.

Wolves

The News of February 1976 quoted the following story from the *Illustrated London News* of 14th June 1879. The author was one 'M. J.'

> 'Captain Sir Allen Young's pet Esquimau dog was either stolen or wandered from the Arctic ship "Pandora" as she lay in Southampton harbour after returning from the polar regions. Quite a panic arose in that part of Hampshire where this most valuable and harmless animal was wandering about, and every sort of story was circulated of the ravages and dangers the country was subject to. The people began to think their sheep, pigs and children were in danger; some said it was a gigantic black fox, others said it was a Canadian wolf. Expeditions were organised to attack it, and after being chased for some miles by people on horseback, it was ultimately shot and exhibited at sixpence a head in Winchester market place. There could be no doubt about the dog's identity, for Sir Allen Young afterwards got back his skin.'

A few years later there was another similar scare, this time with a real wolf *(Canis lupus)*. A letter dated 25th December 1987 from Mr Ted Beverley (former Superintendent-in-Chief of Skegness police) reads:

> '... Whilst I was a village policeman at Messingham, near Scunthorpe, in 1958, I was reliably informed that the last wild roaming wolves were shot on Messingham Common very early in this century. As a coincidence, my Chief Constable, Mr John Bar-

nett, shot and killed the last wolf in this country. He was Chief Constable of Leeds at the time and the wolf had escaped from a local zoo.'

Another story that was most interesting was that of some wolf hunts in the nineteenth and early twentieth centuries, in Scotland and Northern England. I take the story from *Living Wonders* by John Michell and Robert J.M. Rickard. They summarise some wolf scares which phenomenon-investigator Charles Fort chronicled in his book, *Lo!*

On looking through Northumberland newspaper files, Mr Fort, an American, found that in October 1904, a wolf cub escaped from the custody of Bains, of Shotley Bridge, near Newcastle.

There were numerous strange happenings going on at this time, and soon there were mass sheep-killings at Hexham in December 1904. A massive hunt was organised - something like the "Exmoor Beasts" hunt of Spring 1983. The papers stated that when the search failed, the local farmers called upon Monarch, a very skilled blood-dog, and an Indian big-game hunter, as well as an Hungarian wolf-hunter, all of whom failed to catch the mystery predator. However, a dead otter was found on a railway line, and kills around Hexham ceased.

Thirty miles away, on 29th December 1904, 'a magnificent specimen of male grey wolf' was found dead at Cumwhinton, near Carlisle. It was 5 feet long and 30 inches high approximately at the shoulder. Captain Bains examined the dead animal and stated that it was not his wolf. However, evidence suggests that he was lying, possibly because he did not want to pay up insurance for the farmers' sheep. Captain Bains told the 'Hexham Herald' of the 15th October 1904 that his wolf cub was only 4 months old and not capable of killing a sheep. The farmers who had formed the wolf committee stated that they would accept his judgement.

The wolf was photographed for post-cards and named 'The Allendale Wolf killed on the railway near Carlisle, 19th December 1904.' An American, Captain Thompson of Washington State, saw the wolf's head at a taxidermist's shop in Derby. He stated that it was a malmut's head. These animals are a type of husky. Then rumours suggested that a malmut had escaped from a Liverpool exhibition, though this was never proved.

In April 1986, about half-a-dozen wolves escaped from Colchester Zoo. The following article is quoted from the *Daily Telegraph* of April 1985:

> *'Wolves were no risk, says Zoo. Colchester Zoo officials denied yesterday that five wolves which had escaped on Tuesday night had posed any threat to people in the area. Mr D.A. Tropanti, director, said that all were now back in their pen and denied reports that the five had been shot. Only two of the Canadian timber-wolves had escaped from the Zoo. One returned by itself during the night and the other was recaptured by staff yesterday.'*

'The story had begun on a wet Tuesday morning, when the wolves burrowed under their enclosure fence. The number of wolves reported to have escaped differed. Some papers said seven had escaped, while others gave the number as five; yet again others thought six had absconded from the Colchester Zoo.

Police toured the area around the Zoo, advising people - particularly children - to stay indoors. More reports came in - one said that only two wolves had actually left the Zoo, three being recaptured on Zoo premises, while others claimed that the wolves were shot by police marksmen. This rumour arose through residents seeing armed police and Zoo staff milling around.

The lone wolf who had actually left the zoo area was seen loping across an orchard, but it eventually decided to return to the Zoo, where he was captured and returned to his compound. The confusion, which surrounded this 'mass' escape, could possibly have resulted in one or two wolves being unaccounted for, although it did not.

The last British wolf was shot in Morayland in Scotland, in 1743. Who actually shot the animal is something of a mystery. One version says that a Mr McQueen, one of the Laird of Macintosh's shooting party, brought back the mask (head) of the huge black wolf just as the party was preparing to go out and hunt the wolf. In Ireland, the last wolves were killed in 1797, in County Sligo.

Mary Chipperfield had heard that 'wolves were shot in different places' then, but she gives no more details in her book *Lions on the Lawn*.

A wolf is a dangerous animal, as records show. It looks like a larger and greyer version of an Alsatian or German shepherd dog. Wolves have pricked ears, and also like to hunt in packs. Coyotes, or brushwolves *(Canis latrans)*, from North America, are known to interbreed with dogs. Canadian timber-wolves are probably also capable of interbreeding with domestic dogs, if we believe the famous Jack London novel *Call of the Wild*.

Howling is any wolf's characteristic, while its profile could be compared to that of a red fox, to which it is closely related. And as a last word on this subject, at the time of writing, there could be up to ten wolves on the loose in this country.

Wildcats and Feral-cats

• Wildcats: Habitats

The wildcat lives in Scotland; although it used to inhabit parts of England; there are none in Ireland. It prefers areas such as woods and moors.

(EDITOR'S NOTE: The Scottish subspecies of the European Wildcat is *Felis sylvestris grampia*, - one of 18 subspecies -and as Jonathan Downes has shown in *Smaller Mystery Carnivores of the Westcountry* published by CFZ Press, the English populations had died out before the Scottish population was classified. Therefore, although one assumes that the extinct English wildcats were also *F. s.grampia*, we cannot be certain).

- ## Wildcats: Habits

At the outset, the title of this book was to be 'Wildcats, feral-cats and stranger creatures in Britain'. I must therefore pay tribute to the best-known member of the cat tribe in Britain: the 'Scottish' wildcat (*Felis sylvestris grampia*). At one time wildcats were found all over Britain and Europe. However, earlier this century continual hunting reduced their numbers, though the tough fighters survived in the Highlands, where they live elusive and nocturnal lives.

Wildcats are hunters, and some of the toughest cats in the world; dangerous if cornered, and when a man comes upon a wildcat's den, the animal growls. If that does not deter the man, then the animal attacks with its sharp claws.

- ## Wildcats: Distribution and Numbers

Due to cross-breeding with domestic cats and to the changing of the wildcat's breeding season, these animals have become more common. The true wildcat's season for breeding is March to August, when normally kittens are born in an impregnable den where they live for the first few weeks of their lives. At six or eight weeks old, the wildcat moves the kittens to another den. To do this she carries the young in her mouth, one by one, to the new home. Once the kittens are all old enough to be weaned, at about eight weeks, the mother takes them to a number of areas where she has hunted in the past. Gradually she teaches her young kittens the techniques of killing. When they are old enough, they separate, going off alone or in pairs.

As regards the distribution of wildcats, it is true that they are found mainly in Scotland, though some may have returned to England. It is believed by some that the wildcat is found in Wales, and on Exmoor and Dartmoor. Indeed, there is evidence to prove that these areas have a wildcat population. The wildcat was once rare, but it is now more common.

- ## Wildcats: Sizes

Looking at eighteenth century engravings of wildcats, it is noticeable that wildcats were much larger two hundred years ago than they are today. It was called the 'British Tiger' by one author in the 1700s. That of today officially measures two feet long, excluding its bushy tail or, including its tail, about three feet. A really large wildcat would be comparable to a smallish European lynx. When we come to look at Scottish 'mystery' cats, we shall see that they differ greatly in size from Scottish wildcats, being larger in size and different in colour.

- ## Wildcats: Diet

Wildcats survive on creatures such as hares, rabbits, rats and mice, also ptarmigan, pheasants and partridges. Wildcats have been known sometimes even to take deer, though they are really only capable of killing roe-deer. In addition, they are known to take young lambs, greatly to the shepherds' indignation.

- ## The Future of the Wildcat

The wildcat has a promising future. Foresters now recognise their use as a pest-controller, and Scottish conifer plantations now have special entrances for wildcats. The shortage of gamekeepers in the two World Wars left much to be desired, and for the part it played, the wildcat was not held in contempt by the authorities. Now it is totally protected by conservation laws. Luckily for the wildcat, there are fewer gamekeepers intent on shooting it when it pays the keeper back by eating his pheasants, if they are not carefully enclosed! Game-birds are often taken by foxes, and wildcats get the blame for these killings.

Due to cross-breeding with feral ex-domestic cats, the number of wildcat enemies is lower than ever before. So the wildcat is establishing its race as a well-balanced predator in our Isles.

- ## A Description of the Scottish Wildcats

The Scottish wildcat basically looks like a large tabby cat. The head is broad, with wide-set, small, triangular ears. The eyes are normally a yellow colour and it has a brownish-yellow under-coat, flanked on top by blackish-coloured stripes, which go three-quarters of the way around the body.

The main way in which to tell the wildcat from its cousin, the tabby house-cat, is by the wildcat's blunt-ended bottle-shaped, bushy grey-brown tail, when compared with the normal cat's long straight tail. The wildcat's legs are longer than those of the domestic cat, and its hind legs are far more powerful, to help it jump great distances. The wildcat weighs anything from 12 to 20 lbs.

The fur of a wildcat can be quite shaggy under the body, but on the back it seems to be shorter. It has very sharp claws, and sometimes its fangs protrude below the top lip. Its stocky chest is sometimes whitish.

The droppings of the wildcat are large and black, and are useful for the identification of the predator, as they are usually made near to the prey. In March the wildcat male is very noisy.

The creature can be as long as 1.3 metres high, which is equivalent to 51 inches.

Strangely, wildcat kittens have much stronger stripes than those of their parents, while the tail has about five of those stripes or bars.

One of the greatest dangers was thought to be the total obliteration of wildcat genes, through too much cross-breeding with domestic cats. However, evidence suggests that over 60% of wildcats have not hybridised, thus the wildcat genes may be stronger than those of the domestic cats.

According to R.S.P.C.A. figures, until the Wildcats' Protection Act in November 1987, two hundred a year were trapped or snared by Fenn traps and shot dead. Could the new Act stop people from shooting any more Kellas cats, perhaps? Seven Kellas cats have been killed, but could they be a black form of wildcat and therefore protected? Anyway it is unlikely that any more Kellas cats will be shot dead, as live specimens are needed to prove that the breed exists.

Wildcats have home ranges of about 120 kilometres, although one radio-collared cat travelled 35 kilometres in about six weeks. This was a nomadic male wildcat. Adult males have home ranges of about 175 hectares, whereas juvenile females only have home ranges of about 77 hectares. These ranges are much smaller than those of a puma, which may have a territory of about 30 kilometres radius.

The natural enemies of the wildcat are the fox and the eagle. In Joyce Stranger's 1968 novel *Shea!* a wildcat kitten was carried to the local eagle's nest and consumed there. The mother wildcat promptly climbed the eagle's tree and managed to kill a young eagle. There is actually one case where a shepherd observed a wildcat killing an eagle, when the eagle tried to take its kitten. There is at least one recorded case of a wildcat attacking a man, although the animal died in the battle.

Feral Cats

Rathlin Island, off the coast of Northern Ireland, is a prime example of a small cat population isolated from the outside world. Having been to Rathlin, I have met some of the islanders, who number ninety-five in all. If there are thirty families there, and each family has a cat, we have thirty domestic cats. There are also about ten feral cats on the island. These survive on rabbits, rats and the various other small creatures living on the island. (These feral cats are among the few in the world that can dine out on the rare star-nosed shrew). And incidentally, during the nineteenth century, a Pacific Ocean lighthouse-keeper's cat wiped out a race of sparrows unique to that island!

I recently conducted a study of a local 'tribe' of feral cats. The group lived at an old farm, which had become run down, and the old couple who owned the cats were ill in hospital. A neighbour fed the five cats once a day, but they were otherwise wild, spending most of their time patrolling a nearby meadow and the vicinity of the farmhouse.

On my first visit to the cats I found that there were three ginger and two smaller tortoiseshell cats. This immediately puzzled me, as I thought none of the cats were neutered, and surely three ginger tomcats fight, as, for some genetic reason, ginger cats are nearly always male.

On a second visit I found that one of the ginger cats was surprisingly tame, and I was able to see that she was a female. The other two were probably tomcats, judging by the smell. The two tortoiseshell cats were probably kittens, offspring of the ginger cats.

My third visit provided a good opportunity to photograph the tame ginger cat and the second ginger tom-cat, poking his head round the corner through curiosity.

The kittens were not there on my fourth visit. I approached the farmhouse through a meadow and found that the house was uninhabited. It looked filthy, neglected, abandoned, and a haven for rats. There were numerous old sacks around the farm, and while climbing over a fence; I noticed what first appeared to be an old brownish sack, very similar in colour to the ginger cats. On examination this 'sack' proved to be none other than the dead female ginger cat.

On making some enquiries, I found that a local pest collector took all the cats away. The one ginger cat could not be caught and her body was later removed. She presumably died of old age, starvation or some illness. Thus one interesting colony was obliterated.

- ## Feral Cat Control

Mr Bruce Dark, a friend of our family, who is a Fleet Street journalist, put me in contact with Mr Peter Neville, a zoologist who has carried out various studies for the Universities Federation of Animal Welfare (U.F.A.W.), on the control of feral cats.

I wrote to Mr Neville of Chertsey in Surrey, and he was most helpful, sending various papers and photocopied articles on the subject. He also advised me to write to the U.F.A.W., which I did, and obtained more information. My work has mainly resulted through them.

In 1982 the U.F.A.W. published a 12-page booklet called 'Feral Cats - Suggestions for Control'. This booklet clearly sets out the aims of capturing feral cats and controlling them. The booklet was reprinted in 1984 and was revised in 1985. The following short quotation shows their aims:

> *'U.F.A.W. considers the most effective and humane method for dealing with groups of feral cats is population control. It recommends schemes based on trapping, neutering, marking by ear tipping and returning to supervised sites where the long-term care of the cats can be assured.'*

The booklet states that there are twelve million feral cats in Britain, many living in urban areas. These are fed mainly by lonely or elderly people who like to look after them. In September 1980, the U.F.A.W. held a special meeting to find a solution to the problem.

The law states that the owner of the mother cat owns a mother cat's kittens. The owner of the land on which it lives then technically owns a domestic cat that goes wild. If feral cat controllers took a pet cat by mistake they would be liable for prosecution, thus all the local people should be warned about any such scheme. The Acts concerned are the Protection of Animals Act 1911, the Protection of Animals (Scotland) Act 1912 and the Abandonment of Animals Act 1960.

The booklet gives the address from which cat-traps and other equipment can be obtained. M.D. Components, Hamelin House, rear of 211-213 Hightown Road, Luton, Bedfordshire can supply you with all the equipment needed. The *Veterinary Record* has published a number of articles on the control of feral cats.

In 1984, Peter Neville wrote an article called 'Effect of Neutering on two groups of feral cats', which gives an account of how he controlled two feral cat colonies in Regent's Park, London. According to B. Rees's study (from his Ph.D thesis at Bradford University in 1982), about 10% of feral cats in Britain have been controlled by the trapping method.

The problem over the two cat colonies was that the Park authorities discovered that some of their animals - mainly waterfowl - were missing. As it was, after neutering there was an increase in affectionate and aggressive actions. This intensive study gives an excellent picture of all the cats, and it would seem that one colony did not like to mix with the other. In one group the overall operation was totally successful, but the other group was only partly successful, as the Park authorities shot some of the cats which were caught attacking wildfowl.

In the September/October 1983 issue of the *International Pest Control* magazine, an article was published called the 'Humane control of an urban cat colony'. Twenty feral cats were surviving in the basement of a block of flats, multiplying fast as they were all un-neutered. Various kind-hearted residents fed the cats. This was a problem that was to come into the hands of the Environment Services Department of Wandsworth Borough Council, at which point seventeen cats 'were trapped, neutered, marked and returned to the site'. One of the garages was converted into a special sleeping and feeding area for the feral cats. They slept in five tea-chests turned on their sides.

The area was then cleaned once a week by the feeders and the cats were able to have roundworm tablets every six months. The total cost of the operation was about £750. In 75 man-hours the operation was completed. About £100 a year would have to be spent in controlling any cats that planned to join the colony. If twenty feral cats had been shot, the total cost would have been about £4,000, whereas the total cost of neutering the cats would be about £1,700. The benefit is that lonely cat feeders are kept occupied.

- Chapter Three -
THE EXMOOR BEASTS

The Landscape of Exmoor

Exmoor is a national park in North Devon and West Somerset. For centuries writers have praised its beauty and wildness. Unlike Dartmoor, Exmoor has red deer, the remains of the inhabitants of the Royal Exmoor Forest. Buzzards, rabbits, deer and other indigenous wildlife are found all over the moor, which contains a large amount of forestry commission woodland. This has also proved useful cover for marauding animals such as 'the Exmoor Beasts'.

In all truth, Exmoor is like a 'mini-Scotland', to use the words of Trevor Beer, whom we will mention later. It is a hilly area, with deep valleys and long, fast-flowing rivers like the Bane. To the southwest of Exmoor lie the Rivers Taw and Torridge - home of Tarka the Otter. To the south lies Dartmoor, and to the north the Bristol Channel and the south coast of Wales. Exmoor is home to those mealy-nosed ponies, for the well-known book "Moorland Mousie" was about one such animal.

In days gone by, Exmoor was the home of the Doones - those hard-riding villains who became the inspiration for the famous novel *'Lorna Doone'*, by R. D. Blackmore. The Knight family attempted to farm the whole of Exmoor in the nineteenth century, with some success. Since the Middle Ages, sheep have been the main source of income for moorland farmers.

Other features of Exmoor are the old buildings and stone walls which are maintained by the Exmoor National Park authority and by private owners. The rich stock of wild prey has provided an excellent larder for the predators of the moor: foxes, badgers, stoats, weasels, otters, and some elusive creatures termed 'The Beasts', or the 'Beast of Exmoor'.

To find out what the beasts are, we must trace back through the moor's history for any clues as to the possibility of big cats existing on the moor.

The Beasts Long Ago

Trevor Beer, the well-known North Devon naturalist and artist, photographer and writer, once wrote to me:

'big cats'' presence on Exmoor goes back hundreds of years. I was talking to an 82-year-old ex-farmer in the Mole Valley last week, who said his grandfather had seen black big cats at North Molton, and how farmers had tethered out goats to lure them, in the 1870s - 1880s. These very men told of their own ancestors seeing them, so we can either accept it or not; but the phenomenon has been around for a long time.' *Westcountry Mysteries'*, published by Bossiney Books in 1985, notes the cat phenomenon in a chapter

ɘ Beast of Exmoor" by Jillian Powell. Miss Powell relates at one point the story of a cat caught
ιcholls, in the 1920s:

*'He remembers a story Sam Nicholls told him from his rabbit-catching days, when
an extraordinary cat the size of a terrier was found in the trap. This was sixty years
ago, when the risk of being charged by one of the travelling menageries in the area
encouraged the trappers to bury the cat very quickly.'*

Although Miss Powell had interviewed the Nicholls family, of Molland, North Devon, I went along there
and talked to Mr Sam Nicholls, who is now 83 years old. He not only confirmed the story, but added that
the animal was black (the same colour as many witnesses` say the present beasts are). I had hoped that it
might be possible to dig the cat up, but time had passed and Mr Nicholls did not recall the exact spot
where the cat had been buried.

Another interesting clue to wildcats and big cats being on Exmoor still is found in Mrs. Hope L. Bourne's
excellent book *'Living on Exmoor'*, published in 1963. She lives in a caravan near to Withipool, on the isolated moors of West Somerset. Mrs. Bourne is a naturalist, an artist and also an extremely enthusiastic
member of the Exmoor Pony Society.

This is the story of the wildcats of Room Hill, as given in her book:

*By late afternoon my walk has brought me round to the long steep scarp that towers
above the middle Exe. Rocks like teeth thrust through the shaggy lips of the winter
bracken, and thorn and rowan cling to the precipitous slopes that drop to the noisy
river far below. On the farther side the gorse is a yellow fire on the slopes above the
river. It is a wild spot, little frequented except by sheep and foxes, wild enough to be
the last stronghold of the true wildcat in Southern England - for if, indeed, what I believe is true, a last remnant of Felis sylvestris survived here on Room Hill until the
first years of this century, and to within living memory.*

*It was only recently that I heard the full story of the cats of Room Hill. I had previ-
ously heard odd references made from time to time, to the wild cats that used to live
on Room Hill, but I had paid little attention to them, as 'wild cats', that is to say, cats
of domestic origin that had turned feral and taken to living and breeding in a wild
state, used to be of very common occurrence in the Westcountry . Then one day a
farmer friend who has lived all his life on his farm just under the hill, began to talk
about 'the cats' and to say things about them that were most unusual and extremely
interesting. I asked for as much information as he could give, and this is what he told
me:*

*'Long ago, and up to the beginning of this century, Room Hill was the home of a race
of fierce wildcats. In the days when he was a boy, fifty or more years ago, there was
still a family of them living in the rocks on the scarp of Long Combe, or Curr Cleeve,
on the north edge above the Exe. For the most part they kept to the isolation of the
hill, but in a hard winter they would come prowling up over the hill and down to-*

wards the farm, in search of any sort of small prey. Their yowl in the night was a ter-rifying sound. They were noted above all for their ferocity, and if by day one of them was seen lurking anywhere near the farm the children were ordered to gather up all the domestic cats and other small pets and go indoors with them, while father went out with a gun. These wildcats would kill and carry off any domestic cat, and the yard cats were terrified of them.'

Likewise no dog would dare attack such a cat, but just ran away at the first encounter. Now and again he - my friend - would catch a glimpse of one of them, and he vividly remembered how once he came out of the yard just as one came slinking down the lane in broad daylight.

So great an impression did the sight of the thing make on him that he never forgot its startling appearance. It was, he said, about the size of a dog-fox. In colour, it was grey or tawny-grey, marked all over with dark stripes. Its head was huge in comparison with that of an ordinary cat, and its teeth protruded below the lip like fangs. Its tail was thick and blunt and hung in a distinctive curve behind it. The creature seemed tall on the leg, especially in the hindquarters, and it moved with a sort of slouching gait. To a small boy (as he was then) there was something very frightening in the whole appearance of this remarkable cat.

The last of these cats of Room Hill seem to have become extinct in the years immedi-ately preceding the First World War, exterminated no doubt by trap and gun, for sub-sequent to this no more were ever seen about the district. I asked whether any skins had ever been kept from shot animals, but he said No, he had never heard of any.
So the cats of Room Hill remain a mystery and a tale, though I myself have no doubt as to their origin and species, and regret that they could not have survived a little longer.

Anthony Dent, in his 1974 book *Lost Beasts of Britain*, also noted the story of the Room Hill cats. The farmer whom Mrs. Bourne interviewed was given as Mr Fred Milton, a president of the Exmoor Pony So-ciety and farmed at Withypool. Mr Dent knew both Mrs. Bourne and Mr Milton, and he would not lightly disregard their evidence. There was also an interesting note on the Exmoor wildcats, which featured on hunting rights documents: 'On Exmoor, for instance, the last mention in documents relates to the year 1283,' yet wildcats were on Room Hill until about 1914. Andy Roberts quoted this story from *Lost Beasts of Britain* in his book, *Cat Flaps*.

Trevor Beer, the Barnstaple naturalist, tells me that although some people believe that the wildcat lives on Exmoor, there is no evidence to support this. None of the leading Exmoor naturalists, like Mr N Y Allen, have seen wildcats on the moor, but all of them recognise the existence of the feral domestic cats. The Room Hill cats were probably the last wildcats in the whole of the South of England, although Mr Christo-pher Hall says that wildcats were in Surrey until around 1920.

Exmoor Black Dog Legends

Although black dogs are probably not normally connected with black big cats, some of the Exmoor black dog legends could have originated in a black big cat. A large black dog haunts Winsford Hill near Winsford, in West Somerset, which is interesting.

The writer of the 1985 *'Holiday-Maker Tourist Handbook'* gives an interesting reference to this story:

> *'If you walk past the village, about 1 mile, Winsford Hill provides a viewpoint from which to see the Bronze Age Burial mounds known as wambarrows (from the word womb). Legend has it that they are haunted by a black dog, which has some modern relevance.'*

The Blackmore Country, published in 1906 by Adam and Charles Black Ltd. (London) and was written by F.J. Snell: Mr Snell says of the Wambarrows: *'The wambarrows are the haunt of a mysterious black dog.'* In *'Oral Traditions of Wessex'*, Ralph Whitlock includes a short section on black dog legends in Wessex. One story, quoted below, may be in fact sightings of a puma-like cat:

> *'A large, strange, lightly-coloured dog was seen in the vicinity of Porlock in 1910 on a couple of occasions, and each time there was a death in the neighbourhood.'*

A black dog is said to haunt Blackmore gate, an isolated crossroads in North Devon quite near to Parracombe. This legend has been brought alive once again by sightings of a black big cat in this area of Exmoor.

There are many black-dog legends in North Devon, but off Exmoor. The areas where these legends persist are Torrington, Bow, Braunton Burrows, Pinkery Pond, River Torridge and Hollocornbe. Mrs. Barbara Carbonell researched the 'Torrington Hound' at great length, in the 1920s; she found that all the sightings were on ley-lines, and thus she was able to establish some idea as to where the phantom hound might appear. Mrs. Carbonell found out that the dog was seen near Copplestone Cross, a 14-feet high granite pillar dating from the 6th century. The black dog was then observed at Down St Mary, which has an old lane, an ancient Saxon church and various other ancient sites. We also find that the hound haunts the area of Torrington, Aller, Stopgate and Blackgate.

The dog continued to haunt the road through Wembworthy, Hollocombe, Week Hill, St Giles-in-the-Wood, and finally Bow. Many local people had seen the creature, although it would seem that some were reluctant to talk about it. The animal was described as being the size of a calf, with great shining eyes, and was said to be harmless. South of Tiverton there is a hamlet called Black Dog, about one mile from Thelbridge. South Devon is rich in black dog legends, as we shall discover later.

Moving back towards Barnstaple, we find that there is a black animal in that area, for Michael Williams records, under the heading "The Black Dog of Devon - and Strange Cats" in the Bossiney book *Secret Westcountry* .

> *'How, for example, do we account for the experience of North Devon bus driver William Nott who saw the ghost black dog in front of his Barnstaple-Lynton bus?*

William Nott might have remained silent, but for the fact that he had three witnesses.'

Trevor Beer stated that William Nott lived near Fremington, and that this incident occurred in 1939. Mr Nott said the dog was shepherding three sheep and he had expected to run them over. The bus stopped, a search was made, but no sign of the dog was found. The sighting was near Blackmoor Gate, and Trevor Beer says it was known as the Yeth Hound'. Some of the modern sightings refer to a large hound, black in colour, because quite a few witnesses described the creature as a 'hound' to Trevor Beer. These sightings are recorded in Mr Beer's 1984 booklet, `*The Beast of Exmoor*`.

Winsford Hill's black dog, which haunts the wambarrows, may well have 'some modern relevance', if we understand this recent sighting. Mrs. D.M. Okell, of Cadro Cottage, Exford, near Minehead, informs me in a letter of 7th June 1987:

> *'I was interested to read in the West Somerset Free Press about your research into the 'Exmoor Beast' and thought the following might interest you. A friend of mine a few weeks ago had driven onto Winsford Hill one evening to look for a sighting of deer and was suddenly surprised to see two very large black animals moving fast across the moor. They then jumped a fence and went in the direction of Mounsey Hill gate. He then saw what they were - two very big strong black Alsation dogs, and obviously gone wild.'*

I understand that a sheep was killed in that area around that time.

The 1960s Onwards

• Sightings of black big cats

Mr Nigel Brierly, a botanist, naturalist and keen investigator of the `Exmoor Beasts`, provided me with some interesting information on the 1960s happenings regarding the big cats. He showed me two black-and-white photographs of a plaster cast of a paw-print. This was found on farmland, and a plaster cast was made at the time. All the details available indicated that the print was found in the 1960s. The farmer believed it was made by a big cat, possibly an animal similar in size to an Alsatian, judging from the size of the print in the photograph.

In 1970, a black panther was sighted at Wistpoundland reservoir. The sighting was during the summer and involved the Cross family of Ilfracombe. The sighting was the earliest recorded in Trevor Beer's book *'The Beast of Exmoor'*. The cat was 50 feet away from their car, and waved a paw in the air at the noise of a passing car. It then ran back down the reservoir track.

In 1972 the cat was seen again, this time by Mr Ian Tucker of Urnbesleigh, in North Devon.

He wrote:

> *Firstly of course it is true, several people in all walks of life have seen it. A lot of people have claimed to have done, but it's my opinion not many have been lucky*

enough to be as close as I was, unless of course he was at one time in a circus, but on the other hand my sighting was in 1972. How long they live I don't know. This cat I am sure was too big for a puma, as I saw it. He (or she) was a panther about 8 feet from nose to the tip of the tail and all black. He was sitting by the roadside, just off the road from Witheridge to South Molton. It was around 11 pm, and I saw his black form for a few seconds in the car lights before he turned his head towards me. I slowed to have as long a look as possible. He sat until I was within 30 yards, then with his body close to the road, he slowly crossed, watching me all the time. He was in no hurry at all. He then just walked in through the hedge and was gone.

Mr Tucker is of the opinion that the black beast was killing red deer in 1972, and is responsible for more recent sheep-killings. He also thought there might be a whole family of black big cats on the Moor.

In 1977, Mrs. K Sloane of Newport, near Barnstaple, North Devon, saw an unusual black animal, which she described to me in a letter:

It is all of 10 or 11 years since I saw it. I was walking with my two daughters along an isolated lane which goes to Venn quarries. This is on the way to Swinibridge...
We got to a part of the lane and I looked back, as I thought we ought to start going back, and on the top of one of the hills on the left was a bush and sitting upright by the side of this bush was a very large black cat-like animal, outlined by the sky.
Its ears were upright but not very large. I have a black cat myself and it looked like a black panther to me. I was quite alarmed, as I felt it could quite easily have leapt down to where we were, in several minutes. So I hurried the girls back the way we had come.

My husband thought I was mad, when I told him after the children were in bed. I didn't tell them in case they went by themselves, to see if they could see it.

Mrs. Sloane noted that all the sightings of recent years were not very far from the place where she observed her black big cat.

Details of other sightings in the 1970s of black cats came my way. A farmer's wife near West Anstey observed a black big cat jumping a hedge in the mid-1970s. Nobody believed her at the time, and it was only in 1987, when the farmer had a sheep killed in an unusual way, that he believed her story. I learnt this story on my second trip to Exmoor, in May 1987, when I interviewed various farmers and attempted some tracking.

Trevor Beer and Nigel Brierly have collected information about ten sightings of a black big cat, in the 1970s, and Trevor Beer has gone so far as to say that its territory covers a vast area - from South Molton to Barnstaple, including places such as Brayford, Parracombe and Bishop's Nympton. All this evidence tends to suggest that the beast returns to different areas at different times of the year.

The 1980s

The years 1980 to 1982 cover a period when the black beast was only occasionally sighted, and I have no details of these sightings. 1983 was the year when a wet spring stopped wild prey from being hunted by scent and therefore the black big cat turned to sheep-killing. Others would disagree, saying that lurcher dogs were responsible for all the sheep-kills around South Molton. This opinion is based on articles from North Devon and West Somerset newspapers, articles in the national press and letters from the public, as well as official statements made by the police and marines.

- ## Drewstone

The `Beasts of Exmoor` killed (and are still killing) sheep. Some people think that as many as 400 sheep have been killed in a period of four years.

To understand just what could have attacked the sheep, we must delve into my files and pick out all the incidents I have recorded for 1983.

Mr John Fowler of Marlborough Road, Ilfracombe, North Devon, wrote:

> On a winter's evening some three or four years ago I was driving my car on the B3226 in the direction of Blackmoor Gate. It was early in the evening, about six o'clock and quite dark. Just before the little Exmoor village of Brayford I saw what appeared to be a large black dog come out of a gateway. It caused me to brake and I then thought that it was a black calf, but suddenly realised as it crouched and sprang high into the opposite hedge, that it was a large black cat, with a very pronounced cat-like head and feline tail which curved up at the end. I would say it was very dark brown or black in colour and was most definitely a large cat.

> I would say it stood about two feet or more in height, and would be very similar to the pumas one sees at the Zoo. I have seen large cats in the wild in Kenya, and there is no doubt that it was a large wildcat of some kind, as its movements were completely cat-like. It would probably have been possible for me to run the animal down had I thought to. However, apart from the fact that I had no reason to kill the animal, it was of a size, which undoubtedly would have damaged my car.

> I reversed a little way down the road, and shone my headlights on the hedge, but must admit I was somewhat apprehensive with such a large wild creature lurking in the dark.

Following Mr Fowler's detailed sighting, we find that sheep-killing was starting not very far away at Drewstone Farm, to the north-east of South Molton. The farmer at Drewstone, who wishes to remain anonymous, was of the opinion that a fox or a dog was responsible for the first few kills in early February, 1983. As the kills continued, he decided he must kill the animal involved.

He therefore mustered the help of local farmers and a search was organised, producing the usual local press coverage: the *North Devon Journal/Herald* ran a front page article on 21st April, which was headlined: 'Shotgun farmers stalk a South Molton killer. big cat hunter. 30 lambs die on one farm.'

From this day forth, much publicity was given to the beasts.

The farmers searched all the surrounding countryside on foot, with shot-guns and rifles at the ready. Dulverton foxhounds, the Torrington Foot Beagles and a police helicopter all failed to find any trace of the beast. An armed man did shoot at some large animal prowling around at night, but when daybreak came nothing was there. Three nearby farms - Bicknor, Pillavins and Limeslake - also had lost some lambs. The first thing the farmer told the press was: "It strikes when and where you are least expecting it. I have almost lost count. I have lost at least 30 lambs."

The beast incurred the anger of farmers when it killed within fifty yards of a gas-gun. It also killed near the farmhouse, while the farmers were ready to shoot it if it came to take some sheep in a pen some distance from the farmhouse.

Other incidents were also told to Mr Tim Abbot, who reported the story. Susan Fernandez, a young girl of East Street, South Molton who was employed at a farm near Drewstone, saw the creature about a week before the killings. She described the animal as 'Big, black and cat-like'. However, the police issued their first statement to say that the beast was a dog: *We are looking for a large black dog, with white feet. We believe that is the animal responsible for the killings.*

Mr Bob Holmes, stock breeder, journalist and breeding and management consultant of Ash Mill, near South Molton, wrote me an interesting reply regarding the beasts:

> *'I think it is very likely that both puma and lynx have been released in the South-west, but the enormous amount of cover and the availability of food makes it nearly impossible to track them down for identification.'*

After a snowfall, Mr Holmes had found strange prints across his farmyard, but was unable to identify them; this incident was just before all the kills.

Mr George Winzer of Downscombe Farm, Exford, near Minehead, held a similar view:

> *'I am afraid that my only knowledge of sheep being killed on Exmoor by wild animals is that dogs have been the culprits. It is true to say we had a mystery killer of sheep on the Moors during 1983, but although the beast was never caught it was suspected that it was a lurcher-type dog. There is also a theory that someone bred an odd animal and had difficulty controlling it, then brought it to the Moors and released it. That is also a possibility.'*

The police maintained all along that the beast was a dog. When I wrote to the Avon and Somerset constabulary headquarters, Taunton, I was told:

> *'The enquiries that were made in the Exmoor area related to injuries caused to sheep, but they could not be attributed to any specific animal'.*

It is also worth noting that Doctor Henry Durston Smith, a gentleman residing at Burwell Farm, near South Molton, believed that the beast could be shot dead by the farmers waiting at a water-hole in the

Spinney, where Suzan Fernandez had seen a strange animal. He thought the animal might consume water at the spring. He backed up this theory by pointing out that 3 inch wide pug-marks had been found at this spring. The casts that were made there are said to be those of a dog.

So far, £1,000 worth of damage to lambs had been done and the beast was still killing. Mr Charles Trevisick, former Ilfracombe Zoo owner, raised the suggestion that the beast was a rogue bitch dog, feeding puppies. He did not agree that a puma or a panther was on the loose, and he gave good reasons for this claim:

> 'I think it is a big, black bitch with puppies, that has gone to ground. When the pups are about eight weeks they will show themselves and reveal the hideout of the mother. There are a number of fallen trees in the area and it could be that the bitch has a nest in a hole under one.'

Was a big cat loose, or was a rogue dog responsible? These questions remain unanswered, although it seems likely that dogs were responsible for the kills, and big cats were being seen often enough to be mistaken for the killers. However, this solution does not answer all the questions, as we shall now see.

No hound would pick up the beast's scent. Farmers were becoming worried, and as yet the national press had not caught on to the beast story. At the end of April, Mr W.J. Hayes's farm, Sheepwash, near Molland, was to experience the work of the beast. He commented:

> 'We are taking all the precautions we can, but it is very worrying.' Sheepwash Farm lost only one ewe, but as it was three miles from Drewstone, people began to wonder whether the beast was roaming further afield. After April 1983, the farmers decided it was time to call in a new force: the Royal Marines. Sergeant Andy Wilkins was in charge of the operations. The public relations officer at the Commando Training Centre, Royal Marines, Exmouth, confirmed the following details in a letter dated 10th June 1987:

> I can confirm that in May 1983, ten Royal Marines from the Commando Training Centre deployed in the South Molton area, to assist police in the hunt for an animal which had carried out a number of savage attacks on livestock in that area. Armed with SLR5 (self-loading rifles) and sniper rifles with night observation devices they set up camouflaged observation posts in the area, working in two-man teams under the direction of the police.

> No confirmed sightings of cats, pumas or the like were made; however, some members did hear high-pitched cat-like screams in the night.'

The officer thought the best source of information for the Drewstone episode, was through local and national newspapers.

All through the investigations, police took the view that the beast was a wild dog. This seemed a safer explanation than a puma or similar animal. The Chief Superintendent at the Avon and Somerset Constabulary's Taunton branch informed me:

> *'... I regret I am not in a position to supply you with the information you request in your letter. The enquiries that were made in the Exmoor area related to injuries caused to sheep but they could not be attributed to any specific animal.'*

Why did the police, marines and farmers not know what the killer or killers were? The simple reason was that the killer or killers had not been caught 'on the job', i.e. slaughtering sheep. To my knowledge no one has actually seen a big cat kill a sheep, although big cats have been seen, and photographed, stalking livestock. Until somebody photographs a puma or lynx actually killing a sheep, we will have to make do with evidence in the form of pad-marks, hair and sightings near to where sheep are accommodated.

The police have two-inch-thick files on the beast, but as these are private (though they would probably explain the beast story in full) we have no alternative but to leave these files to one side. On the 10th May, the *Western Morning News* reported the fact that the Royal Marines had been withdrawn on the 8th May. This was possibly due to the *Daily Express* offering £1,000 to anyone who could photograph the beast.

Back on 7th May, the *Daily Express* carried a report on Suzan Fernandez's sighting. She was quoted as saying: "I saw a very big black animal with a white front. At first I thought it was a cat, but it was too big for that. It was black and had a long tail. There was white on each foot."

The black-and-white suggests that the animal Suzan saw might have been a rogue collie dog, or possibly a large feral domestic cat. The same report claimed that the beast was a panther, consuming two sheep a day! The Superintendent of Barnstaple Police, Douglas McClary, commented: "Until we shoot the damned thing we don't know what it is."

Two days later, on 9th May, the *Daily Express* published its reward, with the caption: 'The Beast of Exmoor WANTED! Alive ON FILM.' The paper did warn people to obey the country code and not to annoy the farmers or police. However, the farmers were not pleased at this sort of reward.

The *Daily Mirror* reported on the same day that the beast had killed eighty sheep. The column also talked of the farmers' anger against the *Daily Express*; they were also annoyed about the threat of the beast attacking again, because the marines had pulled out, though they had had enough time to set up night observation posts, in one case using a church tower. Also on the 10th May the *Daily Express* brought out a one-page article about the actual events in the beast hunt, and defending their reward offer. Their photographer also provided a picture of the beast's kill, showing the sheep - a ewe - with a gaping throat wound. The M.P. for North Devon, Mr Tony Speller, told the *Daily Express*:

> *Nobody has been seen taking photographs around here today, but there was a gaggle around here yesterday. The* Daily Express *reward is interesting, but not madly popular. We are trying to get the Marines back. They say they will if the police approve, but they will need quiet.*

Following this controversy over the future of 'Operation Beastie', as the hunt was code-named, we wonder what was happening to the beast itself. The same *Daily Express* article carried a sighting by a Mr John

Francis, a local bus driver. He had seen an unusual creature, which he described as follows:

> *Ugly old brute like no dog I ever saw. It had a squat head that did not fit its body, a gleaming jet-black coat and short, powerful legs.*

He was of the opinion that he observed some sort of dog. The article also reviewed interesting points put forward by the local Farmers' Union leader, Mr Denys Smaldon, who was positive the animal was a type of large cat. The way he described the beast's kill was the most detailed account yet:

> *'It kills and eats lambs like no dog or fox ever did. It pulls wool away and attacks the shoulder and rump. This thing eats wool as well, and goes for the chops. It leaves the bone structure of the neck like you would leave a fishbone in a restaurant.'*

The next day, the *Daily Express* published an amusing cartoon showing two people up a tree, with a fierce-looking ram below. The people were beast-hunters and the ram was portrayed as the beast! On May 12th the *North Devon Journal Herald* heard a rumour that a member of the public had spotted a creature, which appeared to be 'black and the size of a Labrador'. At the same time, a Native American tracker was running his expert eye over film of the beast's kill. Mr Connie Davis, a Canadian Native American tracker now residing in Redruth, Cornwall, gave his opinion:

> *'In hunters' terms it's known as the grab hold, a technique used by wolves. It's all over in a matter of seconds. But from the number of throat marks, I believe there could be more than one dog responsible.'*

Somebody wrongly told the *Journal Herald* that the puma strangles its prey. This is not true, for it is known that the puma bites its victim's throat.

The killings continued, and still more theories were being developed by people. Trevor Beer, who joined in a hunt at Drewstone, was baffled and thought the beast was a rogue dog - possibly a dog that had once belonged to a poacher and had gone off, or been turned loose. Most reports indicated a dog as being responsible for some of the Drewstone kills, while some believed that the creature was a lurcher, or a cross-bred lurcher. Another person who held this view was Mr A J Coombs of Plymouth, who told the *North Devon Journal Herald* it was an illegally bred dog, which suggested:

> *'Such a dog would be trained to kill viciously by being encouraged to tear apart small animals. That the beast does not panic at the sound of gunfire could suggest that it has spent its time where gunfire and the sight of armed men are fairly common - perhaps on Dartmoor firing ranges.'*

Yet another man who also thought the beast was a dog was Mr David Mann, a former Master of Foot - Beagles. What he saw one Sunday morning was some sort of dog. He wrote me a long letter, an extract from which is quoted:

> *One Sunday morning in 1983 I and my wife, and also a 'scout' set off from Combe Martin about 8.30 to go to South Molton, some 16 miles away, to train new Scout*

leaders. Nearing South Molton some 20 minutes later, still in the countryside, I saw above me and to the right (about 1 o'clock) and running towards me, an animal I judged to be 30 to 36 inches at the shoulder. My first thought was that it was feline. But it 'cast' as it ran and, as a master and huntsman of a pack of foot-hounds for a long period, I recognised it must be a 'dog' of sorts. It came towards us (it was about 100 yards distant when first seen) and I had slowed or stopped when it came to a standstill no more than 10 to 12 yards away and looked at us and then, when erect, it was clear to me that this was a lurcher and not some sort of 'cat', although I would forgive anyone who saw it running for thinking that it was feline.

It was the colour of dark but not faded creosote, a grey, black, brown mixture, but no question, to someone who has been involved in showing, breeding and working dogs for a lifetime, a lurcher-type canine.

The beast then ran on, and a few minutes later Mr Mann reported his sighting to the police and the Marines at Drewstone. A lurcher, belonging to a local landowner was the creature tracked that day by the Marines. It was on the same day as this lurcher was being tracked that a ewe was killed a mile from where all the hunting was being carried out.

Mr Mann later sorted out the tame lurcher and found it to be much smaller and of a different colour to the beast he had come across on that Sunday morning. Mr Mann also told me of 'travelling people' who use lurchers to poach deer and then sell the venison for a good price. Maybe one of their lurchers went astray...

Many thanks must go to Mr Mann for developing a likely solution to some of the sheep-killing. He thinks the 'Beast of Exmoor' is canine, and he is not sure whether the animal he saw was definitely 'the' beast.

However, a similar animal was spotted by Mrs. Doreen Lock on 26th May 1983. Mrs. Lock of Molland in North Devon, saw the beast in the road between Molland and the 'Black Cock' public house. This stretch of road is fringed on either side by conifer woods, an ideal hideout for a large cat or lurcher dog. She was quoted in the *North Devon Journal Herald* as saying:

'I saw something in the road some distance from me. It was large, black and had pricked ears. I only saw the front part. It then disappeared into the wood on the right-hand side of the road.'

The beast saga took another turn when Wayne Adams (13) and Marcus White (12) came across a weird animal, at the end of May 1983. The press gave full coverage of their sighting, which was remarkably close and detailed. The press reports in the *West Somerset Free Press*, the *North Devon Journal Herald*, *Daily Star* and *Daily Mirror* said that the boys had been staying on a remote Exmoor farm, Willingford near Exford, when they encountered the beast. They were able to give a most detailed account of their sighting, and even produced a drawing of what they saw. Wayne Adams told the *Daily Star:*

I looked over a gate and saw the animal about ten yards away. It stared straight at me with bulging, greeny eyes just like a lion. It was jet black apart from white markings down its chest, and had a head like an Alsatian dog. I was dead scared and said to Marcus "There's the thing everyone is looking for," and it lolloped away. It moved like a cat, but I don't think it was a puma.

Later, the boys came upon its heavy and deep pad-prints in the ground. The prints had claw marks, but because the animal had greeny eyes, I wondered whether it was a large cat they saw.

The press also informed us that the Marines had actually seen the animal, or rather, a 'black and powerful animal', and had attempted to shoot it. The Marines believed that the beast was some type of dog, but how could anyone attribute a cat-like scream to a dog? The press had unwittingly done this. The police started to search old sheds and barns to see whether the beast was inside, and they advised the public to stay away from the area of the police hunt.

On 9th June the *North Devon Journal Herald* confirmed that the police believed the beast was a dog. Knaplock Farm, near to Tarr Steps, lost a sheep early in June. Mr Wayne Hyde, a taxi-driver of South Molton, came across a strange obstruction on Silcombe Hill, near Bishop's Nympton, on a late Sunday evening in June. Mr Hyde's first thought was that the creature was an overgrown fox, but his reaction soon changed, for the creature was cunning-looking, with very powerful shoulders and had *'huge eyes, pricked ears and a long nose'*. The sighting was given in the *North Devon Journal Herald* also on 9th June.

By this time, the Marines, who had withdrawn from the Moor a month previously, had returned some seven days later and had for the past three weeks been searching for the beast. Posters were being placed around the villages, asking people to report sightings. The Marines' operations seemed to scare the beast away, for a spokesman told the *Daily Mirror* on 6th June:

> *"It has either been unsafe to shoot because of nearby houses, or the thing has moved so damned fast and shown itself so little."*

On 16th June, the press noted that Supt. McClary and Chief Supt. Challes, along with the Royal Marines' leader, Major Watkins, met at South Molton Police Station to discuss the progress on killing the beast. The Marines, police and National Farmers' Union all came to the conclusion that the Marines should move their base to West Somerset, which they did for a short time. While this meeting was under way, a local craft shop called '*Togs*' was selling 'Beast of Exmoor' T-shirts, portraying the beast as a panther, snarling. The killings were continuing, but the beast had moved to the West Somerset/Devon border. Kills were occurring at Coombeland Farm, Brompton Regis and at Downscombe Farm, near Exford.

The South Molton police received a sketch of the beast from a witness, a schoolgirl called Alison Healey from South Molton. She had been walking near Bishop's Nympton when she came upon a black, panther-like beast stalking sheep in a field. From 80 yards away she drew the creature for the police. The animal in her picture is undoubtedly feline, although its actual species is not definite. Evidence from the sketch suggests that the animal is either a black panther or a black British big cat, or *even* a black puma. This was reported in the *North Devon Journal Herald* for 23rd June 1983.

According to Alison's drawing, the animal was thinner than a panther and had a larger head, similar to earlier reports of the beast. The animal in her drawing has powerful hindquarters, but is not as stocky of build as the black panther-type animal seen in the summer of 1984 by Trevor Beer, the naturalist.

The police kept quiet about the position of the Marines' new base, so as to keep away the tourists. However, they pulled out in late June of early July 1983. July opened with reports that the beast was feeding upon deer to the east of South Molton. Although some people reckoned that the beast had been killed by the Marines, this was not confirmed as being the case.

Mr G Grimshire, who farms Higher Hudstones, near South Molton, was lucky enough to sight the beast. He wrote to me the following account of his sighting:

> *'Yes, I did see it one Sunday evening. It was two fields away. It was like a fairly big dog, with a very thick and shaggy coat, and his face was like a cat and was all black. And as he was running he seemed to jump along. He didn't have any of our lambs. I went out several times with my neighbours, mostly just as it was getting light, which was about 5 o'clock, to see if we could see it, but we never did.'*

Another person to see the beast was lorry-driver Mr Ray Chilcott, who was driving between South Molton and Brayford, in November 1983, in the early hours of the morning, when he spotted an unusual animal. He described what he observed:

> *'He was black, much bigger than a Labrador dog. Much bigger limbed. He had short ears that were standing up and a much bigger tail than a dog - in fact it was half the length of his body.'*

The creature went off up the road ahead of Mr Chilcott's lorry and, like a cat, went up a bank and into a wood by the road. The animal was in no particular hurry at all, for Mr Chilcott believed it knew where it was heading. This account was in the *North Devon Journal Herald*.

Two other sightings of the beast are recorded for late 1983 in '*Westcountry Mysteries*' by Jilhian Powell, in her chapter on 'The Beast of Exmoor'.

The first sighting was by Major Paget King-Fretts, who saw a black big cat which was grey around the jowls, from only sixty yards away, near Twitchen, South Molton. The second sighting was by Mary Rawle who, whilst out riding, spotted an unusual beast, which was a 'large black cat with a white flash' near Longstone Wells, Heasley Mill.

Before 1983 closed, the beast was in another mystery. A man called 'Bob', who resided near Molland, made a claim that he had shot a bear and buried it on Molland Common. This was on a weekend radio programme. The Devon and Cornwall constabulary followed up his claim, but as he would not give the exact location of the carcass, no-one would believe him. However, the black bear he shot was alleged to have been buried on Molland Common, which is not far from where all the sightings and kills have been. I have attempted to trace 'Bob', but without any luck, but it is worth noting that the *Fortean Times,* No.44, had an interesting end for the story.

Two reporters from the Torbay News Agency had met 'Bob' in a local pub and at first he kept silent about the bear. However, he admitted, after a drink, that the other local farmers had forced him to keep quiet, because they could only claim insurance for kills by dogs, not by any other animal.

• 1984 Onwards - Black Beast Sightings

The winter of 1984 brought news of more widely scattered kills, but it was not until the summer of 1984 that Trevor Beer observed a black panther-type animal. He had been called in to investigate 12 deer carcasses found in a wood. While stalking around, he came upon an unusually large animal, which he told me took him 'by surprise'. A local paper recorded his sighting as follows:

> *'I was crossing a stream when I looked up and saw this head emerging from the bushes in front of me. It was very broad across the top with small ears and wide-set greeny-yellow eyes. The animal ran very fast, and with the gait of a greyhound. It was jet black, sleek, smooth, with very long hind legs, and I would estimate it to weigh between 80 and 120 lbs. It was more like a panther than anything else I have ever seen. All along I have worked on the basis that it was a dog. But now, although I cannot definitely say that it is the sheep-killer, I can say there is a very large cat-like beast on Exmoor.'*

Trevor Beer also noted that the beast ran off, rather than face him. It would seem that most large cats, although often curious, do not like man and therefore take the earliest opportunity to run off. Trevor was also able to see the beast spring over a hedge before disappearing. It was his impression that the animal was somewhat 'otter-like'. He also drew an excellent sketch, showing the beast motionless and in action, thus adding to the details of his sighting.

In October 1984 at least two other sightings occurred in the same area, for a lady picking mushrooms observed a similar animal. Then came another sighting. This time it was a motorist, Mr Sidney Johns, from Ashbridge, near Wrafton, who called at the *North Devon Journal Herald* office to report his sighting:

> *'It was black all over, with a round head, and cat's eyes. It was between 200 and 300 yards away, and I saw it for several seconds. It had a long body and a tail that was about 18 inches long.'*

He and his wife observed the animal while out driving between Swimbridge and Filleigh. In 1984, Mr Niel Brierly wrote a letter to the *'Devon Farmer'*, which gave conclusive evidence that the beasts were feline. He had taken hair samples from the animal's kill and from gaps in hedges where the beast had passed a short time before. He also found pad marks of two cats running together, the larger tracks being four inches across. Mr Brierly was also able to say that the cats involved were not jaguars, panthers, lions or tigers, since by this time he had gathered enough evidence in the form of kills, droppings and pad marks to say there definitely is a lynx and probably a puma on Exmoor. He does not feel that the black cats being seen are definitely panthers, but prefers the explanation of a black puma.

Mr Brierly has also changed his view that the beasts are feral cats grown to a very large size. He considers that the beasts are exotic cats, such as pumas and lynxes, released by their owners.
The sightings of the black beasts were continuing, although many of the incidents to come were from West Somerset. The whole phenomenon of the `Beast of Exmoor` was becoming a legend by this time.

Hardly a person in Southern Britain had not heard of the 'Beast of Exmoor'.

Speculation had started in 1983, but the next three years were to prove the identities of the beasts. The area northwest of South Molton has been a favourite place for a big cat, since 1984. In May or June 1986, the residents of West Cowley Farm near the hamlet of Dean, informed me that they had seen the cat, one of them telling me: 'It was a large black cat with a long tail, which jumped across the lane in two bounds.' Also near Dean, a farmer reckoned he had probably seen the 'beast'. He observed a 'black animal while he was on a tractor, fertilising a field. At the time he only glimpsed it out of the corner of his eye, but on returning to the same place about two minutes later, the animal had gone. This sighting was probably in 1986.

There were other sightings in this wide area between 1985 and 1987.

Another sighting, near Dean, was that by a young man residing near South Dean farm, which is about three miles from Dean Hamlet. His mother told me that he came upon a 'large black cat-like animal, high up on the Moor'. This sighting was in May or June 1986. An earlier sighting was in May 1985, by Mr and Mrs. Derek Castle of Essex. This took place at Wistpoundland Reservoir and was reported in the *North Devon Advertiser* for 31st May 1985.

From the report, Mrs. Castle said:

> *We were still in our car when a large animal crept along the hedge. It was as tall as a Labrador but much longer in the body. It was so close that we could easily see its green/yellow eyes and its small ears. We could easily see its long white teeth and its pink mouth. It was a beautiful animal.*

It leapt over an eight-foot hedge and made off. The couple reckoned it was a panther, which had become known as the 'Beast of Exmoor'.

Another person who has seen the black beast and lost some sheep to it is Mr David Rawle, a farmer residing near to Parracombe, who told a *Western Daily Press* reporter in February 1985: *'The animal was killed where it fell and its shoulder was ripped off. It must be something large and powerful to have done that.'* When I visited Mr Rawle and discussed with him the beast's doings, he told me about the times he and a relation had tried to hunt the beast by 'lamping' from a Landrover. He caught a broad-set pair of green eyes glaring at him, like a cat's eyes. Mr Rawle has lost three sheep to the beast. He believes there are at least two big cats on the rampage.

The Nicholls family, of Molland, have seen the cats a dozen times between them, and have no doubt that the animals' fur is like 'gleaming silver in the sunlight'. They have seen two black cats at the same time. For a fuller record of the Nicholls' sightings, I would suggest that you read 'Westcountry *Mysteries'* by Bossiney Books, referring particularly to the chapter entitled 'The Beast of Exmoor', by Jillian Powell.

I have talked to the Nicholls family, and they have confirmed all the details given by Miss Powell in her excellent chapter.

Other sightings will undoubtedly occur of black panther-like cats in North Devon. For the record, Trevor Beer informs me that he has seen the black panther, or black puma, winding in and out of forestry commission plantation conifer trees. Any other sightings of which I learn will be reported later, in this chapter.

• The Dunster Devil

Since 1978, many sightings and much information about a black beast have come from the Minehead/Dunster regions. The animal seems to reside around Croydon Hill Woods, a vast bulk of forest spanning the old Dunster deer-park and the village of Luxborough.

When I visited Croydon Hill in February 1987, I was able to stalk through the undergrowth. I found that there were almost impregnable places, where any animal could lie up during the day. There were plenty of fallow deer scraps and other signs of red deer. I have since learnt from N. Y. Allen's informative book *Exmoor Wildlife*, that all fallow deer around Croydon Hill came from the Dunster Castle deer park, which was probably abandoned in the 19th century.

Deer provide the panthers and other big cats with a 'larder'. The other predators with which Exmoor's beasts have to compete are foxes, mink, otters, badgers, weasels, stoats and birds of prey. Having noted that the countryside is covered with forest, let us move on to the actual incidents involving this cat.

Sir Edward Mallet, who resides near Luxborough, has not seen the black beast, but he has heard about others who have seen it in the vicinity. On both my trips, I talked to him first, mainly because he had a good knowledge of the surrounding area and of those who might know something about the beast.

The first recorded incident I can find of an animal near Minehead comes from the *West Somerset Free Press* for 6th December 1985, when the beast made headlines on the front page of that paper. Apparently a Minehead smallholder, Mrs. Brenda Cornish, contacted reporter Mr Bob Barron, to inform him that a very large animal had been prowling around her goat-shed. Mrs. Cornish met Mr Barron at her holding at Woodcombe Farm and showed him the foot-prints left by the beast. She was quoted in a later article in the *Daily Express* saying:

> 'Whatever left the print was very big and very strong, to make off with my tripe (dog food). I've heard animals in the woodland screaming after dark, so it's obviously in the area. I'm keeping my gun handy for protection.'

The footprint was found to be larger than that of Mrs. Cornish's St Bernard dog! According to Bob Barron's article, 'Is this the mark of the Exmoor Beast?' Sightings had occurred of a 'large black, un-identified animal' in the same area, two weeks previously. Mr Barron made a plaster-cast, and telephoned the naturalist Trevor Beer who, in turn, informed Mr Barron that the cast was probably of a 150-pound wild dog or wolverine. The animal had been screaming in the early evening, had taken Mrs. Cornish's tripe, and left a large footprint on the hillside.

Trevor Beer also noted that an Exmoor pony had been wounded near Bampton, not long before. There were deep marks in its shoulders.

Since contacting Trevor Beer, I have found out that he does not now believe that the footprint was made by a wild wolverine, but by a large dog. Wolverines, or Gluttons, *(Gulo gulo)* are found in Scandinavia, North America and parts of Siberia. They are as large as an Alsatian, weighing about 70 lbs., and are about 3 feet long. They are not particularly agile creatures. There might be the odd one loose in Britain, although to date I have heard no definite reports. The footprint found at Mrs. Cornish's farm, is 12cm long and 10cm wide. It does not have the large, sharp claws of a cat, but the large, blunt claws of a canine - hence the wolverine theory. I would therefore believe that the animal which was around Woodcombe Farm that day was nothing more than a very large dog - possibly a New Zealand Huntaway, which is almost black all over, and kills like a cat.

Commander Jim Collins, an Exmoor National Park warden, was angry at the response of people who were frightened about coming to Exmoor for fear of being hurt by the beast. He told reporter Christopher Rundle:

> *'There is no beast... If there had been anything there it would have been flushed out and shot months ago. I know what caused those footprints, it is nothing more than a large dog... the people who own it don't want to get mixed up in this nonsense.'*

There had been a sighting by a National Park official at around the same time as Commander Collins made these comments in December 1985.

The year 1986 brought news of fresh sightings and kills. Apparently 'experts' tried to identify the killer of a calf which had had its throat ripped out, near Elworthy, in the Brendon Hills of West Somerset. Another report claimed that the beast had returned with a family, but that there had been no kills as yet. These two reports were in unnamed national papers.

According to a *Daily Express* article of 8th January 1986, the beast had been killing again and was seen twice, at Muddiford and Combe Martin. These two villages are miles from Minehead and the animal, in both incidents, was 'black and cat-like'.

The residents at a Kingbridge Farm, near Luxborough, informed me: "There was a sighting of a black panther at Withicross Village in 1986.'

One witness, to whom I was able to talk personally, was the ganger (a type of Forester) at Luxborough Forestry Station, in May 1987. He informed me that he had observed a 'large, black cat-like animal' crossing the road in front of him, up at a crossroads above Luxborough. He identified the cat as the same one drawn by Trevor Beer in 'The Beast of Exmoor'.

We drove on to the crossroads that windy afternoon, and stopped at the same place where he had seen his cat. We found a break in the hedge where an animal had jumped over. There were broken twigs and signs that a powerful animal had forced its way over the hedge. We also found other clues - droppings! These were analysed by a Dulverton vet, who told me that they definitely contained 'three-quarter rabbit and a quarter cat' remains. This means that the animal, which leapt over the hedge, was a predator, and as badgers cannot jump high hedges, they can be ruled out.

The trail, which we followed, went down a steep hill to a water-hole. I also found wool on some barbed wire, along the trail, indicating that a large predator had dragged a sheep along this trail, the wool being in a most unlikely position for a sheep to have gone. We also discovered that the trail crossed a field and another road, down into another valley, where the trail was lost.

We spent one night waiting up for the animal that used the path. It is my guess that a large animal walked across the open field and ended up at a water-hole which is down at the bottom of the hill running down from the road.

A few months before my investigations, in January 1987, Mr Martin Bosk, a young journalist residing near Luxborough, was driving through Croydon Hill woods at two in the morning. Suddenly, an unusual animal bounded across the road in front of his car. He told me: 'I saw a huge black cat with its tail held high in the air, rush across the road.' Prior to this, in November 1986, two sheep were killed near Minehead, according to a *Daily Mirror* article for February 1987.

To continue with the Dunster Devil, we will now look at an incident which occurred in May 1987.

Mr David Baker, of Styles Farm, Rodhuish, near Dunster, found a dead 160 lb. Border/Leicester ewe, which had lost its shoulder and had received a bite on the back of the neck. This was on the night of 31st April 1987. Two nights later, Mr Baker spotted a big cat near to the scene of the sheep kill. When I interviewed Mr Baker, he gave me a good description of what he saw from a distance of 400 yards. *'The animal was large and cat-like,'* he told me. He also gave me some more information - he had a 'sneaking feeling that this "Lynx" is breeding. Mr Bob Barron, the reporter, investigating the two incidents, quoted Mr Baker as saying:

> *From the evidence I am convinced my sheep was killed by this large cat. It was too clean for a dog or fox, and the killing has all the hall-marks of the so-called "Beast of Exmoor".*

Mr Nigel Brierly, the North Devon Biologist of Bishop's Nympton, who in the 1980s was obtaining information on the beast for the National Farmers' Union, was able to examine the kill and he gave Bob Barron an interview. He was positive that the kill was the work of a puma, or a pair of pumas, killing all over Exmoor 'at least once a week'. He also mentioned that there had been kills near Dulverton about 1st May. The National Press were also told of the story, for the *Daily Telegraph* released two articles which gave the frightening message that farmers were hunting the beast.

The first article, in the *Daily Telegraph* for the 4th May, tells us that Mr David Baker was mounting an armed patrol to catch the beast. He was reported as saying: *'Our greatest fear is that there are two or more lynxes which are breeding.'* However, I do not believe that the animal that caused the killing was a lynx, for one reason: Bob Barron said Mr Baker observed a black cat, not a greyish-spotted cat, like a lynx. Nearly all reports from the Dunster area are of a black cat, but I observed a puma-like beast, which was not black, not far from Dunster. Placing the movements of the cats is very difficult, as their territories over-lap.

One of the most recent sightings of the 'Dunster Devil' was of a 'long, black and sleek' creature, which leapt across a road in two bounds.

Mr Michael Prescott of Minehead observed the beast early in May 1987, and his sighting was reported in Bob Barron's article for 4th May 1987. The sightings of Black Mystery Cats continued. In April 1987, Mr Jonathan Leonard of Exbourne in North Devon was planning to hunt for a beast, which he thought, was a black big cat. The animal, whose identity was not known, had killed a lamb and was heard panting in the bushes. Mr Leonard was able to describe the creature, which he saw after losing a ewe in November 1986:

> The next day I was standing on a bank by some woods when I saw something black running into the hedge. At first I thought it was a black Labrador out with someone shooting, but there was nobody around and it sort of slunk as if it was working.

Since his November 1986 sighting Mr Leonard, who once worked in a zoo, had been able to listen to the beast panting in the bushes, and examine a fresh lamb kill. He also heard that other people in the area had seen such a black cat. In conclusion, he stated: *'There is something wild running around and I think it is a big black cat, and it hunts over a wide area.'*

Other people saw the elusive 'Dunster Devil'. A lady wrote to me, describing her three encounters with a black cat near Croydon Hill Woods. She says: *'The animal is about a metre and a half long and very powerful'.* All her three sightings were in June 1987.

Other sightings and theories still abound all over Exmoor. One strange animal that does not sound like the black big cats, yet is black and shaggy, was the creature seen by Mrs. Anne Waterson of Woolston near Southampton and her family on Exmoor. On 1st May 1986, she wrote Trevor Beer a most interesting letter, an extract from which I use here:

> We were walking along a footpath from Oare to Malsmead beside the river at approximately 4.30 pm. We had entered a gate opposite the entrance to Oare House, and some 100 yards or so along this path there are some trees on the right. This is where we saw the cat, approximately 20 yards away, and we were able to see it quite clearly as the leaves were not on the trees.
>
> It was sitting very still, watching us. It was about 4 ft. in length, 2 ft. high, all black, a definite cat's head, with ears pricked up, whiskers, oval yellowy eyes, very stocky body and legs, short-haired but with longer coarse-looking hair on the belly. (None of them noticed a tail.) We all froze with fright, even though I had a camera on my shoulder I was scared to use it in case the creature felt threatened and attacked us. We stared at it for some seconds and it turned and walked off, turning its head to look back at us several times. The head looked more angular when turned back. It did not move gracefully like a cat, but was rather ungainly. I have drawn a rough sketch, but I am no artist, I'm afraid. (My husband, incidentally, who until that day was extremely sceptical about the existence of a 'beast', thought it was a panther, and he also thought it was slightly brownish-black.

This description led me to believe that the same black/brown dog described by Mr David Mann, in 1983, was still in the area of South Molton and North Devon. I think that on this occasion the beast was not a panther, but a totally wild cross-bred lurcher dog of a darker colour, though I would not swear this was the case.

The Puma Sightings in North Devon and West Somerset

We have already mentioned the possibility that a puma was described as a 'strange lightly-coloured dog that was seen near Porlock in 1910.' Black big cats on Exmoor have differed little in description, but there is no way the 'Beast' of Exmoor can change colour and become a puma-like, lighter-coloured 'beast' - not in my view, anyway! We will therefore have to accept that there are several big cats on Exmoor: at least three types - panther, puma and lynx. Let us start off on the puma hunt.

Although a Mrs. Cooper of Merton twice saw a puma-like beast in the South Molton area, in 1974 (see 'The Beast of Exmoor'), no other sightings of puma-like beasts have occurred, before 1980, in the north Devon and West Somerset areas.

Mendips bobcat	Timberscombe puma
Dark brown shaggy coat with lighter patches	Light fawn-grey coat with lighter under-parts
Size of larger springer spaniel	Size of medium Alsatian dog
Tufted ears	Ears not clearly visible
Length: about 2¼ to 3ft	Length: about 6 ft (including tail)
Short tail	Long tail

However, although the famous mid-Devon Hunt chased a puma in 1980, the reports of such animals really start to come in 1983. Mr and Mrs. George Lewis wrote me a letter explaining their sighting of a beast, in a field behind their home in the village of Fairy Cross near Bideford. The account of their sighting was as follows:

> It was August 1983 that we sighted what we thought was a lioness in a field at the back of our cottage. It was a creamish, fawn colour and was sitting down by the hedge. I went indoors to fetch binoculars and while there my husband said it disappeared into the woods nearby. It had evidently been frightened by a car passing in the adjoining road. The police came straight away but couldn't see any footprints because the ground was so dry. We understand a similar animal was seen in neighbouring parishes.

A second account came from Mr Brian Stevens of Bideford, North Devon, who used to live at Littleham. Following is an extract from his letter to me:

My sighting of the animal, which looked rather like a small lioness, was in broad day-light at about ten o'clock in the morning. I spotted the animal from about 200 yards. Hoping to get closer I climbed over a hedge, walked along inside to where I could have been within a few yards, but unfortunately when I got there the creature had moved off.

I warned my neighbours who lived close by, but I don't think they really took me se-riously. I also told the police who, I think, took it with a pinch of salt. I even began to doubt myself until somebody else living about 3 miles away reported spotting a wild animal, which made me feel much better about it. But I certainly took a lot of stick from my friends and neighbours. To my knowledge there have been no more sight-ings here.

The 'lioness' could well be a large, rangy puma, which I had been told, escaped in 1980, in North Devon. It was one of a pair kept by a local petty criminal, in Swimbridge.

Meanwhile, also in North Devon and in 1983, Mrs. Beryl Knight twice found evidence of a puma-like beast. She resides near the hamlet of Northleigh, not far from Goodleigh in North Devon. She used often to walk on land belonging to the League of Cruel Sports, which had run wild, and she was going from Stoke Rivers village towards some woods, when she first came upon the animal:

On this particular day, it must be two or three years ago, I walked alone. Nearing Hakeford I found the occupants were away, but there were plenty of fowl around (the chickens and ducks). The animal was spotted, quite close, head low, heading away from Hakeford but the colour was more grey and fawn. Height: that of a large dog, certainly not black, which was the colour mentioned of the other sightings. I was dis-appointed that I was unable to see the head, only the back and rear. I was not very sure of the tail either, which must have been held low. This part is not so dense, but covered by reeds and marsh. The surrounding area is farmland, with Exmoor in the distance.

Another day, not too long after, I walked the same way, but apart from hearing the noise of an animal rustling in thick bramble bushes, I had no luck.

The land on which she observed the creature was called Hakeford Chelfham. Other sightings of puma-like cats have come from the area of Parracombe and South Molton. According to Joan Amos, a South Devon U.F.O. investigator, on 7th November 1986, two cats were seen fighting at North Molton. One was black, the other brown. As plaster casts of a mother cat and two kittens were taken at the site, it was pre-sumed that the cats were breeding. Fifteen lbs of meat were consumed at this location.

Another newspaper report, undated and anonymous, claimed that the incident involved two black cat-like creatures. However, the truth emerges that two big cats were seen fighting over a kill. One was the size of a collie-dog, being 'brown and patchy', while the other was black. Trevor Beer took plaster-casts at the scene of this incident. The witness was a lady, who came upon the two cats fighting.

It was on the evening 28th May 1987 that I had a sighting of one of the beasts. My mother and I had been occupied researching all day down near South Molton, and we were returning to a possible cat trail near the west Somerset village of Luxborough. We stopped at a post box on the edge of Timberscombe Village, facing down the valley towards Dunster. I was scanning the hillside through my 8 x 40 binoculars, when I suddenly observed something move on the hillside. As I was an estimated 400 yards, or a quarter of a mile away from the creature, I could only see it through binoculars.

The creature was lying with its paws thrust out in front of it and looked like a strange sort of lioness. A thorn bush obscured its shoulders from my view. Its head was moving from side to side.

The animal, which in size was similar to an Alsatian, was fawny-grey with a lighter underpart visible on the chest. However, as I was a long way off, many details could not be seen, but one thing was certain: it had a small, roundish head and a very long tail. I could not easily see any ears, and facial features were not visible. The animal might have been five or six feet long, if outstretched, including its tail. I had no way of getting closer, for two fields, a river and a hillside separated me from the 'cat'. I had difficulty in judging anything else about the animal, which, if it was a big cat, would be very like a puma or mountain lion. The creature was not black.

We drove on after about three minutes, for I did not have a good enough lens on my camera to attempt a photograph, and it was getting late. The approximate time of my sighting was 8 pm, and I was the only one to see the 'puma'. I am not lying, and all the events above are totally true. I later on sketched the animal and compared it with the creature I had already seen in the Mendip Hills of Somerset and Avon (recounted later in this book). The cats were very different indeed. These differences can best be illustrated in tabular form:

Also, back in July 1986, Mr Jim Gibbs of Limeslake Farm, near North Molton, came upon two dead ewes, and he recognised that their death was the work of the beast. He told reporters of his own sighting of a black big cat and a brown big cat: *"I saw them both among a herd of bullocks."* He asserted that the black cat was a panther and the brown one a puma. Two ewes and a lamb were lost at Ash Mill and Knowstone Farm, where the victims had deep bite wounds in the neck, and ears were missing.

According to a report in the *North Devon Journal Herald* for 24th July 1986, a Mr Garfield Adams of Bicknor Farm near South Molton had also heard the beast's screams at night.

The foregoing evidence suggests that more than one puma is loose in North Devon, while some sightings have occurred nearer to Dartmoor and west towards Cornwall. I can only conclude that five or six pumas have been let loose in an area from Bideford to Dulverton. Just how many of those pumas are alive at the present time I do not know, but I think it is safe to say that two or three are around. It is also strange that the panther-type animal should be seen with the puma-like beast. This is hard to interpret, because pumas and panthers are unlikely to crossbreed. It is possible that these creatures were released together, because nine escapees are known to have occurred around Exmoor. I feel it is safe to say that any British big cat is unlikely to exist in this area.

- ## The Exmoor Lynxes

Since 1983, a number of incidents have taken place on Exmoor, involving a pair of European lynxes. In

1984 and 1985 sightings occurred in the Bane valley area. However, in January 1985 a lynx-like creature was so bold as to walk into the North Devon village of Muddiford. The Mugleston family, who reside at Broomhill Country Hotel, in the village, have had three sightings of such a creature. A lynx-like creature around the back of the hotel surprised Graham, the 13-year-old son of Mr and Mrs. Mugleston. His mother and a family friend, Mrs. Johnston, also saw the creature, which Mrs. Johnston said was 'very dark with pointed ears and a bushy sort of tail'. This sighting took place in January 1986.

At the same time, Mr Brian Chugg, a farmer of Hills View, Muddiford, and Mr Gerald Stevens of the Beeches, Muddiford, spotted a similar creature. Mr Stevens said that he had never seen anything like it, while Mr Chugg felt sure it was not a dog, on account of its 'pushed- back' face. This was reported in the *North Devon Journal Herald* for 23rd January 1986, in an article by Mr Tim Abbot, who had also written on the 1983 kills.

In December of the same year, Trevor Beer and a friend watched a lynx-like creature tracking a scent through a forestry plantation not far from a reservoir. For an hour, Mr Beer and his friend watched the cat moving along the scent trail. Mr Beer was able to pick the lynx up again and again through his 7 x 50 binoculars. He felt sure that the animal was a European lynx. There were sheep in the area, but none of them had been touched, so it was safe to assume that the lynx was surviving on wild prey, such as small deer, rabbits or rodents.

An old lady had seen a 'strange wildcat' several times in the same area. At the same time as the sighting, both men heard a rabbit scream; so maybe that was a victim of the lynx. This information was in a letter dated 11th February 1987, which I received from Trevor Beer.

January 1987 brought news of many other sightings of the more usual black beasts, but it was not until later in that month that some more facts were found on the lynx-beasts. Trevor Beer made a plaster cast of one of nine prints found on the spot where a sighting had taken place, between Muddiford and Barnstaple. The cast was then sent off to Bristol University to be identified.

Dr Steven Harris examined the cast and said it was definitely made by a large cat. Dr Harris, author of *The Urban Fox* and other books, as well as being a Mammal Society Zoologist, was a contributor to the study of urban foxes in Bristol. He and Trevor Beer had a discussion on the beast's footprint, on the B.B.C. 'Natural History' programme, broadcast on Radio 4. Dr Harris had examined the cast in detail, and he said the print was made by a cat 'large enough to be a lynx, and similar to a Scottish wildcat'. He did suggest however that a feral domestic cat might have made the print. However, the size of the print refutes such a suggestion, as it was 7.5cm long by 7.8cm wide. The print showed no claws and had the four toes and three-lobed pad typical of a member of the cat tribe. Therefore a dog can be ruled out, without doubt.

Back in 1986, a fleece had been found in the same valley from which the cat's print was taken. The sheep had been dragged up into a tree, The information given above was taken from the *Daily Mirror* and from the *North Devon Advertiser*, both published in January 1987. February 1987 was to prove another incident-full month for the lynxes. Two adults spotted a lynx-like animal at Tarr Steps, four miles from Dulverton in West Somerset, early in that month. Only a week later another sighting occurred in the same area. According to a letter dated 25th February, which I received from Trevor Beer, the following details emerge:

A Major Dunlop was walking with his wife and their two retrievers when he sighted the creature, which had accidentally been 'flushed' from cover by the dogs. The major described the animal as a huge tabby-cat, twice the size of a Scottish wildcat, and its ear-tufts were very pronounced. Mr Beer also said Major Dunlop told him that the cat spat and snarled at his dogs, but when the major threw a stick at the cat it moved off into the undergrowth.

We visited Tarr Steps a week later, with Mr Beer, to see whether there were any traces of the lynx-like cat. We found small caverns on the inside of the beech woods where the cat had been seen. The caverns were quite large enough to accommodate an animal the size of a lynx. We also came across a number of prints near the caves, but it was fairly likely a dog such as a lurcher made them.

The *Daily Telegraph* has let me reproduce the following article, which appeared in their paper for February 1987:

> *Exmoor Beast "is a lynx"*
>
> *The elusive sheep-killing `Beast of Exmoor` could be a lynx, according to Mr Nigel Brierly of Bishop's Nympton, Devon, who found hairs from the animal near its quarry.*
>
> *'The lynx normally jumps down onto its prey from a tree. This means it could jump down by mistake on a child," said Mr Brierly. The animal would run away when it was on the ground, if it met a child," he added.*

Mr Brierly told me he had not said that there was any danger to any children from the lynx. - Another recent incident involving the lynxes occurred during June of the same year. Trevor Beer had two superb views of a lynx in the ruin of an old farm on Exmoor. He took eight photographs, but as the lynx was under beech trees the resultant pictures were very dark. The cat was estimated to be 130 to 140 cm long. As there were three witnesses, there was no doubt about the identification of the creature:

It was a lynx. And to prove it, Trevor Beer drew a brilliant sketch of the animal which should eliminate any doubts.

Over the past four years, in the national press, the beast has metamorphosed from a dog to a panther, to a puma, to a lynx! This illustrates the truth that three cat types definitely exist on Exmoor, with the possibility of wildcats and hybrids as well.

We will now look at the more unusual side of the beast 'legend' - suggestions that it is an eagle, a were-wolf and even an angry farmer's ghost! The most recent claim is that the beast is a naked man, a long way from an escaped black panther, isn't it?

- **An Angry Farmer's Ghost?**

Mrs I. Chowth of Landkey village stores, wrote me the following letter, describing her involvement with the beast:

Yes, I have said right from the beginning of this thing killing sheep etc. that it is an angry farmer's ghost come back as a beast, as he was disgusted at the way farming was done on Exmoor, and this is the way he is paying out the farmers that is there now. It is very funny the men cannot shoot it, isn't it? My brother saw it on the Ilfracombe Road a while back and he said it ran in front of his car and then went through a thick hedge. He said nothing could get through a hedge like it. So it plainly shows it is not natural doesn't it?

I think Mrs. Chown's theory may have some truth. Could an old farmer have loosed a strange beast, before he died? The way the beast continued to kill meant that people began to think it was a phantom, rather than a flesh-and-blood animal. Just what the creature is that Mrs. Chown is describing is not too clear - is the angry farmer's ghost a panther? Or is it a phantom black dog? (See Trevor Beer's interview with Mrs. Chown in his 1984 booklet *The Beast of Exmoor*.)

• Werewolf?

A number of authorities have stated they believe that the `Beast of Exmoor` could be a werewolf! In *Fortean Times* no.44, Dr Dick Gwynn wrote an interesting article entitled 'The Werewolves of Devon', which gave evidence for this theory. He noted that people foamed at the mouth and wished to kill sheep when they consumed the ergot fungus *claviceps purpura*, which grows on crops like barley.

In the *Devon Life* for June 1984, Professor John Grange wrote about this cause in his article called 'Werewolvery', using a couple of quotations from mediaeval historians. Dick Gwynn was able to prove that the worst affected areas for ergot fungus were Exmoor and Dartmoor, and also went on to say that it is possible that the `Beast of Exmoor` could be none other than a number of werewolves - normal people taking the ergot fungus and then killing sheep.

According to Trevor Beer and others, there is on Exmoor a man who goes mad at times and is known to have killed sheep in the past. As he has been around since the 1950s, it is possible that he is one cause of the werewolf legend. Werewolves have a strange history.

It seems likely that 'were' means 'man' in Saxon and therefore we could be dealing with man-wolves. On the other hand 'were' has a curious likeness to the word 'weird', so we could be encountering weird wolves. The world 'were' also has a curious likeness to 'weir', which might suggest that 'werewolves' originated from water, which dragons sometimes did, long ago.

Turning from this aspect of the name 'werewolf', we might find ourselves thinking more about modern aspects of the werewolf. Wolves often kill for the sake of killing, and some people believe that werewolves were formed out of wolves that were particularly savage - possibly wolves with rabies.

• An Exmoor Beast Hunt - October 1987

We arrived on Exmoor with plenty of very recent incidents upon which to dwell. I had received two newspaper cuttings which showed that activity was proceeding in Devon. The first cutting was from the *Daily Telegraph* of 8th September, and the story was headlined 'Beastly Trips for Tourists'. The story under this headline told us:

> The Beast of Exmoor' - a puma-like cat which has allegedly been sighted many times since it started killing sheep in 1983 - is to become an official holiday attraction in an attempt to boost winter tourism there. Hotels are offering four-day 'beast breaks', which cost £120 for full board and a guided tour of the animal's 'killing grounds'. Mr Trevor Beer, the tour guide who claims to have seen the beast, said yesterday: "This is not gimmickry. We take it very seriously. The beast is a fascinating subject."

The second article appeared in the *Sunday Telegraph* and seemed to be running down these tours. The article was entitled *There's a Beast on the Wilds of Exmoor that's famed for fresh air and sun...* and was by David Brown, Agriculture correspondent. The article was dated 14th September 1987. It seems that local farmers were not happy with the idea of package holidays, because money was being made out of other people's troubles, i.e. farmers losing sheep.

Mr Brown talked to Trevor Beer, who denied that he was 'making a fast buck out of other people's misfortunes.' Trevor appealed to the farmers that he was not going to cause them any trouble, and I believe him, as he is a naturalist and not out to damage the countryside. David Brown continued:

> Trevor Beer.., announced a few days ago that he had taken the first colour pictures of a black panther-like cat which, he claimed, had been stalking Exmoor for years. His colour-slides show a blurred and distant small dark image, which has still failed to prove the existence of big cats in the area.

Trevor Beer treats the beast seriously, as do the farmers, and this article would seem to be misguided. In any case, David Brown found that none of the farmers were willing to talk to him at South Molton market, when 3,000 sheep were being sold. The reason for this unwillingness was because they feared that the value of their farms would drop if they were identified.

Mr Brown continues by telling us about Mr Nigel Brierly's new intention to photograph the beast, which is very interesting. He is growing a large amount of cat-mint as a sex-lure. He aims to photograph the beast at a chosen spot and then prove that it really does exist. Then the Ministry of Agriculture will do something about this animal, or animals. Mr Brierly also reckons that the big cats kill the sheep, but Trevor Beer considers that dogs are the main cause of sheep-killings, for which big cats are blamed. Many of the Exmoor farmers believe that big cats are the cause of all the killing. With this sort of break-up between the beast-watchers, it is not surprising that nobody has yet taken any undisputable photographs of the beast. Trevor Beer told me of his photographs in a letter of 8th September 1987:

> I have now photographed the black big cat, and have nine colour slides of it on an Exmoor hillside. They are not as good as I had hoped, but show it well as a panther-type cat and not a dog. I had a 300 mm lens on at over 100 yards, so it was hand-held photography in fading light, 6.45 pm Bank Holiday Monday. We had amazing views of it hunting rabbits (four of us) and I am now deciding how best to go about things.

We went back to nights later but we didn't see it. This one is as long as a Labrador, two-foot tail, and has brownish tufts on each side of the eyes, yet it is otherwise jet-black. A beautiful animal, definitely living on rabbits when it can. There was a field of sheep beside it and they took not the slightest notice.

The sighting was on 31st August 1987, it would seem. The local T.V news showed some of the photographs, and the cat was seen sitting, standing and walking. After the local television had shown the pictures, the B.B.C. Breakfast television programme also had a feature on the cats. A biologist talked about the beasts' existence for some time, and the interview ended with the biologist saying that the mystery would continue.

- ## A Trip in Search of the Beast

I have recorded this trip in the form of a diary.

<u>25th October 1987</u>

Our first stop was at the home of Mr Nigel Brierly, who has been gathering information on the beast for five years. He told us that there had been two newspaper articles on the beast. The first, which had been published about six weeks earlier in the *Bideford and North Devon Gazette* was on a big cat which had been seen near Bideford.

The other sighting referred to a black animal seen near Timberscome, and was contained in an article published in the *West Somerset Free Press*. Mr Brierly confirmed that photographs that I had received from Eddy Bell of Durham, about the so-called 'Durham Puma', did indeed show paw-prints of a large cat, which was good to know. Mr Brierly is a qualified zoologist.

Then we took photographs of the area around Drewstone. Rupert Bray, who is the official photographer on this trip, took most of the photographs, using colour films. The next place where we pulled in was an old quarry, in forestry commission woodland, where we found plenty of pheasants. Halfway up a forestry track, I found what seemed to be some unusual animal droppings.

These were semi-liquid and extremely like the ones found at Croydon Hill woods, on my last Exmoor trip. We photographed these 'runny' droppings. There was a faint trail on either side of the woodland track.

We then called upon Mr Sam Nichols and his sons at Meadowlands Farm, near Molland, whom I had interviewed on my previous trip. The startling evidence Mr Nichols told me was that the cats followed a circle around their area, which tied in with the droppings that we found. One of sons the told me that there had been a sighting a month previously, by a lorry driver who called on the Nichols to say that he had been watching deer from the A361, looking out over the valley towards Exmoor, and that he had seen a large black animal jump on a sheep. The animal stalked the sheep, but at first the driver thought it was a large fox, though the creature seemed to be like a black big cat. The driver shouted and the creature ran off. Mr Nichols did not know the man's name, but he heard that a ewe was found dead the following day, in the adjacent field.

Mr Nichols also said that the B.B.C. had telephoned him four times since he had been on television, for the *Tomorrow's World* programme, on the beasts all over Britain, in May 1986. He added that he had lost sixteen sheep in the past five years, out of Drewstone's total of a hundred or so sheep. We returned 'home', which was a Dulverton bed-and-breakfast, with the knowledge that Mr Nichols would telephone us, should anything develop on the cats. We shall now start the week with some hope.

Monday October 26th

We started out towards some old quarries, near Croydon Hill Woods, Dunster, where I had heard that the black big cat lived. At the entrance to the quarries some construction work was under way. We then went around the quarries, which proved to be a nature reserve. In a hut, in a woodland grove or clearing, there were a number of maps and brochures to do with the 'Exmoor Natural History Society'. The 1985 *Exmoor Naturalist*, the journal of the above society, edited by N.V. Allen, said of the roe-deer: 'It would seem that dogs have killed deer in Porlock Park. Several deer were killed, especially fawns. This has therefore affected their numbers.' This is an interesting point and was in the reference journal left in the hut.

How could the naturalists be certain that dogs were responsible for those kills? Moving round the reserve, we came upon some droppings in some holes, but a badger could have produced these, for there was a sett further up the quarry. On the way back we encountered some paw prints or spoor, which were very cat-like. The paw-marks showed hardly any claws and were wide rather than long, like a big cat's pad is known to be. We discovered some seven or eight spoor-marks and photographed them, carefully marking where they were found. The pad-marks had four toes and reminded me of a domestic cat's pad, although five times larger. The animal that made the marks would probably have been around the size of a medium dog.

We then drove on to Minehead Library, where I photocopied some old references from various local books about cats on Exmoor. It was about four o'clock in the afternoon that I called upon Mr Bob Barron, of the *West Somerset Free Press* at Willerton. He said that only one newspaper article had come in during the past three months. He was unable to find the article, but these were the details:

About a month before (i.e. September 1987) a driver for the Watchet Bakery, Mr Piere St John, had seen a black animal half-way between Wheddon Cross and Timberscombe. His two other driver-friends had also seen it, on other occasions. I have since written to Mr St John, to find out about his sighting and hope to hear from him in due course. We concluded Monday by stopping at the place where I had seen the puma, five or six months earlier.

Tuesday 27th October

We started out towards Luxborough, where we had a brief examination of the new trail that we had found on our last trip. There were some droppings at the trail entrance, where it crossed over a hedge. We planned to carry out a closer examination the next day. I visited Watchet Bakery, hoping to interview Mr Piere St John. He was not present, but we left a letter for him and planned to contact him later in the week. The next step was to drive to Simonsbath in the pouring rain, and to walk 6 miles to Landacre Bridge, in some very wild moorland country, following the River Barle. We found two lots of very lynx-like droppings, which were photographed. The first were under an oak tree, on top of a cow-pat - of all places! The second set was high up on a hill. We also photographed a sheep-kill, but all that remained was the fleece, which was right by the River Barle. This was all the evidence we found that day.

Wednesday, 28th October

On leaving Dulverton at five this morning, we headed out towards the Luxborough trail. On the way we found a dead, half-grown fox-cub, which had recently been run over by a car. This was photographed by Rupert Bray, with his Praktica Super TL1000 camera. We met a gamekeeper at the Luxborough trail, but as yet no sighting was made. We returned in time for a nine o'clock breakfast in Dulverton, and we planned the rest of the day.

We returned to the Luxborough trail. On the way, about two miles before Wheddon Cross, in the Barle valley, we saw three deer on a hillside, and what we thought was a sheep-kill, high up on the other hill-side. On closer examination this proved only to be a few shiny-surfaced rocks. The deer was a red deer stag, a four-pointer (i.e. four years old) with his two does. We also had excellent views of a pair of buzzards gliding high over the valley. I had one in my view for at least five minutes, and picked out many details as it flew around in continuous arcs.

We drove on to the Luxborough trail, where a close examination of the woods revealed a dead sheep, droppings, and a wealth of pheasants. We found that the ewe had died of natural causes; she had probably rolled onto her back, so that she could not jump up again. There were some strange droppings, but a fox had possibly made these. There were no definite signs that a big cat was in the area, or used the trail. The forestry station at Luxborough was our next port of call. The head forester gave me the address of the people who organise all the Forestry Commission records. He told me that two porcupines had been shot in Forestry Commission woods, near the River Torridge, after killing a terrier dog. I presume these porcupines are related to those, which escaped from the Pinevalley Wildlife Park, around 1970.

The forester remembered that there was a puma cub where he lived, in Surrey, and that he had heard of a big cat in Norfolk when he stayed there, but although he had worked at Croydon Hills for 15 years, he had never seen it. Although helpful, he was a sceptical forester.

We had a picnic lunch at Druids Combe, which is about half a mile outside Luxborough. It was while I was inside the car and my mother was busy clearing up the picnic that Rupert Bray spotted a black animal on the far hillside. In his own words, this is what happened:

> *2.45 p.m. I was standing on a slight incline looking across the valley to a hillside covered in a newly-planted coniferous plantation, which was criss-crossed by many rough tracks. I spotted a black creature with powerful shoulders and haunches. It stood about 2 feet high and four feet long. It was jet black with a long tail and pointed ears. Its coat was in good condition as it was smooth, short-haired and shiny. It came onto a track, paused for a couple of seconds, and then took a few slow steps before bounding up a small slope. It disappeared into some more conifer plantation.*

He described it as 'feline', with its movements being 'un-doglike'. He thought it was like a black panther or melanistic black leopard.

We moved on to the place where Rupert Bray observed this creature. After climbing up the slope, we reckoned the animal had crossed the track in about five bounds. We removed two claw-marks on a log by scraping the bark off around the claw-prints. Some signs of squashed puffball fungus showed us that an animal had passed that way. I also found some droppings, which we decided to take to the Dulverton veterinary practice the next morning. We carried on back to Dulverton, feeling elated at our success in hunting the beast of Exmoor.

Thursday 29th October

Today we did not rise until about ten o'clock. Following this late start, I took the droppings to the Dulverton vets, Fuller, Elliott and Fieldhouse. The vet, stated that they appeared to be the droppings of a dog.
We visited Wistpoundland reservoir, but sighted no big cats. Then we set off towards Muddiford, where I interviewed Mr Muddleston, who had twice last year seen a black big cat (in 1986). He photographed the cat as it ran across the hillside. However, the photograph did not come out well, for he said 'It could have been a post.' It was not worth even seeing the picture. His photos, and Trevor Beer's 19 photos, were - at the time - the only ones in existence of the Exmoor beast. We then drove to Braunton Burrows, where some feral cats are said to live, but I did not see them.

Friday, 30th October

Today, we headed out towards the legendary Doone Valley. Rupert Bray and I hiked 3 miles over the moors and down this beautiful valley. High on the moor, we found the remains of two dead ewes of the Exmoor type. The sheep were just skeletons, and one had been dragged in half. That is to say, it had been 'cut' in half by something very powerful.

We found a large clawed paw-print in the area, about 200 yards from the other kills. There were traces of a fleece in an 8 feet-wide area. We found some cat-like droppings in the middle of this fleece site. All the clues were photographed, and we took some of the evidence home with us.

My mother, riding a horse, met us half-way down the Doone Valley. She had hired it at the foot of the valley, at 'Lorna Doone Farm'.

To illustrate the fact that strange animals have been in this area for a long time, I would be able to turn to the book *Murder and Mystery on Exmoor*, by the editor of the *West Somerset Free Press,* Jack Hurley, which was first published by the Exmoor Press in 1971. The following is the story he includes, which may refer to a black big cat, near Seiworthy, on the coast between Porlock and Minehead:

- **Shivery**

  The most shivery story is one mentioned by the Rev. W.H. Thorton in his "Reminiscences of an old Westcountry clergyman".

  One morning he heard that Mrs. Mary Stenner of Seiworthy had seen a ghost the night before. Thorton went over to see her and found her not far from collapse. She told him:

"I hadn't left Budleigh Hill by two gunshots when there it was, the nasty thing, running along by my side. 'Twas awful. It had four legs and was black and had great fiery eyes as big as saucers, and it ran on until it came to where the water crosses under the road, and they things, o' course, never can abide running water, so it just couldn't get across, and off it went into the air like a flash of fire. I screeched - oh! I screeched!"

Thornton saw John Hobbs, the sexton, who took the story most calmly. *"I know all about it,"* he said.

'Tis exactly twenty-five years since we was bringing a corpse from Horner 'Mill to Selworthy, and the handle of the coffin against the head worked loose, just exactly to the very spot where Mary Stenner met with the ghost last night. I picked up a stone and knocked the handle in again, and no doubt it went into the corpse's brain and let the spirit out. Oh yes! I know all about it.'

We may presume that this account refers either to a black dog or a black big cat. As Di Francis proved in her 1983 book, *Cat Country; the Quest for the British Big Cat*, black dogs often turn out to be black cats. Andy Roberts disagrees with this idea, as the table in his booklet *Cat Flaps! Northern Mystery Cats* shows. The fact that the above black cat/dog hated water and jumped in the air, sounds more like a black big cat.

There are also other things in the *book Murder and Mystery on Exmoor* by Jack Hurley, which are worth noting. Firstly, Mr Hurley mentions another mystery animal: the headless sow running with a litter near Welishead, Exford. Black panthers are easily the size of a sow, which is sometimes black, and big cats run with their head down, so could this 'headless sow' have been a big cat with cubs?

All the murders and disappearances on Exmoor add to the speculation. Could the girl who was found in a bog in 1919 have been followed by a big cat and drowned in the bog? Some of the cases are undoubtedly murder or suicide, but a few may be aligned to the big cats of Exmoor.

We are now nearing the end of this big section on the 'Beasts of Exmoor', and have seen that there is more than one beast. We also know that the cats have been there for a long time and that they are probably breeding. The possibility that some panthers, pumas and lynxes have escaped from captivity during the last ten years cannot be ruled out, and evidence would suggest that this is the case. Some of the cats may be descended from old escapees from travelling menageries, or from indigenous British big cats. These suppositions cannot be ignored.

I conclude with the observation that there could be up to fifteen large cats in North Devon and West Somerset.

The 'Exmoor Beasts' Saga is still continuing at the present date of writing - April 1988, as more letters and articles have reached me during the period October 1987 to March 1988. I have used the information as it has come in.

BIG CATS: LOOSE IN BRITAIN

On 12th March 1988, I received the following letter from Mrs. Julie Stirland of Bratton Fleming, near Barnstaple:

I am afraid that we are unable to help with your enquiries about the Beasts of Exmoor, as we do not own any sheep. However, we did sight two cat-like animals prowling in our farmyard one evening in November (1987). Our farm is situated half a mile from a farm called Ovis, where they had several sheep killed by the Exmoor Beasts, as you most probably have read about in the Western Morning News. 'Our next-door neighbour, Mr B. Gill, has apparently had some sheep killed also. He has photographs to prove this. I suggest that you write to him if you haven't already done so on this subject.

She then gives the address.

The late Miss Theo Brown, a renowned folklorist of Exeter, Devon, sent me an article from the *Western Morning News* of 10th March, as did Mr W. Bennett of the Totnes Museum Trust. This article summarised the `Beast of Exmoor` saga so far. It was by Tim Metcalfe, with the title `Beast of Exmoor` is a 10-1 longshot with the bookies. Mr Trevor Beer was photographed and his views summarised. Once again, Nigel Brierly's new method, on how to capture the beasts using an aphrodisiac lure was referred to by Mr Metcalfe.

The article goes on to give the view of then recently-retired journalist Mr Timothy Abbott. He was able to suggest that the beasts could simply be powerful lurcher dogs loosed by poachers, although he was the first to publish material on the beasts in 1983. Mr Abbott remarked:

'There's extensive deer-poaching on the moor. They hunt with lurchers and, when discovered, the dogs are often left to their fate. A lurcher would still need to eat, and it could take a sheep or a lamb without any trouble.'

At the time of writing, Mr Abbot now takes people on guided walks across Exmoor.

The bookmakers Vickers of Barnstaple offered odds on the proof that the beast is not a dog, announcing they'd pay out £100 after a definite photograph. One had to stake £1 to stand a chance of winning £100. The ultimate photograph would be dated, with a newspaper in the foreground. The possibility of faked photographs was underlined by local photographer Mr Tom Teagan's cut-out cardboard silhouettes of a lion on a background, which fooled the newspaper for a time. The papers were 'pretty angry' after the incident, according to Mr Nigel Brierly.

The following theory was well-known, but it involved an Act different to the 1976 Dangerous Animals Act. This quotation comes from Mr Metcalfe's article in the *Western Morning News* of 15th March 1988:

When the Wildlife and Countryside Act outlawed exotic pets in 1981, no doubt many owners, confronted with stern new restrictions, decided to set their mountain lions and panthers free, rather than put them down. Such pets are known to have been kept in the area.

Rumour suggests, however, that they were turned loose, which does throw light on some of the 'Exmoor Beasts' legend. Other private owners and circuses could have let loose big cats in the 1880s, 1950s, 1960s and 1970s to account for those sightings and big cat sheep kills. I cannot commit myself as to just who turned what out, but the abandoned pets theory will be worth considering. Any released cats may have helped the local tourist industry!

And Mrs. Anne Waterson gave a slightly different description of her 1986 sighting to me. It will be recalled that I used a quotation from her letter to naturalist Trevor Beer earlier in this chapter. Writing from Woolston, Southampton, she recorded her sighting:

My sister, who lives in Devon, passed on your letter in the 'Gazette' to me. My family and I were lucky enough to see the black panther of Exmoor on 1st May 1986. We were walking along a footpath between Oare and Malmsmead by the river when we came to a wooded area. I looked up to see a pair of eyes staring at me, and realised it was a large black cat.

We all stood rooted to the spot, and literally 'stared it out', until it got up, turned and walked away from us, glaring back two or three times. It was a chunky animal about 4 feet long and 2 feet high, mostly black but with brownish shades on the under-belly. There were some lambs on the opposite bank of the river and we assumed it had been watching them until we came along. I wrote to Trevor Beer, who is a well-known naturalist and who has been tracking the 'Beast of Exmoor' for some years. He would be the person to help you with your book. Mr Beer wrote back, saying that he and a ranger had been to the spot where we had seen the panther and found some tracks.

The tracks were found to have been made by a large cat, according to a letter sent to me by Mr Beer. The sighting is very much in keeping with other sightings, but I would make the comment that the earlier description was of a more lurcher-like animal. It does, however, show cat-like characteristics; it stared back at the witnesses, like a cat often does when watching intently. The act of turning round to look back three or four times could also be described as a cat-like characteristic.

As I write, I see that John Fairley and Simon Welfare have produced *Arthur G. Clarke's Chronicles of the Strange and the Mysterious*, which was published by Collins of London, in 1987. It contains an account of the Exmoor Beast, under the section *Puzzling Pumas, Curious Cats*. The 1983 saga was naturally given credit. The Marines of 42 Commando could not catch the beast, despite all their modern equipment. A Marine spokesman said:

The animal moves like soldiers themselves do, from cover to cover, and it rarely crosses open ground. It kills ruthlessly, ripping open its prey, and it can eat 35 lbs. of meat.

At 5.30 on a May morning in 1983, Marine John Holton saw a strange beast in the valley below the moors, and he told the press:

"It was very big, all black and looked very powerful. It was crossing a railway line, but there was a farm-house in the background and it wasn't safe for me to shoot." The services of game park chief Philip Lashbrook, who had served in the South African bush, proved fruitless and a farmer lost a cow which had "the skull crushed by one incredible snap of the jaws". There was also a photograph of a marine pointing his rifle over a hedge. As commandos, marines are trained for sharp-shooting, using night-sights. These were all the details that have not been referred to already, in the *Exmoor Beasts* chapter of *big cats Loose in Britain* from the *Arthur C. Clarke's Chronicles of the Strange and Mysterious*.

The next information came from Mr Nigel Brierly and referred to a photograph of a paw-print that was taken in October 1987 by Rupert Bray. He also told me about a foal that was killed, or died, on Broomhill country estate, Muddiford, Barnstaple. Mr Brierly's letter was dated March 1987:

> *The photograph of the paw-print:*
>
> *It is difficult to assess the size from the print, but it would have to be in the region of 4 inches across, to be that of a puma. Furthermore it appears to be slightly narrower than it is long, which points more to canine than feline. Cats' paws spread out more. Sorry I can't be more positive. I am sending you a photograph of the Haflinger foal, which may be useful to you, together with the negative. This is quite typical of the kills we have had around here, although it does appear that a fox has scavenged afterwards, by the bites on the nose.*

The 'Clippings Files' in my *Exmoor Beasts* chapters file was most helpful, and I have been able to add these notes to each year, starting with 1983. I am also sure that these facts give us a further insight into whom the beast has attracted. The reports come from both local and national newspapers.

- ## THE EXMOOR BEASTS: A Summary with Excess Newspaper Articles 1983:

1) The *Express and Echo* of 22nd April 1983 had a large report by Jonanne Row called 'Bright-eye to catch a killer'. This was devoted to the hunt, informing people that there had been two good sightings, and that 60 lambs had been lost, so far. The police contacted Paignton Zoo but they were unable to identify the killer. Back in April 1983 the police also had started to say that it was a dog, as a Bristol police spokesman remarked:

> *We are keeping an open mind about what sort of animal it is... but it appears on balance that it is some kind of big dog.*

The killings had started in early March. They did not finish until July 1983 for the South Molton farmers - five months of 'Beastly' killings. Mrs. Ruth Ley, the drewstone, was quoted as saying:

> *All night and every night we are keeping watch... We will not give up until we find the killer. If we do not get it this year, the killings will go on next season. We will get it in the end, but at great expense.*

2) On the 3rd June 1983, the *Exeter Express and Echo* reported that weird animal screams were being heard at East Anstey, near Dulverton. The village of East Anstey is ten miles away, on the edge of Exmoor, but the police knew that the beast could cover big distances in search of food. The police were planning to use new tactics.

3) These tactics did not work. The 17th June 1983 *Exeter Express and Echo* reported that the beast had killed a sheep over at the isolated Leigh Farm, Exton, near Dulverton. The sheep was savaged, as was a Hampshire Down Suffolk lamb at nearby Mr Philip Land's Hillview farm, Exton. The Leigh farm killing was at night. Chief Superintendent Michael Charles, the head of Taunton Police, who was coordinating the Somerset operation, said:

> We do urge all farmers, in spite of their heavy work loads this time of year, to check their flocks more frequently, particularly at late evening and early morning. By doing this they will detect any attack on their sheep more quickly, which will give police a greater chance of getting close to this animal earlier.

4) The *Express and Echo* of Exeter told their readers that, on the claims of three builders, another black panther sighting had taken place. These men told the press and Trevor Beer that they watched it for five minutes at a range of 200 yards. Mr Bird told the *Exeter Express and Echo:*

> 'We caught a glimpse of something and stopped the car. We started whistling and shouting, and it jumped out of a hedge to run across a field. It bounded up a hill from the valley and disappeared into cover. We were dumbfounded. I always believed the `Beast of Exmoor` was someone's lurcher dog, but this was not a dog - we are all certain of that. It was stocky, with strong legs, a straight tail and roundish face.
>
> It was a lot bigger than an Alsatian. It was like watching a big cat on a survival programme. It ran off like a flash when we started making a noise.'

The animal was fit and well-fed - on sheep? The sighting was in a quarry in the Bray Valley, near South Molton.

5)   An un-dated clipping from the Exeter *Express and Echo* informed readers that the beast had returned with a family. Two black cat-like animals were seen running together on East Exmoor. The beasts were stated by the National Park Wardens to be large feral cats. The Wardens thought that the cats had killed sheep and deer. (These must have been very large feral domestic cats.)
A police spokesman stated:

> There have been no recent reports of large-scale sheep-worrying.

6) In the same year, Minehead councillor Mr Tony Holman lost a sheep on his land. The sheep was partly eaten, leaving only a skull, ribs and two legs. The local police chief inspector, Mr John Kelly, said: 'We are investigating'. The *Sunday People* article also quoted Mr Holman as saying:

It was horrible to see an animal stripped of flesh like that and with so many bones missing. I have always scoffed at the idea of a beast, but when you hear so many reports and then this, it does shake you a bit.

7) On the 7th November 1986, Joan Amos heard a report on the local news, which she recorded in her scrap book. A number of sightings had occurred at North Molton of a black and brown big cat. Sheep were pounced on from a tree, and plaster casts of paw-prints were taken. A mother cat with kittens was thought responsible. The cat, or cats, consumed 15 lbs of mutton.

8) The beast had been in the North Molton area since 25th July 1984 because the *Daily Telegraph* of that date reported:

'The beast is back! Farmers in the Westcountry fear that the so-called 'Beast of Exmoor' could be on the rampage again. Five sheep have been found savaged to death at Ash Mill and at North Molton where the 'Beast' first appeared'.

9) The *Western Morning News* of 29th November 1986 had an article by Mark Dough, called 'Bid to tape the Beast of Exmoor'. It would seem that a farmer from an area north of Barnstaple, who wished to remain anonymous for fear of trippers on his land during lambing, had heard 'really horrific' screams at night. He had lost a ewe to what at first appeared to be human black magic rituals. Two of his neighbour's sheep were also found savaged. The farmer's brother-in-law and niece were terrified by the beast's screams. The farmer planned to use a series of tape-recorders and microphones to capture the animal's screams on tape. Then he planned to get the screams positively identified by an expert.

He said: *'We are country people and have lived in the country all our lives, but we have never heard anything like it before. Regularly over the years I lose some stock to foxes. It is almost an occupational hazard. But this is something a bit different.'*

In the previous three weeks there were two sightings near the farm. Mrs. A Shirwell saw a large black cat run along the road in front of her car, and another woman was walking her dog on the outskirts of Barnstaple when she observed two huge cats fighting.

10) The editorial comment section of the *Exeter Express and Echo* of April 1984 states:

'Remember the Beast of Exmoor?

It was a year ago that reports began of a panther-like creature preying on sheep and lambs in North Devon. Most of the killings were around the South Molton areas, but in later days they spread over Exmoor and even moved towards Taunton. The deaths of more than 100 sheep and lambs were attributed to the beast. Farmers formed night patrols, and several dogs were shot in a bid to protect flocks. The Royal Marines were called in, amateur big-game hunters, national newspapers seeking a large reward, and even just sight-seers flooded the area.

The killings continued for months. The beast was never caught. Was there ever really a beast? Was it just a large rogue dog? The arguments rage on even today. Mr Ralph Lacey, National Farmers' Union group secretary, said:

'I think it is true to say that anybody who had seen the carcases at the time would say there was something very peculiar about it, because of the way it killed and the amount of meat and bone it ate at a sitting. There is no official line on whether it existed or not. The farmers who suffered the damage are absolutely convinced that something peculiar was in the area.'

So what has happened to the beast?

A report of a large, cat-like animal being seen in the Colliepriest area of Tiverton is being treated seriously by police.'

11) We shall now look at the 1986 to 1988 'Beast of Exmoor' saga through articles from newspapers and B.B.C. radio broadcasts, starting in July 1986. This is about the same time that I first became interested in the 'Exmoor Beast'.

The *Western Daily Press* of 25th July 1986 reported that farmer Mr Jim Gibbs of Limbslake Farm, North Molton, had seen a black panther lik type cat and a fawn puma-like cat on his land. He told reporter Christopher Rundle:

'I saw them both among a herd of bullocks. I have had sheep killed here every year in this way, ever since the beast was first recorded. No dogs would ever have done this.'

There had also been a number of sheep-killings in the area at the time of the sighting. The paper said that the beast was first seen in 1982. The Royal Marines were said to have killed nine semi-wild dogs. The 'Radio Devon' news was supplied with some information by *Devon News* of Barnstaple, which was announced on 5th November 1987:

'Beast - A new theory that the `Beast of Exmoor` is a lynx has been advanced by a man who has been making a close study of the series of sheep killings for the past four years. Nigel Brierly of Bishop's Nympton said that hair from the site of one of the killings had been identified as coming from such an animal, and thinks it is probably that of a European lynx. He says that the killings are continuing on Exmoor at the rate of about one a week and that because of the amount of meat eaten at the kills, it is probable that several cat-like animals - possibly a female and her kittens - are feeding together.'

The Bristol press and picture agency supplied BBC Radio Devon with the following information, which was broadcast shortly afterwards:

Beast - Chief Inspector John Kelly of Minehead police said, "We keep an open mind on the question of the beast. There have been a number of reported sightings over the years and it is always difficult to know how much is fact and how much imagination. But we are certainly investigating this attack."

More than 130 killings have been attributed to the beast by some residents, and recently two men who crashed their car in North Devon told police they had swerved to avoid a large animal in the road.

This broadcast was part of a longer statement telexed to 'Radio Devon' by the Bristol Press and Picture Agency, on 17th November 1986. The statement concerned Mr Tony Holman's dead ewe, which was found only a hundred yards from his home in Periton Lane, Minehead. Maybe the sheep could have met a dog.

On 10th December 1986, Richard Howe, for 'Good Morning Devon', interviewed Bernard Simms on 'Radio Devon'. The introduction and newsreader's broadcast ran:

Dingo Dogs: All kinds of attempts are being made to try and catch or identify the so-called "Beast of Exmoor"... from drafting in the Royal Marines, to cage-traps, photography and tape recorders. Now the British forensic scientist who testified against Linda Chamberlain in the famous Australian dingo trial has offered his services. Bernard Simms is a specialist in orontology in London, and wants to see the bite-marks of the beast, to try and find out what it is.

By 21st January 1987, Richard Howe was announcing on Radio Devon that Dr Stephen Harris, a top zoologist at Bristol University, who said that the marks shown to him are definitely those of a large feral cat, a kind of British wildcat, had identified the beast. But he says that it is not as big as a puma or a panther. The BBC's Natural History unit at Bristol has sought Dr Harris's opinion, who had a plaster cast of the track found by Barnstaple naturalist Trevor Beer on a farm north of the town.

Dr Harris described the track, saying that a feral cat had been the cause of the beast tracks. He blamed dogs for killing sheep, considering that they were killed by pet dogs out of control, or people out hunting hare and deer at night, with lurchers. The plaster cast was taken by Trevor Beer at a place where two cats were seen fighting by a dog-walking lady, on the outskirts of Barnstaple. The cast was apparently too small for a puma, but large enough to be a lynx. Dr Harris told the *Western Daily Press* reporter:

The pads on the print are spread out because the animal had jumped down into soft mud, so it looks bigger than the paw actually is. It is the sort of size of track that could be made by a particularly large feral cat, certainly not a leopard or a puma. Their paw-prints would be massive compared to this. What must follow is that an animal this size would have difficulty in pulling down a normal-size ewe, and in any case cats usually kill with one single bite or blow.

The *Somerset News Service* telexed the following message to BBC Radio Devon on the 7th May 1987:

'Beast: A Somerset farmer, who's become the latest victim of the `Beast of Exmoor`, has warned other farmers not to take a long-range shot at it. David Baker fears it

could turn on humans if it is wounded or cornered, and he believes the beast could be a lynx. Evidence of the remains of a sheep killed on his farm at Rodhuish, near Minehead, suggests an attack by two animals, and it is thought a missing shoulder could have been taken off to feed kittens holed up in a lair in the dense woods nearby.'

The article, 'Gory Clues to predator's identity,' in the *Western Morning News* of 25th July 1987 was yet another summary to the beast saga.

This article said that the beast had become a myth, like the Loch Ness Monster. The only people who could be 100% sure of its existence were Nigel Brierly, Trevor Beer, the farmers and the witnesses.

On 4th October 1987 there arrived another telex to "Radio Devon", this time from the *Somerset News* of Taunton:

> *Town Beast: The Exmoor Beast came to town today with a sighting in Taunton. Pub, landlady Mrs. Warrington of the Waggon and Horses inn saw what she describes as a lynx leap about 20 feet from a conservatory roof into a tree. It had pointed ears and a striped back, and was three times bigger than a large domestic cat. Staff at the pub. say that Mrs. Warrington was wide-eyed with shock after she saw it and called in police and R.S.P.C.A. officers.*
>
> *They searched the area and contacted zoos and wild-life parks, but found nothing. The `Beast of Exmoor` has killed hundreds of sheep since it was first reported four years ago, but this is the first sighting in a town.*

The following broadcast was made in December 1987 or January 1988, on Radio Devon:

> *Beast: The `Beast of Exmoor` is back. Police in North Devon say that since December, 13 sheep have been killed at Ovis farm, Bratton Fleming. The killings have all the hallmarks of the so-called beast. The year-old lambs have been slaughtered individually, leaving the rest of the flock undisturbed. The killings are carried out every five or six nights. Police say the hind-quarters of the animal are eaten on the night of the attack, with the forequarters devoured the following night. Neighbouring farms have not been affected.*

The beasts appeared to be enjoying killing sheep, and the Bratton Fleming killings were a long way from the next beast encounter.

Mr D. Henderson of Barnstaple sent the following report to Radio Devon on 29th January 1988:

> *Beast latest: In one of the most savage attacks yet the `Beast of Exmoor` has struck again - this time killing a foal only a few hours old, near Barnstaple. The foal was discovered by its owner, Chris Mugleston who, with his parents, runs the Broom-hill Country Hotel at Muddiford. The Muglestons breed horses and the new-born*

foal was found with its throat torn out in one of the fields of the 160 acre hotel grounds. Beast expert Nigel Brierly who was called in today to investigate the killing, said he had found the largest prints he had so far discovered in his study of the Beast's activities and said they obviously belonged to a large male cat.

Mr Mugleston said that he had contacted the Ministry of Agriculture, and added that they didn't seem interested. He said:

'Quite apart from our loss, we think it is high time something was done about the beast because of all the killings over a long period. We've had damage by foxes before, but nothing remotely like this. Nigel said that he was quite shaken by what he found.'

The foal kill merits a deeper look, so I turn to the main sources of information - the *Western Morning News* and *Western Daily Press* of 30th January 1988. The foal was a rare Heflinger from Austrian Mountain Pony stock and was worth an estimated £1,000. The foal was only a day old, and it appeared that the foxes found it, for there were bite marks on the legs. The foal was partly eaten, and it seems that something smelt the animal's after-birth. Several guests at Broomhill a number of years ago saw the beast.

Nigel Brierly and Mr Trevor Beer both visited the scene of the kill. Mr Brierly told Tim Metcalfe, *Western Morning News* reporter, that the cats were responsible:

It was definitely killed by the so-called `Beast of Exmoor`. A puma covers a territory 100 miles wide. I think that they (the puma and European lynx) were in captivity together and both were released into the wild a few years ago, when the Law against keeping pets like that was tightened up. They are very protective over their territory. If any other cat strayed into the area it would be chased off. I am convinced that the animals feed most of the time on red deer calves, rabbits, foxes and squirrels.

The Eurasian lynx *(L. lynx)* was once a native of Britain. Officially, the last native lynxes died out 25,000 years ago, but there is evidence to show that they roamed Britain more recently.

The foal had only lived about two hours and could have died from hypothermia. Then animals such as dogs, foxes and big cats could have scavenged from it. Many theories could be offered. Mr Muggleston found huge, cat-like paw-prints in the area, which confirmed his suspicions that the beast had paid a visit during the night. Christoper Rundle in the *Western Daily Press* of 30th January quoted him:

Our foal may be dead and gone. It's a pretty distressing sight, even when you are fairly hardened to country life. But now I am concerned for the safety of every other animal in North Devon. It is getting a very serious matter when it starts taking large animals, and it's time that serious steps were taken to stop it. I was staggered when I 'phoned the Ministry, after the attack. They said they simply weren't interested, and that technically it was not their problem. There is no way this could be a dog or even a fox. They are both frightened of horses and wouldn't have gone near the mare. But cats are different. I've never seen an injury like this. The foal's neck was ripped out from ear to shoulder, and right back to the spine.

Two hundred yards away was where Mr Mugglestone's brother Graham had seen the beast in 1986.

Trevor Beer wrote to me:

The foal killed at Broomhill last week is the cause of controversy 'twixt the owners and Nigel Brierly and the Ministry of Agriculture. Their Ministry vet was called in and says 'Hypothermia followed by fox scavenging'. Nigel says 'big cat.' Mugglestone has a marksman in there at present. There have been sightings of a black and a chocolate-coloured big cat nearby in recent weeks. This exactly bears out my territory-theory, and prediction of Broomhill for January/February.

I have had a long talk with the Ministry of Agriculture doctor from their Wildlife and Storage Department, and he says that their examination also included nearby fox scat with foal hair in them; while black hairs on the foal carcass were typed and found to match those of the Alsatian owned by Mr Mugglestone. He accepts that the dog was at the kill before him, and says he found a four-inches wide cat-print near the scene. A pantherish cat has been seen since, chasing after horses in the field, and the observer says that the horses turned on the animal and chased it out of the field. The brown big cat was seen at Challacombe Hill by a Derek Jones, who lives at Arlington.

This last statement was dated 13th February. The Ministry of Agriculture are now interested in Mr Beer's territory theory and his maps of their territory. A doctor at the Ministry (the one mentioned in the letter) was going down at Easter 1988, to look into the above theory with Mr Beer. The sceptics who went on the first "Exmoor Beasts" tours have come away thinking that it is true, according to the same letter. Three of the tourist sceptics are taking serious steps to study cryptozoology. The controversial statements over sheep kills and other data seem to be slowly disappearing, as more people are convinced about the beasts. The Bratton Fleming kills were recorded in the *Exeter Express and Echo* of 22nd January 1988. Mr J. Bustin of Tedburn St Mary, South Devon, sent me the cutting. Thirteen sheep were killed at Mr B. Gill's Ovis farm, Bratton Fleming, North Devon. The sheep were all one-year-old lambs and were killed on different nights. No neighbouring farms had lost sheep. The Barnstaple police were investigating, and a spokesman said:

From what we can tell, they were all killed quickly and swiftly, without any disturbance to the rest of the flock. All their hindquarters were eaten on the same night, and their front-quarters on the following night. All that was left was the fleece. It seems to have been the work of one large animal.

Mr Trevor Beer investigated the case, and he told me the following evidence had emerged, in the already referred to letter of 13th February:

The Brayford killings at Ovis Farm are interesting. I spent a day there but any prints

I found were dog prints which, as the farmer breeds Belgian shepherd dogs, did nought to help prove anything at all.

The Ovis farm killings occurred at a time when there had been other sightings on 30th January 1988. The *Western Morning News* had a report of a 'leopard-like' animal, seen by Mrs. Doris Reed of Eastercombe Farm, Henton, near Barnstaple. She had seen this unusual creature bounding through a field behind her home. She watched it from a bedroom window. The animal was 5 feet long, but low to the ground, at 2 feet 6 inches high. It was a rusty ginger colour with dark sides, a long curly tail, and a small, round head. The police from Barnstaple carried out a search of the area, without any success. The sighting was thought to be of the Exmoor Beast. Mrs. Reed was familiar with leopards and lions, as she had lived in Kenya. She was positive about what it was, for she noted:

> *'It was without doubt not a dog. I spent some time in Kenya, and I am convinced I saw a cat-like leopard.'*

Leopard or puma? Here we have another classic cat-sighting. The Radio Devon broadcast could only add the details that Mrs. Reed was 35 to 40 yards from the animal, and that it had a russet brown top and dark underside. The sighting was made from a bungalow bedroom window, so vision would have been pretty good, as most bungalows are designed to give its occupants a good view.

The *Mid-Devon Star* published the first close-up photograph of the Exmoor Beast on 1st January 1988. The evidence was all coming from the Colliepriest area, near Taunton, and Tiverton. Colin Richey was the reporter assigned to the case. The photograph shows a seemingly large bear-like beast, black in colour, against a background of snow. Its tongue is visible. The animal could be a large black dog, a bear or a panther. The *Mid-Devon Star* had recently reported on beast sightings near to Tiverton. An enlargement of the photograph appeared on the first page, with this caption underneath:

> This is the Exmoor Beast, says mystery "Jungle Man". A mysterious animal trapper known as the Jungle Man claims that the photograph proves that the notorious `Beast of Exmoor` does exist. This week's revelations come as once again the Star hears of reported sightings. A Tiverton man said he saw the black panther-like animal just before Christmas. For a full report on the latest sighting and the Jungle Man, see page three today.

The local people were sure that the beast existed, as a number of them had seen it. The Jungle Man, an anonymous 'mystery animal trapper, had been 'trapping'(?) the animal for some time and had visited Colliepriest on a number of occasions. The Jungle Man, who had managed to photograph it, before it ran off, saw the 'black panther-like creature with tufted ears'. The Jungle Man was obviously afraid of ridicule and did not want his name disclosed in the newspaper. He was not a Colliepriest man, but maybe he was a local Tiverton resident. He may come forward one day. Mr Peter Bailey of Colliepriest Farm Bungalow, near Tiverton, knew the Jungle Man did exist, as he had met him. Mr Bailey sighted the beast himself before Christmas 1988, and he commented to the *Star*:

> *'People may think I have been drinking when I say I have seen this animal, or that I am letting my imagination run away with me.*

'Well, that's up to them. But I can tell you that on more than one occasion I have seen this creature. It is a very big black cat, very much like a panther. And it is frightening suddenly to come across such an animal.'

He had also seen this animal and not long before Christmas he managed to photograph it before it ran off. ('He' is the anonymous Jungle Man photographer). The reporter, Mr Colin Richey, contacted Mr Trevor Beer of Barnstaple, who stated that he had never heard of the Jungle Man.

The fear of humans always seems to show through in sightings. Trevor Beer told Mr Richey that 'April fool-type jokes' did not help investigators. Was this a joke? No, it would seem not to be a hoax, and Mr Beer gave his views in this long quotation from the newspaper:

'Over the past five years I have made an exhaustive study of the so-called `Beast of Exmoor`. And let me say at the outset, such an animal does exist.., but it is in the plural, not the singular, so it is more than likely that one such creature has turned up in the Tiverton area on more than one occasion. I have not been to the area myself, but of course over the years I have heard the rumours.

> *They are no Loch Ness Monster fantasy. They do exist. Some are a fawn colour rather like a puma, and the others are jet black, rather like a panther to look at. And in one form or another they have been seen as far apart as Scotland and Cornwall. To a naturalist like me they are known as a feral breeding population - animals that have escaped from some form of captivity and bred, and continued to breed with other animals in the wild. By now there must be literally scores of them roaming all over our countryside as they look for food. Their diet is mainly rabbits and other small animals and birds. In my experience, if approached they will run off as fast as they possibly can. I'm firmly convinced that it is more likely the work of rogue dogs, but of course it is easier to blame the Beast. We have to expect this and just put up with it.*

> *The fact that these animals can be seen in one place and shortly afterwards turn up in a completely different area is not surprising. They can easily travel 30 or 40 miles in a night, especially when they are looking for food. If anyone honestly thinks they have seen one of these so-called "Beasts of Exmoor", I would ask them to contact me.*

The latest piece of news comes from the Quantocks, near the village of Nether Stowey. I believe that the *Western Daily Press* of April 1988 said that sheep-killing was going on. I have yet to find out more about that story. This beast 'legend' will no doubt continue, and I can inform all the North Devon/West Somerset residents that the beasts are not going to die out fast! Six books already refer to the current beast 'myth', and an estimated 200 newspaper articles have appeared concerning it. Some of the South Devon and Cornish chapters in this book may well tie up with the `Beast of Exmoor`. Many of my contacts will continue to send reports, no doubt.

There were a few sightings back in the late 1960s and early 1970s. The *News* became the *Fortean Times* in the mid 1970s, and the February 1977 issue of this magazine, number 20, contained these two anecdotes in the editor's (Bob Rickard) introduction to "Out of Place":

> *The first case is from a letter to me from John Michell, dated 8th May 1976:*
> *Here's a good story to fill a gap in your puma record told to me today by my friend*
> *Mark Palmer. On Christmas Eve 1968 he and his friend, Maldwyn Thomas were*
> *taking horses across Devon and camped on Knowstone Moor, near Tiverton. In the*
> *late evening a local policeman roused them to ask if they had seen a puma, as one*
> *had been reported there that day.*

'Next, another anecdote, from Auberon Waugh's column in the *News*, 26th December 1975:

> *'... A few years ago... I was standing at an upstairs window (of a house in West*
> *Somerset) in the late afternoon with about four cricketers and their wives or girl-*
> *friends - one of whom was a teetotaller - when we distinctly saw a black panther*
> *run across the fields in front of the house. Waugh suggested writing a letter to the*
> *press to record the event but "several of the witnesses started to back down...*
> *they thought it might have been an extremely large black cat." Then Waugh says*
> *wryly: "The modern mind isn't interested in ghosts; it rejects them as unwelcome*
> *reminders of some discredited past." (Credit John Michell, John Rimmer, Roger*
> *Sandell),'*

Following is a quotation from a letter received from the naturalist Trevor Beer, dated 9th August 1987:

> *'Re: Roman escapes and travelling menageries. This aspect may not have been the*
> *subject of books on big cat phenomena, but it always enters into conversations on*
> *the subject and is simply common sense to accept that escapes occur whenever*
> *and wherever animals are housed for whatever reason. They always have and*
> *always will. At present there is much on the local news of a Chinese woman*
> *down this way who is rearing a black panther. She is in some conflict with*
> *neighbours and local authorities as to risk to life if it escapes etc.'*

The fact is that there have been some escapees on Exmoor and it seems that they have bred in the wild. The Exmoor Beasts are not going to die out for a long time - if ever. A live or dead specimen will be the final solution to the question of their existence.

Note on the 'Exmoor Beasts' chapter:

Mrs D. Lovett of North Molton, North Devon, wrote this in a letter dated 13th May 1988, which I quote with her permission:

> *I was most interested to hear you speak on the radio this morning and about the*
> *book you hope to publish about wild cats. We, like everyone else in the area, have*
> *heard quite a lot about the `Beast of Exmoor`! But to my surprise last week at about*
> *8 p.m. I was doing the dishes and I looked up the field that is directly behind our*
> *row of council houses (normally there are sheep in this field) and I saw what I*

thought was a lioness. So I called to my husband and we both watched it walk slowly along by a row of trees on the brow of the hill.

The description was just like the one you gave on the radio this morning. We haven't seen it again. I know a couple of years back there were several sightings in this area because they called the Marines in! I expect you know all about that.

A lioness wandering around North Molton? I think that this lioness must have been a puma, as they are similar creatures in appearance at a distance. I wrote back to Mrs. Lovett, asking more about the colour of the beast.

- Chapter Four -
SOUTH DEVON AND CORNISH CATS

• South Devon Cats

The first mention of anything vaguely cat-like coming from this area was recorded in the 1700s by a traveller, according to a letter dated February 1988, from Mr John Bastin of Tedburn St Mary, near Exeter.
In February 1855, the famous case of the `Devil's Hoofprints` occurred in the Exe estuary area of South Devon. The prints covered snow-clad fields, went along walls, along narrow window ledges and over roofs. On the 9th February of that year the people found hoof prints all over the countryside. *Arthur G. Clarke's 'Mysterious World'* notes one relevant reference to the hoof prints in a section called 'A Cabinet of Curiosities': *'A farmer said they must have been cats' paw-prints that had thawed out and then refrozen.'*

In her brilliant work, *Cat-Country: the Quest for the British Big Cat,* Di Francis gave the possibility that the 'Devil's hoof prints' might have been made by a British big cat. Alternatively, a kangaroo is known to have escaped from Mr Fish's zoo at Sidmouth, South Devon, around the same time as the hoof prints were found. The hoof prints are reported as being attributable to badgers, donkeys, cattle, sheep, mass hysteria, the Devil (Satan), dogs, foxes and all native mammals of a fair size.

The following sources should be referred to, when tracing material on the paw-prints:

1) Fursdon, Henrietta (daughter of Dawlish Vicar): *Devon and Cornwall Notes and Queries*. 1855.

2) *Torquay Directory*, Friday 9th February and Saturday 10th February 1855.

3) *Woolmer's Exeter and Plymouth Gazette*, Lympstone, 9th and 10th Febuary 1855.

4) *Illustrated London News*, 24th February 1855 (Revd. H.T. Ellacombe).

5) Brown, Miss Theo: *Transactions of the Devonshire Society*, 1950s/1960s/1970s.

6) Francis, Di: *Cat Country: the Quest for the British big cat* (David & Charles, Newton Abbot, Devon, 1983. See *Black Dogs and Devil's Hoof prints*, Chap 1)

7) Fairley, John and Clarke, Arthur G.: *Arthur G. Clarke's Mysterious World*, 1982. (See *A Cabinet of Curiosities*)

8) *The Times*, 15th February 1955.

There are undoubtedly a great many other sources, but the above should be an introduction to this mystery. There can be no doubt that there were big cats in the Exe estuary area in the 1700s and 1800s, when they could have made some of the paw-prints while on a prowl. The animals must have been almost starving, due to the cold and snow.

We now travel from the Exe estuary to the ruined rectory at Luffincott, Launceston, near the Devon/Cornwall border. From 1838 to 1893 the incumbent of the parish was the Revd. Frank Parker, who was a rather eccentric gentleman. In the book *Ghosts in the Southwest*, James Turner discusses the Revd. Parker's ghost returning to haunt the Rectory. Parker kept a library of old books on magic, of which he was both proud and protective. The servants wanted to look at them, but he would not allow them to do so, even interrupting a sermon he was giving in the church to stop people from looking at the books in his house.

The Revd. Scott, who was a Rector of Luffincott in the mid-20th Century, collected stories of this strange incumbent. Mr Scott told James Turner one story that was related to him by a local parishioner:

"My Gran," said one, *"used to say that folks believed that Parson Parker could turn himself into a lion."* The incumbent who followed Rev. Parker left hurriedly in 1897, leaving everything in the house. People vandalised the Rectory when they learned of this comparative treasure-trove just sitting there. The incumbent left because, when about to eat his supper one night, he observed the ghost of the Revd. Parker. The foundations of the Rectory can still be seen, but all else has gone, as the building was burnt down in a fire. The reference to a 'lion' could have something to do with our mystery cats, could it not?

Judy Chard wrote an interesting book called *Devon Mysteries*, in which she quotes a story from Mr Honeywell, a local historian of Ipplepen. I have a letter from Mrs. Chard dated 30th May 1987:

> *'The story of the cat was given to me by the man quoted in the book and I would think you should ask his permission, not that of Bossiney to quote it. I don't have his full address as it is some years ago, but he lived in Ipplepen which is not a very big village so you could probably contact him there.'*

I was unable to trace this gentleman, but I *do* have the permission of Bossiney Books to quote the following story from *Devon Mysteries*:

> *'Mr Greig sends a story dated 3rd December 1957. It happened when living near Holsworthy, he saw a great ghost-cat with eyes as big as saucers, which used to sit on top of a stone gatepost near Morwenstowe. A man there said he wasn't afraid of no ghost, and hit it with a stone. The cat jumped on his back and clung there while he ran home. Ever after he was bowed down as if with a great weight on his back - which proves the truth of the story.'*

I think Mr Greig observed a large cat such as a lynx. It is certainly a lynx habit to jump on the victim's back. Could the man who threw the stick at the poor creature have surprised it? In anger and desperation the cat would have leapt upon his back. Then he dug in his claws, and when they neared Mornstone the cat jumped off and disappeared into the woods. A ghost-cat would surely be weightless, and quite unable nearly to break a man's back. This story could be a folk tale dating from the early part of this century.

This story is not the only one concerning cat-like creatures from the early part of this century.

On page 66 of *Cat Country: the Quest for the British big cat*, Di Francis says:

> 'The earliest report of a cat sighting that I have read occurred sometime in the 1930s. An archaeologist working on a dig on the Moor reported that whilst working he had seen a puma-type animal.'

There is time here to examine the black dog legends, which I consider have a great similarity to the South Devon big cats. For this section I am indebted to Miss Theo Brown, who has researched into black dogs since the 1950s. Later on we will quote from her letters to me. The black dogs instil fear wherever they appear; John Harman, who went on a holiday to Devon in 1982 says, in his *Reader's Digest* article 'Glorious Devon' for May 1982:

> '... Nor did we meet the jet-black hell-hounds breathing fire and smoke which prompted Conan Doyle to write The Hound of the Baskervilles".' *

Dartmoor guide-books often refer to Squire Cabell of Buckfastleigh, who lived at Brooke Manor in the 1640s and 1650s. He kept a pack of large hounds which were similar to bloodhounds, and possibly black. He was considered to be a rather evil squire and these devil-hounds no doubt helped to keep his estate in order. He hunted over the Moor for polecats and foxes. Polecats are now no longer common, if found at all, in South Devon. Black dogs are common enough still.

Most of the encounters date from the 1800s, when people often observed these fearsome black dogs on deserted roads and lanes. Here are the localities of which I have heard where a black dog haunts. I have also added such details as I have come across:

---

* *The Hound of the Baskerviiles*

Sir Arthur Conan Doyle (1859-1930) wrote *The Hound of the Baskervilles* as one of a series of Sherlock Holmes stories for the *Strand* magazine in the 1890s. First published in book form by George Newnes Ltd. in London in 1902, this popular story has resulted in many editions, and in two films.

The book was inspired by a Westcountry legend of a large black hound that Sir Arthur Conan Doyle had heard about from his friend, Mr Fletcher Robinson. It seems that Sir Arthur stayed at Parkhill House, Ipplepen, on the Totnes Road. He used to go up onto the Moor for walks, and Mr Robinson's coachman was named Baskerville.

In her book *Devon Mysteries*, Judy Chard refers to the well-documented fact that Squire Richard Cabell, who died in 1653, kept a pack of large jet-black hounds at Brooke Manor, Buckfastleigh, Dartmoor. He used these bloodhounds to chase fox, polecat and hare. The squire had a formidable local reputation. He vowed to terrorise the local people after his death, so he was buried in a tomb with a 12-foot high gravestone over it. Judy Chard believes that Conan Doyle was inspired to write this book because Squire Cabell's hounds 'turned rogue'. Hound Tor and Wistman's Wood, both on Dartmoor, were places visited by Sir Arthur. *The Hound of the Baskervilles* was described as "a foul thing, a great black beast shaped like a hound. Yet larger than any hound that ever mortal eye has rested upon... blazing eyes and dripping jaws..."

a) Wistman's Wood, Dartmoor. This old wood of curving branches and trees is the home of a fearsome black dog, which haunts an old trackway there. It was recently the scene of a fawn puma sighting.

b) The same black dog was also haunting Hembury Woods in the late 1800s. (See Judy Chard's book, *Devon Mysteries.*) These woods are near to the town of Buckfastleigh.

c) The Princetown-to-Plymouth road is haunted by a murdered man's dog seeking revenge on passing travellers by flying at their throats. This dog is also a black colour, and only haunts one spot.

d) There is a black dog sometimes seen around Hound Tor, Princetown, Dartmoor. The hound gave the name to the large rock tor landmark.

e) The black dog, which haunts the Lydford-to-Okehampton road, could be the manifestation of a Lady Okehampton, who murdered three of her husbands.

f) The black dog of Dean Wood is said to be a weaver called Knowles, who has to bale out a pond with a holed acorn. Some foxhounds died in the pond in the 1960s while on a sporting chase.

g) In the area of Dog village, Broad Clyst, Exeter, on the Dorset-Devon border, is a famous black dog haunting. There was a sighting by a woman in 1852, but although her husband was with her, he did not see the large black dog.

Trevor Beer saw a strange black animal at Lydford Gorge recently. He told me in a letter dated 31st December 1987:

> *'I spent several weekends at Lydford in 1985 and 1987, following up various bits and pieces. On one visit we observed a huge black creature looking not unlike a black hind, on the pathway below us at Lydford Gorge. When we arrived at that same spot the animal 'was crossing the stream beneath the White Lady cascade, and clearly visible against the white water. We watched it move up along the path in the woods, and I have to admit to feeling the old spine tingle. I even let it get ahead, rather than have it turn back on us in alarm or anger. We then had one further glimpse as it headed into the cul-de-sac of the Devil's Cauldron. As it was a 'dead-end' in there, we sat awaiting its return. It did not come out. We waited half an hour and decided it was daft for any animal to be in there that long, so we went in ourselves, as far as is humanly possible, and it wasn't there! I haven't mentioned this as I felt a bit silly about it. There just isn't a way out without retracing one's footsteps! There were no footprints on the pathway, nor across the plank bridge in the Cauldron. We had no subsequent sightings at all.'*

The black dog haunts about ten locations in South Devon. There are references to this character in most local guide-books and also in the landscape. The names 'Hound Tor' and the 'Devil's Cauldron' must have some connection with the phantoms. Here we have large black creatures of an elusive nature appearing again and again.

BIG CATS: LOOSE IN BRITAIN

I have written as a footnote to this chapter an account of the truth behind Sir Arthur Conan Doyle's novel *The Hound of the Baskervilles*, which was set on Dartmoor in 1889.

We now come to what Miss Theo Brown has to say about black dogs. She told me from her home in Dog village, Broad Clyst, Exeter, in April 1988:

> *'I'm afraid I can't help you much as I am a folklorist, not a naturalist. Also I have been working on black dogs, not cats since about 1950, and have a huge dossier, which I couldn't begin to photocopy for you - it would take years and cost a mint of money. Anyway, though I have read Di Francis's Cat Country and met her, I don't agree that black dogs, when seen in broad daylight, could possibly be confused with big cats. And in a bad light it might sometimes happen but not often; the characteristics are so different. And I don't think it is reasonable to suggest that there's a native big cat that has survived from pre-historic times without being spotted. Have you any solid evidence of it? I have never seen any mention in old histories. All sorts of strange creatures were reported, odd things in the sky, even a 'dragon' at Horsham in Surrey, but not big cats. What one does hear is that it was fashionable for kings and very rich men to have private zoos, and no doubt some of their exhibits escaped from time to time. I've probably got one or two references to this if you'd like it. I'm sure we have lots of various big cats around, as you and Di Francis have found. Pumas are not the least like panthers or lynxes. I remember one man spotted a 'puma' in North Devon when it crossed the road in front of him, but from the very clear description he gave the animal was obviously a hyena!*
>
> *Trevor Beer has recently said that he's sure that rogue dogs are responsible for a lot of killings, but there are certainly lots of various big cats around.*
>
> *I see you write from Warminster. Have there been UFO activities there lately? That's an intriguing problem! I have been the Folklore Recorder for the Devonshire Association for over 30 years.' ***

We now move on to more modern South Devon cat sightings and incidents. Firstly, I am most grateful to Mrs. Joan Amos, who has built up a scrapbook of sightings and done some research herself, interviewing farmers and collecting newspaper reports. She is a member of the Plymouth UFO Group and is interested in the connections between mystery cats and UFOs. Her theory could tie up with the 'military' theory I have developed, so to speak. She very kindly photocopied the material for me.

Now we come to the first sighting from Mid-Devon. Janet and Colin Bord record an interesting sighting by Colonel W.H.C. Haines of Brushford, in June 1969. He was travelling down a country lane near Witherbridge, ten miles west of Tiverton, when he spotted an unusual creature by the roadside. Janet and Colin Bord and the publishers of their book, *Alien Animals*, have very kindly allowed me to quote what he saw. Their source was the *Western Morning News* of 25th June 1969:

> *'I have seen many leopards in Malaya, and it was exactly like one but smaller, although it was the size of a calf. At first I thought of a Great Dane or a fox gone*

wrong, but it was far bigger than a fox. I am non-plussed - I just do not know what it was. It had a brown head, large, prominent eyes and a nose extraordinarily like a pug. Its left ear was pricked, but the other hung down as if torn. Its ribs were a bright pale chestnut, turning to a sort of dirty gingery brown, and its hindquarters were darker still. On its hindquarters were three black spots about the size of a penny, and along its spine was a ridge of hair about two inches high which waved in the breeze. Its body was smooth-haired and thin. Its tail, long and thin, looked like a piece of dirty rope. Its legs were very long for its body, and pale in colour.'

The colonel saw the creature in good light for three minutes. He also noted that other witnesses had seen the creature two years earlier in 1967. Was this a brown-coloured, old and possibly ill big cat such as a puma? The answer is undoubtedly 'Yes'. I doubt very much that the colonel would mistake a mongrel dog for a seemingly large cat. To back up what the colonel observed, we can look at the sightings of the late police sergeant, Mr John Duckworth of Tavistock. He later moved to Okehampton, where his colleagues informed Di Francis that he had died in tragic circumstances. The book *Chronicles of the Strange and Mysterious* by John Fairley, Simon Welfare and Arthur G. Clarke, says of the two sightings:

> *'A beast of some description has been seen by reliable witnesses around Exmoor for at least twenty years. Police-constable John Duckworth of Tavistock saw the beast twice and collected eye-witness accounts of many other sightings. The first time he saw the animal was at Coxton in October 1969. He and his son had been flying a kite, but had got back into their car to warm up. Then, about 40 yards in front of them, they saw a strange animal coming towards them. "It was about the size of a pony," said Constable Duckworth, "with a dog's head and ears, wolf-hound head, and a short tail. It was slatish grey with heavy shoulders and a smooth coat." Three years later he was shooting, also in October, about two and a half miles away from Coxton. The same, or similar creature appeared, loping across some fields about 100 yards away. This time P.C. Duckworth had some binoculars with him and followed it until it disappeared over a wall.'*

In 1970 a panther scare was caused when a motorist sighted a black big cat at Telegraph Hill, Exeter. The scare came to an end when the Exeter R.S.P.C.A. were brought in. A large fat, elderly, half-blind black Labrador was found wandering by the roadside near Exeter. This dog was thought to be the alleged 'black panther'. (See Grant Dean 'On the big cat Trail', *Exeter Express and Echo*, 13th August 1982.) In this article Mr Dean also mentions the sighting of Mr Bill Harris, a postman. He was watching deer near Tiverton in 1973, when he spotted a 'light brownish' creature, with the gait of a cheetah. The animal was the size of an Alsatian. Mr Harris had apparently seen cheetahs in East Africa in 1942, during World War II.

• The Tedburn St Mary Panthers

These cats have been seen around Tedburn St Mary for some time, since at least the 1970s. Perhaps we should start by noting that a full account of this can be found in Di Francis's book *Cat Country: The Quest for the British Big Cats*.

Mr John Bastin of Tedburn St Mary, near Exeter, gave me this description of the cats in February 1988. He is a witness himself. The letter said:

'It seems we have a mutual interest in these strange cats. Incidentally, we have brown ones as well, and some that have been described as ginger. Not many weeks pass here between sightings. Not in the main village area, but in a five to ten miles radius. As you may well know, the terrain here in Devon is hilly. And in our area very hilly, which means many steep-sided valleys, wild and natural as they have been for a thousand years.

There is one valley about a mile from the village, which was never affected by the rabbit disease Myxomatosis, and this is the reason that I think that Tedburn attracted, and enabled the cats to live in our area. The first record of cats here was in the 1700s; a traveller in those times recorded them. If there was a population of something like twenty cats here in Devon, they would have no trouble surviving relatively unnoticed.

You will unfortunately have had to bear your share of teasing, but perhaps the saddest fact of this whole thing is the scorn that has been heaped on the whole idea of our country having its own population of large cats, and the stance taken by most established naturalists against the possibility. One wonders which comes first: science or their reputations. I wish you every success with your efforts. Maybe it will take a young man such as yourself to make the whole subject respectable. If anything of importance happens I will keep you informed."

This description seems to give us a starting-point from which to launch into the sightings around Tedburn St Mary.

At Kenton, Exeter, in the late 1970s, a large hind deer was blamed for the sightings of a black panther-type cat. In about 1979, a farmer's wife, Mrs. Pat Broumel, was riding past Tillerton farm when her horse shied. A large black animal with cat's paws frightened both horse and rider. The horse bolted, not wishing to make the acquaintance of the large feline. A quarter of a mile away, Farmer Mr Bruce Burton saw 'a mysterious pair of eyes' in the light of his torch, one night in about 1980. His wife was interviewed about this sighting by Grant Dean for his *Exeter Express and Echo* article of 13th August 1982, called 'On the big cat Trail'. Mr Dean found landlord Mr Eric Mattock of the 'King's Arms', Tedburn St Mary, had offered a reward back in January 1982. Mr Mattock had a large bottle of Bell's Whisky ready for anyone who could capture the 'puma'. The 'Cardboard Reward' advertisement said: 'Gallon of Whisky for the man or woman who captures the Puma.'

He had no answer to his reward by August 1982, but he had been quoted as saying, back in January of that year:

'I am determined to scotch this mystery one way or another. I tended to put the story in the pink-elephant category, but so many reliable people have been scared by this thing I am now beginning to think there must be something in it.'

Ide farmer Mr Martin Bragg, aged 23, saw a large animal dash across fields just outside Exeter, in August 1982. He was 'puzzled and amazed'. It was too fast for a dog and was not a fox. He said: *"I couldn't be-*

lieve my eyes."

Mr Peter Pattison heard dreadful noises one night in August 1982 but he found only one paw-print "which could have been the dog's" in the garden. He telephoned the police at Exeter, who informed him that they had checked the circus. No big cats had escaped from there. Mr Pattison was a vet from Ide and he had often attended to the claws of a pet puma in Paignton. He was in favour of there being cats, when he issued this statement to Grant Dean:

> *The night before the circus opened in Exeter (about two weeks ago) my wife and I heard a low guttural, cat-like sound in the garden at about 3 a.m. I thought it was the kids being sick at first. Horses were neighing and performing in the nearby field, and our cats were shrieking and rushing in and out of the cat doors. It frightened us. It was a controlled noise, which went on for 15 or 20 minutes - not particularly noisy. When we put the light on it stopped instantly. There are feral cats - domestic animals which have gone wild - living in the countryside without being fed. There is plenty of cover, and a bigger cat could sleep in trees during the day and hunt at night.'*

The Devon and Cornwall constabulary spokesman, at Exeter, told Mr Grant Dean: *"There have been many reported sightings of this kind of animal in Devon over the years."*

The *Fortean Times* had a piece on the 'Dartmoor Panther' in 1981. In issue No.35 there were descriptions of three cats sightings around Tedburn St Mary. The *Western Morning News* of February 26th and 27th 1981 had two articles on these three sightings. The *Fortean Times* used the *Western Morning News* as its source.

The 'Terror of Tedburn', a large cat similar to a panther or puma, was seen by Mr Nick Hallett, a lorry-driver from Tavistock, on the A30, near the Cheriton Bishop junction. He stated to the *Western Morning News* reporter: *"I knew it wasn't a dog or a fox or a badger, because I see those all the time."*

The cat ran across the road in front of his lorry. It was black in colour. And the next night, about 15th February, the same cat again ran across the road, at almost the same place. Mr Hallett again observed it. Some readers will already be muttering 'Black dogs', as by coincidence these creatures appeared at the same place. Maybe this was just a prowling panther or puma.

On 21st/22nd February 1981, 8-year-old Ben Huggins and his friend Peter Tremeer, aged 7, came upon a black big cat in woods near Spicery Farm, Tedburn St Mary. The owner of Spicery Farm was Ben's father, and he knew about the creature. The big cat chased the boys' dogs out of the woods, but was frightened on seeing them. On returning home, Ben went through his wildlife books and came to the conclusion that the animal was like a puma, but black like a panther or black leopard (*panthera pardus*).

In 1982 there was an outbreak of sheep-killing in the Peter Tavy area, near where Mrs. Amos lives. This was miles from the previous sightings, which were nearer to Exeter. These kills were occurring in the area of Tavistock. The *Tavistock Times* gives us no definite clues that the beast-killer was a big cat, although they do give it the title of a 'Mystery Beast', so speculation was open. Mr George Palmer and Mr Tony

Cossens joined forces to watch 'their flocks by night', to use a Biblical quotation. Mr Palmer, a farmer of Horndon, Peter Tavy, Tavistock, lost two lambs over Easter weekend 1982. He stated:

> 'I had two more lambs killed. One was on Friday night, the other on Saturday night. They were killed the same way. They were tiny day-old lambs.'

Mr Palmer had lost a total of eight lambs in the past week, all savagely ripped apart. The killer was definitely the same animal. Mr Cossens, also of Horndon, stated:

> 'I've not had any more lambs taken. I've not seen anything around to account for it all. I wonder if it is dogs, and people read the papers last week and kept them in.'

This was in the *Tavistock Times* of April 1982, under the title of 'More Lambs Killed'.

The early 1980s, up until 1983, were a trying time for smallholder Mr Kingsley-Newman of Stoke Gabriel, South Devon, who had at least two big cats on his land. The cats were jet black and had red eyes, it seems. In her book *Cat Country: the Quest for the British big cat*, Di Francis provides an account of Mr Kingsley-Newman's experiences. I telephoned the Kingsley-Newmans in February 1987, when I talked to his wife, who said that her husband was ill, so we could not visit them. She did say that Di Francis had actually gone to investigate at the farm after a calf was lost. She also said there had been no activity for 'three or four years', since about 1983. Mrs. Kingsley-Newman had never seen the cats, but her husband had seen them at least twice.

In April 1982, Mr Maurice Knowles of Prescombe Farm, Inglebrake, Lydford, South Devon, saw a large cat-like creature on his farm. The *Tavistock Times* of 16th April carried an article on this subject. I received a photocopied clipping of the article from Mrs. Amos' collection, which I quote:

> 'Eerie creature seen by Lydford Farmer.
>
> An eerie creature has been reported in Lydford. The creature is said to be about four or five feet long, built like a greyhound but with the back legs and face of a colt. Its eyes reflect no light. It was seen at about 3 o'clock one morning by farmer, Mr Maurice Knowles on his land... He spotted it as he went out to look for one of his ewes, which was about to lamb. It was snuffling its way alongside a hedge, looking, he thought, for a dead lamb. Mr Knowles had the creature in the light of his powerful lamp for ten minutes, and then tracked it as it made its way beside the hedge. 'Before he frightened it off by shouting at it, he was able to look at its head, which resembled a colt's face.
>
> '"The funny thing was," he told the Times, "when I shone my torch in its face, its eyes didn't shine back at all. I've heard that stags' and hinds' eyes don't shine back, but I haven't seen other animals like that." He thinks the animal may have been blind. The BBC say they were not filming The Hound of the Baskervilles that night, and the creature was too small to be the probably mythical Dartmoor puma. But there are many stories about giant and black dogs in Devon.'

Mrs Joan Amos investigated the case a few days later. She talked to Mr Knowles, who told her that the animal's eyes 'reflected no light', and showed her some paw-prints, which had been unfortunately damaged by rain. She was told that the farm dog was terrified when it encountered the large cat. I wondered whether the beast could have been a large black fox, as Northern foxes are large. The Countess of Faversham's book, *Strange Stories of the Chase; Fox-hunting and the Supernatural*, has a case of a black fox in the Sinnington area of Yorkshire, in 1803 (See the 'Canines' chapter of this book). Black foxes have not necessarily to be jet black; they could be just dark brown. At night, a big dark brown fox would look rather strange.

But whom have we here? An experienced farmer who is good at identifying known native animals. There is no mention of a tail, which one would have expected in most big cats. I also pondered over the possibility of a deer and a dog, but decided that these two animals would be well-known to Mr Knowles.

Joan Amos spells out her idea very clearly in her scrapbook when she states: 'Paw-print of Big Black Puma'. The whole description of this animal is somewhat baffling, but the clue may be when we understand that Lydford Gorge, near-by, is haunted by a large black 'dog'. Trevor Beer, the well-known naturalist, whose sighting we mentioned earlier, said that he had seen 'a huge black animal not unlike a hind' near the Devil's Cauldron and Lady's Cascade, Lydford Gorge. The animal could just have been a black panther. One lady telephoned the beast investigator, Trevor Beer, to say that she knew of a farmer who keeps a Tasmanian Devil to loose on the sheep of 'anti-conservation' farmers (See 'The Beast of Exmoor'). Mr Beer also quotes one sighting which is definitely of interest to us. I am most grateful to Mr Beer for allowing me to use this sighting quotation from page 36 of his excellent booklet. I think the animals seen were a panther and a lynx cross-breeding:

> 'One such woman who was prepared to give her name even though her story had been 'knocked' by locals is Mrs. P. Champion of Yeovil, who had an amazing sighting when out walking with her dogs during the spring of 1981. She was on a bracken-covered hillside when she observed what at first she thought was a fallen log, yet there were no trees in the immediate vicinity, nor had she seen it there on previous walks.
>
> As she drew close and one of her dogs was only six yards from the 'log', it suddenly moved and Mrs. Champion realised that she was staring at two huge cats, one having been on top of the other. "They must have been mating, as they had been in that position on the hillside for some minutes," she said, "then, realising we were so close they suddenly ran off in a wide circle, to disappear into the bracken." The one she thought was the male was jet-black, smooth-coated and with a long curved tail. It stood about two feet or more at the shoulders. It had a round head and small ears. "The female was really beautiful," said Mrs. Champion. "It was like a giant Manx cat. I could not see a tail at all and her hair was very long, almost nine inches, and black, but with touches of rust-colour in it. She was bigger and squarer in build, about three feet at the shoulders, and like one huge bundle of fur."
> Mrs Champion says she has not seen the creatures since, but would let me know immediately she does.'

BIG CATS: LOOSE IN BRITAIN

In May 1983, the *Exeter Express and Echo* published an article remarking on:
> 'Panther Spot - 1; Couple sight Beast at beauty spot'.

> *Mr and Mrs. Edwards from Clapham, London, observed a big cat at the narrow entrance to a country lane, near Southcott, off the main Bovey Tracy to Manaton Road. Mr Edwards said:*

> *At first I thought it was a large dog, waist-high, black and athletic-looking, though very thin. It was suddenly there, face on, with a rounded face and big looping tail, about 30 yards away. Then I rounded the corner and there was no sign of it. I just did not believe what I had seen; I could not believe that I had just seen a panther. It seemed almost tame, and did not bolt or take up an attack position.'*

> *Mr Edwards stated: 'I thought it was a joke at first, because I did not see the animal, but I was amazed when we told friends later and they knew about this panther.'*

A very badly-typed article appeared in the *Exeter Express and Echo* of 1984 or 1985, entitled:

> *Village in terror of cats:*

> *It seems that a plague of feral cats had occurred around Holcombe, between Dawlish and Teignmouth. The "wildcats" left several pet cats badly injured. They were large, as one was described as a 'monster', almost the size of a dog. The cats could not be captured, as they stole the meat off specially baited traps. They were not harmed doing this; some of the villagers were prepared to shoot the cats. Some cat owners were scared to let their pet cats out as they figured that they might be harmed.*

> *Mrs Millicent Groves of the Cats' Protection League said: "They are dangerous and could attack children, and even adults."*

The *Daily Mirror* of 8th March 1984 had a relatively short piece on the cats, called "New Hunt for Moors Beast". A mystery black animal had been sighted three times south of Dartmoor. The police had even brought in one of their helicopters to help in the search. Market gardener Jane Derbyshire said after seeing a big cat in a field near Modbury, Devon: *'It was jet black, four times the size of a fox, and moved like a cat.'*
The paper was making a suggestion that the animal was a puma. The *Fortean Times*, No.44, has a summary of the Devon sightings, along with many others. The relevant South Devon sightings were:

- 'Devon: April 1984 - Holcombe, near Dawlish: (feral?) cats, plague of wildcats, size twice normal, one big as dog, *Exeter Express and Echo*, 4th May 1985).
- July 1984 - Yelverton, Dartmoor: black animal, size, large. Hundreds of chickens killed. (*Daily Telegraph*, 30th July 1984). 5th August 1984 - Mile End, near Newton Abbot: Huge cat, colour fawn, size, fox. *Western Morning News*, 14th August 1984)

- 13th August 1984: East Orwell, Newton Abbot: Leopard, colour brown, size, small chasing pony. *Western Morning News*, 14th August 1984).

- 1st November 1984 - Buckfastleigh, near Dartmoor: Lamb almost totally devoured (see photo). *Western Morning News*, 31st October, *Daily Mirror*, 2nd November 1984).

The photograph in the last instance showed a half-grown black-faced Moorland lamb totally eaten, except for the head, backbone and ribs, as well as the hind legs. The *Torbay News* was also called in to report on this incident.

The *Tavistock Times* of 5th October 1984 carried some conclusive proof. The article published was boldly lettered: 'Giant cat paw-prints spotted in Bere Garden'. The article was by regional reporter Angela Larcombe. 83-year-old retired engineer Mr John Rose reckoned that the lynx-like, 3 feet high cats with long tails arched over their backs were the cause of livestock killings and 'savage' black beasts sighting. Mr Rose and his wife had first seen cats fifteen years earlier, when they went to live at Bere Alston. He saw the pair of cats several times and thought that they lived in some local old lead mines. Mr Rose kept on finding the same paw-prints in his garden.

He stated:

> My wife and I watched them from our bedroom window many years ago. I noted then they left strange paw-prints the size of the palm of my hand. They are unmistakable - one behind the other quite unlike a domestic cat or dog. A lion or lynx leaves prints like that because it rolls from side to side, and these creatures move the same way.

> It was about the time of the harvest moon (15 years before). I could measure the height of the cat which I thought must be the male one, because it was sitting next to some plants which had stakes over three feet tall supporting them. Its head when it was sitting down reached the top of the cane. They were black and very smooth-coated. They kept their tails up over their backs when they moved. It looked very strange.

On the 5th November 1986 an article appeared in the *Western Morning News* entitled 'Beast (of Dartmoor) seen near town

> Mr Christopher Richwell, an employee of the 'Sloping Deck' Restaurant, Dartmouth, crashed his car early on 5th November. He is a baker and was travelling to Brixham along the Dartmouth/Totnes road at 4.30 a.m. A large animal the size of an Alsatian, dark in colour and with swift movements, sprang into the road, in front of his car headlights. He swerved the car, smashing the headlights, and the car had to be towed away. Mr Richwell's sighting was near to the Norton Park holiday centre, a couple of miles north of Dartmouth. The police at Dartmouth warned local farmers to keep a close watch on their livestock.

> Mr Richwell stated: "It shook me. It could have been a cat and it was certainly

quick."

A Lieutenant from the Royal Naval College, Dartmouth, had seen a large cat with very green eyes and pointed ears the previous night, the 5th October. He had seen the mottled, cat-like beast at a Heliport, and he informed Dartmouth police of his sighting. This is one of the first indications that the military are interested in these felids.

Shortly afterwards, the 30th October edition of the *'Daily Express'* had a small piece called 'Beast Riddle'. Mr Aubrey Paull spotted a lynx-like cat on the A38 Plymouth-bound carriageway near Dean Prior. He thought it looked more like a cheetah than a lynx.

No doubt this sighting was reported elsewhere. Another cheetah description can be found in the following extract from Mr Mike Sullivan's article 'The British Bigcat - fact or fiction?' in *The Shooting Times and Country Magazine*, 24th-30th December 1987. The extract is in keeping with sightings:

> *'I have a report from a farmer who used to live near Tiverton in Devon. During a regular visit to his ewes and lambs, he tells of a large animal, at least 200 lbs, 5 feet long, with a long tail. It was smooth-coated, with a short stubby face like a cheetah.'*

The strange thing is, that one would have expected all the sightings to come from the Moors, but relatively few sightings have actually been made there. I decided to write to as many organisations and authorities as I could, in Devon, in the hope of obtaining information. The Devon Hunts number up to twenty, and no doubt caught up with the cats on a few occasions. I know that one cub was killed on Dartmoor, and Di Francis has the skull of this 'monster' at the present time. It is a big cat cub skull.

On the 5th January 1988, the Devon and Cornwall constabulary - Tavistock Division Devon Community - constable told me:

> *'With regard to your letter dated 31st December 1987, relating to a book you are researching about 'big cats Loose in Britain', I can supply you with the following addresses and telephone numbers of local area newspapers who could possibly be of assistance to you.'*

He then listed various local papers and Tavistock local radio, as well as other publications. I wrote to these. The Exeter Police Chief Superintendent, G. Burgess, based in Heavitree Road, Exeter, gave me the following information in a letter of 4th January 1988:

> *'Unfortunately I am unable to assist you with your work as I have no relevant information on this subject. However, I can supply you with the address of our local daily newspapers: the Western Morning News and the Express and Echo (evenings) at Sidwell Street, Exeter. I am confident they will be able to assist you.'*

Mr Paul Westaway, of the Kingsbridge and District Tourist Information Centre, said in a letter of 16th February 1988: *'I have enclosed an Exmoor paper which I hope will be of some help to you. You may also care to contact the Dawlish Tourist Information Centre, the R.S.P.C.A. at Plymouth, and the N.F.U. at Exeter, who may also be able to help.'*

I obtained a long list of Devon newspapers and wrote to all of these.

I advise that any readers of this book should also read the following directories:

1) *'Welcome to Historic Totnes and the Dart Valley'.*

2) *'Welcome to Dartmouth, a Town for All Seasons'.*

3) *'Exeter and District Citizens Guide and Trade Directory'*, (1987-88)

4) *'South Hams Handbook'* (1987-88)

Mrs Ethel Green of Modbury, South Devon, runs the Modbury Tourist Information Centre, and said, in a letter of 18th February 1988:

> *Surprise! Surprise! The day your letter came re big cats, there was an article on local TV. A Mr Nigel Brierly has set up 'Love potion traps' made of catmint to try and get evidence, so there's one lead. I will see if it is in the local paper and send it on to you. But, no doubt, a letter addressed to Westward TV will rustle up Mr Brierly for you... Also there have been several reports in our local paper over the years, so I suggest you contact them or come down to Plymouth and look up records with this in mind.*
>
> *I am enclosing the South Hams Gazette with a mine of information and addresses. You could try museums, Dartmoor National Parks, zoos, sanctuaries. Anyway, I hope I've been of some help. I enclose my address as our Information Centre is only open during the summer months.*

She enclosed the leaflets on two local parks, and I later obtained a copy of another. The only three wildlife parks in South Devon are:

1) Dartmoor Wildlife Park, Sparkwell, near Plymouth
2) Paignton Zoological Gardens, Paignton
3) Shaldon wildlife Trust Ltd., Shaldon, Devon.

The Dartmoor Wildlife Park is set in 25 acres and has over 100 species of animals and birds to enjoy, from lions to guinea pigs. They have a large collection of big cats, including leopards, lynxes and pumas, but I have not heard of any escapees from here.

The following extract comes from a letter, dated 13th February, sent to me by Miss E.G. Brown of the Tourist Information Centre in Newton Abbot:

> *'I am sorry I can not help you much. Apart from having seen mentions of cat-like*

animals of a large size being seen on Exmoor from time to time, I know nothing on the matter. I enclose a copy of the "Exmoor Visitor" in case it might contain something of interest. The R.S.P.C.A. is not represented in Newton Abbot, but is in Plymouth, though the telephone directory does not give an address. Plymouth Information Bureau, Civic Centre, Plymouth, might help you.

The Young Farmer's Club in Newton Abbot has a secretary - Mrs. Vooght, West Hayes Farm, Luton... Newton Abbot police station is at Baker's Hill, Newton Abbot. Information on Dartmoor could be obtained from the National Park HQ, "Parke", Bovey Tracy.'

I went ahead, writing letters to all of these organisations. Mr Roan Beaman, Enquiries, Cullompton police station, wrote:

'You are quite correct in saying that a gentleman came to the police station on the 20th July 1987 to report a sighting of a cat-like creature at Westleigh, near Burlescombe. This morning I have spoken to the gentleman concerned, and I explained to him that you are writing this book. At the time he had made the initial report to us, he purposely asked that his name and address were not given in the press. This is why the newspaper article did not mention his personal details. I have explained to him that you are writing your own book on this subject and he has kindly agreed to let me pass on the sighting of the animal. You can either write to him at the above address or you can telephone him on the telephone number below.'

The article was in the *Western Morning News* of 22nd July 1988. The press figured that the animal might be a 'Beast of Exmoor'. Mr Beaman was quoted as saying that the animal was seen at Westleigh, near Burlescombe. The man was driving on an unclassified road when the strange animal came out of a disused quarry at Rocknell Farm. Mr Beaman, who is a civilian enquiry officer, said this of the Exmouth man's sighting:

'It came out of the quarry entrance and stood in the middle of the road, forcing the driver to slow down. The animal snarled at the vehicle before jumping over a hedge and disappearing. The man described the animal as having a ginger-brown head and body with a grey tail, and the tail was between 18 inches and 2 feet long. He said it was similar to the size and appearance of a lynx, with large eye-teeth.
'I have no reason to think the man is anything but genuine. He was most sincere. Although it seemed odd, I had no hesitation in believing that whatever he saw, he saw.'

Dr G. W. Wills, the Assistant for the Amenities and Countryside Officer, remarked in a letter dated 17th February 1988 upon Mr Beer's and Mr Brierly's activities on Exmoor. He also wrote:
"For information on Dartmoor I would suggest that you write to the National Park Officer, 'Parke', Bovey Tracy. You might also contact the two Biological Databanks that serve Devon. These record information on wildlife in the County and may have records of interest to you. Mr K. Boot, of the Royal Albert Memorial Museum, Exe-

ter, and Mr D. Curry, of the Plymouth City Museum should be able to help you. My colleagues in the Devon Tourism Office will send you some of the information you have asked for. You might also find 'Devon's Wildlife - a Guide to Nature Conservation in in Devon,' a useful source of information."

I wrote to the three named authorities.

The letter from Mrs. le Roux, Assistant Secretary to the local branch of the R.S.P.B. in Exeter, said:

'I am afraid I cannot help you with your research into 'big cats in Britain' as the R.S.P.B. is concerned solely with wild birds.... I know there have been tales of the "Beast of Exmoor" but cannot say that there has been much in the news lately. Certainly at that time there were a number of sheep savaged in a particularly brutal way, and it was thought that a creature larger than a dog, or otherwise an extremely large dog, was responsible, but nothing was ever established for sure.'

Mr William Bennett of the Totnes Museum Trust told me the following in a letter dated 7th March 1988:

'I have been trying to help you by referring to our library here, and last Friday I attended a meeting of our Museum committee, and I read out your letter. However, we have no knowledge of the big cats here, although some of us read articles in the Western Morning News and we suggest that you write to the editor of that paper at Harmsworth House, Plymouth, Devon who may be able to help you.'

Many people referred me to the three main papers that cover Devon, while the Guild Hall, Totnes, sent me a note saying:

'I enclose the 'Exmoor Visitor' and advise you to write to the Dartmoor National Park, Bovey Tracy Devon, for information you require. Also, I suggest that you contact Mr Martin Lufthouse, Tourist Information Centre, Shepton Mallet.'

On 22nd February 1988, my birthday, a letter arrived from Mr Montagne, for the Dartmoor National Park Centre, Bovey Tracy, to say:

'I am interested in your idea for a new book called "Big Cats Loose in Britain". I am afraid that I know very little about this. There was, however, a ranger, Tom Pridmore, who took a considerable interest in the subject. He has now moved, but can be contacted at the following address (which he gave). I never seem to meet people who have seen it, only people who have met other people who have seen it.'

I was soon talking to Mr Pridmore on the telephone, on 4th March 1988. He has talked to many people who have seen the Dartmoor cats, but he has never seen them himself. He says: *"It is a beast of woodland, I think, as there have been few sightings on Dartmoor itself."* As Exmoor is only 50 miles away, he thinks the same cat could be involved in all the sightings. He knows a farmer who observed a white cat, and of a number of people who have seen a black big cat. The earliest sighting was in 1983. He thinks that many of the sightings were by 'broad Devon Farmers' who would talk to me on the telephone, but are not so good at writing of their sightings on paper. He would try to trace a Moretonhampstead policeman who tried to follow a big cat while out with the Mid-Devon hunt in 1980 (See Graham J. McEwan's '*Mystery Animals of Britain and Ireland'* (Robert Hale, 1986).

Mr Pridmore also thought that he could contact two farmers who might write back. Mr Pridmore was one of those who attended a three-hour long lecture given by Miss Di Francis.

Mr Pridmore remarked upon the fact that she had offered to track the cats with the Dartmoor National Park Officers. He describes some sightings of 'very dangerous wildcats', and is planning to send me a map of sightings and the addresses of some witnesses. It is interesting to note that Mr Pridmore believed the cats left a smell like 'boiled cabbage'. There have been a lot of sightings on Manaton, Miston or Mardon Down, South Devon. My thanks to Mr Pridmore for his help.

On 22nd February 1988, I received a letter from E.A. Pollitt, BA, WRNS, a second-officer at the Britannia Royal Naval College, Dartmouth. She gave me the following guarded statement about military sightings and involvement, concerning our phantom furry felids:

> *'I very much regret that I am unable to provide you with any information on 'big cat' sightings, as none have been made in the location of the Royal Britannia Naval College, probably because the College is in the town and not in the middle of the countryside. In answer to your questions about the use of 'big cats' in the Royal Navy, they are not used for either tackling animals or in jungle warfare.'*

We are thus left at a dead end over any military involvement. The curator of Natural History, the city of Plymouth Museum and Art Gallery, told me on 25th February 1988:

> *"The enclosed are copies of press cuttings taken from local newspapers over the past few years. I hope that they are of some interest."*

The cuttings are all of great value and interest.

A gruesome find by a couple from Brixham, Devon, really sent some excitement to Paignton Zoo. Mr Tony Jonas and his wife and daughter came across the skeleton of an unknown or unidentified animal on the Moor. Mrs. Jonas was quoted in the *Western Morning News* as saying:

> *'My first thought was that it was a dead lamb, but when I saw those teeth I knew that it wasn't. The feet look webbed and there are no signs of any paws at all. We cannot understand why no one else discovered it because it was in quite an open spot off the Bovey Tracy - Haytor road. It cannot be a hoax because there is no sinew on the back of the head. Tony has grown quite attached to it, but it's staying in the shed because it stinks to high heaven.'*

> *The skeleton was over three feet long, and Paignton Zoo's Executive Director, Mr Peter Stevens, said:*

"Judging by the description it sounds like some sort of dog. It's too big for a domestic cat or a fox. The front paws could have been carried off by a buzzard or a crow. There are all kinds of predators on Dartmoor."

The animal might have been a porcupine, or just a dog such as a mongrel lurcher. I have yet to contact Mr Jonas, who was obviously planning to mount it. The paper was trying to claim that the skeleton was none other than the 'Beast of Dartmoor'. Until 1985 there was no other 'hard' evidence. In the next two years, another skull, a dead leopard-cat, and many more sightings would occur.

Mid-Devon District Council Chief Executive's assistant, Mr Philip Talbot, sent me a letter on 1st March 1988:

> *'Unfortunately, I fear my reply will be something of a disappointment to you, in that the Council does not hold any records, articles or information of the type which you are seeking. There have, of course, been many reported sightings in the fairly near vicinity (for example, the 'Beast of Exmoor') but, as far as I am aware, they have been outside of this Council's area. It is possible that the Mid-Devon Natural History Society may be able to help you in your research. Their secretary is listed as Mrs. Sylvia Keen-Hammerson of Tiverton.'*

Mr G.L. Cullen is the chief executive and secretary of the Devon County Agricultural Association in Exeter. On 1st March 1988, he wrote the following:

> *'I very much regret to inform you that we do not have any information to hand. I will be attending a meeting in April and will mention your request for information then.'*

M Gail Hall, the acting news editor on BBC Radio Devon at Exeter gave me some useful publicity. She informed me of this in a letter of 2nd March 1988:

> *'We will be broadcasting your plea during the Help section of the Ian Brass programme. We've asked listeners who may have any anecdotes about big cats either to give you a ring, or write to you c/o Radio Devon. If you don't get any response you might try the following people we've interviewed several times about the 'Beast of Exmoor'. Trevor Beer is a naturalist who says he's seen the Beast. Nigel Brierly has laid several traps for the beast, including a special trap and using catnip.'*

Mr David Smeeton of the BBC, in Plymouth, who is a special correspondent, stated the following in a letter dated 2nd March 1988:

> *'The Exmoor Beast, the big cat, the lynx, or whatever it is, is elusive! Perhaps these cuttings may be of some help, but be warned - some of them are highly journalistic and could relate to sheep and cattle-worrying by dogs. But they may give you some idea of the range of interest in 'tracking' down the beast. They may also give you some names of people to contact.'*

Mr John Jones of Yelverton, Devon, wrote the following to me on 14th March:

> *'Your letter to David Holmes of Devon Bird Watching and Preservation Society was passed to me because David has moved and is no longer the secretary of the Society and I live nearby. I enclose a recent cutting from the* Western Morning News. *It shows Trevor Beer, who is the only person that I know of with a particular interest in such sighting in Devon. I do not know whether he is interested in such sightings on Dartmoor, however.'*

The enclosed article was of great interest, and I have mentioned it in the chapter on the 'Exmoor Beasts'. Devon Books, are the official publishers to the Devon County Council. Mr Simon Butler, the publishing manager, wrote the following from A. Wheaton and Co. Ltd., of Exeter:

> *'Concerning the Beasts of Exmoor and Dartmoor, I'm sorry I can't help much. We haven't published anything that contains mention of these animals. I enclose an article which appeared in the Western Morning News recently. It may be of interest to you.'*

Mr David Smeeton, the special correspondent whose letter I quoted earlier in the chapter, wrote to me on about 10th March, 1988, to say that the May 1986 *Tomorrow's World* programme called 'On the Trail of the Big Cat' was not available on video yet. He advised me to contact the BBC Enterprises Video Inquiry Unit in London, which I did. They said they were not able to help me, as they have many similar requests. Mrs D.Wood, Assistant Reference Librarian, Barnstaple, said on 16th March:

> *'Your enquiry about "big cats" has been passed to us by the Tourist Information Centre. There have been reports of sightings in the local paper, but you would need to visit the Library to see these. Two books which you would find of interest are: 'Cat Country' by Di Francis and 'The Beast of Exmoor' by Trevor Beer. They would be available through your local library. The address of the Devon National Farmers' Union is: Agriculture House, Queen Street, Exeter. The R.S.P.C.A. address is: Market Street, Exeter.'*

This was some more mixed old and new information. If I repeat myself, you will understand that these are statements from as many authorities as possible, who have somehow been involved with the cats.

The *Tavistock Times* have published two of my letters, as have the *North Devon Journal Herald* and *West Somerset Free Press*. The following letter appeared in the *Exmouth Herald* on Friday, 4th March:

> *'Have you seen the `Beast of Exmoor`?*
>
> *Sir - I am writing a book called 'big cats Loose in Britain' and am hoping your readers could tell me about their sightings of the pumas, panthers and lynxes which have been termed the 'Exmoor Beast' and 'Dartmoor Puma'. I would be grateful for any information regarding sightings etc.*
>
> *I have 550 letters in 15 files on these cats, and can say that they do exist. I would be*

happy to answer any queries.'

My name, address and age were also on the printed text. This letter must have brought a few results.

Mrs F.M. Sellick is the Hon.Secretary of the South Hams Society, which is registered with the Civic Trust and affiliated to the CPRE and Men of the Trees. On 9th March, she wrote:

> *'We had a committee meeting on Monday and I read your letter to everyone and was asked to write and say how interested we found your letter and to wish you well in your endeavours. None of us had seen a puma or a lynx around here, but if we do we will certainly let you know.*

> *Have you written to Mr Ian Mercer, Dartmoor National Park Officer? He might be of help.' Mrs. C. Hughes of the Cats' Protection League, Exeter, told me in February 1988:*

> *'I am afraid we do not have any details on the "Beast of Exmoor" or "Dartmoor Pumas". However, you might try our group at Hatherleigh, which is closer to Dartmoor.'*

(A name and address was given, to which to write.)

On about 20th February, I obtained a photocopy of a letter in the most recent issue of *Devon Life*, a local magazine. I had forgotten, but the 'Letters to the Editor' contained one of my appeals. It was adjacent to a piece by an acquaintance of mine, Mr Graham J. McEwan of Wallasey, who is writing a book on 'Holy Hauntings'. My letter simply suggested:

> *Big Cats:*

> *Dear Devon Life, I am writing a book called "Big Cats Loose in Britain" and I hope that your readers might be able to send me some information on this subject. I have seen a puma on Exmoor and a bob-cat or lynx loose on the Mendip Hills of Somerset and Avon, and if anyone can send me any information on escaped pumas, panthers and lynxes, I will send back the photocopying charge.*

> *A puma or panther was often seen around Tedburn St Mary in 1981, and perhaps readers may have heard of the Dartmoor pumas and Exmoor Beasts.*

The appeal was to bring forward some more witnesses. Mrs. Carol Bankes, of the Woodside Animal Welfare Centre, Plymouth, wrote me the following on 21st April 1988. She was writing on paper, with two delightful drawings of a cat and a dog at the top.

> *'It is very interesting that reports are always cropping up in the press. I am enclosing one in our local paper of today, which you may find helpful. We do not keep any large cats in our Centre, just domestic, so we cannot let any escape. We live*

*near a large forest in which we walk the dogs every day. We cannot see any big cats
in there, nor had any reports of anybody seeing any. However, it is very interesting
they exist.'*

My next sources of information are a number of articles and letters that describe all the 1988 South Devon
sightings.

In late 1987, Mr Trevor Beer sent me the address of Mrs. Rosemary Bunbury of Thorverton, near Exeter,
who, on 27th February 1988, wrote describing her September 1987 sighting.

*'I hope it's not too late to send you details of the puma we apparently saw, but any-
way, here they are. We were due to move into the village of Thorverton in September, and drove there about mid-day one day in the middle of August with my parents, who had not seen the house. We parked outside it and went for a walk along a
lane towards the centre of the village.*

*On our way we passed the village school and I happened to glance into the school
field next door. Sitting by a hedge about 100 yards from us was a fawn-coloured
animal, which I assumed to be a sheep. I remember commenting that it was unusual to see a sheep all on its own, and especially in the school-field.*

*We all stopped and leaned against the gate to take a look. The animal was staring at
us and then it slowly got up and started walking down the side of the hedge towards us. We saw plainly by its shape and the way it walked that it was of the cat
family, but it was the size of a sheep. As it came towards us, we beat a hasty retreat!
I went to look an hour later, thinking I had imagined the whole thing, but there was
nothing to be seen. I am sorry that I have no one else's address who have sightings.'*

Back in 1985, a similar cat with pointed ears was seen by a Dartmouth farmer. The man had not been
drinking, according to the police, whose spokesman told BBC Radio Devon, in November 1985, that the
animal was *'a huge cat-like creature'*. The same broadcast and a later, 5th November 1986, encounter described similar sightings. A year later, on 18th July 1987, BBC Radio Devon gave the following announcement:

*A new Beast of the Moors sighting has been made by a Devon bus-driver. The slate-
grey animal, about the size of an Alsatian, was spotted in daylight near Honiton,
near where a sheep was killed recently, and eleven miles from where a similar
sighting was made last year.*

*The driver, Mr Joe Lake of Honiton, returned to the spot to look for tracks but was
unsuccessful. Naturalist and author Trevor Beer, who is on the trail of the `Beast of
Exmoor`, says there are wild pumas in the region and the sparsely-inhabited loca-
tion would be popular with them.*

"People should not worry about them. They are wary of humans and generally

make off if they see anyone," said Mr Beer.

After these 1986, 1987, and early December 1987 sightings, we are now going to refer to some evidence on film - on 22nd January 1988. Security cameras at the Electricity Generating Board's Whimple Station, between Exeter and Honiton, recorded sightings of a number of very large panther-like black cats. This information was included in both the *Western Morning News* and on BBC Radio Devon. The latter team broadcast the announcement as follows:

> *'Panthers spotted. Panther-like beasts have been recorded by security cameras in East Devon. And today villagers were being warned to be on the alert because the creatures could be dangerous.*

> *Staff at the CEGB's Whimple station watched as the cameras homed in on the black, sleeky, cat-like creatures, resembling the fabled `Beast of Exmoor`. Maintenance workers at the station saw the Alsatian-sized beasts near the perimeter fence where TV security monitors picked up the scene on screens relayed to other staff in a control room.*

> *Meanwhile a motorist in the area has reported seeing one of the animals, and last year similar sightings were reported in Dunkeswell on the outskirts of Honiton.'*

The *Western Morning News* have very kindly let me use some of the witnesses' reports to their reporter. The cats were the size of an Alsatian, and the staff were surprised at the sightings. Butcher, Mr Keith Turner of Bradninch, stated:

'It was on the road and it was like a panther. I stopped and stared at it, and it went over a hedge. When I got to the top of the hedge, it glared at me and I stared back.' He saw the cat while on his way to Whimple.

Mr Tim Powell, a maintenance worker at the sub-station, saw another black panther when he worked near a perimeter fence. Station attendant Mr Gordon Hicks saw another black panther coming out of nearby woods, and he was quoted as saying: *'It was black and I thought I saw a long furry tail. After about two minutes, it went back into the wood.'* I think that these cats were seen by the men at the Electricity Control Room, but I have yet to find out whether they were captured on film, as a video. I wrote to all the witnesses who were named.

On 30th January 1988, headlines were broken by a story that was to cause some excitement in the cat world. A large skull with sharp teeth had been found by two youths - Simon Hopwood, and Sebastian Carnell - of Lustleigh, a small village near Newton Abbot that is only a few miles north of Dartmoor.
The boys discovered the skull on the far side of a hedge, five miles from Newton Abbot. When they first found it, the boys recognised that it was unusual, as Simon is a collector of moorland skulls. The press thought the boys were telling the truth about its origin, and they suggested that it could have belonged to a puma. Simon told the *Western Morning News* of 30th January:

'We don't think it's very old. But it would be nice if we could get it properly carbon-dated, so we could discover how old it is.'

His friend, Sebastian, described the skull:

> "It is about six or seven inches longer than a puma's skull, and has jaws which can only be those of a large cat - a leopard's skull, almost certainly. It couldn't possibly be a domestic cat or dog. It was just lying on the other side of a hedge." Paignton Zoo had not positively identified the skull, according to the Director, Mr Peter Stevens, who said: "We have never seen this skull and certainly have not made any official statement on it."

The *South Devon Sunday Independent* newspaper ran two stories on the skull. The first was headlined 'Skull of "Beast" found on Moors. Experts check lad's big find.' The first story, like the *Western Morning News* mentioned the fact that the skull had been found in the same week as a foal was ripped apart at Barnstaple. This time, Simon and Sebastian were photographed with the skull, which has four powerful canines, and three rows of incisors. The shape of the skull suggests that it was probably that of a large feline. Sebastian was the first to find the skull, then handed it over to Simon.

"It is in good condition, so we don't think it's very old," said Simon. The *Sunday Independent* of 21st February quoted zoologist, Dr Karl P.N. Shuker as saying, about the skull, after studying detailed photographs of it:

> 'Structurally the Dartmoor skull is insufficiently massive to be that of either a lion or tiger, and has none of the features of the cheetah. The only remaining cats are the puma, leopard, jaguar or snow leopard. The chances of it being either of the last two are very remote. The only real contenders are the puma or leopard's, but the skull's lower jaw displays marked differences from the puma. It is in fact very similar to that of a leopard. In addition, the upper jaw section also appears to match that of a leopard. I would hesitate to pass a conclusive opinion without first having the chance to examine the skull, but from the photographic evidence it would seem to be a leopard and not a puma. This is particularly interesting when one considers that over the past few years many sightings have been reported from the Dartmoor and Exmoor areas of black leopards, which are in fact no more than abnormally coloured leopards.'

Dr Shuker did suggest that the skull could have been placed on the Moor by hoaxers. It was also thought that a large black cat had been seen by a motorist travelling north of Tavistock. This sighting was probably in the third week of February 1988.

Simon Hopwood wrote to me on 15th May:

> 'I cannot give you a lot of information, as I have not an awful lot myself. I can tell you that we found the skull just outside of Lustleigh around the 25th January 1988. I'm afraid I have not many photos of the skull and I have no slides. The best I can do for you is to send a negative labelled in the envelope, which is not the best in the

world. I have also enclosed a photo, which if you want to make a few copies for your book, you may still do so even without the negative. The photography group Bonus Print can do this, and the information on how is in the envelope.'

The photo and negative were interesting, and a reproduced photo of the skull is produced in this book. The *Western Morning News* of 22nd April 1988 quoted Di Francis as saying that she had matched up the creature's fang-marks on a Highland sheep-kill of a lamb with the 3 inches wide teeth of the skull. They matched perfectly, so one presumes the same type of big cat killed the lamb.

As Francis stated, *'It's now very likely that this is the skull of the so-called beast.'* She obviously thought it could belong to a British big cat. She also knew that the experts disagreed over what it belonged to. One expert thought it was a lion or tiger-type of cat's skull, which was due to be put through further tests in America and Britain. It appeared to be one of the first pieces of conclusive evidence to reach the national press. One supposes that there must be a whole skeleton out there somewhere, to which the skull belongs. The skeleton found on Dartmoor in 1985, by the family, is not the body, as it had a head. The skull could have come from any one of a number of places. It is not clear who owns the skull legally. It probably belongs to the boys, as it is unlikely to be of much interest to a local museum, although I could be wrong.

(EDITOR'S NOTE: However, when a CFZ researcher contacted the boys in 1995, they admitted that although the skull had, indeed, been found on Dartmoor, exactly where they said it was, that it was wrapped in a plastic bag when they found it. Another promising snippet of evidence bites the dust.)

What was now needed was an actual carcass from South Devon. The following sighting occurred after the skull was found. The independent local newspaper, the *Tavistock Clarion* (No. 41), gave a front page account of two local cat sightings. It was dated 2nd March 1988, and stated that Mrs. Mary Connett and her sister Mrs. Dixon, of Tavistock, had seen a black puma-like cat in a field between Green Lane and Mount Tavy Road.

Mrs Connett saw the cat on two occasions, both with a clear view and for several minutes. She was quoted as saying:

> *'It was much too big to be an ordinary cat. I thought it was like a puma. It was quite thin with a curved tail. When it moved it seemed to be stalking and went up a tree, then disappeared into some bushes. We had a good view of it.'*

Tavistock police searched the area, but as they found no trace of the cat, they decided still to keep an eye out for it.

Paignton moor walker Mr Mark Turner was the other witness. He told the *Clarion:*

> *'It was a brief sighting but I am sure it was not a fox. It was just like an ordinary cat. I'd love to know what it was. I came upon it about 100 yards away, up-wind, so it wasn't immediately aware of me. It was crouching down as if it was stalking something. When it spotted me it moved off fairly quickly, but not in a panic.'*

The cat was *'a mottled ginger colour and about the size of an Alsatian.'* He sighted it a few miles from the sisters' sighting at Burrator Reservoir, Combeshead. He was sure the creature had a cat-like shape and body. The *Clarion* noted that he even went to Paignton Zoo when he reached home, but they could not think what it was.

"They couldn't suggest anything that it was like," he stated. The mystery animal was seen near Loveton, where there had been a number of ewes and lambs savaged over the Christmas period of 1987. At the time, a pack of dogs was blamed for the killings, according to the *Tavistock Clarion* article.

The above two sightings were also recorded in the *Western Morning News* of 1st March, and the *Tavistock Times* and *Gazette* of 4th March. Mr Ken Thatchley of Kingsbridge sent the former article to me.

He wrote on 2nd March:

'Unfortunately I have no information myself on this subject, only the reports I read in the press from time to time. As it happens, there was a report in yesterday's *Western Morning News* which I enclose. I am so glad that you are interested in wildlife.'

Apparently, hundreds of sheep and lambs were lost around Loveton and the farmers were carrying out all-night vigils, though nobody ever caught sight of the attackers.

Mr J. Lake, a bus driver from Honiton, Devon, is a witness twice over. He wrote the following on about 15th March 1988.

I know for a fact that these cats, or wild beasts, do exist. The sighting of the one I saw was very clear, as I got to within 30 yards of the animal, and have seen it since, on 2nd March, at a quarter past eight in the morning, about 500 yards from the spot I saw it before. In a bus you can see over the hedges. This animal is evil-looking. More like a wolf, very heavy coat, probably due to the wild living. This animal leaves no scent for some reason because greyhounds tried to pick up the (scent) trail, but lost it immediately, which is very unusual, especially when it crossed the road fifty yards in front of them. In the paper, a couple of months after my sighting, a man was travelling past a quarry near Cullompton and an animal like the one I saw stood in the road and snarled at him as he stopped the car. It frightened him very much, as he went to the police station and reported what he had seen.

The police are becoming quite concerned about these things now. They have been seen at night by drivers who have told me, but it's difficult to distinguish the facts at night. The eyes of the one I saw are like cat's eyes - very slinky, but the head, which I saw the second time, as it looked at me, is longer, as I said, more like a wolf's, but not quite so big.
It stood in the road the first time I saw it, and from a distance it looked something like a large fox, but as I got nearer, as I said, I realised it was too big as it stretched from the grass curb to the middle of the road with its tail, which is very long and the road is quite wide at that spot. Its coat is very bushy, slate-grey colour, with a white stripe on its tail, left side only. I know a lot of people don't believe what you say, but some do. It doesn't worry me. I know what I saw. They can believe it or

not, it's the truth. If I get any other information I'll pass it on to you.

This was a kind and most truthful letter. The animal in question obviously had distinctive markings. It could have been a puma or a lynx. The long wolf-like head sounds more like a lurcher's, but some cats *do* have long muzzles.

We now come to one of the most conclusive forms of evidence yet, a dead leopard-cat (*Prionailurus bengalensis*), which was shot by a farmer, near to Widecombe-on-the-Moor, after it had killed some of his poultry. Miss Hilary Hoad of the Ministry of Agriculture, London, sent me all the articles that appeared in the press on these cats. The anonymous farmer contacted Mr Neville Harrison, a veterinary surgeon of Bickinton, near Newton Abbot. He thought there might be a risk of rabies, so he contacted the Ministry Vet, in Exeter. The papers covered the story widely, as the following list of articles will show:

1) *The Times* 22nd April: 'Exmoor beast Mystery lives on' (2 editions)
2) The *Birmingham Post*, 22nd April: 'Rabies alert as leopard-cat is killed.'
3) *Western Morning News* 21st April: 'Exotic leopard-cat sparks rabies alert'
4) *Today*, 22nd April: 'Beast of the Moors'
5) *Guardian* 22nd April: 'Rabies Alert'
6) The *Daily Telegraph*, 22nd April: 'Leopard-cat Shot on Dartmoor'.
7) *Evening Standards* 21st April: 'Leopard Shot on Moor'.
8) *Western Morning News* 22nd April: 'Experts still puzzled over creature's identity. Skull may hold key to the riddle of Exmoor Beast'.

The authorities involved were the Devon and Cornwall Constabulary, the Ministry of Agriculture, Paignton Zoo Shaldon Wildlife Trust and the local vet, Mr Harrison. Let us examine what each was quoted as saying.

Mr Harrison came upon the leopard-cat, when he was called to the farmer's home at Widecombe-in-the-Moor, Dartmoor, on 14th April 1988. The cat had been chasing his geese and a young lamb had lost its head, nearby, a week before. Mr Harrison stated that he was worried about it having rabies, as he told *Western Morning News* reporter Colin Bradley:

> *'Because this cat is not a native of this country, I am very concerned about rabies. No one knows yet how a cat like this got on Dartmoor. It may have been brought in illegally and its owner ignored the quarantine regulations.'*

He told the *Today* newspaper: *'The cat could have been brought in illegally, without quarantine.'* He was quoted exactly the same in the *Western Morning News* and London *Evening Standard*. The *Birmingham Evening Post* quoted one sentence of the above. Mr Harrison thought it might have been a leopard-cat, but it was a Paignton Zoo Director, Mr Colin Bath, who identified the animal as a leopard-cat. It was a young male, and some authorities thought it had only been loose for a few weeks. The Ministry of Agriculture vet, Mr Tony Keele, informed the *Western Morning News*:

> *'We take action whenever there is a case of an animal being brought into this country illegally, but at the moment there does not seem to be any evidence of*

that.'

Leopard-cats come from South-east Asia, but they generally only live on small rodents and other small mammals, or birds. A leopard-cat could bring down a small deer, on some occasions. Continuing to inform the press about the leopard-cat, Mr Keele remarked to Today: 'It is unlikely that an animal like this could be imported easily. If they are breeding there, the cat's parents could be the beasts.'

He was also ready to say to the *Daily Telegraph*:

'This cat, which was little more than a kitten and the same size as a domestic cat, was almost certainly bred in captivity. My guess would be that it had only been at large for a few weeks. It was aged less than a year, and would only just be capable of finding its own food, and would have lived to some extent on carrion. There is no chance it could kill a sheep, and was probably living on birds and small mammals, such as rabbits. At most, it might have a go at a very young and very sickly lamb. The animal is not the so-called `Beast of Exmoor` or Beast of Dartmoor. It is just possible, although extremely unlikely, that its parents are.'

Mr Harrison agreed on this possible point, as he stated to a London *Evening Standard* reporter:

'And there might be more of them about.' The beasts are often described as black, and leopard-cats are sometimes black. An adult leopard-cat would weigh about 20 to 25 lbs and be about 3 to 4 feet long, including tail. Some of the larger-cat sightings could have been of some leopard-cats. However, a leopard-cat could not kill a 200 lbs ram, as the beasts have done on Exmoor'.

Mr Keele told me in a letter of 13th May 1988:
'Re what the newspapers called 'the Leopard Cat', I regret that there is not a lot of factual information available. Paignton Zoo identified the body as a tiger-type cat from South-east Asia, a young male about six to eight months of age. The farmer who shot the animal reported that it appeared healthy and was stalking his geese. Enquiries were made about licensed keepers of such animals in the county and no-one reported the loss of any animal resembling this. As to how it arrived near Widecombe, we can only conjecture that it escaped from an unlicensed owner. In my opinion the stories about it being related to the "Beast of Dartmoor" are very unlikely.'

The local police were able to warn people to keep a close watch on their livestock in case the leopard-cat had been a rabies-carrier. The police spokesman was carrying out an investigation into the affair, and he commented to the *Western Morning News*: *"With so many odd-balls these days you do not know who is keeping what in their home."*

The Devon and Cornwall police thought it was 'highly likely' that the young male leopard-cat was the animal which killed lambs in the area. They thought that the sheep-killer was just a 'rogue' animal, i.e. a dog. The spokesman told the reporter for *The Times* that *"The media idea that there is a 'Beast of Dartmoor' or a 'Beast of Exmoor' is probably just mythology."*

The police were sceptical about any wild claims.

Another authority concerned was the curator of mammals, Mr Colin Bath, at Paignton Zoo. He carried out an investigation by contacting all the Wildlife Parks in Devon - there are only about five others. He found no positive leads, but he did believe that the cat had been set free on Dartmoor within the past few weeks. Mr Bath issued the following statement to *Today*: *"It may be an escaped or abandoned pet, but there could well be others out there."*

The London *Evening Standard* quoted him as saying: *"It was probably dumped by its owner, who risked falling foul of licensing regulations under the Dangerous and Wild Animals Act."*

Mr Bath told the *Daily Telegraph* more about the cat:

> *'Leopard cats are slightly bigger than an average-sized tabby, but nowhere as tame as domestic cats. They are hunters and can be quite vicious. In South India and South Asia they will take on animals the size of a small deer, although they are most fond of catching birds. We may never know how this one got here. I think it is a case of someone releasing the animal irresponsibly and illegally on to the Moor.'*

The other authority who was quoted was Mr Stewart Muir, of the Shaldom Wildlife Trust, and who keeps a pair of leopard-cats. He knew that leopard-cats could be bought from 'cowboy' dealers (pet-shop owners) who sold these animals for only £50. He said: *"It's possible that someone bought this cat as an unusual pet, realised he could not cope with it and decided to get rid of it. These cats are untrainable."*

This was in the *Western Morning News* of 21st April, and a similar quote appeared in the London *Evening Standard*, except that the cat was described as being 'wild'. He obviously also was calling on the government to tighten up the present laws on Dangerous Animals. Rabies is dangerous, but it normally appears to affect cats only of the domestic variety, and dogs. There have been a number of cases of monkeys with rabies. I do not think that any of the Devon cats are likely to be carrying such a killer, as they would all be dead by now.

Miss Di Francis apparently spoke to the *Western Morning News* reporter Mr Colin Bradley, about the leopard-cat, on 22nd April. She referred to the Pine Valley Wildlife Park, Okehampton, which closed down, probably around 1975. She remarked:

> *'I remember a wildlife park having to close down in the Okehampton area in the early '70s. A pair of porcupines were known to have escaped, and a listed colony is now living in the area. I would not be surprised if this cat was part of a leopard-cat colony which over the years had grown from a pair which also escaped from the same wildlife park. There could be as many as twenty out there because they prefer wooded areas. They would have kept themselves hidden from view. And with their diet consisting of rodents they would not have tackled any sheep, so that farmers*

would not have noticed them.'

The late Mrs. Joan Amos, UFO investigator and witness of Peter Tavy, Tavistock, Devon, told me in a letter dated 25th April: *"Maybe you have heard about the leopard-cat that was shot on Dartmoor in 1988. It belonged to a band of hippies who were camped on the edge of the Moor."* She later remarked upon the fact that in March 1988 there was quite a lot of UFO activity. She wrote: *"We have recently had a spate of UFO activity, when about a week afterwards the cats appeared again!"*

(EDITOR'S NOTE: Joan Amos was a very dear friend of the CFZ and we miss her very much. She told us about the 'band of hippies' as well, and because the CFZ have always had friends in low places, we managed to reach the bottom of the problem. A pair of these cats was owned by a well known, semi-aristocratic drug dealer just outside Widecombe. He may or may not have had a license, but when he was busted in the middle of the night and hauled away protesting that 35kg of hashish was 'for personal use only maaan', the two cats escaped. The other – to our knowledge – has never been found).

Mrs. Liza Jay of Ashburton, Devon, which is on the edge of the Moor, gave me another lead in a letter dated 13th May:

> *'I listened with great interest to your interview on Devon County Radio with Perry Downes. I do believe everything you are saying about these cats because I am convinced there is one living up in the woods opposite my caravan. I hear it regularly at around dusk, letting out a deep throaty cat-like yowl. It is loud and quite startling, almost as though some creature were in pain. Very few people walk in the wood because it is privately owned, quite large and very overgrown, and riddled with old mineshafts. Some say there are deer there, though not as many as in the past, before a plantation higher up near Buckland, was felled. Anyway, I am sure you will want to know the name of the wood - Borough Wood, a large wood on a hill north of Ashburton. Follow the A38 to Ashburton, turn into North Street at the 'T' junction and at a stone bridge turn right and go up the valley. Just before a tall stone mill building which is wedge-shaped (and a distinctive landmark) called Bellford Mill, you will find a track - overgrown, of course - which leads into the wood. Good luck if you decide to go in there and hunt for it!'*

The South Devon sightings are bound to continue. I feel that there are pumas, panthers and lynxes in South Devon as well as the odd leopard-cat. Undoubtedly some are ex-exotic pets, but others could well be British big cats. Di Francis has done a lot of research into the South Devon cats and is still well-informed about their existence. The cats will probably continue to breed, just as they have done for centuries, I hope that we shall soon have conclusive proof.

'The *Daily Telegraph* of 5th March had a small piece which was headed 'A scare deal for Tourists':

> *'The Westcountry Tourist Board was advertising for a fearsome looking person with a working knowledge of the "Hound of the Baskervilles" territory. The employee's job was to act as a guide on a set of horror holiday trips. So now we know*

what to look out for, as well as the cats!'

"Devon Attractions" (Devon Tourism, County Hall, Exeter, price £1.00) is worth reading.

- ## Cornish Cats

The first instance of a possible Cornish cat arose when Tony 'Doc' Shiels, the wizard, monster-hunter, busker and writer of Ponsanooth, Cornwall told the *Fortean Times* he thought the 'Lost Land of Lyonesse' could be interpreted as 'Lioness'. He wrote a letter, a sentence of which was published in the 'Once More with Felines' article in No. 44 of the *Fortean Times*:

> *'Our Cornish "Mystery Cat" hasn't been seen for a few weeks, but a Cornish naturalist has just been killed by a tiger in India. He was from the Scilly Isles, sometimes thought to be part of Lyonesse (Lioness?).'*

The letter was dated 4th March 1985. Lyonesse may have been one of the last pieces of land to connect Britain to France. Is it not possible that European big cats, some species the size of lionesses, in prehistoric times, have come along this causeway of land, to reach England's shores? The name 'Lyonesse' may have many other connections, which are not of interest to us.

Mr John Rose, the 83-year-old retired engineer of Bere Alston, South Devon, told the local *Western Morning News*, after finding giant cat pawprints in his garden, that in the 1920s he had seen black big cats at Tregantle firing range, south-east Cornwall, while on guard duty. The cats were not sighted again until the 1970s, according to the records I have. I am grateful for the help in this chapter, of Dr Frank Turk, his wife Stella and Mrs. Joan Amos. In a letter of 28th May 1987, Mrs. Amos of Tavistock told me:

> *'Having read your letter in the* Tavistock Times, *I decided to write to you right away. I think you will be interested in what I have to tell you.*
>
> *I live right under Dartmoor, and have my own reasons for being interested in the cats, since 1982. I have therefore kept a scrapbook on all reports. I am enclosing a copy of the latest one, only a month ago. I interviewed a local farmer at Lydford in 1982, and took a photo of the beast's paw-print which, owing to five days of rain, was not as clear as I would have liked. I have a friend down in Camborne who has also seen a 'golden cat'. There is a valley near Redruth that has a colony of large wildcats, and a gentleman living nearby has kept watch on them, and is trying to photograph one. I am enclosing one of his letters to me from last October. Included too, is a recent sighting on the Isle of Wight.*
> *I must tell you here, that contrary to your letter, which mentioned lynx, most descriptions I have received were of 'cats' with rounded heads and ears; also of red eyes, or dead eyes with no reflection.'*

In her second letter it emerged that Mrs. Amos was a UFO investigator, and that she was interested in the connections between cats and UFOs. Her theory is very different from that of Dr Turk, whom we shall look at in a minute, but I do feel it should be examined here. The second letter was dated 1st July 1988:

As you will know, I did not divulge my interest in the Alien Black Cats (ABV), but you are right - my interest is research into UFO phenomena! I belong to the PUFORG, Plymouth UFO Group, and I am the coordinator of South-west groups. I keep in touch with all our contacts and link them up with the Plymouth Group. I investigated a case of a GB Breaker on Dartmoor, in the early hours of the night, who was frightened by a UFO, 40 feet in the air, which had a pony caught in its search light beam. Within a week the black cat turned up, on a farm on the edge of the Moors.

As I knew there is a suspected connection, I wrote to the Bords, but their reply was non-committal. Then I heard about Di Francis, on our local TV, so I contacted her. But as she is a naturalist, she would hear nothing of UFOs. I continued to report other sightings in our area to her, till she moved to Scotland.

There are two points I would like to put to you, which support a suspicious UFO connection: one is, how the hell does a colony, recently found, get on the Isle of Wight? Secondly, if you have read the account of the policeman in Yorkshire who was abducted, you would know, from the transcript of his hypnosis session, that he spoke of a black animal on board the craft. While he was being examined, he said, "a big black creature" (was what it was). I had a farmer who said its eyes had no reflection", and another report which spoke of the eyes being red. All I know is there are too many everywhere to be escapees, and the farm-dog was terrified.

For a transcript of Alan Godfrey's UFO abduction hypnosis, please see Jenny Randle's 1983 book *The Pennine UFO Mystery*. Judy Chard's book *Devon Mysteries*, and her *Tales of the Unexplained in Devon*, have references to Mrs. Jinos's own five UFO sightings, two of which were in daylight. She has seen UFOs without lights over Brentnor, Dartmoor, and the front cover of Mrs. Chard's book depicts this. I am sure that there is something in these UFOs, and they could have military connections. See also Michael Williams's book *Strange Lines of Power*, which has a chapter on Mrs. Amos's UFO sightings.

On 2nd January 1985, an article appeared in Exeter's *Express and Echo* about the 'Beast of Bodmin'. I have learned from a relation that in the 1970s and 1980s there were always rumours of an escaped orang-utang ape in the area. Farmers coming home from the public houses at night were used to seeing a strange pair of eyes looking at them, and a hairy human-like figure disappearing quickly!

But returning to this article in the *Express and Echo* of the 2nd January, it appeared that in 1973, Mr David Nicholas, a young man from Camborne, had seen a "big brownish cat", like a puma, in Camborne's woods (see *'Cat Country'*). By 1980, reports of a black panther-type cat had come in from Stithians Reservoir, Lewdown, and the outskirts of Launceston. Mr Leonard Mingo of Burthey Farm, west of Bodmin, Cornwall, had lost a sheep in December 1984. He contacted the local *West Cornish Guardian*, who published his story and a picture of the sheep kill. The cutting came to the attention of Di Francis, then based in Torquay. She drove down to the farm, where she photographed the paw-prints and the dead sheep, which she felt had been killed by a big cat. She noted that only a little meat had been torn from it, and that 'two independent sightings' of Alsatian-sized cat-like beasts had occurred in West Cornwall. No North Cornwall or West Devon Hunts had come across any big cats. Miss Francis thought the big cats were living on rabbits and small mammals. She was also puzzled by the fact that only one creature had died, as ravens - those large black birds - had already been killing lambs.

Only a couple of weeks after this incident, respected zoologist Dr Frank Turk of the Camborne area, announced that he had positive evidence that pumas were roaming Cornwall, and other parts of England. Dr Turk was asked to examine some possible puma hairs from an over-grown orchard in Surrey, where they were found on bramble bushes. Dr Turk reported to the *Western Morning News* of 14th January 1985 the following facts of interest here:

> *'Puma hairs are quite distinctive, and I am absolutely certain these animals are living wild in Britain. I think pumas are responsible for killing the sheep. They probably escaped or were released from small private menageries and are now breeding successfully. Pumas are usually quite amenable to humans. There have been only four incidents in the past 150 years of pumas attacking a human. They have wide hunting areas and can easily travel up to 100 miles in a night.'*

Dr Turk was given the hairs by Miss Di Francis, who obtained them from a witness in the Peaslake area of Surrey. After this announcement, the Natural History Museum stated they thought his discovery of wild pumas was 'very exciting', but they maintained an open mind on the `Surrey Puma` hairs, although they did say that Dr Turk was well-qualified to judge such an incident.

The next sighting was reported in the *Western Morning Herald* of 31st January 1985, under the headline 'Mysterious Wildcats seen on Farm', and the summarised story runs:
Mr Gordon Philips, then aged 71, crossed his yard one day in January 1985, when he observed an unusual beast outside a shed where he kept five young cattle. The tawny-brown animal might have been a puma. Mr Philips knew that his neighbour, Mr Garfield Willey, had had some of his sheep disturbed about the same time. He also was aware of the fact that an animal of a similar description was seen crossing a field three miles away.

Mr Philips told the *Western Morning Herald:*

> *'I've never seen anything like it before, but it was definitely a cat. Part of its tail was missing, and it was not looking in very good condition. It ran off down towards the village, but it was thin and moved as if it was very old or ill. As a farmer, you get used to looking at animals and judging their condition. The animal looked hollow, and as if it did not have many days left.'*

Mr Philips lives at Bridge, near Redruth, Cornwall. He told me the following facts in a telephone conversation of 15th February 1988, after I had written to him. He is now 74, and his son manages their farm. He was told by somebody that he saw a lynx, on account of the fact that the tail was missing. He knows animals well, and he now says that he definitely saw a puma. The Redruth police are aware that a puma escaped from Newquay Zoo, 15 or 20 miles from Mr Philips's farm. I found out from another source that a puma had escaped eighteen months before, in 1983. It is possible that Mr Philips saw that puma, which was now elderly and sick-looking. He said farmers were warned to look out for the cat, as it might attack their sheep. He found droppings in the yard that were not from a dog, or domestic cats' excrement, so he thinks these could have been made by the puma. Mr Philips killed about 100 foxes on his land, when he was younger, and he has badgers on his land, so he does know his animals well enough.

Mr Philips contacted Dr and Mrs. Turk concerning his sightings. About this time, I had a letter from Mrs. Ruby Lamb of Exmouth, Devon. She wrote to me on 7th March, after reading my appeal in the *Exmouth Herald*.

> *'Between five to seven years ago we were living in Truro and every week had a trip to Penzance, walking miles around the highways and byways. During one of our jaunts we saw what must have been a black puma. I saw it first around fifteen to twenty yards away, in a private garden, and was intrigued to see what I thought was a large black cat washing itself in the sun. My husband said at once, "It's a puma." We then asked a passing man on a farm vehicle if he knew of a private zoo, but he, after look-ing, went on his way.*

> *'At this time the next-door neighbour arrived home, and we asked her about it, still visible, but it started to spot with rain and she went in to take her washing in'.*

> *'I'm sorry I never pursued my nosy instincts now, but hope my narrative is of inter-est.'*

The sighting was in about 1981, and was not far from Penzance seafront. It seems that Mrs. Lamb and her husband sighted the cat behind a *'house with high iron double gates'*, which was next to a road, with a ditch. The house is to the left of a main Penzance road, which is running parallel with the sea-front road. I plan to follow this sighting up in due course. Maybe it was a private owner's pet black panther, within its owner's property, or maybe it was an escaped exotic pet. We will have to see. The incident could have taken place a few months before the 'Wildlife and Countryside Act' was introduced, and people would be reminded about the '1976 Dangerous Animals Act'. The black 'puma' is unlikely, as the puma is dark brown. We now refer to the cuttings collected by Dr and Mrs. Turk. She runs the Cornish Biological Re-cords Unit in Redruth. She said in the note of 4th March 1988:

> *'I am sending you copies of the cuttings that we have collected on Cornish sightings of 'big cats', and I hope that you will find something of interest.'*

The cuttings were also enclosed with a report from ASSAP, Cornwall, and a number of typed summaries of telephone calls. The articles ran as follows:

'Black beast may be puma' was the heading of an article in the *West Briton* newspaper of 17th January 1985. It was similar to the one to which I have already referred, in the *Western Morning News* of 14th January 1985. The article mainly drew attention to the puma hairs from Peaslake, Surrey, obtained by Di Francis, but given by her to Dr Turk for analysis under a microscope.

The article also mentioned the sighting of Truro Councillor, Mr John Cockle, who recalled how three or four years earlier he was cycling down a lane near Truro, when he sas 'a large cat-like animal' leaping over a hedge. Dr Turk told the press that the animal was later identified as a puma. The same man later telephoned the Turks. The typed summary of the conversation ran:

'To Mrs. Stella M. Turk, but he asked for Dr Frank A. Turk. 'Phone call on 14th January 1985 (at 8 a.m.) from John Cockle, who had just heard talk/report on 'Radio Cornwall' concerning puma sightings. He said that two to three years ago he had two sightings, spaced by one year and one mile apart... He talked to the press a few months ago, but there was disbelief. Sea-faring man, much travelled, says that he is not easily deceived, and he knows a cat when he sees one!'

Second sighting near Malpas. Both were seen in the half-light, 'when he was on a bicycle. They leapt over hedges.'

A close look through the files shows that the 8th December 1984 edition of the *Western Morning News* has an article by Jeanette Taylor, called 'This Puma is no pussy-cat'. Mr Cockle's first sighting was in St Clements Road, and the other was at 6 a.m. in Malpas Road, Truro. He stated:

'I have seen it twice. Perhaps there are more than one of them. It is definitely not my imagination. I was on my bicycle and was within 20 feet of it. It was crouched down in the road and when it saw me it leapt over the hedge. It was a sandy-brown colour with a big tail. I don't see any reason why there should not be a large cat living around here and I am sure many people must have seen it.'

These two sightings probably occurred around 1982-1983. They are obviously genuine, considering that Mr Cockle is a much-travelled sailor and a town councillor.

b) The 7th February 1985 edition of the *West Briton* and the typed summaries gave some more details of Mr Philip's sighting at Bridge, Redruth. Mr Philips told a reporter:

As soon as it spotted me it ran down towards the village. It was tawny-brown. When I read about the sightings at Stithians I admit I laughed about it.'

The report said that a local lady had found paw-prints of a large animal near her home and some other villagers had heard catlike shrieks. Mr Philips also told the press that he was of the opinion that the cat might have been living off scraps given to the birds in his back garden. On a Saturday in January 1985, a 'black puma' was seen in the St Stephens area. However, the *West Briton* discovered that a young black-and-tan Dobermann Pinscher dog was rescued from a disused clay tank in the area, so the assumption was that the Dobermann was the big cat. Mr Philips gave the Turks the following information, which I quote from the typed summary:

Sighting of large cat.

On 30 January 1985, at 6.50 a.m., Gordon Philips of Bridge, a farmer aged 71, saw a cat, the size and build of a medium-sized lurcher dog, against the window of a shed with young calves. The calves were terrified, but when Mr Philips appeared the animal moved off slowly towards the village, during which time two cars came up the village and should have spotted it in their headlights. (He saw it under powerful quartz lights.)

It was fawn-coloured and it looked thin and what he described as 'hollow-gutted'. Also it had part of its tail missing, as if it had been in an accident. He told the police, so that other farmers could be warned to protect their livestock. A nearby farmer with sheep said that his had been disturbed and frightened on the night/ morning of 29th/30th, and a girl who works for MAFF at Nance Duke actually heard a curious noise from an unknown wild beast.'

c) The sighting of Mr Walter Berry of Redruth was in 1980. He told the *Western Morning News* of 8th December 1984:

'I was in the lane when I saw it. It looked like a leopard or a puma, was about four feet long and a small head. I banged my walking-stick on the road and in one leap it was over the hedge. My wife had seen something strange by the pond and she won't go out at night. My son is also convinced and makes sure all his horses are locked up before darkness.'

He knew that other people had seen the big cat.

d) The sighting of a lynx-like cat at Chancewater was recorded in the *Western Morning News* of 16th January 1985. This article and another in the 17th January issue of the *West Briton* referred to the sighting of Mr and Mrs. Sydney Bowden of Stithians. Mrs. Bowden stated she first saw the cat in a field near their cottage, stalking another animal.
It had a thick tail, was a dark brown colour, and looked like a cat. The Bowdens had lived at the cottage for 50 years. He was/retired builder and a choirmaster, well-known in musical circles. He and his wife saw the animal in a field near their cottage before it jumped a hedge. They contacted Dr Turk. The sightings were through a window, from which they had a good view. Mr Bowden stated:

'It was like a cat, but much bigger and darkish in colour. We often see foxes, but this was bigger. It looked like an over-sized cat. We are used to seeing all kinds of wild animals, but we have never seen anything like this.'

Dr Turk said: *"There is no doubt that wildcats, including pumas, are living in the British countryside."* Dr Bowden said that in the second sighting the cat was 'nibbling corn'. Dr Turk also told the *West Briton*:

'This was just one piece of small correborative evidence which helped his theory of there being different types of British wildcats. But I cannot say that this definitely was a puma.'

Newquay Zoo did not deny that there were pumas in the countryside.

Maybe they are reminded of their own puma, probably a male, which allegedly escaped in 1983. I have written to the Zoo, but received no answer. However, I can say that the then Manager, the late Mr Norman Marshall, thinks the 'Cornish cats' are pumas. He told Janette Taylor, for the *Western Morning News* of 8th December 1984:

'Pumas prefer a cold climate and would be very suited to the Cornish countryside. Sightings would be few because they lay up by day and hunt by night, when they could catch sheep, goats or young horses. It is unlikely that one would have escaped from a zoo, but this sort of animal is privately owned and there have been incidents in circuses where animals have escaped.'

The manager advised anyone seeing a puma just to carry on walking, ignoring it, as it probably would not attack.

e)   The sheep kill at Mr Leonard Mingo's farm in December 1984 was examined by veterinary surgeon Mr Dixon Gunn. He knew that if a puma had been the killer, the bones would be crushed to pulp. The vet who examined the Fraddon, West of Bodmin sheep-kill, said: 'It was the most complete demolition job I have seen in my 25 years as a vet.' He played on the theory that a pack of dogs was responsible for the kills, not a big cat, as Di Francis believed.

f)   The typed summaries of telephone calls to the Turks contain this item:

'Phone call on 23rd February 1985 from young woman who preferred to remain anonymous, as she did not want her name to appear in the press. On 19th February she saw a large cat, the size of a red setter, in the headlights of her car. Its eyes were large and green, and it was by the hedge. It appeared to be black. Although she did not distinctly notice the tail at the time, on reflection she believed that it was long and thin. The sighting was near Mabe on the road above the reservoir at Argyll. She spoke to Mrs. Turk, but had asked to speak to Dr Turk, having seen him quoted in the recent press notices of such sings.'

Mr David Thomas of Redruth, Cornwall, wrote the following information to Mrs. Turk:
'The sighting of cat reported to D. Thomas on 24th June 1987. The witness was a woman who had lived in the village for most of her life and who saw what she claimed to be a 'cat-like creature' on a still summer evening. With her was her 20-year-old son.

My son and I were walking out one Sunday afternoon. I said: "Oh, look at that cat!" It was huge. We stopped and I said to my son, "That is no cat!" It was stealthily hunting just like a cat would but it was much too big to be a cat. We watched it, and it seemed as if it was looking for something in the hedge. We were watching from two fields away... It wasn't a cat because of its size. It had a cat's face and ears but the body was big and sleek, not long-haired. I can't remember what the tail was like, but we must have watched it for ten minutes to a quarter of an hour. I watched it with a bit of fear. I would not have gone over the hedge to get any closer as I felt that there was something a bit "out of the ordinary" about this creature. It was a lovely golden colour like a golden Labrador. It was not a dog, it was not a fox. It was cat family.

It didn't seem to see us and as we walked on we lost sight of it. We did venture back a few steps but it had gone.'

g) The *Shooting Times and Country Magazine* of January 1987 had a small piece on a Cornish cat sighting:

S.W. Puma spotted: The fabled `Beast of Exmoor` - a large, dark, puma-like creature has been spotted again, but it has moved, it seems. Reports of the beast - after an initial rash of sightings in various parts of the Exmoor area some time ago - have been non-existent lately, but now a motorist claims he saw the creature, again described as 'puma-like', jump a 15 feet hedge near Liskeard in Cornwall.'

Trevor Beer told the *Western Morning News* that the Exmoor Beasts could be coming off the high moors and searching in the North Cornwall area. We will remember that biologist Mr Nigel Brierly told the newspaper reporter that the puma can travel up to 100 miles in a relatively short space of time. Such factors would limit the number of cats, one would have thought.

j) The *Fortean Times* (No. 44), lists six sightings of cats in Cornwall in 1984 and in 1986.

k) We now refer to the two sightings of Mr Sydney Tucker of Redruth. There had been the sighting of a cat-like, crouched-down feline, feeding with a long black tail out behind it, at St Keyne, near Liskeard in 1986. Mr Tucker wrote to Mrs. Amos three times in 1985. He received a copy of the Plymouth UFO Research Group's Newsletter in March 1985, and noted the interest it took in the black-cat reports. Mr Tucker said on 4th March 1986, in a letter to Mrs. Amos:

'These things have been seen in four places down here over the past six months. I have seen the same thing twice, but did not think it was of sufficient importance to broadcast, as very few seemed to be interested. However, the circumstances are as follows:

Last September... second week... I went out on Sunday morning with my camera, and saw a cat, sitting up exactly like the same position as the cats in the old Egyptian tombs, and this cat was the size of a greyhound. No doubt you have seen cats which have been surprised out in the open, and they invariably crouch, before they take off. This one did not. It just turned and scampered. Tail full and not tapered. All black.
Just before I became ill in the same area but Todpool (near St Day) I saw the same creature, moving like the cats out of the devil's residence. It was a cat. Readily admit to being in my first dotage, and find it hard to differentiate between gin and whisky, but I do know a cat when I see one! Head about the size of a decent-sized teapot, and full length, including tail, four feet.'

By 29th September 1985, Mr Tucker was saying:

'Everything is, and has been quiet down here, except for the fact that I have seen the cat again - and it really was, and is a cat. Saw it two weeks ago, in the fields half a mile from where I first saw it in Todpool Valley... travelling very fast as if it was chasing something, but I could not see what. Distance from me about 300 yards. I should say that it was definitely the size of a normal greyhound, but fatter in the body, with a round head, and its run was in leaps as well as running straight and flat. All black, no brown or white colour that I could have seen. I am going out as often as I can with camera and field-glasses, and with an open mind.'

Mr Tucker gives further details of the animal:

'About height and length of medium-sized greyhound, but much fatter and rounder. Head: typical cat, with normal set ears. Length, I should think total (from nose to tail) 3 feet to 4 feet. End of tail rounded and not tapered as in most cats. When sitting, before it turned in the bushes behind it, had the impression that the eyes were red.

Now to give some idea of the different ways in which it acted when it saw me. As I said on the 'phone, while out with my gun over many years, I have come across and seen very many pet cats which have gone wild. All colours and all types and breeds, from pure white-haired to tortoiseshell and marmalade and pure black - all these have acted in the same way when they have seen me: crouched down and watched me, to see which way I was going, and what I was going to do.

Not this black one. It took off at once. If anyone wanted me to give the best description I could, I could only say that it was the same size and shape as a panther or puma, but not so fat or big around the body; higher than a puma, with a longer tail. For a comparison with any dogs, I would put its size near to a Weimaraner pointer, or fully-grown Dobermann Pinscher - that size round body, but of course, head of a cat, and size of a medium teapot.

Three reports came in from different parts of the country within three weeks of my sighting. Where do they come from?

I have heard of it raining frogs, and it is true, this does happen. But these cats are a different matter altogether. As for the kitten-sized one shot up in Cumbria, what I saw was an adult one. Male or female - could not be sure, but thought it could be male, from the female of every species. The Egyptians worshipped cats, but there may be reason for it. They even embalmed them in special tombs, but no other animal was treated in this way by them.'

This was most interesting, and the whole story was undoubtedly true. There can be no question that Mr Tucker was telling the truth. The two sightings were also expanded in two letters that I received from Mr Tucker:

'Regarding my sightings of the big black cat (or cats), there is 'very little more I can tell you than you already know from my letter to Joan Amos. I can only add the following:

1) I do not live in the valley - it is half a mile from my house.

2) I could not swear an oath in a court that the second cat I saw was the same cat, as it was at a distance from me, but I am certain in my own mind that it was, as the chances of two cats of this size in such a small area are far too great.

3) The nearest I can get to a true description of the cat I saw is that it was about the same size as an American cougar, but much thinner, and not so fat or rounded.

4) Although I did not mention my first sighting to anyone, within three weeks of my seeing this big cat, reports came into the local press of the same thing being seen at the village of St Stithians, four miles south-west of me, and also at the small seaside place of Portreath, three miles due west of me. The whole animal was black. Tail roughly a half to two-thirds the length of the body. At the second sighting the animal was at a distance of about three hundred yards, and really moving (bounding) very fast, as if it were chasing something. My other reference was to the (kitten) which was shot in Cumberland.'

By 16th July 1987 I had received another letter from Mr Tucker, one part of which ran:

'You may certainly use any information which I have given in the past regarding the two sightings of these cats, provided that nothing is added to what I have already stated. There are, however, two points which are worth making, regarding what I saw:

1) Small, domestic cats have been known to travel quite long distances, to return to a house or home from which their owners have moved. It stands to reason, therefore, that a much larger cat (i.e. the animal which I saw) could travel much further.

2) As previously stated, at the time of my sightings I mentioned them to no one and yet within three weeks of these sightings, there were two reports in Cornwall, the furthest only four miles from me. It is well-known that if someone says they have seen something, someone else 'will see the same thing' immediately afterwards! In this case, as stated, I reported what I saw to no one.' The Western Morning News of 13th November 1987 had an article entitled 'Pensioner Sees Beast of Bude'. Mrs. Grace Tiffley, aged 72, observed a large animal outside her house in Meadow Drive, Bude, Cornwall. The animal was black, but it was not a fox, dog or domestic cat, The animal was seen early one morning from her bedroom window. Mrs. Tuffley told her husband about the sighting and she also told her son. She said: "It was enormous."

Twenty-four hours later, Leisure Industries consultant Mr David Kay saw a similar puma or panther near Stratton, Cornwall., He told the *Western Morning News* about his sighting, and Mrs. Tuffley read about it. She then contacted the paper, who published her story. Mr Kay's sighting was also of a large black big cat like a panther or puma.

The most recent sighting at the time was published in the *West Briton* newspaper, on 14th April 1988. Mr. Jim Andrew, aged 72, a retired farmer, went to check one of his three-day-old calves on his small-holding. He entered the field at Penryn, Falmouth, and observed the cat-like faced beast, which had a brown hue on its black fur, stalking the calf. He said to me later, on the telephone: It was 'broader than a fox' and could have been a puma or a panthers Mr Andrew saw the animal for three or four seconds, but he was sure it was not just a domestic cat or a fox, as I see lots of these". He warned farmers that the cat-like beast might kill their livestock. Mr Andrew told the *West Briton* newspaper:

> *"I found the calf, its mother and a steer all staring at something about ten to fifteen yards away in a big stack of brambles and ferns. Suddenly the calf jumped up and the cow bleated - I have never seen animals look so frightened. Then I saw this black beast dart out across the meadow and disappear in the heavy cover of a railway cutting. I have never seen an animal move so fast. I know animals - I was reared on a farm, and farmed nearly all my life. I could recognise any wild animals, but I have never seen anything like this before."*

Mr Andrew also told me that he went to a local cattle-market afterwards, and while talking to another farmer about his sighting, the farmer stated that he had seen a black big cat in Cornwall, forty years before, so we now have two clues to suggest there have been "Cornish cats" since the early part of this century!

Mr David Thomas, of the Association for the Scientific Study of Anomalous Phenomena, [ASSAP]wrote to me on 26th March 1988, giving me the following information:

> *"I was delighted to receive your letter, and it goes without saying that I, and all in AS-SAP, Cornwall, will offer you every help we can. I do not think we can say all 'cat' sightings are of escaped animals, although I do feel some are, and I will cite one case that was reported to me some months ago.*

> *A workmate, who was aware of my interest in his home village, was driving to work about 2 a.m. when down one of the village lanes just outside the village, about 12 ft high on both sides and no opening in either side, or houses, he saw what he describes as a large black Labrador which crossed the road in front of him about 50 yards away.*

> *He saw this beast dissolve into the hedgerow at a point he later found to be solid granite wall. He also said the beast seemed to be a dog, but it definitely had the head of a cat.' This writer had previously expressed a total disbelief in anything supernatural, and did not want this sighting to be general/known because of his stated disbelief. I still think that when writing a book such as yours it is more important to be objective than subjective. I would recommend that you contact Richard Dufton on this matter. He was involved in many 'cat' cases, as well as other earth mystery subjects and ancient Norse mythology. I was not sure whether you wanted me to supply you with Cornish authorities who could help with your research, but have included a few addresses you might find useful. One final comment: have you considered the link between these "black cats" and the "black dogs" or Norse mythology, also the links in local folklore*

such as the"Hound of the Baskervilles" and "Beast of Exmoor". I shall keep you in-
formed of our investigation when it resumes again in May.'

He sent me the address of Mr Dufton, who lives in Brighton, and he requested the confidentiality of witnesses. He also sent me a list of addresses. The magazine, *The Magpie*, is a free publication edited by Mr
Thomas, about 'People interested in, and practising, the out-of-the-ordinary experience'. Mr Anthony
'Doc' Shells, of Truro, Cornwall, who is interested in lake monsters and sea serpents, told me, on 18th August 1987, in a letter, his own theory:

'There's not much I can tell you about the Cornish "big cat", "Puma", or whatever it is. I
have never seen it myself, though there were several sightings reported around this
area, Ponsanooth Stithians, during the winter of 1984/5. I suggest you write to Janet
Bord, who has collected most of the newspaper cuttings relating to these sightings.
There seems to be a link between big cat sightings around the Great Glen, and sightings
of the Loch Ness Monster, which suggests some kind of psychic or paranormal inter-
connection. The animals seem to be both 'real' in the organic sense, and paraphysical or
hallucinatory, but they can be photographed and filmed, sometimes.'

We now come to a rather long statement by Dr Frank Turk, who is an extra-mural research fellow, and
formerly university reader in Natural History and Oriental Art, at Exeter University. As a zoologist he is
an expert on all sorts of animals and can positively identify the remains and clues that big cats leave behind. The support he has given to Miss Di Francis, Mr Nigel Brierly and Dr Karl Shuker has undoubtedly
helped them in their individual quests for these cats. I am very grateful for his help, and I hope that the
following statement from a letter of 15th February 1988 will pay tribute to his valuable work.

I am interested to know that you propose writing a book on this subject, but it is go-
ing to be difficult for you because a lot of work is now taking place on this subject.
Miss Di Francis 'phoned me yesterday to say that she has a grant to set up a small re-
search unit in Scotland to investigate the 'big cats' there.

All of them, I am sure, are pumas and indeed, I understand that a few have been shot
but cannot vouch for this.

Mr Nigel Brierly also recently sent me further news of the "Exmoor Beast" and of the
cage he has had made in which to trap it. There is also a young graduate of Birming-
ham University who is most active in this field. Although I am not myself at all
deeply involved in the subject of 'big cats in Britain', I have found myself in the posi-
tion of giving advice and providing 'back-up' services to other people. This possibly
has given the very little 'hard' evidence that we have.

I have identified puma hair from an orchard in Surrey, and the hair of a lynx
(surprisingly possibly European?) from Exmoor, and the bone identification of small
mammals from an Exmoor wood, in a collection, which suggests they were the prey
of the lynx. I was, I think, the first zoologist to examine the "Kellas cat" and to iden-
tify it as a melanistic mutant of the wildcat, and probably an animal very closely re-

lated to a "species" (?) described by a Russian zoologist from an area near the Black Sea many years ago.

I have also examined a set of X-rays of the skull of the Kellas cat, and casts of the footprints of a very large cat, which Miss Francis made. It is natural that, in the course of these events, I have accumulated a big file of letters and newspaper cuttings - many of the latter from Scottish newspapers. You would be very welcome to see these and copy out what you wanted if you are ever in Cornwall.

Some fifteen years ago I founded the University's Biological Research Unit, housed at the Institute of Cornish Studies, University of Exeter, Redruth. Since my retirement my wife is now the Director of the Biological Records Unit, and currently engaged, with the help of Dr Colin French, in putting on computer all our one and a quarter million zoological and botanical records.

We also have a bibliography of Cornish Natural History of nearly 10,000 items as well as massive holdings of the site surveys etc. If you are ever in Cornwall and wanted to make an appointment by 'phone, my wife at Trevenson House would be very pleased to show you all we have on Cornish sightings of big cats. It is curious that all the animal species tentatively involved seem to be American.'

This last point is interesting. Are there any fur farms in England which keep lynxes for the purpose of making coats?

A few of the lynx kills and sightings could be explained by this. We would have to make careful enquiries to see whether any lynxes were kept on English fur-farms, like the coypu and mink. The mink first established itself in Britain in 1929, as did the coypu in the 1930s. They expanded rapidly, though coypu are now almost extinct in their main stronghold of East Anglia, thanks to a military-style operation by the Ministry of Agriculture, Fisheries and Food.

The mink is now widely found throughout the Westcountry and Southern England, I believe. The Cornish cats are larger than the coypu, or the mink.

- Chapter Five -
OTHER SOUTHWESTERN CATS

- ## THE WINTERSLOW LIONESS

To start this chapter, let us go back to the days when horse-drawn coaches travelled throughout Britain, and examine the story of the Winterslow lioness. An escapee, she attacked a mail-coach on the night of October 25th 1816 at Wintersiow, near Salisbury, Wiltshire. She was an African lioness, about five years old at the time of the incident. She somehow detached herself from the menagerie with which she was travelling, and the thought of supper was in her mind at the time of the attack.

The Exeter-to-London 'Quick-silver' coach pulled up at the *Winterslow Inn*, then named the Winterslow Hutt (but now called the *Pheasant Inn*). A 'calf' was seen to be running alongside the coach, but the driver suddenly realised, to his horror, that the beast was none other than a lioness. She then proceeded to attack the lead horse, an ex-racehorse named Pomegranate. The horse was unable to escape, but, with eyes rolling in fear, attempted to lash out at the lioness. The guard, on the back of the coach, took up his blunderbuss and prepared to cut short the life of the lioness.

However, an extremely brave menagerie owner, who shouted at him not to shoot the animal, which was very valuable in those days, being quite hard to replace, stopped him from doing this. Either a Newfoundland dog, or a bull-mastiff then set upon the lioness. The dog was able to hang onto the lioness for some time, but in due course the enraged lioness attacked the dog, which was either killed, or badly hurt, as its attacker had sharp claws and an array of fearsome teeth.

I wrote to the proprietor of the *Pheasant Inn*, and they sent me a photocopy from an unnamed local guidebook and a postcard depicting the lioness's attack on the mail-coach. The guidebook, containing an account of the inn's history, refers to the lioness's attack, as follows:

> 'As the Exeter Mail drew up at the Winterslow Hutt one night in 1816 it was attacked by a fierce lioness. One of the horses, called Pomegranate, a famous ex-racehorse, gave a good account of himself, but he was hampered by the harness. A mastiff was set upon the lioness, who promptly made short work of the dog and then retreated under a granary, where it was later secured. The lioness was owned by a local menagerie owner, who prevented the Mail guard from shooting the animal, which he sold for a good price at Salisbury Fair.
>
> It seems that the passengers of the coach in their terror, after fleeing into the inn and barring the door, locked out one of the slower passengers, who then witnessed at close quarters the attack on the horse. This had such an effect on him that soon after he became an inmate of the Laverstock Asylum for twenty-seven years.
> The postcard bears a print by Mr Robert Pollard, showing the coach in the foreground and the inn in the background. The inscription under the picture read:

'The Lioness attacking the horse of the Exeter mail-coach.

To Thomas Hasker, Esq., Superintendent of His Majesty's Mail coaches. This print by permission is most respectfully dedicated by his servant Robert Polland'. Under the main inscription, in very small print, these words can be made out: 'Drawn from the information of Joseph Duke, Guard of the Mail at the time of the event on the night of Sunday 26th October 1816 at Winterslow Hut, near Salisbury. The ferocious animal had escaped from the custody of the exhibitor of wild beasts etc.'

The picture was painted and printed only five months after the actual event, on 17th February 1817.

The 'Lioness of Winterslow' inspired other people to draw and write about the event. On arriving in London, the news must have travelled fast as the passengers told others of their ordeal.

Mr Daniel Howell, editor of the *Wylye Valley Life,* a local magazine that is published in Warminster in Wiltshire, wrote an article for his February 1987 edition. It was entitled 'The Winterslow Lioness'. Mr Howell also published, very kindly, a letter from me concerning an escaped black panther. In addition to recounting the actual lioness incident, he also says that the famous essayist, Mr William Hazlitt (1778-1830), lived in the Winterslow Hutt, and he must have witnessed the aftermath of the lioness affair.

There is some confusion over the story, for each account differs somewhat from the next. Take, for example, the fate of the dog. Some say the dog was killed, while others say it was just badly wounded. One thing is certain: people heard of the event and a lioness vogue gave the animal an almost legendary place in history. Lioness beer-mats, paintings and other articles came into being. The *Pheasant Inn* has made a collection of the 'Lioness' articles.

Three artists who drew the lioness attacking the mail-coach were Robert Pollard, A. Sauerweid, and a German artist from Nuremburg city.

Sauerweid's rather dramatic painting was done using as a background a London pub beer-garden. The 31st July 1984 postage stamps contained one stamp on 'an attack on the Exeter mail in 1816', which shows Pollard's print, and was issued to mark 200 years of the mail-coach introduction.

Robert Pollard's print also shows three top-hatted gentlemen watching the lioness's attack from an upstairs window of the inn. The men are supposed to be Charles James Fox (1749-1806), the famous politician, of Farley village, the writer Charles Lamb (1775-1834), and William Hazlitt, whom I mentioned earlier.

Mr Howell's article inspired Major A.T. Edmunds, of Wylyes, Wiltshire, to write in to the *Wylye Valley Life* of 18th April 1987, and to inform readers:

'I am in the fortunate position of having a copy of both Pollard's and Sauerweid's Illustration of the incident. However I also have a coloured print of the incident, painted by a German artist which has an indecipherable signature but whose first name may be Nurnberg. (of course that may be the name of the place he came from.)

If you, or the source of your article, has any knowledge of this print I should be most grateful to hear about it.'

Mr Howell had no knowledge of such a print and neither have any of the four people who wrote accounts of the lioness in their books. I would recommend that any one interested in the lioness should go for a drink at the Winterslow Pheasant Inn, where there/several paintings depicting the lioness event.

I end this section by noting that there are modern reports of a mystery cat at Farley, just down the road from Winterslow, on the Wiltshire/Hampshire boundary.

References

1) Hodge, Lornie Leete, *'Moonraker Country'*: Alan Sutton, 1982. See pp. 37-38.
2) Milkson, Cecilia, *'Tales of Old Wiltshire'*: Countryside Books, 3 Catherine's Road, Newbury, Berkshire. 1982. See pp.44-45.
3) Whitelock, Ralph, *'The Folklore of Wiltshire'*: B.T. Batsford Ltd., 1976. pp.154-5.
4) Whitelock, Ralph, *'Salisbury Plain'*: 1955. pp.54-55.
5) *'Wylye Valley Life* 13 George Street, Warminster, Wiltshire. See issues in Vol.2, Nos. 4 and 6. (For photocopies send a self-addressed envelope to the above address.)
6) *The Pheasant Inn Guidebook* - undated. Obtainable from The Pheasant, Winterslow.

The Salisbury Plain Panther

I once overheard a conversation between two hunt servants. They were talking about a black panther or similar big cat, which had escaped after a train crash in the Wylye Valley area of Wiltshire. The crash took place during the 1970s, and the panther was hunted down into Great Ridge, a long band of woods near the Wylye Valley. This conversation must have been around 1982 or 1983, and from what I heard the panther had been on the way to a circus. To satisfy my curiosity, I began a number of enquiries in this area, writing to many people and receiving a number of replies, which led to new fields of enquiry, and more information. The following is what I discovered.

The first letter was dated February 1987, coming from the Manager of the famous Longleat safari park, Mr Roger Crawly:

'In reply to your letter, addressed to Mrs. Chipperfield, neither she nor anyone else here has kept any record of wild animal sightings in Britain. On occasions we have been involved in searches for alleged wild animals, but they have always turned out to be large dogs. We are not convinced that there are any wildcats living free in the British Isles.'

He doubtless said this because he was probably tired of suggestions that all the big cat escapees had come from Longleat, which does not seem to be at all true. When Longleat was opened in 1965, the safari park received a great deal of bad press, for people complained that the fifty lions in the enclosures were liable to escape. However, the local council was finally convinced that this would not ever happen and Longleat went ahead. The Managers of the safari park were the Chipperfields, and you can read about their exploits in Mary Chipperfield's two books: *Lion Country* and *Lions on the Lawn*. There are interesting pictures of lions in the Pheasantry House, where the Chipperfields lived. In all this time, not one large cat has gone missing from Longleat, although there was one instance where a seal escaped in the August of 1986, but it was soon recaptured, halfway down the River Avon, heading for the Bristol Channel.

Longleat's lions are very dangerous, and there have been a number of nasty incidents when lions have attacked cars, but to my knowledge, nobody has been badly hurt.

To see what had arisen during February 1987 on mystery cats in this area, it is necessary to look at the letter I had published in the *Wylye Valley Life* of that month:

> *'I am very interested in the big cats of Britain. I have a book entitled 'The Runaways', by Victor Canning, published by Penguin Books in 1973. It is the story of a runaway boy and a cheetah. The cheetah has cubs on Salisbury Plain. I wondered what caused this book to be published.Here are two possible reasons:*
>
> *1) Halfway between Warminster and Salisbury a crash between two trains occurred.*
>
> *2) Mr J. Chipperfield, of Chipperfield's Circus, kept a pet tiger called 'Rahat Longleat' for a few years, when the safari park was being started. I also believe there is a species of British big cats which has a leopard's body, a puma's head and hand-like paws. I have photographs to prove this fact.'*

The photographs in question were the ones taken by Di Francis, and used in her book *'Cat Country'*, and I am now not certain whether those photographs were of an unknown species. (See the chapter on 'Welsh Mystery Cats'.)

Soon after sending off the above letter, I began to receive replies from a variety of people. A smallholder who lives near Chitterne, on Salisbury Plain, told me of seven 'mongrel lurchers' which had gone missing from gypsy camps and had all been shot dead. I heard from somebody else that these lurchers had packed together, and that they were more like long-haired whippets. These dogs had consumed deer on the Plain for some years, but had never bred in the wild.

The first record of sightings near the Plain was included in Janet and Colin Bord's book, *'Alien Animals'*. I quote the two cases with permission of both Mr and Mrs. Bord and their publishers, Granada Ltd. These cases appear on page 54 of their book:

> *'The avalanche of sightings continued throughout October (1964). At Farley Mount, West of Winchester, Hampshire, a gamekeeper shot at a 'black slit-eyed animal'. There were reports of a 'wounded puma', but a police search found nothing. Another gamekeeper reported seeing the 'puma' on two occasions at King's Somborne, seven miles west of Winchester.'*

On page 55, another incident in the same area was recorded:

BIG CATS: LOOSE IN BRITAIN

'Early in February 1965, Michael Lewis, a gamekeeper with his brother David, found large footprints which they thought might be a puma's, at Farley, Near Salisbury, and photographs and plaster casts were sent to London for identification.'

The sources of the first cases were the articles in the London *Evening Times* for the 24th and 28th October 1964. The third case, with no name, was recorded in the newspaper of 12th February 1965. All these cases come within easy reach of the Wylye Valley, but as they were in the 1960s, I doubt whether the same creature could be alive today. However, on the other side of Salisbury Plain, three sightings came straight to me.

In January 1987 a 14-year-old boy named Edward Bridges saw a large black cat crossing the road between Bratton and Earistoke. This sighting was late in the evening, on the Westbury side of Salisbury Plain. Edward, with his father, saw the cat in their car headlights, and described the creature as being 'larger than a Scottish wildcat, and with a bushy tail.' He thought it was not as large as a black panther, and likened it to one of the Moray beasts - the Kellas-cat type, which is like a spaniel-sized dog. Edward Bridges also said that he had heard of a tabby-cat, which was captured near Westbury and was later released back into the wild. It was like a ferocious Scottish wildcat, he said. Then a second 14-year-old boy, James Barrett-Gray, informed me that he had seen a black panther in woods on the edge of the Plain. He said:

'It was a black panther, longer in the body than a Labrador dog.' The beast was seen jumping a log. (One gains the impression that there might be two cats around.) James also claimed to have seen a deer carcass, not far from the woods. However, a dog could be responsible for this killing. The third sighting from this side of the Plain came from Duncan Robinson, of Potterne, near Devizes, Wiltshire, who saw a strange animal o'clock while watching television at 10 one evening, early in December 1987. He looked at the creature, which stared at him through his living-room window, and then he looked back at the television. When he looked again, the creature had disappeared into the night. He is a reliable witness and described the creature quite well. He said that it was large and white, but too small for a dog. The creature was cat-like, but it was not a normal cat. He also observed that the creature had black spots. When I showed him a newspaper article with a photograph of a genet, he stated:

'That is most like what I saw.' Genets * are about the size of a large mink and are half cat-like and half weasel-like.

---

* **Genets** are Old World carnivores of the family Viverridae, related to civets and linsangs. There are ten species, all contained within the genus *Genetta*, except the Aquatic Genet, which is housed in its own genus *Osbornictis*. Genets are superficially cat-like creatures, despite being only distantly related to cats. Most of them have spotted coats and long, banded tails, small heads, and large ears. Like civets, genets have strong musk glands, which are used to mark territory, and they are known to perform handstands when doing this. Genets are highly agile creatures, and are the only Viverrids that stand bipedally. All live exclusively in Africa except for the widespread Common Genet *Genetta genetta*, which can be found in Northwest Africa and throughout Europe and parts of the Middle East, including countries such as France, Spain, Portugal and the Balearic Islands. The Ibizan subspecies, *G. g. isabelae* is listed as vulnerable on the IUCN Red List.

from *Wikipedia*, the free encyclopedia

Following these sightings, I decided to question people in the Wylye Valley about the black panther escape. What came up was very different, and most interesting. The first person I contacted was Mr M. M. Sach, the Area Manager of British Rail, to see whether there was any record of such a crash. All he told me, in a letter dated 19th March 1987, was: *'I regret I have no information for you.'*

So then I tried Mr David C. Holton, who was mildly interested in the UFO sightings, at the Warminster during the 1960s. He is a chiropodist, living in Crockerton, near Warminster, in Wiltshire. In a letter dated 19th May 1987, he told me:

> *'I have never heard of any such animal as a panther escaping from a train crash in the Wylye Valley in the 1970s, but I noted with great interest reports of a lion having been seen by a number of witnesses in the Norton Bavant area, as they were travelling by train to Bristol. Intensive enquiries and searching by both the police and military failed to show any physical justification for the reports, though a phantom lion has been seen in that vicinity on many occasions.*
>
> *As you may know, the Romans had an encampment at Norton Bavant, and Roman witchcraft (of which we have very little knowledge) centred very largely on animal/ etherial/astral forms through their Lunar cult of Diana. People who are sensitive to such sitii may interpret them, on occasion, as physical beasts and have very disturbing experiences on this account.'*

When I talked to Mr Holton at a later date, he informed me that the witnesses may have mistaken a deer for a lion, or something similar. I was anxious to find out more about this event, so I looked through the files of the local paper, the *Warminster Journal*, and came up with the article covering the lion search.

The article was dated 8th February 1980, and was entitled *'And the Lion danced with the Kangaroo'*. The guard on the Portsmouth to Bristol train had reported that some of his passengers had seen a lion browsing in a field near the village of Codford. At least one of the passengers had seen the lion. Later in the day (a Friday) a kangaroo was said to have been seen on the Thursday in the same area. The police checked Longleat safari park, who quickly denied that anything had escaped from the park. Then a search was conducted, with twelve policemen, led by Inspector Robert Eades and two Army Air Corps helicopters overhead.

The search lasted the whole of the Friday morning, but no trace was found of either the lion or kangaroo. All the farm animals seemed very peaceful, so the police declared the search a false alarm and stopped searching. Nobody in the area of Norton Bavatt and Codford had seen anything.

I then contacted the local hunt servants of the South and West Wilts Foxhounds, who reckoned that the search had definitely been a false alarm. Roger Crawley's statement seems to confirm this. The *Fortean Times* (No.32) included in its 'Escapes and Discoveries' section a reference to the above incident, quoting the article of 2nd February 1980. The passage runs:

> *'On 1st February 1980, the area around Warminster, Wilts., not far from Devizes, was searched by police marksmen and two Army helicopters. Two separate reports - one*

of a kangaroo and the other of a lion near the railway line jusbutside Warminster - caught the police by surprise. "It began to look as though there had been a mass escape from a safari park," a police officer said. Ten miles away is Longleat House, with its famous collection of lions, but they had none missing. The police search found nothing at all, and there the mystery lies.'

The same *Fortean Times* also notes the case of two escaped lionesses at Devizes. The London *Evening Standard* of 28th April 1980 had the story, which ran:

'Two lionesses burst into the grounds of Southbroom Comprehensive school, Devizes, Wiltshire, on 28th April 1980. They had escaped from Sally Chipperfield's circus on the village green nearby, and were re-captured within two hours. The children were at their lunch break when one lioness, chased by circus men, jumped through the window of a mobile classroom, sending kids screaming into the playground. Some of the kids were shocked, but the rest became quickly excited as the circus men closed in. The other lioness made for the main building and dived through a double glazed door. She was badly cut and wrecked the classroom as she paced the floor.
A spokesman for Devizes police said that they had not established how the animals got out.'

Note that all these events happened in a very short time. The Chipperfield circus has close connections with the Chipperfields at Longleat, of course.

Black dog legends are also in existence in Southern Wiltshire. In *'Moonraking: a Little Book of Wiltshire Stories'*, the most recent account of a black dog encounter is recorded. The book was published in 1979, and the account is entitled 'A True Story':

'I was sitting, some years ago, in the little white lodge on the Salisbury Road, waiting for my husband to come to tea. It was mid-winter and quite dark at 5 o'clock, and I was somewhat nervous after being alone all day. Suddenly I heard his step, and he opened the door and walked in.

I looked up and exclaimed at his extreme pallor. "Why, whatever is the matter?" I cried. "How white you are!"

"Yes, and so would you be white if you'd been with me tonight," he said. "Why, what's happened?"

"Give me a cup of tea, and I'll tell you." He then said, "It was pitch dark when I left the Avenue and turned into Wilbury, and I had just entered the Grove when I found something trotting beside me. It seemed to be a big, black retriever dog. I spoke, but it did not bark, and continued trotting by my side, and panted as if it had been running hard. It left me at the double shuffle and although I whistled and called he did not return. It was only then that I realised it was no real dog, but a ghostly one.'

UFOs are also found in the Warminster area, and a local journalist, Arthur Shuttlewood, wrote four books on the subject during the 1960s and 1970s. The UFOs often appeared over Warminster and there are many photographs showing strange lights at night, and even some daytime encounters have occurred. UFO5 are still active in this area, and therefore we might have a connection between them and the mystery cats.

There are other possible theories behind the panther on the edge of the plain and the Norton Barrant lion. Maybe people are just seeing deer and dogs, and making mistakes. However, I will not comment on theories that deny the existence of mystery cats, because I am convinced that they are out there. It is just a matter of seeing them.

• The Mendips Bobcat

On the 20th November 1986, my mother and I were driving near Priddy in the Mendip Hills of Somerset and Avon. As we entered a rocky-outcropped valley, with a stone-wall-flanked minor road in the middle, we observed a cat-like animal.

It was definitely not a domestic or feral cat, although at first I mistook it for a large specimen of the latter. It was sitting on its haunches, watching the wall as I jumped out of our car, with a camera. The cat, which by now I thought was a sort of lynx, looked at me and hissed like a cat does, after jumping onto a four-foot high stone wall. While on the wall, the cat arched its back and also snarled at me. It looked quite fierce.

I photographed the cat. with my Olympus trip camera, as it disappeared under a five-bar gate. It was running at some speed and when the picture came out, the cat was only a small speck in one corner. The cat ran away into a shed, but I did not follow it, as I thought it might well try to attack me. It was thirty yards away from me when I closed in on it, so I had a good view of it for about five seconds, on top of the wall. I also took a photograph of it perched up there, but unfortunately this photograph did not develop.

This 'bobcat', as I called the animal later on, after consulting a wildlife book, was definitely a largish cat of some type. It was 2* to 3 feet long, with shaggy 2-inch long hair. The coat was a striped, dark brown, tabby colour. It had lighter yellowish patches in the coat, and possibly some black also. If you were to have a darker version of a clouded leopard's coat, then you would have this cat's coat.

The animal I saw was the size of a springer spaniel, and weighed about 30 lbs. at a conservative estimation. It had a roundish head, with pointed ears like a Lynx, and had no visible tail. It was about 12 inches at the shoulder.

We returned to the same area in December 19 and I found a number of possible clues that proved the lynx's existence. I went inside the shed into which it had disappeared, to find razor-sharp claw-marks four feet up one of the wooden posts supporting the tumbled-down corrugated iron shed. I also found a number of strange droppings in a hole, which might have been made by a large cat. Badgers had undermined the shed, having established a sett. At that time I thought the lynx like cat might be living in one of the badger holes; one was more than the standard 25cm in diameter, which is the normal size for a badger sett entrance.

On a third visit, in April 1987, I found a large brown dead badger by the roadside. This was definitely not the creature I observed.

The badger had obviously crossed the road and had been run over by an on-coming car. I also talked to the people at a nearby bungalow, who told me they had never seen the cat. They said that someone had owned a large tabby-cat at a farm nearby, but those people had moved out long before my sighting in November 19, taking the cat with them. There were no other known cats in the district.

At Charterhouse hamlet I talked to a couple, who said there were wild soay sheep near the sheds. When we returned to the area of the sheds, I saw these wild sheep. The countryside around Pridd is dotted with rocks, thorn-bushes and lead mines dating back to Roman times. These mines, which were frequently used in the nineteenth and early twentieth centuries, held a whole range of wildlife.

Sheep kills are not unknown on the Mendips. Signs read: 'Keep your dogs on leads by Order of Mendip District Council'. *The Fortean Times*, No.44, is very useful, for it contains details of sheep kills on the Mendips. This particular passage tells us:

- *'July 1984 - Rodney Stoke, nr. Axbridge. 19 lambs killed; blamed on escaped Alsatian named Percy.'*
- *29th July 1984 - Charterhouse. 16 lambs killed; blamed on Percy.'*
- *1st August 1984 - Tarnok, nr. Axbridge. Dog shot while attacking flock, identified as Percy from collar'*

The sources of these passages were the *Bristol Evening Post* and the *Daily Mirror*. When I questioned the people at Charterhouse about the kills, they said Percy was a 'wild dog' and that he had caused considerable damage.

My aunt told me that Girl Guides, on a camp in 1985 at Burrington Combe, on the Avon side of the Mendips, had heard 'yowling' at night. They thought some sort of cat was responsible. Could it have been a lynx? These animals certainly 'yowl' when mating and guarding their territory, so it may well have been a lynx.

I then wrote to a number of people in the area. The Forestry Commission, Mendip Forest, Hunters Lodge, Priddy, near Wells, told me:

> *'I have seen or heard no mention of any "big cats" loose in the area I cover, from Bristol down to Wincanton. I do have a cousin who is a vet in the Exmoor area, and who is convinced that there is one loose in that area. You will no doubt be aware of that one though, as it has had plenty of publicity.'*

The above was from Forester Mr R. N. Gosslin and was in a letter dated 14th August 1987. The local Somerset Wildlife Park Manager, Mr S. J. Standley, who runs Cricket St Thomas Wildlife Park, near Chard in Somerset, was most helpful:

> *'We have never been involved in any searches for feral big cats in this country, and we wish you luck in your endeavours to find them.'*

He was very helpful because he offered me some lynx droppings from their two Siberian lynx, with which I planned to identify any strange droppings I came upon on Exmoor.

I also wrote to the BBC Natural History Unit, in Bristol, to see whether they could come and film the lynx with their expert photographer, Simon King. Unfortunately they were too busy to do so. Bristol Zoo's Director, Mr G. R. Creed, would only stress, in a letter dated 5th April 1987: *'We regret, however, that we have no relevant information we can send you and we have no knowledge of any big cats loose in Britain.'*

The *Western Gazette* Co. Ltd. told me, in a letter dated 18th August 1987: *'Our paper does not cover the area surrounding Exmoor. To our knowledge we have not printed anything regarding mysterious cats.'* It looked as though I had come up against a brick wall, but then things started to brighten up. Bristol Zoo had some trouble with people breaking into its wildlife park, for the *Fortean Times*, No. 44, said:

> *'A "vandal" broke into a wildlife park in Bristol and shot dead a rare Scottish wildcat (see* Daily Telegraph, *30th October 1984).'*

The Mendip Hills have a long history of mystery cats. Trevor Beer told me he had heard of a panther-type pre-historic cat called *"Panthera gombaszoegensis"* which was found at Westbury-sub-Mendip, in 1938. He said there was a scientific paper on it by a Mr Bishop in 1974. Dr Karl Shuker was Trevor Beer's source, and he has since written to me a number of times. Dr Shuker, a zoologist with a longstanding interest in cryptozoology, sent me a photocopy from A. J. Sutcliffe's book *On the Track of Ice-Age Mammals*, published by the British Museum in 1985. On page 137 Mr Sutcliffe gives this description of what was found at Westbury-sub-Mendip:

> *'Westbury-sub-Mendip Fissure, Somerset:*
>
> *'A cave, discovered in 1969 in a working quarry in the Mendip Hills, Somerset, with a rich mammalian fauna, including the Etrus-can rhinoceros and Deninger's bear, suggesting an approximately Cromerian age for the deposits. Other interesting species include the Sabre-toothed cat, Homotherium; the lynx, the European jaguar,* Felis gombaszoegensis; *an extinct dhole,* xenogyon, *and the vole* Pliomys episcopalis.*'*

A local vicar told me that human bones which were 50,000 years old had been found in the cave.

In 1905, at Great Badminton, Avon, some sheep were killed and their throats had been ripped as though something like a vampire had killed them. It seems that the blood had been sucked from them, though none of their flesh had been taken. Dogs were later shot. big cats are known to drink blood on occasions, and Nigel Brierly stated that the beasts on Exmoor sometimes do this.

• The Beast of Brassknocker Hill

In *Phenomena: a Book of Wonders* by John Mitchell and Robert J.M. Rickard, it is recorded on page 124: 'As we write (April 1976) the *'Bath Evening Chronicle* reports another puma in West Wiltshire.' This was one of the first facts I heard about the "Beast of Brassknocker Hill", near Bath, in Avon. This creature, or creatures, has variously been described as a black panther, a puma, a huge dog, a bear and a monkey! The following is an account of an intensive study I did into this mystery animal.

I sent off for all the articles on the beast ever produced in the *Bath and West Evening Chronicle*. The story dates back to 25th July 1979, when Mr Ronald Harper, a cabinet-maker, found the tree above his goat-shed stripped of bark. Mr Harper, of Sun Cottage, Brassknocker Hill, said to the Chronicle:

> *'On Saturday the tree was perfectly normal, but on Sunday morning something had stripped a third of its bark away. It would have taken more than 200 squirrels to do that damage and, anyway, they seem to have disappeared. I don't know what sort of a creature has attacked that tree, but it has frightened our goat half to death. She lives in a shed under the tree and is locked up at night. The morning after the bark had disappeared she was shaking all over and her eyes were popping out of their sockets. We have lived here for 21 years and nothing like this has happened before. I just can't think of any creature living in this country which could do such damage. The only thing I can think of is that some animal like a raccoon or monkey which escaped from some zoo.'*

The bark had been stripped off on the lower side of the branches, and on the lower branches up to half an inch thick of bark had disappeared. Even two local experts were confused by this act of bark-stripping. Naturalist Mr John Harris was asked to give his opinion of the matter, and he simply stated: *"It is most strange, and I have never heard anything like it occurring before."*

However, at least Bristol city council's leading tree expert, Mr Harris, stated:

> *'The only thing I can think of is that a horde of squirrels stripped the bark looking for water, but I do not think this is very likely. It is a most odd phenomenon.'*

On 3rd August 1979 it was announced that the International Primate Society was going to search for the "Beast of Brassknocker". The General Secretary of the Society, Mr Cyril Rosen, said this from London:

> *'Our man is sifting through the evidence, and if he decides there is a primate loose in the wood, we shall send down a team of experts. It sounds as if it could be a chimp, but until I have made an investigation I cannot say.*
>
> *There is also a strong possibility that the creature could be a baboon. Several of them escaped from Longleat in 1977. A baboon would have no trouble surviving an English winter or covering the distance from Longleat to Bath. If the existence of an ape is established, the Society plans to ask the owner of the wood, Mr Malcolm Farrant of Bathampton if it may track it down. Our experts should be able to clear up this mystery in a couple of days. If we find that there is an ape in the wood it should not be difficult to catch it.'*

Monkeys, apes and other primates are all very dangerous, according to Mr Rosen, and he thought it was vital to catch the creature if it really was there.

Less than a week later, reports started to come in. Mr Frank Green, an 81-year-old retired lorry driver of 1 Brassknocker Hill, started to patrol the area in which the beast was supposed to be. He carried an old converted rifle. Mr Green said:

> *'I am very fond of some animals like horses, but I reckon this creature could be dangerous, and I am taking no chances. I wouldn't like to catch it alive, because any wild animal will turn on you if it is cornered. I think I have heard it screeching and barking several times. If it goes on stripping the bark off those trees many of them will die and that's bad. If I manage to shoot it, this mystery which has been puzzling everyone will be solved.'*

The local RSPCA inspector, Mr John Hobhouse said:

> *'I can see no good reason for shooting an unfortunate creature which has obviously escaped from captivity, unless he has done serious damage to other animals. I do not see any reason why it should not be left to live in the wood.'*

The wildlife expert, Mr Jonny Morris, was convinced that the "Beast of Brassknocker" was a cunning old male baboon. The first sighting of the beast was when two fishermen spotted a three-foot-high, grey-furred, broad ape-faced creature just outside Monkton Combe. The kitchen staff at Ciaverton Down hospital found a few monkey-like prints next to a tree that had been stripped of all its bark. The prints were on a flower-bed.

It was on 14th August 1979 that the International Primate Protection League made an intensive two-hour search of the area. The lone investigator asked people not to go near the area while he was searching. He said to a reporter from the *Bath and West Evening Chronicle*: *"I have no proof, but certain clues have made me decide to return."* He continued to say that he was looking for overnight beds made in tree-tops by chimpanzees, particularly. The investigator, who was a chimp expert, also said:

> *"A chimp makes a different bed each night. If we had found one, it would have been conclusive proof, but there appeared to be none."*

However, he believed that the bark-stripping was in keeping with a primate's work, but the lack of leaves on the oak trees was unexplained. A week and a half later, on 23rd August 1979, 'Curiosity keeps the beast alive' - or so ran the headline in the *Bath and West Evening Chronicle*.

A number of sightseers were to be found patrolling through Brassknocker Wood. The International Primate Protection investigator was still around, and he had some interesting evidence, in the form of a monkey's print. He said this time: *"It's all very baffling. There is an element of hoax and real mystery here."* A lady naturalist from Surrey who had heard about the beast on Radio 4, was carefully picking pieces of bark off a tree, using a pair of tweezers to do so. She explained:

> *"I hope to find some hairs or fur."*

BIG CATS: LOOSE IN BRITAIN

The Chronicle was beginning to treat the whole matter as an interesting joke, but more evidence and ideas were to come.

Mr Ronald Harper was positive that the beast was an aye-aye, a miniature lemur found in small numbers on the island of Madagascar. He was the owner of the goat, which had been frightened by the beast. He was continually boiling up his kettle, to give cups of tea to the investigators. A naval commander from Plymouth brought his binoculars, for he had a 'more plausible theory' as to what the beast might be. Unfortunately we are not told what that theory might be. During the past month the beast had been seen only once, yet people had described it as a spider-monkey, chimp, baboon, golden eagle, Japanese deer and an aye-aye. The majority of people who gave these theories were not named. Bananas were put out to see whether the beast would take them.

In August 1980 a chimpanzee was seen on Claverton Down by 23-year-old taxi-driver Mr John Elphinstone, who said:

> "I was on my way back from Fox Hill, driving towards the University. In the dip past Brassknocker Hill my lights picked up the chimp about to sit on the edge of the roadside. It was about two feet six inches to three feet tall. I didn't stop but I must say I was surprised."

A policeman, P.C. Christopher Roberts, searched the area and he himself saw the chimpanzee, so it seems one was loose, for policemen do not lie just for the sake of it! RSPCA inspector Peter Meyer searched the area for thirty minutes and planned to return to the area the next day, for a more detailed search. He said: *"Chimps can be very dangerous and put you in hospital for months."* The Claverton Cats' and Dogs' Home did not keep a chimp, and Longleat and Bristol Zoos were not missing any chimpanzees.

During 1979 and 1980, birds had stopped singing in Brassknocker Wood. Mr Green, the 81-year-old lorry driver who had lived next to the wood for 80 years and had unsuccessfully hunted the beast, said, on 14th November that a lorry driver had called on him to say that he had seen the monkey, and wondered whether Mr Green had lost a pet monkey. Mr Green had not lost such a pet, but of course he had often heard the creature *"screeching and barking"*.

On 12th August 1980, Mr Ronald Harper of Sun Cottage, Brassknocker Hill, spoke out about the beast. In the *Bath Evening Chronicle* he was quoted as saying:

> 'It's all monkey business in my opinion. In my opinion it's a monkey. Chimps are fruit-eating animals, and the animal that I believe has been living in the wood for the past year ignores my fruit trees. It's an animal with two front teeth which enable it to tear off the bark of trees. Then it sucks out the pith, which is like a sweet syrup, from underneath the bark. I reckon it was a pet that escaped when its owner probably stopped his car beside the wood, and opened the windows.'

Mr Harper thought that the owner did not report that the chimp was missing as he might have brought the animal into the country illegally.

Mr Harper's 10-year-old cat has been frightened out of his life from time to time by the mystery beast. 18th October 1980 saw the first theory to dispel the existence of the mystery beast, for Mr Harry Gray of Grove Street, Bath claimed:

> *'It is about time this myth was quashed. I drive through the district two or three times a day and I have never seen anything resembling a monkey, but I have seen a limping stag three times in the last fortnight. Yesterday I tried to go to its aid when it went down into the trees below Monkton Grove Hotel, but it had gone by the time I could reach it.'*

Mr Gray felt that the stag was responsible for stripping the bark, but he could not explain the monkey sightings.

It was in December 1980 that the `Beast of Brassknocker` became a little more cat-like, which spurred on my own interest in the creature. Firstly, Mr Huntley of Warminster Road observed three mysterious beasts in 1977, and he described them as being a dirty yellow colour, with a stomach and hindquarters that were large. The creatures often sat up straight, and when they did they were a pear-shape (i.e. thick at the bottom and narrow at the top). He saw the creatures at Dundas Aqueduct, Monkton Combe, while he and his wife were picking blackberries in the summer of 1977.

Mr Huntley also believed that there was a third, smaller creature, possibly the young of the other creatures. He described it as *'a dirty yellow, with a faint black marking.'* A few days after his sighting, Mr Huntley found a dead, much smaller creature, 100 yards from his earlier sighting. Countrymen gave their view that the picture was of a stoat *(Mustela erminea)* or a ferret *(M. putorius furo),* yet Mr Huntley felt he had seen a type of 'wildcat or polecat' (polecats are the wild ancestors of ferrets and are only found in Wales and Scotland, although CFZ research has suggested that there are relict populations in parts of England). Nobody could identify the creatures he observed. However, the night following his sighting of the three creatures, he took a photograph of one of them at a distance of 40 yards. The creature involved could not definitely be made out, but it was of a fair size. Mr Jim Mead had a sighting, in 1980, of a similar creature. Mr Mead worked at the Gas Works and was living at Turnleigh. His sighting prompted Mr Huntley to come forward. It is interesting that the picture of the dead animal does show similarities to a ferret. Mr Mead also said that he had seen a stag in the area of Claverton Hill, but Mr Huntley stated that it was first seen three years earlier (i.e. in 1978) at Comwell, and had been around ever since. What this had to do with the `Beast of Brassknocker`, I do not know.

7th November 1981 was the date of the fourth actual monkey sighting, when 16-year-old Miss Sally Carr was riding her moped up Brassknocker Hill. Miss Carr, of Combe Down, who was studying at a Bristol Nursing College, told the *Bath and West Evening Chronicle*:

> *"My lights were down low. Then I saw something in the bushes and turned them up. The lights caught the eyes. I saw some thin 4 feet high with a dark kind of tan colour. It darted quickly into the bushes. It was kind of hairy and had small eyes.*
>
> *I was frightened and wanted to get home as quickly as possible. It was like a human being, but it wasn't... "*

BIG CATS: LOOSE IN BRITAIN

This report was by Mr Gerald Goodman. Earlier reports had been written by Mr Michael Dolan and Mr Robert Foulkes, both of the *Bath Evening Chronicle*.

On 19th August 1982 there was a sighting by Mr Bruce Parfitt, who was a colleague of Mr Jim Mead at S. W. Gas, Bath. Mr Parfitt, 24, was hunting rabbits with a shot-gun and a powerful lamp in the Claverton area. It was at about 11.30 p.m. that he spotted the creature in a field, near some apple orchards. The creature was described as being cream in colour, with brown markings, with peering eyes and a shaggy coat. It was said to be about 30 inches long and had four-inch high legs. Mr Parfitt said:

> *"I picked it up for five seconds in the beam of my lamp. As it rushed out across me - less than 20 yards away - I was startled and said 'Hell!' We would like to catch it. It would be quite a thing if the Shockerwick Shocker turned out to be the Beast of Brassknocker Hill, wouldn't it?"*

Mr Parfitt returned to the area with a camera and a friend. Mr Parfitt reckoned that the creature might have been a polecat. The rough sketch he drew for the *Bath Evening* a short, four-legged creature not unlike a badger or otter in shape. Mr Mead thought Mr Parfitt had seen a polecat, or a wildcat.

Only a year later, on 6th June 1983, the *Bath and West Evening Chronicle* carried this article on the 'Beast of Brassknocker':

> *'Llama Alert:*
>
> *Is there a llama on the loose near Bath? One was spotted at the top of Brassknocker Hill this morning by Mr Alan Sandall, editor of Wessex Newspapers' Avon and North Somerset series, near where the famous 'Beast of Srassknocker' was seen a few years ago.'*

The next day, a photograph of the llama was produced. The article in the *Bath and West Evening Chronicle* said that the llama had lived for years near Claverton Down, in a field and had broken loose onto Brassknocker Hill. Twenty cars queued up on the hillside, to get a view of the llama. Some of the drivers approached the creature, which belonged to a local resident and had for years lived near Brassknocker. At any rate, the article finished up by saying that the question now was:

> *'Could the `Beast of Brassknocker` be this llama?'*

The *Bath Evening Chronicle* then printed my letter appealing for information about mystery cats. What was intriguing me at the time was how could the beast be a llama, a monkey, a baboon, a chimpanzee, a Japanese deer, a big cat, a bear, an aye-aye, a golden eagle, a stag, a panther, a puma, a wildcat and a polecat?

Moving back to the Mendips, I found out that the local writer Mr Ralph Whitlock wrote in his 1975 book, *'Somerset'*:

> *'Banwell cave, near the western end of the Mendips, contains a curious wall of bones.*

It was built with meticulous care by a pioneer excavator, William Beard, early in the nineteenth century. The bones are those of mammoths, cave bears, cave lions, woolly rhinoceroses, hyenas, wolves, bisons and reindeers, which he found in huge quantities in the floor debris of the cave. A similar collection of prehistoric animal bones was discovered in a cave near Wookey, now known as the 'Hyena's Den'. Here too were found traces of fibres made by prehistoric men, as well as bone and flint implements. This was one of the first sites in Britain to yield proof that men were contemporary with such animals as the cave bear and woolly rhinoceros.'

Is the "Beast of Brassknocker" and other such beasts around the westcountry possibly some left-overs from this period of the Stone Age? Could the cat I saw on the Mendips be the British indigenous lynx? We shall just have to wait and see.

In his book *'Ghosts of Somerset'*, Guy Underwood noted that there was a phantom cat at the King John Hotel at Axbridge, and that it was seen only in the evening hours. The cat has appeared to archaeologists who were visiting the museum in the hunting lodge. Six people have seen the ghostly tabby-cat as it disappears into the doorway of the panelled room at the top of the stairs. It has also been seen by various members of the Museum Society, and Mrs. Frances Neale, of the Museum Management Committee, had some belief in this phantom cat. A thorough search always proves that there is no cat. An Elizabethan lady also haunts the hotel or hunting lodge. Axbridge is a beautiful town, at the foot of the Mendips in Somerset.

I was now receiving many replies from people who had been involved in the saga of the Brassknocker Hill beast. Mr A.G. Harper, the first person to start the 'Beast of Brassknocker' legend, said in a letter dated 5th November 1987:

> *'I would like to help you all I can, but my composition would not be a match to a budding author as yourself. Perhaps it would be better if you would call at Sun Cottage where I have a scrap book of newspaper cuttings and radio tapes. Give me a call when you wish to see me. Sun Cottage is near the top of Brassknocker Hill.'*

I decided to visit Mr Harper and obtain some more information, but must first quote the other letters I received. Mr S. Huntley of Monkton Combe, near Bath, wrote on the 5th November 1987:

> *'I'm afraid I cannot add much to the Bath Evening Chronicle articles, except to say that two of the animals were very large and of a dirty yellow colour, and the third one was slightly smaller and of the same colour, but with greyish patches, probably a young one. They were too large to be ferrets etc. My wife and I were about fifteen feet away from them. We watched for about five minutes, then we moved on without disturbing them.*
>
> *There have been no further sightings of them and the land has now been developed. I have never seen a polecat, so I can't compare them to the animals we saw.'*

This was a sighting that occurred in 1977, and is covered in my earlier review of the *Bath Evening Chroni-*

cles.

The third letter was from Mrs. Shelley of Turnleigh, Near Bradford-on-Avon. She wrote to tell me that Mr Jim Mead, one of the witnesses to whom I had written, had recently died. She had been his next-door neighbour. The next letter, dated 12th November 1987, was from Mr J.S. Hobhouse, Chairman of Bath R.S. P.C.A. All he could say was:

> *'I am sorry but we cannot give you any useful information. The 'Beast of Brassknocker' turned out to be a myth.'*

However, I now have details of one monkey on the edge of Salisbury Plain. To quote from the *Fortean Times* (No. 43), under the heading 'Monkey Business':

> *'On 1st August a male rhesus monkey was first spotted on the outskirts of Frome, Somerset, bounding across a road. The next day the 18-inch-high monkey was seen at Westerbury in Wiltshire, just north of Warminster. Attempts to catch it proved futile, and on the 3rd it was hit by a car at the ominous Black Dog crossroads near Devizes. It was so badly hurt that it had to be put down. The police of the two counties were unable to trace an owner, and the keepers at Longleat safari park said it wasn't one of theirs.'*

This is very near the sightings of the Salisbury Plain Panther. I remembered that about five years previously I went with a friend to see some monkeys that were kept privately on the outskirts of Warminster. There were three of these monkeys - two females and a male, if I remember rightly. They lived in a cage at the bottom of somebody's garden. One was particularly vicious and we were warned not to go too close, as they might bite.

They were dark brown, about one to two feet tall, with sharp teeth. They were not baboons or chimpanzees, but they were quite large.

I heard from the North Devon naturalist, Mr Trevor Beer, that a security guard at the ICI plant near Avonmouth, Bristol had seen a puma. He was told by the guard that the puma was living in an 8 by 2 miles area of scrubland there. The guard had Mr Beer talking on the radio, and he was certain that the mystery beast was definitely a puma.

Then I heard of another sighting, this time of a chimpanzee. P.C. Downes observed one of the 'Brassknocker Beasts' at Bath University in about 1980. He wrote to me in November 1987: 'My recollection of it is a little vague. From what I remember I was on night duty when I was directed to the Bath University area, where a taxi-driver reported seeing the animal sitting in the middle of the road. On my arrival I glimpsed what I thought was a chimp quickly disappear into the trees, making a loud screeching noise. A search of the area proved negative and in fact was never really confirmed.

It would seem that from 1979 to 1986 a largish monkey or ape was loose near Bath. Were there several of them - the baboons that escaped from Longleat in 1977? Or were they possibly the (rhesus?) monkeys from the cage near Warminster? I think I saw these monkeys in about 1979 or 1980, and as I understand it they had belonged to the previous owners of the house, who are no longer there, so could the animals have been let loose? Maybe there is now a breeding colony of these monkeys in the Bath/Salisbury Plain area.

One man who allegedly actually saw the `Beast of Brassknocker` wrote to me, but stated he had only heard of it. He was Mr Reg. P. Piper, who works at Bath University and lives at Larkhill in Bath. He wrote on the 2nd December 1987:

> *'I am afraid I have no knowledge of any wild animals, cats or otherwise, only on hear-say of unconfirmed sightings. I have not heard of any report about a puma at Avon-mouth.'*

However, I am sure that we now have a puma, a black big cat, a lynx-like cat and several monkeys loose in the general area of North Somerset, Wiltshire and Avon. I also read in the *Daily Telegraph* of 22nd November 1987 of an unusual theft. The brief article said:

> *'Lion lifted. Thieves have stolen a hundred-year-old stuffed African lion from a furniture shop in Ludgershall village, Wiltshire. "It probably took four men to carry him," said a police spokesman.'*

There have been no reports of any lion scares, yet. Maybe someone will photograph the lion and exhibit their belief that a lion is on the rampage!

I heard in 1986 that a green monkey was seen swinging through the trees near Chippenham, Wiltshire. The presence of the monkey was a puzzle and was seen near a motorway. The *Daily Telegraph* of August that year recorded this. In 1987 I was informed by a local resident that the monkey belonged to somebody 'up the road', and that it was recovered near Ford village. There was great excitement at something like this happening in the quiet rural village of Ford, near Chippenham.

The *Daily Mirror* of 1st November 1986 published this article:

> *'Swinging times: 'Zacherie', an African green monkey who escaped from his owner four months ago, has been spotted chasing deer in Dyrham Park, near Bath, Wilts."*

The monkey absconded in July 1986, and must have been the same one that was seen near the motorway, or main road, in August 1986.

There are other tales to consider about animals loose in Wiltshire, as we shall soon see. The Wiltshire Trust for Nature Conservation, based at Devizes, has not heard any accounts. Mrs. Sale, their administrative officer, told me on 14th January 1988:

> *'I am afraid we are not able to supply you with any information on this type of subject. We have not had any reports of such animals within Wiltshire. When you publish your book, perhaps you would like us to review and/or publish it for you?'*

This was most helpful, but still did not give me the information that I needed. Strangely enough, I had a letter from Mr Charles Nodder, the public relations officer at the same Conservancy Trust in Fordingbridge, Hampshire, around this time. He gave me some unusual information that may apply here. It was written on 4th January 1988:

> 'Whilst in certain circumstances the wildcat can be a severe predator on game-birds, I am not aware of any problems experienced by gamekeepers in the past as a result of escaped big cats. 'I was interested to note that you have some details of pheasants being taken by big cats. If you ever produce anything in print on this I would be interested in a copy.'

This statement makes it clear that although gamekeepers *do* link kills with big cats, they do not publicly talk about their views on these cats. The animal I saw on the Mendips may have been a Scottish wildcat. Although unusual enough, which part of the country had the lynx/wildcat come from, I wonder? Have wildcats stayed on the Mendips since prehistoric or Ice Age times? The *Fortean Times* (No.19), of December 1976, notes the case of a 35 lbs. porcupine in woods on Salisbury Plain. The porcupine was sighted and identified as a North American porcupine.

According to the Scunthorpe *Evening Telegraph* of 21st April 1975, some experts were trying to track it down. Maybe the porcupine was an escapee from Longleat Safari Park or from a private menagerie.

The 'Beast of Brassknocker' was reviewed by the *Fortean Times* (No.30) when they quoted Mr Harper's account of the beast stripping his oak tree. He said:

> 'It must be some kind of creature which can cling upside down and lean over. I suppose it could be a bat, but it would need to be a terrific one to strip bark like that. I think it's some sort of monkey.'

He also said that it has got to be a rodent, because a Bath parks official made a joke about his having a "squirrel ten times larger than normal". The *Sunday Express* of 29th July 1979 carried these extra details; the *Fortean Times* also notes four or five other incidents involving the beasts:

1) 'In February 1977, three baboons escaped from Longleat Wildlife Park, not ten miles south of Claverton Down, and as far as we know were never caught.' *Daily Mirror*, 1st March 1977. This theory has already been dealt with and is worth bearing in mind. Do baboons eat tree bark?

2) Mr Albert Miner of Claverton was sitting in his garden when he saw ua strange animal come through the gap in my garden wall. I followed it to the garden gate but did not get a look at its face. It crossed the road and went into the wood apposite." The sighting was at dusk. The animal was 2 feet high, with a grey, bushy coat and upright, being twice the size of a cat. This sighting was mentioned in the *Guardian* of 23rd August 1979.

3) On 9th August 1979, according to the *Guardian*, three men had almost caught the beast. Mr

Alan Heaslop, the team leader of Combedown, near Bath, said they had been in the wood for a number of hours, when they spotted *"this black creature swing from tree to tree above our heads"*. It dropped to the woodland floor 20 feet away and peered at them, in a curious or tame manner. The men surrounded it and dived. Mr Heaslop said:

"I caught it by the leg and it let out a high-pitched scream and jerked free." The fully-grown chimpanzee was *"about 3 feet tall, with a flat face and patches of grey and white on its chest."*

This incident, and Mr Miner's sighting, were not reported in the local newspaper, the *Bath Evening Chronicle* for some reason. This sighting was again in poor light.

4) The *Guardian* later gave the sighting of Christopher Morris, who was returning from a fishing trip with a friend, and he saw a strange beast in Monkton Combe. The sighting was in August 1979. We told the *Guardian* of 23rd August:

"We were driving through Monkton Combe at about 12.30 a.m., and it stood in the middle of the road, right in our headlights. It was 3-4 feet high and scrambled through a hedge. To me it looked like a baboon. My friend thought it looked like a chimpanzee. It had bright white rings around the eyes, rather like speacles. We had not been drinking."

5) Mrs. A. Lawless of Bath wrote to the *Guardian* and had her letter published on 25th August 1979. She had apparently thought of an answer to the beast's identity. She believed that a bespectacled bear had escaped from a local zoo. All the local zoos assured her, as did the police, that no such beast had escaped.

I am sure that the Brassknocker beast existed, but I think it must be dead by now. The three wildlife parks nearby are Cricket St Thomas, Longleat and Bristol zoo. None of them have lost anything other than those three baboons. However, we must not forget the monkey that was run over at Black Dog crossroads, Littleton Parnell, near Devizes, or the escaped African monkey that was caught near Ford, Chippenham.

Now we will look at a black dog legend.

In her 1986 book 'Our Neighbourly Ghosts (ex Libris Press, Bristol) Mrs. Doreen Evelyn wrote a story, based on truth, called 'A Dog's Chance'. The story was about two women who went for a walk near Witham, Upton Noble, on the Mendip Hills of Somerset and Avon.

The two ladies were chased by some cattle across the fields, and then they saw a dog. It appeared from a wood, jumped over some broken-up stones and disappeared The ladies thought must have jumped back over the wall, although they could not see him. One of the ladies realised that she had left her stick back by the gate. They return, and again saw the dog. The writer describes him:

'As we approached the wood we saw the dog again. He was trotting back alongside the wall where we had first seen him. I looked at him more carefully this time. He was quite a tall dog, thin, black-and-white short-haired coat, a bit like a pointer but with

floppier ears, distinctly of mixed lineage.

He turned his head towards us. Odd, I thought. His eyes have no life, they are just like two dull black holes. The next minute he was gone, exactly at the spot where he disappeared before.'

Later, she meets an old man, who tells her that, forty years before, he buried such a dog up there, after sadly shooting it. A fierce black dog now haunts the woods near Frome.

- ## The Chiddock Lioness

I interviewed a friend of the family, P. C. Russel, about the Chiddock Lioness. Chiddock is a large village in Dorset.

In the 1920s or 1930s a lioness escaped from a runaway caravan on Chiddock Hill. The travelling menagerie tried without success to recapture the lioness. She was eventually shot dead by an angry farmer, who discovered the lioness on his land. He must have been very lucky, for one supposes he used a 12-bore shotgun, which is hardly the weapon to shoot a lioness. Russel told me had heard the story from the farmer's son, when he was village policeman in Chiddock. He has now retired from the force and runs a farm.

The Bournemouth beast is another animal, which has been seen only once. On 7th April 1974, Mrs. Joan Gilbert of Bournemouth was driving along Western Avenue, Branksome, on the outskirts of the town. The time was 3.30 a.m. As Mrs. Gilbert turned the corner from Bury Road, she watched a 'strange striped creature, half cat and half dog' crossing the road. She was surprised and on arriving home she looked in a wildlife book, only to find that the animal was like a rare Tasmanian wolf. She contacted the local paper, the *Bournemouth Evening Echo*, who published an article on the sighting, later that day. Mrs. Gilbert was quoted as describing the animal like this:

'It was the most peculiar animal I have ever seen. I had stripes, a long thin tail, and seemed to be all grey, though it might have had some yellow on it. Its ears were set back like a member of the cat family, and it was as big as a medium-sized dog. It was thin, and it definitely was not a fox.' To my knowledge, the Tasmanian wolf is very rare, and it would be highly unlikely that a rare animal such as that would be in this country. Mrs. Gilbert could have seen a mongrel dog, a greyhound or an unusual British big cat. Di Francis thought that a striped big cat was one type of feline that was found in Britain. Reports of striped tiger-cats have come in mainly from Inverness-shire, but there are others from other places.

Mrs Gilbert's sighting was noted in *Living Wonders*, the *Fortean Times*, the Bords' *Alien Animals*, as well as *Cat Country*. Bournemouth is a relatively suburban area, so it would not be a likely place for a big cat to survive.

Notes on Chapter 5: 'Other South-Western Cats'

1) The 'Folklore of Warminster' by Victor Stode Manley. On page 6 there is an interesting story that will serve as a footnote to this chapter. The book was first published in 1924, and was republished in 1984 by High Street Publishers and Newsagents, Coates and Parker of Warminster. The passage reads:

> 'Black Dog: Black Dog is the name of the dangerous hill on the Bath road haunted by this animal with large fiery eyes (see Somerset Year-Book 1922). Sometimes it is left behind by the wild hunt (see under 'Horses', below). To have a black dog on one's back is a local idiom for a bad temper.'

The 'Wild Hunt' section of the 'Folklore of Warminster' reads:

'Horses: A place called the Vicar's Walk at Norton is haunted by a headless, galloping horse at night. The church lane at Crockerton has a similar spectral horse, and Longbridge has three, besides the wild hunt at Gun's church, a barrow on the hill. Even after the introduction of Christianity the ignorant northern folk still dreaded the on-coming storm, declaring that it was the wild hunt sweeping across the sky

2) On page 186 of *The Secret Country* by Janet and Colin Bord (Paladin, London, 1976) there are a few brief references to Wiltshire black dogs. This book connects such hauntings with ancient sites, like dolmens and barrows. West Kennet long barrow near Avebury, Marlborough, Wiltshire, is haunted by a red-eared or red-eyed hound, which is huge and white. It only appears with a Celtic priest or druid on the longest day's dawn. There is also a ghostly guardian dog at Doghill Barrow, Knighton Down, Wiltshire, and a white hound at the Devil's Deiolmen, Fyfield, Wiltshire. The 'eyes of burning coals' are a feature of this dog.

3) *A Shepherd's Life* by W.H. Hudson is a classic book, first published in 1910. This book has a chapter entitled 'Concerning Cats' which has various anecdotes about cats and is well worth reading. There is one tale of cats being transfixed by the shiny metal of railway lines.

For this reason cats were constantly being run over. There is no reference to Scottish wildcats on Salisbury Plain. However, some of the cats described are very large.

4) On 13th February 1988 I talked to a Maiden Bradley man who was once a poacher. He said it was a challenge not to be caught, and he did not like killing animals. He knew that one of the Duke of Somerset's gamekeepers had shot dead a (Scottish) wildcat in the 1930s, in woods near Frome, on the Wiltshire/Somerset border. It was thought to be a 'great thing', as it was the last wildcat in Wiltshire. These animals officially died out here in the 1850s. I believe that the skin was not preserved. The former poacher is a countryman born and bred, and he learnt of the tale from an old man of 80 odd, who still lives in the village. Was the Mendips Bob-cat a wildcat?

5) *An Introduction to the Archaeology of Wiltshire*, from the earliest times to the pagan Saxons, with chapters on Stonehenge, Woodhenge, Avebury, Silbury Hill, Barrows, Earthworks etc.', by M.S. Cunnington and Mrs. B.H. Cunnington (published by George Simpson and Co., Devizes, 1933) has a sec-

tion on 'The Life of an early Iron Age village'. On page 26 we read:

> 'The villages were generally, perhaps always, enclosed within walls or barriers of some kind, as shown by the banks and ditches often found surrounding them. There is reason to believe that the banks carried stockades, and where earthworks are absent, as at All Cannings Cross, it is probable that stockading only was used. The entrances were barricaded, and sometimes at least it was thought worth while to make a sunken pathway by which it was possible to leave or enter the enclosure screened from observation (easterly). The walls and fences were perhaps necessary chiefly to keep out marauding animals (a necklace of teeth of wolves was found in a barrow on Salisbury Plain); but although the defences were not calculated to stand a siege, they were no doubt useful on occasions to withstand raids from unfriendly or 'cattle-lifting' neighbours and generally to deter unwelcome visitors.'

This quotation shows that early men obviously had a fear of large predators. Were some of these predators still around in the Iron Age? I remember seeing, a few years ago, the site of an 'Iron Age' settlement, which was created for a BBC 2 documentary series. A bank and a ditch surrounded the settlement. The bank was topped by a wattle hurdle fence. The 'residents' lived in the camp for a year, being filmed. They had Jacob sheep and other old-fashioned farm animals. The site was burned down, after the filming, which took place in the late 1970s. The site can still be found in a remote part of Cranbourne Chase, on the Wilts/Dorset border. It seems that there were plenty of wolves in Wiltshire during the Iron Age.

These villages obviously kept dogs, but there is never any mention of cats. The first British domestic cats are thought to have been brought to south-east England in the Roman occupation. One believes that they were pampered pets which lived around the Roman Villas. There are numerous bones in museums which have been identified as Roman-age domestic cats.

Before going any further, perhaps we should note that wildcats were still living all over Britain in Roman, Saxon and Norman times. They are unlikely to have caused any great amount of trouble, but was there on the scene a larger predator, other than the wolf? I understand that unknown species of leopard bones have been found in widely separated caves, both on the Mendips and in Norfolk. Are these the bones of the British big cat?

It is interesting to know that there are numbers of Viking brooches, sword hilts and carvings which portray lions and big cats. The Vikings imported many things from Rome, and I believe that the native craftsmen of Scandinavia must have copied Roman ideas. We should remember that the Devon black-dog may have Norse or Viking origins, in the name 'Hound of Odin'.

• 'The Beast of Brassknocker' - Further investigations.

On 7th June 1988, Swindon G.W.R. (Radio station) announced that there had been a sighting of a large cat at Coombe Grove Manor Hotel, Monkton Coombe, Bath. The announcement was made at 8 a.m., on the 'News'. I heard it while on a bus, the *Daily Telegraph* of that day had an article on the subject called 'Beast of Bath strikes again', by reporter Mr Paul Stokes.

It seems that on 6th June at about 6 a.m. a large cat-like creature was seen prowling around the above named hotel. Mr Needham, the night-porter, was making his rounds when he observed a 'panther-like creature' at a short distance. He told Mr Stokes:

> *'It was the biggest cat I have ever seen, and was covered in shiny black hair. It chased*
> *a rabbit, caught it and literally ate it as I watched.'*

The police were called to the scene. WPC Maria Hooper and Mr Needham approached the animal, which ran off at speed. Mr Needham was not the only witness with WPC Hooper, for he stated:

> *'A taxi-driver drew up, carrying one member of staff at about 6 a.m., but when he*
> *saw this creature he locked the doors of the cab and stayed inside.'*

Miss Jennie Mailer, the hotel receptionist, had noticed a 'very large cat' prowling the grounds in the past few months. She said:

> *'I have seen it in the distance a couple of times. The strange thing is that it only*
> *ever seems to come out at early in the morning and late at night.'*

The Bath constabulary were rather curious in their statement to the press, as they would only say: *'One of our officers attended and said she saw a small wildcat the size of a rabbit.'* Rabbits are smaller than domestic cats, and I gained the impression that the last statement could have been a printer's error. I also thought there could have been two cats involved: an adult nocturnal black panther-type cat, and its small black cub, which might be little larger than a rabbit. Apparently the paper said that the local people all knew about the beast, as since 1979 there had been sightings of bears, baboons, monkeys and wallabies. It was since 1983 that people had begun to think of the beast as a large feline responsible for ripping apart local cats and dogs. People had even set traps in a vain effort to catch it.

I decided that it was time to carry out an investigation, believing that this cat could have been the same creature which I saw on the Mendips, and the 'puma' which had turned up at Avonmouth. There had also been sightings at Nether Stowey, a village on the Quantocks, of a 'puma', which had killed various sheep or lambs. A report appeared in the *Western Daily Press* of February or March 1988, on that cat-like beast, so on 18th June I went to the Monkton Coombe area of Bath.

I had had an interview on 'BBC Radio Bristol' the previous month, which was broadcast on 10th April. The interview was with reporter Mr Roger Bennett, in the early morning programme he runs, from 7 to 9 a.m. I thought that this would help witnesses to come forward, as I mentioned the 'Beast of Brassknocker' and the 'Avonmouth puma'.

I spoke to Mr Harper on 19th June - we made an appointment earlier. I photographed the tree from which the monkey had eaten the bark six years previously. The creature, which had a long tail, sharp teeth and was dark brown, arrived at Mr Harper's home in the early spring of 1979, and left it in the winter of 1981/82. It could possibly have died from the cold. It was only 18 inches high, and was not a chimpanzee or a baboon, as was suggested by some. Mr Harper observed it only once on his garden wall. It frightened his old goat into charging across the garden one day. Mr Harper has seen wild monkeys and cats in India, during World War II. In June 1988 Mr and Mrs. Harper watched a young deer move down one side of the garden. Suddenly a large black cat leapt out of the bushes. It missed the deer, but Mr Harper could see that it was the size of a medium-sized dog, possibly a young panther. The animal had only been in the area about a fortnight. The porter and police at the Monkton Coombe Grove Hotel, just down the road, also chased it.

There was a sighting of a lioness at Cuffley in Hertfordshire in 1983.. According to the London *Evening Standard* of 16th May, the lioness was seen roaming through gardens in Cuffley. The first witness, a Mr David Messling, told the "*Standard*" reporter:

> *'I looked out of the window and there was a lioness in the back garden. First I thought, "I can't believe this." And then I thought, "No one else is going to believe this." It was definitely a lioness as it had no mane.'*

The police were confident enough that there really was a lioness loose. They even bought in a police helicopter, in an attempt to track the beast. A police spokesman gave the following information:

"We have not found the lion yet, but we have had several sightings from people in the road. One of the sightings is by a policeman." It would seem that he was called to the scene of the sightings and saw the animal at quite close quarters. Mrs. Vera Duncombe, a resident in Sutherland Way, told the press that the gardens of each house backed on to woodland, so an animal could easily be hiding in those woods. She was very worried by the thought of an escaped lioness. The expert from nearby Broxbourne Zoo, Mrs. Vickers, pronounced some paw-prints as belonging to a large dog, puma or lioness. It is interesting to note that mystery cats have often appeared over the border, in Wales.

These three images were taken on Exmoor on August Bank Holiday 1988 by Devon naturalist Trevor Beer. They are used with his kind permission and enhanced by Mark North.

Dunkery Beacon on Exmoor - a good place for mystery cat sightings in 1988.

Footprint taken at Munstead Stables, Surrey in September 1964, during the `Surrey Puma` flap, compared with puma cast (right)

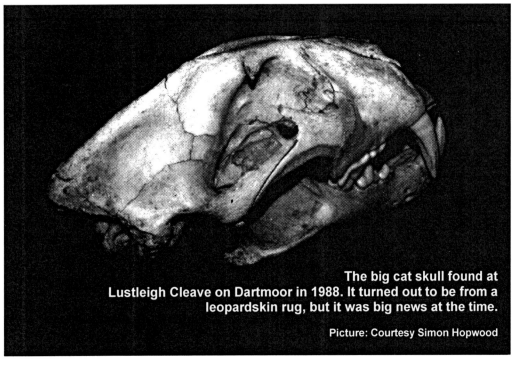

The big cat skull found at Lustleigh Cleave on Dartmoor in 1988. It turned out to be from a leopardskin rug, but it was big news at the time.

Picture: Courtesy Simon Hopwood

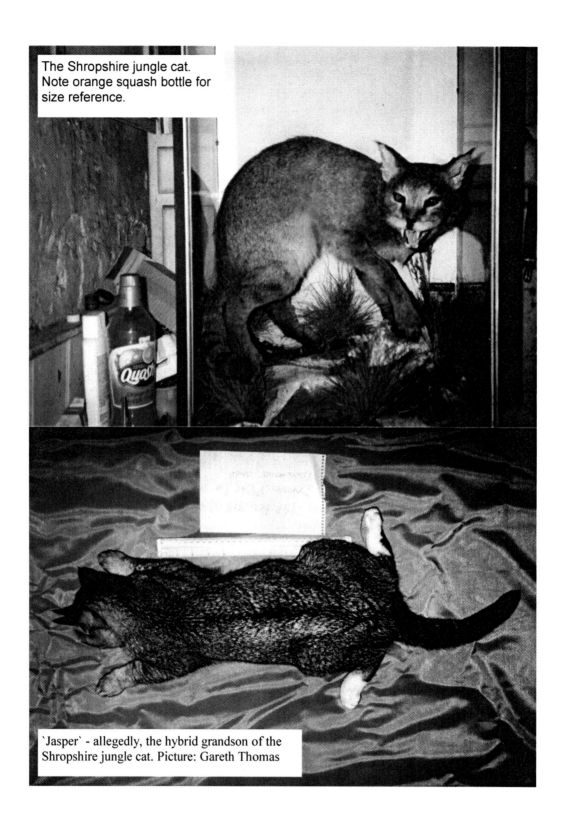

The Shropshire jungle cat. Note orange squash bottle for size reference.

`Jasper` - allegedly, the hybrid grandson of the Shropshire jungle cat. Picture: Gareth Thomas

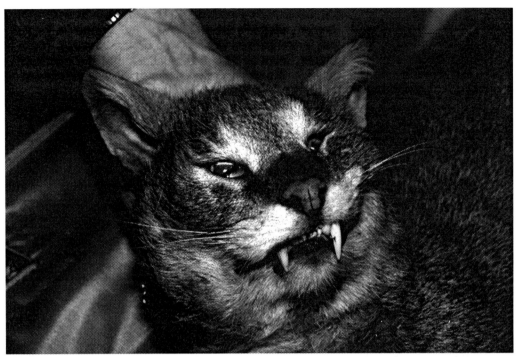

The Shropshire jungle cat, found as a road-kill in 1989. Now in the possession of Dr. Karl Shuker, these pictures, (which are copyright Gareth Thomas, and included with his kind permission), show the creature before it was mounted, and appear here for the first time.

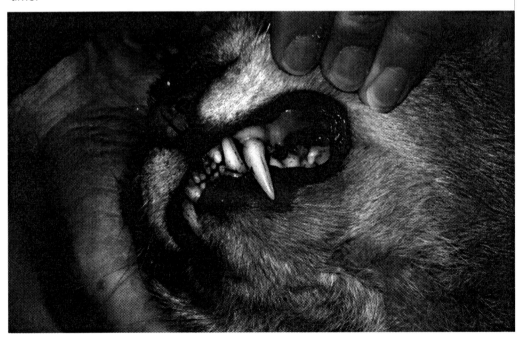

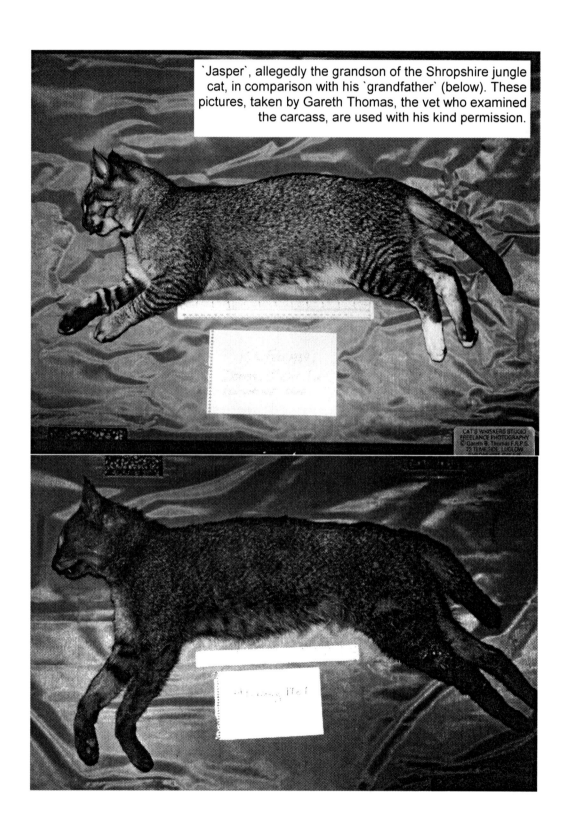

`Jasper`, allegedly the grandson of the Shropshire jungle cat, in comparison with his `grandfather` (below). These pictures, taken by Gareth Thomas, the vet who examined the carcass, are used with his kind permission.

`The Beast of Exmoor` (1988): These two images by Nigel Brierly (used with his kind permission) show a pawprint from Exmoor, and an alleged victim of the creature: a dead, and half-eaten, Halflinger foal, from Broomhill near Barnstaple.

The author's 14th birthday `party` at Tarr Steps on Exmoor in 1987. The author (left) stands next to his mother, and the family of naturalist Trevor Beer. They celebrated a long day's cat hunt with chocolate cake!

A big cat footprint from the River Findhorn near Fores in Scotland, photographed by Alan Lawrence in 1988, and used with his permission. Bizarrely, the print has five toes, which has led some people to say that it was made by an otter. However, it has the characteristic rounded lobes of a big cat.

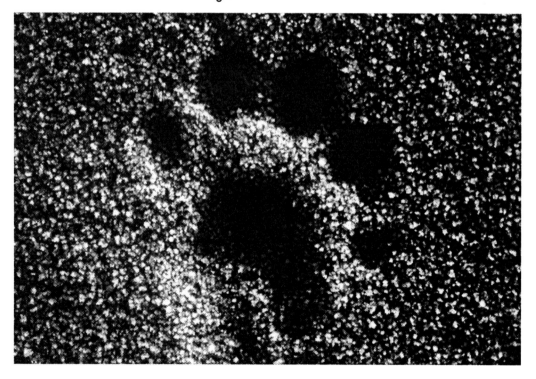

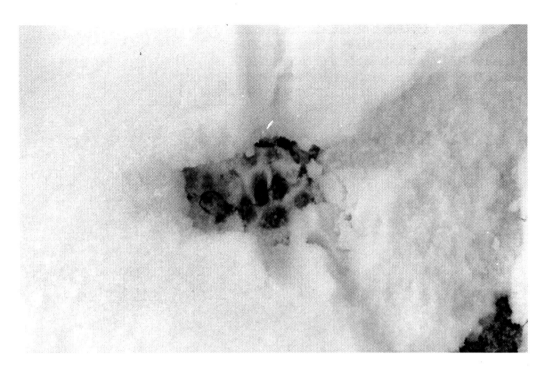

Two images of what appear to be big cat footprints from The Forest of Dean, photographed by Danny Nineham in 1990, and used with his permission.

Another striking snowbound image from The Forest of Dean in 1990. Again, courtesy Danny Nineham.

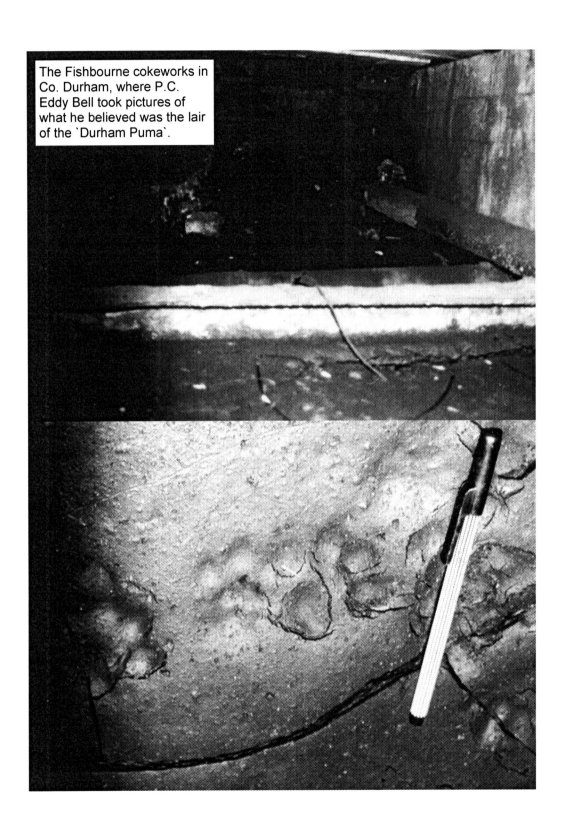

The Fishbourne cokeworks in Co. Durham, where P.C. Eddy Bell took pictures of what he believed was the lair of the `Durham Puma`.

Bengal leopard cat shot by Mr Willie Thomas, gamekeeper on the Minto Estate, near Jedburgh in the Scottish Borders in 1988, and used with his permission. It killed seven out of a hundred pheasants in their pen. The cat originally came from Edinburgh Zoo, and was sold to a Curnbrian lady, from whom it was stolen by burglars.

The ultimate proof that big cats have lived wild in the UK. `Felicity`: the puma caught alive by farmer Ted Noble near Cannich in Scotland during 1980.

`The Beast of Brassknocker Hill`: The tree in Ron Harper's garden, with bark stripped by the beast. All these pictures used with his kind permission.

Brassknocker Hill near Bath.

`The Beast of Brassknocker Hill`:

(Top) Ron Harper in his garden, near the tree with bark stripped by the beast. All these pictures used with his kind permission.

(Bottom) Another view of his garden.

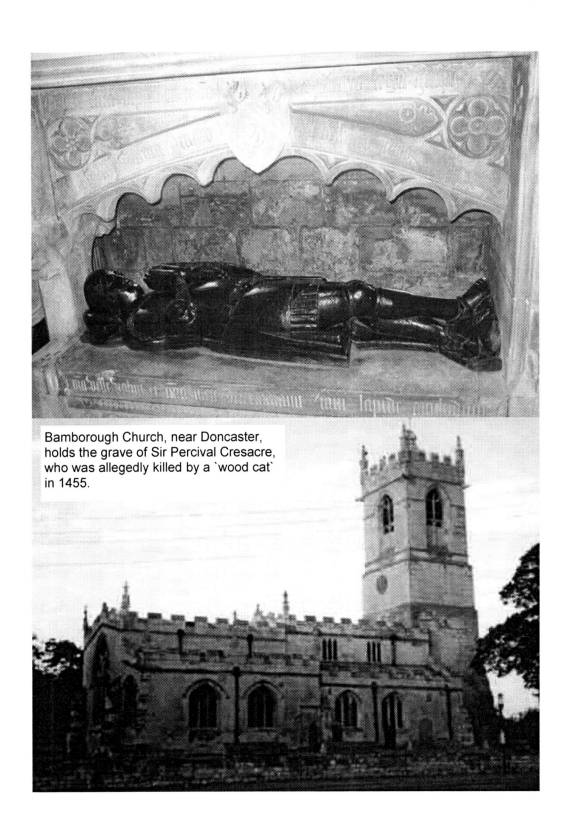

Bamborough Church, near Doncaster,
holds the grave of Sir Percival Cresacre,
who was allegedly killed by a `wood cat`
in 1455.

PART TWO

- Chapter Six -
THE SURREY PUMAS

The first account of a strange animal in Surrey comes from long before William Cobbett's sighting of a strange cat in 1770. It came to me in the form of a photocopied page from an un-named Surrey guidebook, from the Young People's Trust for Endangered Species. Mr Cyril Littlewood, the founder and director, told me on 23rd April 1987:

> *'I have been trying to find some information for you on big cats loose in Britain, but the only thing I have come up with is one tiny mention in a local history book of the 'Surrey Puma'. The legend of the puma roaming Surrey is quite popular, and even today many people believe there is a wildcat in the area. Perhaps your local library will have a book on myths and legends which will include details of wildcat reports, as I am afraid that our own library of books on wildlife does not give any information on mythical beasts.'*

Mr Littlewood, who was awarded the MBE for his conservation work, was most helpful, and I must thank him for assisting me. He also said:

'We do get the odd request from time to time about big cats roaming in Britain, and in future I will give these youngsters your address!' This was a useful contact, and a starting point for tackling the puma saga. The passage from the book ran as follows, mentioning other mystery animals:

> *'In Surrey the savage excesses of King John were said to be perpetuated by a werewolf for many years after his death. A curious reflection of this story is found in frequent modern reports of a puma seen roaming wild in the country, although official attempts to see and subsequently catch the animal always fail. Other strange southern creatures include the dragons of St Leonard's forest, near Horsham.*
>
> *These beasts, now often amusingly portrayed by local Morris dancers, had their heyday in the Dark Ages and were not supposed to reappear after a particularly fearsome example was slain by St Leonard himself in the sixth century. From the seventeenth to the nineteenth century, though, there were numerous reports of foulsmelling, monstrous creatures of dragon-like proportions.'*

I then purchased a copy of Janet and Colin Bord's 1976 book '*The Secret Country*', which proved to be the key unlocking many doors. They have a chapter on the dragon legends of Britain and it would seem that in August 1614, a pamphlet was produced all about the Monstrous Serpent that was killing cattle and even men. They also note many other dragon stories, and when alluding to the possibility that the dragon was a reptile that had escaped from a private menagerie, they make the following comment about the 'Surrey Puma':

'The most noted case in recent years is that of the `Surrey Puma`, though it has been seen in places far distant from Surrey, and even in two widely separated places at the same time! It is most unlikely that pumas are escaping from private zoos all over the South of England...'

This comment means that there must be more than one `Surrey Puma`, in my mind. The 'were-wolf' scare probably referred to a particularly savage wolf, as these lived in Surrey until about the sixteenth century, although by then they were rare. Surrey is very near to London and since Roman times there have been menageries in and around the city. big cats were kept at the Tower of London, and they were only moved out of there in the nineteenth century. The first actual sighting of the puma dates from approximately 1770 and may refer to a lynx. The witness was that essayist, politician and farmer, William Cobbett, who lived from 1763 to 1835. The scene was Waverly Abbey, in the heart of `Surrey Puma` country. I quote the whole reference from a Victorian edition of his 1830 book *'Rural Rides'*. When aged eight or so years he used to play in Waverly Abbey Grounds, as he was the son of a farmer. Cobbett was a countryman at heart, so he probably had a fair knowledge of wildlife. In 1825, while on a rural ride from Chillworth to Winchester, he showed his 11-year old son Richard around Waverly Abbey. The date was 27th October 1825, and Cobbett was recalling an event which took place between 1766 and 1770, some fifty or sixty years previously. The tree involved in the account was still hollow. Richard measured it as sixteen feet in girth.

William Cobbett wrote:

'I showed him an old elm tree which was hollow even then, into which I, when a very little boy, once saw a cat go, that was as big as a medium-sized spaniel dog, for relating which I got a great scolding, for standing to which I, at last, got a beating; but stand to which I still did. I have since many times repeated it, and would take my oath of it to this day.

'When in New Brunswick I saw the great wild grey cat, which is there called a lucifee; and it seemed to me to be just such a cat as I had seen at Waverly.'

The Victorian editor of *'Rural Rides'* assures us that Cobbett observed a native wildcat (*Felis sylvestris*). Chris Hall, a leading expert on the 'Surrey Puma', assures us in *The Unexplained*, (No.29) that Cobbett could have seen a wildcat, as they were resident there until about 1920. I have records of a possible wild-cat colony on the Isle of Wight during the 1940s. However it was in *Alien Animals* that Janet and Colin Bord suggested that Mr Cobbett saw a puma (which is native to New Brunswick). British big cat expert Di Francis gives her view that Cobbett observed a lynx, in 'cat country'

Latterly, I see that in the year 1966 Dr Maurice Burton, the distinguished naturalist gave his view that Cobbett saw a feral domestic cat. If Cobbett had seen a puma, surely he would have noticed its long tail. Pumas are larger than spaniels; or did he see a puma cub? We shall never know. I myself believe that Cobbett was not lying about his cat encounter, but that he saw a large, unusual cat. There were no definite sightings of a large cat in the 'Surrey Puma' country until about World War II. The first detailed account of a puma that I have managed to find dates from about 1955. Mrs. Christine Reynolds, now a naturalist in her own right, told me in 1987 how she used to ride her pony in woods on

Hurtwood Common during the 1950s. In 1955 there was a puma scare, and she was worried about riding her pony through these woods, in case the puma leapt out.

Graham J. McEwan, writing in his 1985 book *'Mystery Animals of Britain and Ireland'*, recounted:

> *'Earlier, in 1955, a woman walking her dog in Abinger Hammer in Surrey came across the half-eaten remains of a calf and saw an animal resembling a puma skulking away.'*

Mr McEwan also records that in 1959 Mr Kilham, an Aldershot taxi-driver, springing over a hedge at Teeziedown Racecourse, in what was to become puma country, saw a 'huge lion'. There was a puma around Winchester in the 1950s and 1960s. The *Unexplained* Magazine, No.29, records the sighting of Mr A. Burningham near Preston Candover, not far from Winchester. Mr Burningham, now in his 70s, was driving along a country lane at about 6 p.m. on a day in August 1959. From about 40 yards away, Mr Burningham saw a Labrador-sized cat.

Its feline head and walk confirmed that it was a large big cat of sorts. He also observed that in size it was halfway between a domestic cat and a dog. It had a very short neck and was a yellow colour, with a rough coat. It watched a number of lambs from the trees and then moved off. It was not until 1962 that Mr Burningham read of another puma report - Mr Ernest Jellet's sighting - and he realised that the cat was probably a young puma, as he had seen one in a zoo. There were several other sightings in the same area during the 1950s.

In 1960 there were alleged sightings west of Farnham, if we are to go by Mr Matthew Alexander's 1985 book *Tales of Old Surrey*, which has a three page chapter on the puma, based on what Dr Maurice Burton and folklorists told him about the beast. I have no records of any sightings other than this mention in the above book, which may refer to the next sightings for the period 1960-1961.

In 1962, the *Farnham Herald* carried the following short article in one of its July editions:

> *'A large sandy-coloured cat-like animal "resembling a small lion" charged a Crondal man in a wood at Ewshot. Moving at great speed, the animal was only a few feet away when the man shouted and screamed and it turned aside and vanished in the undergrowth. Mr Ernest Jellett of Green Springs said afterwards: "It gave me a real scare".'*

This sighting took place on Monday 16th July 1962 at 7.45 a.m. on the Heathy Park reservoir track, west of Farnham. The creature was sandy-coloured, long and thin-tailed, with a round, flattish face and what appeared to be large paws. The cat ran towards him, chasing a rabbit, and was startled by him shouting. Of course, the police searched the area and found no definite sign of the 'phantom feline' save a flattened patch of bracken. Mr Jellett was certain that the cat was not a fox. His sighting was reported in the Mid-Wessex Water Board Magazine of August 1962, and in the Farnham Herald of July 1962. This sighting was also noted by McEwan in *'Mystery Animals of Britain and Ireland'*, and in *'Alien Animals'* by Janet and Colin Bord, Chris Hall in his *'Stalking the Surrey Puma'* article of *The Unexplained* magazine, (No.29), and Di Francis in *'Cat Country: the Quest for the British big cat'*, so it has been well-published, one could really say!

There was something disturbing Mr Edward Blank's Aberdeen Angus cattle at Bushylease Farm, a few days later. In December 1962, the Water Board magazine carried another short mention of the creature, saying that the station superintendent for the southern area, Mr L. Noble, had seen the cat at Heathy Park. Suggestions were made that the beast was only a large feral domestic cat, and although this is unlikely it cannot be ruled out.

In 1962, a woman was walking near Crondall when she spotted a large cat-like beast. According to the *Sunday Times* or *Sunday Telegraph* of December 20th 1964 the lady saw what might have been a puma cub. Duff Hart Davis ended this Sunday paper article by suggesting:

> *'Finally, the crucial question: where did it come from? As anybody can buy a puma cub for about £125 from an animal dealer, it seems most likely that this one was reared as a domestic pet and escaped. This theory is supported by the fact that one of the early sightings, about 18 months ago, was of ua large wildcat with spots"; a puma cub is spotted until it is about four months old. A domestic infancy would also explain the puma's odd combination of cunning and naivete. Although it has eluded all pursuers, it has made some distinctly ill-judged appearances - for instance, in a council house garden in full daylight. In any case, whoever let it out is clearly not going to own up now. If the animal were to attack someone, the owner might be sued for heavy damages, so it is hardly surprising that he is lying as low as the puma itself.'*

This was the first time that the puma's origins were discussed. The woman observed the animal in a field and came to the conclusion, after consulting a wildlife book, that she had observed a Jaguarundi - an otter-like cat from South America, which is very shy indeed.

1963 brought more sightings and rumours. To start off with, I shall reproduce a lengthy passage from Mrs. Ginny Dowden's letter. She lives near Albury, a small village near to Guildford, in Surrey. On 7th July 197 Mrs. Dowden wrote:

> *'I cannot give you any real information to help with your book 'big cats Loose in Britain', but I certainly remember the excitement and the speculation, though none of my family ever actually saw the puma... At the time we lived on Albury Heath... which is open country, high heathland with occasional farms in the valleys...*
>
> *In 1963 (I think) there was a scare that a 'lion' had killed and maimed dogs, cats and farm animals. Foot-prints had been found in many places in the area. There were enclosed lions near Wonersh to the west, but none were missing. Some said the footprints were those of a large dog. Dr Maurice Burton, the famous naturalist, who lived in Albury, also said it could be a dog, but the prints were never clear enough to be certain. However, there were more "sightings" and we were warned not to let our children out of doors alone. Tracks were found from the heath.., crossing the road, into the forest north of the roads very near our house.*

*Our children, and all others who attended Albury primary school, then had to be ac-
companied to school, and we families went up to school in a group, not straying from
the road! The school, which is now closed, is in heath and woodland, with no road or
driveway leading to it, only a sandy track, which ran out some 100 yards from the
school.*

*The children played in the trees and bracken at playtime, but at this time I think they
were kept in the playground. I never saw the puma or its footprints. I do not doubt
that it existed, as those who saw it gave good and consistent descriptions, and it certainly seemed to be a puma and not a lion. It was said to be honey-coloured or beige,
and not the right shape for a lion.*

*There is plenty of rough country here for such a creature to live, plenty of rabbits and
deer. The complaints about farm and domestic animals being savaged soon died
down. A family in Peaslake said they saw the puma, with cubs, on their lawn... These
people arranged for the BBC to film the pumas, as they were frequent visitors. I never
heard what came of this, if anything. Hope this is of some help to you.'*

Many thanks must go to Mrs. Dowden for letting me use this information. The scare she refers to may not
have been the 'Crondall cougar' scare of August 1964 onwards, but a different one: the Shooter's Hill
cheetah scare of 1963. This was a scare that had widespread publicity at the time. The following summary
of the events come from newspaper articles of the time, and from Janet and Colin Bord's article 'Big cats,
Tail Stories?', from *The Unexplained* magazine, (No.114), as well as two articles from the early editions of
the *Fortean Times* (or as it was then called, the *News*).

The sightings started on 16th July 1963, when lorry-driver Mr David Back was driving on a main road,
near Shooter's Hill, in south-east London. He thought that there was an injured dog at the road-side, so he
stopped to help. It turned out to be a big cat eating something. As it was one o'clock in the morning, it
must have been pretty dark. Mr Back commented about his sighting to the National Press:

*'I walked over to it, and then it got up. I knew then it wasn't a dog. It had long legs
and a long pointed tail that curled up. It looked as if it had a mouthful of food. It ran
off into the woods.'*

The *Kentish Mercury* of 19th and 20th July 1963, as well as the London *Evening News* of July 18th and
19th provide us with a picture of what happened. The cheetah jumped over the bonnet of a police-car near
to the first sighting, and the police radioed for help. A search was mounted, involving 126 policemen, 21
dogs, 30 soldiers and ambulance men, as well as animal welfare officers from the R.S.P.C.A. The public
joined in the search, with schoolboys and Scouts involved also.

The police seemed to think the beast was a cheetah, as motor-cycle police drove through the woods
around Shooter's Hill, and would have chased the animal, which can go at speeds of up to 70 miles per
hour.

850 acres were searched, looking for the cheetah. Some of the parties were armed with weapons such as

hockey-sticks and pick-axe handles. A large set of paw-prints was found in the bed of a stream. These clawed prints showed up clearly in the mud, but they could have been made by a dog, on account of the claw marks. Sniffer-dogs were used in the search. No cheetah was ever caught, despite this search.

On the 23rd July 1963, five car-loads of London police turned up at Kidbrooke sports ground. They had all come to search out the animal that had made a loud, cat-like snarling. It is possible that the local domestic cats were yowling, or that some other animal was responsible. The same night a man at a local RAF base observed a 'large dark animal' against a screen. The animal disappeared but it did make loud catlike snarling sounds. Was a cheetah really on the loose? It was never caught, but rumours of it hung around the area for a longtime. It was one of the first mystery cats to become an urban legend.

The Shooter's Hill area has a number of golf courses, also Jack and Oxleas woods. There is also a place called Eltham Common, where a beast could just about have survived. One presumes the urban life did not suit the beast, which headed for the slightly more rural countryside of North Kent. In his article 'Phantom Felines: Part 5: Animals of the Mind', Mike Goss quotes the saga from Janet and Colin Bord's book 'Alien Animals'. He suggests that foxes and domestic cats could have made the noises, while a very large dog could have made the clawed paw-prints, which were larger than those of the Alsation police dog; while a number of animals could have been responsible for the sightings. However, it is possible that somebody did release a puma or a cheetah around here. I doubt that this beast was the same one that turned up in Crondall in Hampshire the next year, but you never know.

Incidentally, cheetahs do walk with their claws out.

It was in August 1964 that a mystery beast was said to be wandering around Crondall in Hampshire. The following passage comes from the *Farnham Herald* of 30th August and is one of three articles the same paper published on the puma:

> *'Surrey Puma:*
>
> *The mystery animal which had been haunting the Crondall district for the previous two years has reappeared. This time the evidence showed that it may be a killer. Its only victim, a 4-cwt steer at Bushylease farm, Crondall, has fortunately been mauled and not killed. The steer was examined by a veterinary surgeon who gave the definite opinion that the animal had been clawed. Its attacker could well be dangerous to children, he said, and he added that from the descriptions he had been given, it might be a puma. A flesh-eating, hunting feline, the puma could have existed in the neighbouring woods by preying on rabbits and other small animals. Shortage of food might have driven it to attack the steer, and in the opinion of the veterinary surgeon, something had disturbed it before it made its kill.*
>
> *The manager of Bushylease farm said:*
>
> *Forty cattle had broken out of their field after having knocked down the fence. One steer was missing and eventually we found it in the woods.'*

A vet was called to examine the steer which had been bitten and mauled about the shoulders, flanks and legs. He said that the steer had been clawed. He would not consider that the injuries had been caused by a domestic cat run wild, or a badger or indeed any wild animal normally found in this country. From the descriptions he had been given of the attacker and from the claw-marks, he thought it could be a puma. He agreed that it could be dangerous to children and added that it had probably been disturbed by something or someone while it was attacking the steer. The steer survived the attack, although it was covered in talon marks and was also hurt internally where it had been fighting and had rolled in the ditch.'

We shall see that this search for a killer's identity was to lead to positive evidence of the `Surrey Puma`. I shall return to Crondall shortly, but let us look at the police records, kept by Farnham police. They cover the puma period 1964 to 1967, and contain details of 52 sightings. They were sent to me by Inspector Bridgeman of the Public Relations Office at Guildford. They are unique and I quote them in full:

*   3 September 1964 During the early afternoon a man was picking blackberries near the water Tower, Munstead, near Godalming, when he was confronted by a very large cat-like animal which spat at him. Its description fitted a puma.

*   7 September 1964 Sometime between 9 a.m. and 4 p.m. hundreds of identical footprints appeared on the surface of a wide and firm sandy track at "Stileman's", Munstead, nr.Godalming. The footprints, which were in groups of four, each measured about 5" in width and about 5" in length. They stretched in almost a straight line, completely uninterrupted for a distance of half a mile.

*   Night of 22nd/23rd A heifer was badly attacked in a field at Hindhead. September 1964. Its injuries were consistent with it having been attacked by a puma or similar wild animal.

*   23 September 1964. During the afternoon people at Hascombe, including several police officers, saw a very large cat-like animal lying in the sun on the slope of a hill at Hascombe. Its description resembled a puma. The animal then disappeared into nearby woods. The fresh remains of a rabbit were found at the spot where the animal had been seen.

*   23 September 1964. About 7.20 p.m. a farm worker saw an animal, the description of which fitted a puma, walking across a ploughed field in the Cranleigh area.

*   24 September 1964. During the afternoon deer were at a waterhole in the Hascombe area. A local man heard a screech whilst they were there. The deer then made off. An official of the Zoological Society and police officers investigated. They found a dead deer, the injuries to which were consistent with it having been savaged by a puma or similar wild animal.

*   25 September 1964. During the afternoon a farmer was driving his Landrover along a road at Duñsmold when he saw a very large cat-like animal cross the road just in front of his vehicle. The description of the animal fitted a puma.

*   27 September 1964. About 10.45 p.m. a man was driving his motor-car (with headlights full on)

along a road at Loxwood when he saw a very large cat-like animal walking along the road to ward him. The animal then ambled into the roadside hedge and disappeared. The description of the animal resembled a puma.

- 28 September 1964. About 6.15 p.m. a woman saw an animal, the description of which resembled a puma, near Witley.

- 29 September 1964. About 6.45 a.m. a road worker who was working on a motor mower in the Puttenham area came almost face to face with a very large cat-like animal, the description of which resembled a puma.

- 29 September 1964. About 12.30 p.m. a schoolmaster saw a very large animal jump up into the branches of a tree in the Witley area. The animal resembled a puma. An official of the Zoological Society examined the tree and found claw marks, in keeping with those of a puma, on the trunk of the tree.

- 3 October 1964. About 3.30 p.m. a woman saw a very large animal, the description of which resembled a puma, in the Witley area.

- 3rd October 1964. About 4.35 p.m. two women were walking on a bridleway in the Shackleford area when they came almost face to face with a very large animal, the description of which resembled a puma. The animal then jumped over an 8 ft. hedge.

- 6th October 1964. About 11 a.m. a police officer was cycling along a road in the Elstead area when he saw an animal cross the road just in front of him. He was satisfied that it was a puma.

- 16th October 1964. About 5 p.m. a woman saw a very large cat-like animal in a field near Winkworth Arboretum, Hascombe. The animal resembled a puma.

- 18th October 1964. About 5 p.m. a woman who was exercising her dogs in the Hindhead area saw a very large animal about 100 yards away. It then disappeared into undergrowth. The animal resembled a puma.

- 24th October 1964. A sheep was found dead on a farm in the Lurgashall area. Its injuries were consistent with it having been savaged by a puma or similar wild animal.

- 25th October. A sheep was killed and almost completely devoured on a farm in the Northchapel area.

- 31st October 1964. About 1.30 p.m. two workmen saw a large animal running across a field in the Elstead area. The description of the animal fitted a puma.

- 11th or 12th December 1964. A sheep weighing 110 lbs. was killed and eaten in a field on a farm in the Northchapel area.

- 13th December 1964. A sheep weighing 80 lbs. killed during the early hours of the 13th December, in the Lurgashall area. It was dragged some distance after death and partly eaten. Its injuries were consistent with it having been savaged by a puma or similar wild animal.

- 15th December 1964. About 4 p.m. a man saw a large animal running across a field near his house at Ewhurst. The description of the animal resembled a puma.

- 19 December 1964. About 4 p.m. at Hurt Wood, a man saw an animal which resembled a puma.

- 3 January 1965. During the early evening a motorist was driving along a road at Brook when he saw a large cat-like animal bound across the road. The description of the animal resembled a puma.

- Night of 17/18. During the night a sheep was killed on a farm at Ewhurst. January 1965 It was then learnt that on two occasions about two weeks previously a very large animal, the description of which fitted a puma, had been seen in the same area.

- Between 23/25 January 1965. A sheep was killed and almost completely devoured in a field in a farm in the Northchapel area.

- 27 January 1965. About 5.15 p.m. a man was driving along a road in the Hurtwood area when a large cat-like animal crossed in front of him.

- 15 February 1965. About 12.40 p.m. a woman who lives at Holmbury St Mary saw an animal which resembled a puma, walk across the bottom of her garden and go in the direction of the local cricket ground.

- 17 May 1965. About 10.40 p.m. a man was driving a motor vehicle in the Dunsfold area when he nearly ran over a large animal which resembled a puma.

- 18 June 1965. About 10 p.m. a woman was taking her dog for a walk at Dunsfold when she saw an animal which resembled a puma.

- 6 August 1965. At 11.45 a.m. a woman saw an animal, which resembled a puma, cross a road in the Ewhurst area.

- 20 September 1965. About 5.45 p.m. a man saw an animal, which resembled a puma, in a copse in the Cranleigh area.

- 16 October 1965. About 5.20 p.m. a young lady saw a large cat-like animal, which resembled a puma, near a water trough in a field in the Chiddingfold area.

- 10 November 1965. At about 10.15 p.m. two men in a motorcar saw a large animal which resembled a puma, cross the road in front of them between Shillinglee and Plaistow.

- Night of 23/24th November 1965. A sheep was killed and most of it devoured on a farm in the Plaistow area.

- 11 December 1965. About 1.10 a.m. two men in a motorcar saw a large animal which resembled a puma, cross the road in front of them between Bramley and Godalming.

- 8 April 1966. At 7.30 p.m. a woman saw a large animal, which resembled a puma, loping across Whitmore Common, Worplesdon.

- 24 April 1966. Shortly after midnight, a motorist saw a very large cat-like animal in Catteshall Lane, Godalming.

- 6 May 1966. During the afternoon a man saw a large animal, which resembled a puma, in Woodcock Bottom, Hindhead.

- 22 May 1966. During the morning/was fishing with his son in the Chiddingfold area when nearby he saw a large animal, the description of which resembled a puma.

- 6 June 1966. During the afternoon, a person saw an animal, the description of which resembled a puma, in a copse in the Dunsfold area.

- 6 June 1966. About 10.30 p.m. a motorist was driving along a road in the Chiddingfold area when a large animal crossed the road in front of him. He was positive that it was a puma.

- 4 July 1966. About 11.40 a.m. several people, including a police cyclist, who were all together, saw an unusual, large cat-like animal in a meadow in the Worplesdon area. They clearly saw the animal for several minutes and were firmly of the opinion that it was a puma.

- 11 July 1966. During the morning a lorry driver saw a large animal, which he thought was a puma, in the Puttenham area. Several people living in the same area had sighted a similar animal in that district during the previous two weeks.

- 14 July 1966. About 9.30 pm a man saw a large cat-like animal, which he thought was a puma, in the grounds of his house at Ash Green. The animal ran off across adjoining fields.

- 24 July 1966. About 6.30 a.m. a man who lives in the Worplesdon area saw a large animal, which he thought was a puma, in the garden of his house. He was only about 25 yards away from the animal which then sprang into a neighbour's garden.

- 6 August 1966. During the evening a person saw an animal which resembled a puma in the Cutt Mill area.

- 9 August 1966. About 8 p.m. two men saw a strange animal, which resembled a puma, in a paddock on a farm in the Stringers Common area.

- 15 August 1966. During the evening a man saw a strange animal, which he thought was a puma, in the Pirbright area.

- 16 August 1966. About 2.45 p.m. a man saw a strange animal, which he thought was a puma, in the Woking area.

- 22 August 1966. About 9.45 p.m. a man was driving his motorcar along a road in the Grayswood area when in the beam of his car headlights he saw a strange animal, which he thought was a puma, walking along the side of the road. It then disappeared into some roadside bushes.

- 29 August 1966. At 11 a.m. a man saw a very unusual animal, the description of which resembled the puma, very close to him in a copse at Shillinglee.

- 30 August 1966. About 3.30 p.m. a woman who lives at Wormley saw a strange animal in a field at the rear of her house. The description of the animal resembled a puma.

- 31 August 1966. About 9.45 p.m. the same woman at No.48 above saw a strange animal, the description of which resembled a puma, near her house at Wormley.

- 4 September 1966. About 7.30 p.m. a man saw a strange animal, which he thought was a puma, on Rodborough Common, near Milford. He says he saw it come out of a tree and run away.

- 7 September 1966. About 7.30 a.m. a lady saw an animal, the description of which resembled a puma, at Thursley.

- 9 September 1966. At 7.5 a.m. a man saw a strange animal, the description of which resembled a puma, in a field at Chiddingfold. He saw the animal run away and jump across a wide stream.

- 3 September 1966. About 11.30 p.m. - dog badly attacked at Witley.

- 8 September 1966. About 2.45 a.m. a man who was driving a motor-car in the Hindhead district saw a strange animal cross the road, in front of his car. He was positive that it was a puma.

- 21 September 1966. About 7.10 a.m. a man saw an animal which he thought was a puma by the second tee at Worplesdon Golf Course.

- 22 September 1966. About 7.15 p.m. a farmer saw six of his cows grouped together in one of his fields at Whiteways Corner, Hogs Back, Runfold. They were staring at another animal in the field. The farmer got quite close to the animal and, when he was 15 - 20 yards away from the animal (which was playing about in a kittenish manner) it saw him and bounded away in large leaps. The description of the animal fitted a puma. GOOD SIGHTING.

- 23 September 1966. About 4 a.m. two men in a motor-car travelling along the Hog's Back from the direction of Farnham to Guildford saw a most unusual animal on the offside of the road, by a five-barred gate. The driver swung the car across the road, so that the headlights were on the animal which then crossed the road in three or four leaps or bounds (but it did not appear to hurry). The men were very close to the animal after the car had been slowed down and its headlights focused on the animal. The description of the animal fitted a puma. VERY GOOD SIGHTING.

- 23 September 1966. Between 5 p.m. and 6 p.m. a woman saw a strange animal, the description of which resembled a puma, at Stringers Common.

- 2nd October 1966. At about 1 a.m. a male motorist travelling along the Hog's Back road, between Farnham and Guildford, saw an animal at the side of the road. He felt positive that the animal was a puma.

- 14 October 1966. During the early hours of the morning, two men travelling in a motorcar along the Hog's Back road, between Farnham and Guildford, saw a strange animal on the grass verge at the side of the road. The men stopped in their car and saw the animal run away across nearby fields. The description of the animal, as given by both men, resembled a puma.

- 28 November 1966. During the evening a man who lives at Lower Bourne, Farnham, was in the very large garden of his house when he saw an animal in the garden. The description of the animal, as given by the man, resembled a puma.

- 8 January 1967. At about 11.45 a.m. at Effingham, a man saw a strange animal walking along a road. The description of the animal, as given by the man, resembled a puma.

- 14 January 1967. At about 5.10 p.m. a lady was walking in the Punchbowl at Hindhead when she saw an animal, the description of which resembled a puma.

- 12 May 1967. During the early evening, several people, including a man who has seen a number of pumas in captivity, saw a strange animal in a field at Wood Street. The description of the animal, as given by the people, strongly resembled a puma, and the above-mentioned man felt sure that it was a puma.

- 18 July 1967. During the evening a man at Pirbright saw an unusual animal in some bushes. The description of the animal, as given by the man, resembled a puma.

- 21 July 1967. During the morning, a retired Royal Navy captain, who lives at Thursley, was looking out of a window at his house when he saw a very large animal strolling about in bracken on common land close to his house. The description of the animal resembled a puma.

- 17 August 1967. At about 10 p.m. a man who was riding a motor-cycle along a road at Chiddingfold, saw a very large animal on a grass verge at the side of the road. The description of the animal, as given by the man, resembled a puma.

The following events are recorded in the *Surrey Advertiser* of the l960s. I have also used all the other possible sources - letters, interviews and the like.

Before looking at the police records, I quoted an article from the *Farnham Herald* of 30th August 1964. A large dog such as a Great Dane could have caused the cattle breaking out and the wounded steer; or, as has been suggested, a calf could have been frightened and the cows, sensing danger, could have broken out. One of them could have been wounded by barbed wire, perhaps. However, as there had been sighting of a mystery animal, such as a puma, a search was mounted by police, and also helping them was Canadian tracker Mr Billy Davidson, who was giving up part of his English holiday to hunt the puma.

Mr Flanks, manager of Bushylease, suddenly found himself being interviewed by the press and other people. There are numerous sources that have come my way, and I shall now use them to describe the events. Firstly, when I visited Bushylease farm in April 1987, I found the land to be wooded, with a number of roads in the vicinity. The area could easily support a number of big cats. Mr Blanks was the manager of the farm throughout the 1960s and early 1970s. He had seen the puma in March 1962 and in March 1963, and once again in March 1964. In September 1964, the puma hunt was on.

Mr Billy Davidson, on 'definite evidence', said there was a puma around, but he did not know where it came from. The animal made a lair, which could mean that the cat was having cubs. Certainly there were reports of a lynx, puma and black big cat around Crondall during the 1960s. Mr Peter Barclay, of Bushylease, told me in a letter dated 11th April 1987:

> 'The Bushylease estate has been split up for some years now. The farm where Mr Blanks lived is now a separate property and he no longer lives there. We have lived here for four years and seen nothing like a puma, though the publican at the Queen's Arms at Ewshot said he had heard stories about a puma in this area. So far as I know no one living in this area at the moment has seen a puma.'

Mr Barclay had heard of the Essex puma. The publican at the *Queen's Head*, Ewshot, had been there twenty years before and knew about the scare, as he mentioned to my mother, in April 1987. In September 1964, a motorist observed a puma crossing the road next to the *Queen's Head* at Ewshot. It was on the A287, and was on the weekend of 6th/7th September 1964. The man had not visited the *Queen's Head*.

In No. 2 of the publication *Touchstone*, Mrs. Cara Trimarco notes her own lion sighting, in an article called 'A Surrey out-of-place cat sighting'. She lived on Folly Hill near farnham in Surrey, as a young girl and learnt about the `Surrey Puma` at primary school. When she was about five or six she saw a lion in her parents' very large garden, which had a 6 ft. high fence separating it from Wildhale Common and the main road. She describes how while playing one day, she observed the lion on a heap of dead leaves under a tree, three feet from an old wire fence separating the two homes.

She states:

> 'My own personal alien cat sighting, however, was not of a puma but of an adult male lion - a huge, beautiful, honey-coloured animal with a splendid mane, instantly recognisable, and impossible to mistake for any cat, dog or other animal.'

The lion looked satisfied and did not see her, although she was only six feet away. It was moving its head slightly and flicking its tail. Then she ran off back to the house, and finally managed to make her mother come and look at the lion. Her mother thought she had seen a white poodle, which was on the lawn. Mrs. Trimarco was always sure she had seen the lion, and she also now believes it was a manifestation caused by 'energy from water'.

Strangely, a friend of her father's was the motorist who observed the puma at the *Queen's Head*, Ewshot in 1964. Chris Hall analysed what Mrs. Trimarco stated in her article and suggested that it must have occurred in late August/early September 1964. He notes that there was one report of a male lion from this area of Surrey. I now know that several private owners keep lions in the Surrey area. However, I do not know whether any of these lions had escaped.

We will now have to study the reports that were coming in from Crondall, which was a puma-base for 25 years.

On the 3rd December 1987, Mrs. Christabel Arnold of Crondall told me the following in a letter:

> *'My encounter took place back in the 1960s, when I came face to face with this creature, on the lane where I still live. But I always maintained that the creature I saw was definitely not a puma. I still do; more so now, after years of searching for a picture, which I first did with the police to whom I reported this sighting. A zoo-man came and spent half a day with my late husband and me, and after looking around zoos that we travelled to, where we went on holidays, I never came up with anything that resembled this creature.*
>
> *However, the farmer here (on whose land it roamed) said he and his wife thought as I did - that there were two different creatures around here at that time, as the wife saw what I saw, and he said it was a puma. Anyway, having said that, I still followed my own private investigations, writing to my friends in Canada, as I did say if the creature had a lovely tail like the one I saw and was a deeper red colour on top, instead of being beige-grey, it could have been a bob-cat. But it had this tail and was a red-fox colour.*
>
> *Now, 20 years after (approx.) having become a widow and having to go through my husband's papers and drawings (he did a lot for the "Church Harvest" and the seasons etc. and wildlife pictures for various clubs etc.) I found someone had sent him a picture of a little animal to copy, called a desert bobcat and her kitten. This was the colour and pattern (spots and stripes) of the creature I had seen. I can't judge the size of the animal. It was quite big, taller and longer and heavier than a wildcat (which I imagine to be the size of this desert bobcat). I hope I'm not wrong. I must add that when I told the police that first time, that it had "spots and stripes", the three of them fell about laughing, but it was true, and they took it all down.*
>
> *I admit I was very frightened, especially as it spat at me all the time. It is twenty odd years since.*
> *Incidentally, I've mislaid the picture of the cat. I think my grandchildren may know something about it. However, we know the name, I think, of it.'*

Mrs Arnold describes what I believe could be a type of lynx. The caracal , which lives in North Africa and is also known as the 'desert bobcat. She might have seen the Spanish pardel lynx, which is now rare, but does have spots and stripes on a reddish-coloured background. I sent Mrs. Arnold a photograph or drawing of a caracal, so that she might identify it as what she observed.

Firstly, on 3rd September 1964, a set of large paw-prints were found that stretched from one part of a sandy gallop at Stileman's Racing Stables, Mudstead, to a fence and woods. The prints showed no signs of claw marks, which was unusual for a dog. The prints were considered to be the size of a man's hand with the fingers outstretched. Mr Roy Pettit, the trainer of the stables, telephoned the local police and a reporter of the *Surrey Advertiser'*, who came and viewed them. The prints were the size of a very large dog, but they ran in a straight line for a half to one mile. Experts from the Zoological Society of London stated that a puma made the paw-prints. Plaster casts were made and photographed for various newspapers around Britain.

The track was in fact made of cinder. Dr Maurice Burton, the naturalist, in his 1966 article in the *Wildlife and Countryside*, shows that a bloodhound, which apparently was kennelled near Stileman, probably made the prints. It could have had its claws clipped, so the prints would look cat-like. But did the bloodhound have the capability of jumping a six-foot chain-link fence, which it or whatever made the paw-prints must have done.

The Zoological Society was now on hand to investigate any reports, along with the police, the Ministry of Agriculture, Fisheries and Food, as well as Dr Burton and various 'puma-hunters'. With so many authorities about, it is no wonder that so many conflicting views appeared. The 'Mudstead Monster' prints were made by something larger than a normal puma - an escaped male lion, perhaps? Superintendent Robert Hagley was called in to answer the press's questions; he was in charge of the puma-hunt at Godalming station. His view of the prints was recorded in *Telegraph* colour supplement article 'Hunting the Puma' by Duff Hart-Davis. The Superintendent was quoted as suggesting:

> *'If there'd only been a few prints, I'd have believed it was some young fellers having a lark with us. But no one's going to keep on for half a mile.'*

London Zoo officials and the Zoological Society of London agreed that a large puma made the paw-prints; they were 5 inches wide.

The next event was an actual sighting by Mr George Wisdom, a bricklayer. The *Surrey Advertiser* records the event:

> *'... On September 7th, Mr George Wisdom... living at Croydon, was blackberrying near the Mudstead watertower, when he stumbled upon a large, tawny, cat-like animal which, he said, spat at him.*
>
> *He gave a vivid description of the beast, saying that it was about three feet high and five feet long, was of a dirty brown-gold colour, with a long tail and a black mark running from the tip of the tail along the back. Its legs, he said, were short, its paws*

large and its head small and cat-like. Allowing for a slight magnification in size - due possibly to fright - the description best fits that of a puma.

Arising from this incident, the hue-and-cry started and reports of sightings came in thick and fast," commented Supt.Hagley.'

The puma - which was what Mr Wisdom probably saw - was as surprised as Mr Wisdom and did not wish to have a closer confrontation.

On 23rd September 1964, the puma decided to appear at Hascombe, in Surrey. Two builders, working on their site, spotted the puma basking on a hillside above the village. Two members of the Surrey constabulary drove to the scene of the sighting and approached the animal on foot. The police later stated that an animal was seen at a distance, but gave no more details of the sighting until September 1965 - a police cover-up, perhaps? It seems that the two officers advanced to within a hundred yards of the beast by creeping through a wood. They recalled how it was 'lying with its legs thrust out and moving its head'. Obviously the puma sensed them and in the tradition of mystery cats, it made off across the hillside. There was a dead rabbit where it had been seen, and the rabbit had been partly consumed.

Also on the 23rd September 1964, a dead roe-deer was found at Cranleigh. The deer had a broken neck, and claw marks were found on the body. The killer was said to be the puma. On the same day a farm-worker saw the puma in fields near the Leathern Bottle, on the Guildford-Horsham road. That night a heifer was attacked near the village of Hindhead. She was found to have deep scratches on the left side, and along the stomach. It was suggested by some that barbed wire was responsible for marks such as these.

The 24th September proved to be a busy day. Godalming police were receiving many calls from people who wanted to catch the puma, offering all sorts of suggestions, but the police knew that London Zoo was their only real help. The Zoo provided an expert opinion, although I cannot find any direct statements made by them. I do know that their fellow experts of the Zoological Society of London were prepared to give views and equipment to Godalming police, for a tranquilising gun, cage and nets were provided by the Society. Mr V.J.A. Manton, MRCVS, the curator of Whipsnade Zoo near Dunstable, told me in a letter dated 9th April, 1987:

'I am sorry I cannot help you much about big cats loose in Britain, although I gather a book will be published about them in the near future. There was a programme shown on BBC1 last year on "Tomorrow's World", and it might be worth you writing to the editor of this programme for further information.'

This was all Mr Manton could tell me at first, but he made another statement in a second letter of 15th May 1987:

'The book I was referring to has yet to be published, and unfortunately I have forgotten the name of the author, but suggest you write to Eddie Orbell at Highland Wildlife Park. As far as the Society's involvement in the `Surrey Puma` is concerned, investigations took place between 7th September and 31st October 1964, and I had no

evidence, at the time, that there was more than one animal around. I hope you get a useful reply from the BBC.'

The BBC's "Tomorrow's World" programme of 22nd May 1986 covered the `Surrey Puma`, Exmoor beasts and other large cats, but the second half of it was largely concerned with the Moray beasts or Kellas cats. The Zoological Society believed that the puma existed, and they have their own confidential file on the affair. It is now known, through Victor Head's article 'Trailing the `Surrey Puma`' in *The Field* of 8th April 1965, that a roe deer was killed near Hascombe Place, Hascombe. It was found with a broken neck near a waterhole, on 25th September 1964. A major puma hunt was under way, involving both Godalming police and the Zoological Society. There were no other signs of the puma until late in the afternoon, when Mr Charles Oakley of Pound Farm, Dunsfold, spotted 'a puma', which bounded across the road in front of his farm Landrover. It was a classic sighting. Mr Oakley mentioned the sighting to a *Surrey Advertiser* reporter and also noted that 'it had whiskers like bailing wire'. Clearly, Mr Oakley had had a detailed sighting.

While all this was going on, a local taxidermist and formerly curator of Charterhouse Museum, Mr Percy Mountney of Godalming, was shown a scale drawing of one of the plaster casts taken at Mudstead. Having stuffed three pumas previously, he felt that he was expert enough to say that the paw print was of a puma. It was not until 1966 that Dr Maurice Burton turned against the puma. He did not dismiss every sighting as an old wife's tale, which some people have done. Thus the Mudstead prints were considered firm evidence of the puma's existence.

On 29th September 1964, Mr Bert Aylward, a Surrey county council road-worker of Puttenham, observed the puma in a narrow and isolated lane in Puttenham village. The time was approximately 9 a.m. and Mr Aylward had a 'close-up glimpse' of the puma. Also on the same day a teacher at Barrow Hill School, Witley, telephoned the police to say that he had just seen the puma trying to jump into a tree. This was between the Haslemere and Portsmouth roads. An official from the Zoological Society found claw-marks at the scene, which were consistent with a puma, or another similar wildcat. Did the teacher just see a large ginger tom-cat trying to jump into the tree? I doubt it, as the animal was the size of a large dog, 3rd October 1964 proved to be another puma-spotting day. At Mare Hill, near Witley, a lady encountered a very large puma-like animal, at about 3.30 p.m. Also that day another unnamed witness or witnesses spotted a puma at Gatwick (not the airport), near Shackleford village in Surrey.

This close encounter left the two ladies involved rather stunned. The animal jumped an eight-foot high hedge, and as dogs cannot jump eight-foot high hedges, it must have been a feline, I feel - and a very large one at that!

On his bicycle, PC Taylor, a village policeman, encountered a black puma at Somerset farm, on the Elstead-Shackleford road. He could not actually identify what he had seen, as it was moving at speed, but it was black and apparently 'moved like a cat'. The officer was 100 yards away from the animal. The beast crossed the road and made off across a field. I think it was a black panther or black leopard.

By now the puma was spreading its range all over south-east England, and evidence suggests there was more than one cat about. On 16th October it appeared at Hascombe, on the 18th at Hindhead, and on 24th at Lugershall a sheep was found dead. These three incidents can be read in detail if you look at the police records. I have nothing to add to them, as they are not recorded elsewhere.

At the end of October a puma appeared at Bunch Lane, Haslemere. It was this time described as 'a large black animal', which frightened the life out of some horses. Sightings also came in from Grassham, near Petworth and Crawley in Sussex. (Such sightings outside 'Surrey Puma' country but in south-east England will be dealt with in the 'Other southeastern cats' section.)

On going through reports I have found that there was a black animal on the Surrey/Sussex border during the 1950s. I take it that this was not a puma but a black panther or black melanistic leopard; or maybe people were just seeing black dogs. However, during October reports came in of black animals in Bury St Edmunds, Suffolk, from Princes Risborough, and various other far-flung towns and villages boasted a puma witness. On 30th October 1964 an unusual cat-like beast appeared on the eighth green of the West Surrey golf links, near Enton. The animal bounded away, leaving prints which were too vague to be positively identified (of course!)

The 18th November 1964 was the day on which a puma appeared in the council house garden of somebody in Slough, which is separated from the rest of the puma sightings by a motorway. Earlier, on 12th November, it was seen by two policemen at Stoke Poges, in the graveyard and near to the memorial to the poet Thomas Gray. The puma was also seen around Nettlebed in Oxfordshire, on 20th November 1964.
Mr H.L. Holden, a farmer who lost a sheep on 11th/12th December at North Chapel in Surrey, stated to Duff Hart-Davis for an article in the *Daily* or *Sunday Telegraph* of 20th December 1964: *"people don't mind having it around as long as it leaves them alone. But when it kills something that belongs to you, it isn't so funny."*

The ewe was 112 pounds and was in lamb at the time of being killed. The killer had actually eaten her.

The year of 1965 was to prove to be yet another puma-spotting year, and I have attempted to chronicle all the material that has come to my notice.

To start, on 27th January 1965 Mr Robert Ware, Ranger of Hurtwood Common and publican at the Hollybush Tavern, Holmbury St Mary, was driving on the common near Peaslake. Up ahead of his car was a cat-like creature - 'the puma' - that crossed the road in front of the car. The time was 5.00 p.m. and presumably dark, so we can presume Mr Ware was watching the animal in his headlights. He was warden, or ranger, of Haslewood in 1983, when he was mentioned in the '*Touchstone*' magazine.

This sighting was followed by a series of paw print findings in the snow. The paw-prints, which were large, were found in the same area of Hurtwood and the animal was considered to be wintering in the 4,000 acres of common consisting of heathland and woodland.

On 14th July 1965, a motorist reported seeing the puma in the Golden Valley, near Hindhead. By 6th August the puma had moved to the Shere and Ewhurst area. At 11.45 p.m. on that date it was observed crossing the road between Shere and Ewhurst villages. The driver reliably told Godalming police that it was a large, unidentified beast, with a reddish-brown coat and an Alsatian-sized body. The police searched the fields, but with no success. This no doubt prompted an irate Superintendent Hagley to stress:

'All incidents continue to receive the fullest attention by the police. We request that in the event of a sighting taking place, no time is lost in telephoning Godalming Police Station.'

The puma continued to appear, for on the 30th October the *Surrey Advertiser* published an article called 'Puma rears its head yet again'. The puma had been on the move, for three separate sightings occurred around Chiddingf old.

Mr Stanley Lintott of Robins Farm, Chiddingfold, noticed one day that all his sheep were in disarray - two of them were scratched, and five sheep were missing. Why had they broken out of their field? Mr Lintott discovered that the sheep had a habit of breaking out, and he also had a sighting, some time after 14th October. He told the *Surrey Advertiser*:

> *'I was a mile or so away from where my sheep were. When we were taking them away on the following Saturday, I saw something which I had seen before. It was a large cat-like animal, but it was about 200 yards away, running in long strides at terrific speed.'*

On a Friday morning in October 1965, Mr S.A. Francis of Okelands, Chiddingfold, spotted an unusual animal jumping over a fence. It left large paw-prints in the snow or earth. The police sergeant had no doubt that the animal was a puma. It was no dog. *"By the time I got near,"* said Mr Francis, *"it had disappeared."*

The beast jumped up from Nitthurst farm and went down through Okelands farm to another property. No doubt this beast was the puma. Other sightings were made by the residents of Hazelbridge Court near Chiddingfold, who were Viscount Chelmsford and his family. On a Thursday in October, Lady Chelmsford told a reporter how her daughter had seen the puma on four occasions. After looking at pictures of wildlife, the Hon. Philippa Thesiger came to the conclusion that she had encountered a puma. She watched it once for some minutes at a distance, and another time discovered it had taken food from the Court's boilerhouse. Lady Chelmsford said:

> *'My daughter went to feed her horses in a field adjacent to where the sheep had been. My daughter, shaking like an aspen, was looking over the gate. The mare looked away in the corner of the field. The puma was lying beside the water-tank about 20 feet away from my daughter, crouching down, looking at the horses. Two horses there had already been damaged. My daughter looked at the animal for five minutes, during which it didn't move at all. Then when she made a noise it went through the hedge and over the hill to Pickhurst.'*

The horses were brought nearer to Hazelbridge Court, for their safety's sake. On Saturday night, both daughters of Lady Chelmsford drove their Landrover around the fields, looking for the puma. The Sunday was another day when the family was worried "because we knew it was round all the time." When on the Sunday the Hon. Philippa entered the store sheds, she came upon the puma lapping up the milk left for the eleven cats. Lady Chelmsford informed the reporter:

'We had about eleven cats there, and they have all disappeared. As my daughter noticed it, the puma sprang off the bales of hay and went practically over her head as she ducked, sensing the presence of the intruder. Dogs were "screaming their heads off".'

Monday morning was the fourth day of a puma sighting, and the Hon. Philippa Thesiger was milking the cows at the time. She observed the puma cross the paddock. Foxes, deer and other wildlife fled the wood as soon as the puma entered it. By the Monday night, things were still going on, as Lady Chelmsford recounted:

'On Monday night we put out some bait and got in a friend who is a good shot. He said he would have a preliminary look around. He had his gun, but saw nothing.'

Two local sportsmen prepared to patrol one night, but as usual, nothing was seen. The following Friday, the Hon. Philippa was going into the boilerhouse when she encountered the puma at the doorway. It was apparently after the dog meat. A year was to pass before her next sighting.

The puma was observed at Cranleigh by Polish-born cowman Mr Frank Schebedly, on Snoxhall farm. He was bringing the cows in on a Monday morning when he saw it 'asleep and basking in the sun' in a field some 300 yards away. The puma awoke and bounded away through the thickets. Mr Schebedly told a boy to go back to the farmhouse and obtain some more people. The group beat through the undergrowth for two or three hours, but the obviously frightened puma had made off.

The following day Mr Walter Thomson of Weybridge was riding his bicycle along a lane in Cranleigh when the puma jumped over one hedge, crossed the road and ran into a field on the other side. Mr Thomson told the *Surrey Advertiser.* "It looked very fierce as it sailed through the air with the greatest of ease." Farmers had put guards on all their sheep, and the paper reckoned that a hundred people had seen the puma in the past fifteen months. Its lair was thought to be somewhere near Godalming. People believed that one animal was responsible for sightings in Surrey, Hampshire and Sussex.

At about the same time as this, a flamingo was observed in Witley Park. Godalming police contacted London Zoo, who came and took it away. Flamingos, pumas... what next?

The year 1966 proved to be one of the best years for puma sightings. The first newspaper report appeared in the *Surrey Advertiser* for 12th January. 'The Puma: £100, dead or alive' was the caption above the article. It seems now that Miss Joan Palmer, Secretary to the National Dog Owners' Association, spoke from Gray's Inn Road, London to the *Surrey Advertiser.* She stated that they were offering a £100 reward because the puma might harass dogs. Owners were apparently afraid to let their dogs off the lead because of the possibility of a puma attack. No actual reports had come in of dogs being attacked, but Miss Palmer was taking no chances. She said:

'We have a great many members in the Guildford and Godalming areas, and we have had a number of telephone inquiries asking what we are going to do about it. Obviously we would rather it was captured unharmed and presented to a zoo.'

The reward was part of the Association's obligation to people in Surrey. At the same time as this reward was offered, Mrs. E. Beerli, a member of the Association who lived in Merstham in Surrey, was having a close encounter of the feline kind. Her dog was in the garden with her and it decided to run into a near-by sand-pit. What happened next is best described in Mrs. Beerli's statement to the *Surrey Advertiser.*

> *'I followed naturally and saw this animal running away. I think my dog had disturbed it. It was a very long, cat-like animal, greyish in colour, with a black ring in the middle of its tail. It was about 20 yards away when I saw it.'*

She identified the animal as a puma, when she looked in an encyclopedia. She telephoned the Association on the day of her sighting and lodged a complaint about her dog's safety. By 30th April 1965, London Zoo was asked to supply puma urine to entice the puma, during a new hunt, which would have involved thirty people, over a 3 month period. The hunt was in the densely-wooded area around Godalming, and involved an animal psychologist, a lecturer, research fellows and students from Oxford University. Mr Michael Dowse, of Northwood, in Surrey, led these scientific people. He told the *Surrey Advertiser.*

> *"We are using lures adopted extensively in America by puma hunters. Others are a mixture of catmint and petrol, which is said to attract pumas half a mile away, and horsemeat. We are also considering using recordings of puma calls amplified. Our object is to study the animal. We have no intention of trying to catch it."*

If somebody makes 'contact' with the puma, a 'safari' of people with tents, caravans and cars would move there. Then the group would have the time to study and photograph the puma.

However, the expedition was not quite so simple. The spokesman for London Zoo confirmed that they had been asked to supply the expedition with puma urine. He continued: "You will realise it is not a very easy job to collect it, but we are doing our best." The police at Godalming said there had been no recent sightings of the puma.

A week later, on the 4th May 1966, the *Surrey Advertiser* announced that a hunt for the puma had been made the previous weekend, involving the 16 scientific expedition members and anybody who wanted to join them. The expedition's leader, Mr Mike Dowse, was a London psychologist, and he had his own glimpse of what might have been the puma - an Alsatian-sized, very long-tailed large animal, moving off through the trees. He and another member both observed the beast, and a third member heard some 'cat-like sounds'.

The group was also using tape-recordings of a puma's call to attract the puma, while horse flesh baits had been strung up in trees. At one of the baits, nearest the Windmill public house, Ewhurst, scratch marks were found. Mr Dowse thought that if they had not been made by a very large member of the cat family, they were very difficult to account for. The puma urine was also considered very valuable, for Mr Dowse commented:

> *"This is a very precious commodity. We want to make pretty sure that a puma is somewhere about before we start spreading it about. On safari, we had better luck than we expected at this stage."*

They were obviously keen to carry out more searches, which they did later in the year. About this time a Mr George Turner of Godalming wrote to the *Surrey Advertiser*, complaining that his sighting on a road on 23rd April 1966, of a 'strange animal' had been omitted in an earlier report. Both he and his wife had seen the animal and a Godalming police spokesman said there had been an unconfirmed sighting on 23rd April 1966. Presumably this sighting was now confirmed as such. The puma hunt was centred on Dunsfold, a village south of Godalming and in the heart of `Surrey Puma` country.

On 22nd May 1966, the *Surrey Advertiser* published a new article detailing the fact that a search was to be mounted the following week-end, involving a hundred people. The search was to cover 100 square miles of Sussex, Hampshire and West Surrey. However, evidence suggests that the expedition actually took place in late October 1966.

Strangely enough, during the whole time of the 'Surrey Puma' scare, UFOs had been seen over Surrey. I feel that at least one sighting occurred during 1966, and it would be worth our discussing the Surrey UFO business. To open, I quote from the No. 4, July 1984 edition of *Touchstone*, the newsletter of the Surrey Earth Mysteries Group. The magazine or newsletter is mainly concerned with ley lines and related phenomena in Surrey. The editor is Mr Jimmy Goddard of Weybridge in Surrey, and he sent me all the issues containing references to the `Surrey Pumas` on 1st July 1987. He was carrying out ley-line field-work on the Hurtwood Common track, which goes from Winterfold forest through Holmbury St Mary and ends up in Hurtwood. The track was of Roman origin and had various ancient sites along the way. Mr Goddard contacted another gentleman who was interested in ley-lines, Mr Philip Heselton, who had walked the ley-line in May 1966, at the height of the puma saga. The relevant passage reads:

> 'There is an interesting anecdote regarding the track told to me by Philip Heselton. When walking the track in May 1965 he met the Hurtwood ranger (there is only one). After a short conversation the ranger pointed to the ridge and exclaimed, whats that?" On the ridge was a rather strange object, round, and standing on some kind of legs. The ranger then drove off to investigate and Philip, not particularly interested in UFOs, at that time, simply carried on down the track and did not know the outcome of the incident when I contacted him, but he did mention that 1966 was the year when a puma had been sighted several times in Huftwood. On enquiring of Chris Hall, currently researching the puma, I was informed that 1966 was indeed the peak year for the puma, and Hurtwood was the centre of activity.
>
> Only one account linked it to a UFO, however, and that was very tentative. So the mystery of the object of the ridge must unfortunately remain a mystery.'

The ranger of Hurtwood was Mr Robert Ware, who had actually seen the puma, in 1965. I thought the object on the ridge might have been the puma itself, but the UFO suggestion sparked off my imagination, and I now find that there are other references to UFO5 in Surrey. The Surrey police have seen UFO5 at Ash, and I believe there is a group that investigates UFOs in this area. However, in 1964 or before, Mr Edward Blanks of Bushylease farm, Crondall in Hampshire, had an encounter with what may well have been a UFO. I quote a relevant passage from the editor of the *Flying Saucer Review*, Mr Philip Bowen's 'Mystery Animals' articles which appeared in the *Flying Saucer Review* of November-December 1964, No.16. Mr Blanks met Mr Bowen at the farm and told him that it was his custom to make the rounds of the farm every night. Mr Blanks was described as a 'very down-to-earth type of man'. This quotation comes from the article and was mentioned by Brinsley le Poer Trench in his book *The Secret of the Ages*

The passage runs:

> *'On two occasions he suddenly became aware of a mysterious light on the roofs of the farm buildings. The light moved from roof to roof, yet he could not see the beam which produced the light. It was certainly not produced by car headlights from the Odiham road: the local topography precluded that possibility. Mr Blanks could not trace the source of the light, and he was puzzled by the phenomenon, because on each occasion the mystery puma arrived on the scene shortly afterwards.'*

Brinsley le Poer Trench was the 8th Earl of Clancarty. He researched widely on the UFO phenomenon, and has come to the big cat's origins, in his 1974 book *The Secret of the Ages*. In Chapter 25 he discusses the probability that pumas are transported by Aliens to places where they would not normally be found. On pages 164-5 he summarises this theory, and I quote an extract here, with the publishers' permission:

> *'Thirdly there is the landing of pumas and possibly other creatures, in various coun- tries. These pumas have been landed at night, and it is a well-attested fact that sightings of them have coincided with UFO 'flaps' in the same areas. Pumas are not indigenous in some of the countries in which they have been seen. For example, England and Ireland are not the natural habitat of pumas. They are, however, indigenous to our planet, and not necessarily to another world. Therefore, the earth being hollow, with very likely a sub-tropical temperature, it is reasonable to assume that is where these 'out-of-place' pumas originated. Another fantastic but perfectly feasible idea has just made its way through my 'little grey cells'. In an earlier chapter the brain-washing of surface people was suggested. Perhaps the inner-earth people, with the aid of their hypnotic machines, could program the pumas to do a job of work on the surface. Now that really is an idea! Not so crazy when you think about it; possibly the first thing to do with the puma.*
>
> *We have made a fair amount of progress in communicating with the dolphin. Then with the aid of the machines, the animals could be programmed for whatever work was required. In short, the puma would be landed from a UFO, under cover of darkness, go about its programmed business and, at a pre-arranged time, the UFO would return at night to pick up the waiting animal.'*

We now move on from UFOs to the next well-publicised puma sighting. This comes from *The Times* of 6th July 1966, and as the reporting is of a high standard, I quote it in full, with permission of *The Times*.

> *'Puma is seen stalking a rabbit', from our correspondent, 4th July.*
>
> *The elusive puma that has been roaming the Surrey-Hampshire border for three years came out into the open today, and was watched and followed by police, post office of- fice engineers and villagers for more than twenty minutes. The last shred of doubt among the police about its existence disappeared when it stalked and killed a rabbit in*

full view of a police Inspector.

It appeared today in a meadow adjoining the home of the Queen's cousin, the Rev. Andrew Elphinstone, at Worpleston, near Guildford, and among the first to see it was Inspector Bourne of the Special Constabulary, who watched from his garden only a hundred yards away. Inspector Bourne said tonight that a post office engineer working 20 yards away yelled: "Look at that puma!" I went to where he was standing and sure enough, without any doubt whatsoever, there was the puma. I watched it come out of a copse and walk along the side of the meadow, keeping to the cover of the hedge, to within a hundred yards of the bottom of the garden. Then it lay down out of sight.

It was a ginger-brown colour and the size of a Labrador dog, with a cat-like face. I rang the police. Just as they arrived it got up and sauntered back at a leisurely pace to the copse as I watched through field glasses. I do not know whether it saw us watching, but it was in no hurry as it went into Mr Elphinstone's copse and disappeared. We went over to where it had lain in the grass and found a half-eaten rabbit.'

A motorcycle patrol officer, P.C. Robin Young said:

The animal was in sight for 20 minutes and there was no doubt it was the puma. It was ginger-coloured and had a long tail with cat-like face. It was just walking casually I had a good look at it through binoculars One of the villagers there had a shot-gun and the animal just took off. We followed it for then lost it when it reached the road.'

While trying to trace more about this sighting, I noted that Inspector Bourne was interviewed by Mr Michael Vestey of the now defunct *London Life Magazine*. Mr Vestey quoted Mr Bourne as saying:

"A blooming puma it was. It slunk across that field in full view. I tell you, I'm not up the pole. I know a badger from a puma. And it was definitely a puma."

At this stage of the affair, the existence of the puma was accepted as existing by most people. However, Dr Maurice Burton was following up every case and a white tip and a round the meadow, from 50 yards away took a pot-shot, then about half a mile and by the end of 1966 he was prepared to attack the puma legend, with some success. It was during this year that people continued to report seeing pumas, but some of the descriptions were of normal animals, such as badgers, foxes, dogs and domestic cats. The local papers covered the stories, and one of the papers to do so was the *Farnham Herald*, which had covered the first publicity back in 1954 of Mr Edward Blank's injured cow. I quote the following letter from Mrs. B. Sprules, editorial assistant on that paper. She wrote this on 13th October 1987:

'With reference to your enquiry regarding articles in the Herald on the `Surrey Puma`s, I am sorry to disappoint you, but although there have been stories about the cats in the paper some years ago, no record was kept of when they actually appeared in the paper, which makes them extremely difficult to find and we do not have the staff to undertake this type of search. We know that at the height of the various sightings Godalming police station kept a file, and it might be worth your contacting them. We are putting the

request to our readers on this week's letters page, and hopefully you may get some response.'

It would seem that a month before all these incidents, on 4th June 1966 the *Surrey Advertiser* published an article called 'Probe puma clue: 'This might be it' - police?' It would appear that Mrs. M. Wallach of Dunsfold in Surrey was walking her dog in Burnwood copse, when she noted an unusual cat-like beast sleeping in the undergrowth. Mrs. Wallach left for London, but before going she reported the sighting to Godalming police, and her neighbour, Mrs. Enticknap told the *Advertiser.*

> *'Mrs Wallach is not the sort of person to imagine things. She saw this animal at about 4 p.m. on Monday, then she came to tell us and I ran to telephone the police immediately. She described this animal as about the same size as a Labrador dog, of marmalade (orange) colour, and with a cat-like head. She was within about 30 yards and watched it for quite a time.'*

The Godalming police carried out a search of the area and found some hair, which they thought might belong to the puma. So they handed the tawny-colour tuft of hair over to the Ministry of Agriculture, who were considered experts. The Ministry planned to have the hair analysed by the following weekend. A police spokesman was confident enough to say on the Tuesday: *"There is a strong possibility that this might be it."* Mr Mike Dowse, the puma research group leader, was asking people to carry a camera with them, just in case they had an encounter with the puma and were able to photograph it.

In a second sighting, on the day following Mrs. Wallach's sighting, a Southsea motorist saw the puma, in his car headlights, while going through Chiddingfold village at 11 p.m. The police spokesman said: *"He was positive it was the puma because he knows a lot about animals."*

The 2nd August brought more news of the puma. Mr Martin Hedger and his wife were driving back from Godalming to their home in Aldershot, in Hampshire. He observed the animal on the outskirts of Seale. It turned off up a lane and they followed it for a mile. He told the Aldershot policeman on duty: *"I know you will laugh at me, but my wife and I have just seen the puma. In fact we chased it for a mile at about 35 m.p.h. in our car."*

The policeman said he had an open mind on the puma and took down all the particulars. Then he contacted Godalming police and told them of the sighting. Mr Hedger gave the following description of the event:

> *"I never believed the puma story myself. I always used to laugh about it. Now I know it is true. The animal had a long tail that it kept out straight when it ran. And when it turned to look back at us I could see that it definitely had a cat's head. It went like a bomb. It just ran in a straight line, cutting off all corners. I thought it was a dog at first until my wife yelled 'It's the puma!' Then I raced after it."*

On 20th August 1966 the *Sunday People* published the first photograph of the puma. Mr Ian Pert, an ex-police photographer and a friend were hiding in a Worplesdon garden at the time. To my mind, the beast was either a large feral tomcat or a female puma. The photograph was taken at a distance of 35 yards, just after a cat-like beast had been seen in the area. Mr Pert gave a description of the beast, which bounded off as soon as the camera clicked. As you can see from the photograph, the animal does have a feline appearance and unless it is a feral cat, the only other option would be a puma-like member of the cat family. The cat is about three feet long and one can just make out stripes on the beast's flanks, but this may be a trick of the light. The windows of the house in the background give us some scale. The cat appears to be about the same length as the width of the windows - some 3 to 4 feet. It might at first be mistaken for a fox, but closer examination does show that it would be a very unusual fox, dog, badger or otter. Experts were divided over the beast's identity, so we can only say that it might have been the puma, rather than it definitely was the puma.

Underneath the *Surrey Advertiser's* article of 20th August 1966, the puma's identity was being explained away by Dr Maurice Burton. The week before, a Mrs. Julian Stode from Mayford, near Woking, had reported seeing the puma. Dr Burton was invited by the *Advertiser* to comment on the sighting. He drove to Mrs. Stode's home and showed her photographs of a puma, but they did not conform to what she had seen. She was convinced that what she saw was not a fox, but an unusual animal. A single paw print in her garden was found by her gardener, and Dr Burton stated that this print belonged to a dog.

He also commented that Mrs. Stode believed that only one of the puma pictures he showed her was like the beast she had observed. Later in the week, Mrs. Elizabeth McLaughlin of Courtenay Road, Woking, stated that Mrs. Stode probably described one of her former neighbour's stray shelty sheep-dogs. Miss Nola Muir Rolfçe had bred shelties at her kennels near Maybury Hill, Woking The dog was a strong, powerful beast and could easily look after itself for 2 years, the time during which it had been lost. Miss Rolfe had moved away to Effingham, obviously sad at losing her dog. Mrs. McLaughlin said:

> 'Two and a half years ago Miss Rolfe lost one of her loveliest shelties, Daffodil. If anyone approached her, she would riot go to them. I'm sure this is what Mrs. Stode saw the other day, and not the puma. Her description fits Daffodil exactly.'

It seems that the dog was large, timid and strange-looking to those who did not know the shelty breed of sheep dog, so I think we must presume that this is what Mrs. Strode encountered. However, Dr Burton had not finished explaining away sightings. He believed that a young fox in moult, playing with ponies, was responsible for the sighting of a puma-like animal on farmland at Stringer's Common. Ponies on the same land had been injured in August 1965

In August 1965, Mr Hart of Ottershaw was driving over the six crossroads at Woking, when he reported seeing the puma. He knew the appearance of mountain lions and described the animal as having a long smooth tail, 'pricked ears' (like a puma), rippling muscles and a four-foot long body. The tail was out of proportion to its body. The puma crossed Shores road only ten yards away from his car. Mr Hart remarked: *"It came out of the undergrowth on one side, crossed over the road and disappeared in the bushes on the other side. It was a beautiful animal, coloured like a washed-out golden retriever."*

This sounded like a genuine puma, and only a few miles away and on the same day, Mr Bowler of Sandhurst, near Caniberly, reported seeing the puma on the Guildford-to-Bagshot road. He observed the puma again on the Pirbridge road in August 1966. He stated: *"It looked like a cat, but it was four foot long."* He noticed that it pondered before crossing the road. As it appeared from a hedge, the beast crouched down low - a most un-doglike action.

A later *Surrey Advertiser* article of August 1966 contained details of more sightings. A puma was seen by three young girls near Chiddingfold. Jane and Fiona Cunnington, aged 11 and 12, were walking on their father's farm at Shillinglee with a friend aged 10. They were not surprised at seeing the beast because they first thought it was a fox. However, Catherine said it was a puma. One of the girls told the *Surrey Advertiser* the full story, as follows:

> *"It did not have a bushy tail, but a long straight tail like a cat's - horrible. The animal was as big as a bulldog, with a face shaped like a cat but bigger. When it saw us it jumped the wire fence, then ran into the field, where the cows went frantic. After it had jumped another and lower fence which is electrified, it stopped and looked at us. We didn't know what to do. Then it chased a little heifer into the wood. We didn't dare stop any longer, but ran off home."*

> *The sighting was just after 7 p.m., when the girls went to bring the cows in from a field between two woods. The eldest girl gave a more detailed description of the animal:*

> *"It had long whiskers on each side of its face. I have never seen anything jump so well in all my life. It cleared the fences easily."*

The cattle were described as 'very unsettled' the next morning, but the heifer that had been chased was unharmed.

One of the girls had apparently won the 'Bonniest Baby' competition with the *Surrey Advertiser* eleven years previously. Thus one could be led to think that the whole sighting was a publicity stunt. However, the mother of the two girls stated that when they arrived home they were *"absolutely white and terrified"*.

Earlier that same week the puma had been seen at the Witley railway station, although I have no details of that sighting.

Mr and Mrs. F.D. Newman of Burpham discovered some possible puma-hair on a barbed wire fence on Albury Heath. Mrs. Newman told the *Advertiser* on the day after the Shillinglee sighting, that the hair was almost certainly that of the puma, as it was the same texture as the stuffed puma at the Farnborough Show Puma Exhibition. Mrs. Newman said:

> *'My husband and I found the fur one evening last month. We had been watching a cricket match at Albury Heath when, as we were walking down a lane, we saw it on a barbed wire fence. There was blood on the fur and a paw print nearby in the mud. We waited until the show opened, knowing that there was to be a puma exhibition. The fur is the exact colour and texture as that on the stuffed animal. An official there agrees with us. This practically convinces me.'*

That weekend in August 1966, a recruit at the Deepcut depot and training camp of the Royal Army Ordnance Corps reported seeing an unfamiliar creature from 15 to 20 yards away. The soldier thought the beast was the `Surrey Puma`, so he reported his sighting to Godalming police. A search found no trace of the animal. An Army spokesman confirmed the sighting, but made a sceptical statement: *'We're a little bit sceptical about this, as there are a lot of foxes in the area.'* The sighting was at 8 p.m. in fading light, so the man could have seen a fox, although he was quite close to the beast.

The next sighting was at Shillinglee, on the Surrey/Sussex border. A search by Sussex police showed no sign of the puma. This sighting was quite near to Chiddingfold and was reported to Godalming police station.

One evening a resident of Farncombe village observed the puma on Rodborough Common. The following week, two reports came in from the Woodham and Windlesham areas.

One morning in August 1966, a Windlesham resident observed the puma while motoring through Thursley village. He described it as being 'golden brown in colour and the size of an Alsatian'. A Woodsham resident stated that at 3 o'clock one morning he observed a strange animal in his garden. It was between 4 ft 6 ins, and 5 feet long, with a height between 3 ft 6 ins, and 4 ft. It had a small head compared with its body, and its colour was 'whitish' in the moonlight. The beast was in the garden for ten minutes before jumping over a 5 ft. high fence. 3 in. by 3 in. paw-prints were found in the garden after the sighting.

August was the month when the Guildford/Farnborough show was held. The `Surrey Puma` exhibition was organised by Mr Colin Smith, a chief reporter on the *Surrey Advertiser*, and Dr Maurice Burton, the distinguished naturalist of Albury, in Surrey. Mr Smith was secretary to the Guildford Town Society which staged the exhibition. It had a three-year-old stuffed puma on display, lent by Mr Max Rynish of Farnham. (How did he acquire this puma...?). The puma surprised one of the first visitors, a local lady,, and she apparently stated: *"That can't be the puma. It's nothing like the one I saw at the bottom of my garden."*

Other items on show were plaster casts of paw-prints of 'a large cat-like animal' seen at Ayot St Lawrence, in Herts, in April 1966, and the pug marks of an adult Labrador bitch, taken on the same day in the same place at Ayot St Lawrence were on display, for comparison. Other items of note included a puma pug-mark plaster cast from a zoo, and paw prints of a small dog and a domestic cat. There were even the Godalming police records on display. These covered 362 sightings, and were destroyed around 1975, for some technical reason.

There were also a number of copies of an article entitled 'The `Surrey Puma` - Fact or Fiction?' BBC Bristol lent the recordings of all the wild creatures' calling and screeching. A boy at the exhibition was heard to say that he knew of a family, which had kept three puma cubs and let them go. This would explain sightings at more than one place at once. The boy disappeared and despite efforts to trace him, he could not be found.

On 3rd September 1966, the *Surrey Advertiser* published an article entitled *'I trod on the puma's tail - and hit its nose'*. Before puma lovers jump up in arms, let us examine this case. Lord Chelmsford's daughter, the Hon. Philippa Thesiger, was out in a field collecting some cows one morning. She described this encounter - her fourth or fifth - to a reporter:

> *"I went up to our big field to bring the cows in for milking. I was walking up the field. There are a lot of thistles. It was lying between the clumps. I was looking at the cows and it was raining. I was squinting into the rain and did not see the puma until I trod on his tail and it reared up at me and struck at me with its paw. I thought at first it was my Great Dane, and lashed out with my stick, hitting it on the nose and breaking the stick. As I did this I saw the big cat head and realised it was the puma. I did not have time to be frightened and I was not hurt. The puma I saw on Thursday was bigger than the animal I saw then. It must have grown considerably in the last year."*

Miss Thesiger had seen the puma a number of times before, in autumn 1965, as we have previously mentioned. The puma ran off through the field, scaring cows, horses and other animals before scuttling up an oak tree on the edge of the field. From there it watched Miss Thesiger for a few seconds and then leapt down into the woods and made off. The next day she was driving through the same field and she again noticed the puma. She drove the family's Landrover right at it. She commented on the second sighting:

> *"The cows seemed pinned down with fright. I did not get out of the Landrover as I was not going to give it the chance of attacking me again. I drove at it and it slipped back into the woods."*

Godalming police searched the area, but they found no trace of the puma. Early one September morning 1966, a puma was seen crossing the Hog's Back road, by two lorry drivers. Dr Maurice Burton later showed how a mongrel dog could account for the sightings on the Hog's Back.

At Newdigate, in August or September 1966, a former game-keeper encountered a 'ginger animal twice the size of a cat'. Another puma was seen at Wormley, and another at Farnham. I have no more details of these sightings.

A family at Woking claimed to have seen the puma, in September 1966.

In September 1966, at 7.10 one morning, Mrs. Diana Prime of Hook Heath, looked out of her bedroom window onto the scrubby railway land behind her house. She observed something in the undergrowth and quietly called her parents. They knew that a painter doing a job of work nearby, had seen the puma at midnight several weeks before. He had chased it up the road and it went into the undergrowth near a deserted house. Mrs. Prime's mother told the *Advertiser* about her daughter's sighting, and stated:

> *"She called us quietly, because she didn't want to disturb it. She had her window open. We all saw it. It galloped up past the houses and then back. It might have smelt something. It was a sort of golden colour, brown or fawn. I particularly noticed its bounding movement. It was not like a fox. We haven't been here very long and we saw a fox when we first came."*

Mrs Prime thought the puma was living on local grey squirrels, as their numbers were now down, she thought. She had some difficulty in judging the puma's size, but she later saw a programme for children which featured a puma.

At 5 o'clock one September morning in 1966, Mr A.J. Gartery, a Farnham gamekeeper, observed the puma at Glade farm halfway between Bentley and Crondall villages. It came out of a copse and Mr Gartery rushed home for his gun to kill it. He gave the following account to a reporter on the *Surrey Advertiser.*

> *"The animal saw me and trotted off. It did not gallop, but just trotted off as if it wasn't frightened. I saw it go into some kale so I jumped into my car and dashed up the road to try and cut it off. When I got there I saw it was going the other way. The nearest I got to it was 100 yards. I wondered what it was when it first moved, but the thing that made me know it was not a fox was its tail. This animal had no brush and held its tail at an angle like you see lions. I have always said there is no puma, but now I think differently. I could not have mistaken this animal for a fox, because I spend a lot of time trapping them and know what they look like."*

The beast was the size and colour of a gold retriever dog, and thus a much lighter colour than a russet-red fox. He saw the animal three hours later for a short time. This sighting was by one who knew local wildlife and who had spent all his life in the countryside.

In September 1966, an enterprising businessman, Mr Oliver Moxon, who owned a Farnham Hotel, advertised for 'Ten intrepid gentlemen' to hunt the puma on a Sunday. A number of cars contained hunters, reporters and photographers. They visited all the surrounding areas. On 22nd October the *Surrey Advertiser* came back to the research team, led by Mr Michael Dowse, a psychologist, and Mr Robert Mash a zoologist. They had been lead in expeditions since March 1966. The men planned to take cat-naps in their cars over the weekend search, which was setting off from Dunsfold. There had been one definite and two doubtful sightings at Pitch Hill and further south-west in April 1966, by members of the team.

A mixture of paraffin and catnip, along with horse-meat and puma dung, from London Zoo, were to form the lures with which to bring the puma for photography. The public were allowed to join the hunt, provided they contacted research group members at Dunsfold cricket ground, on the day of the article's publication (22nd October 1966), before 5 p.m. Mr Dowse commented about the searching:

> *"While this is the biggest thing our research team has yet organised, it is not quite the finish. We still have other things to do before we bring out our report. A great deal of evidence has to be obtained to support the hypothesis that there is a three-year-old female puma roaming the woods of Surrey and simply dying to be photographed."*

A half-eaten sheep was found at Loxwood in Sussex in October 1966. The Godalming police referred the kill to the Ministry of Agriculture Fisheries and Food.

In October 1966 a resident of Hambledon heard a 'roaring' noise near her home at night. She telephoned Godalming police, who recorded the incident in their 'Puma Book'. The following day a male motorist on the A3 road near Shackleford spotted a dark, puma-like animal crossing the road, heading towards Shackleford.

29th October saw the publication in the *Surrey Advertiser* of a full-page article called 'The Diary of a Puma-Hunter'. An *Advertiser* reporter was sent along to join in the weekend safari, which proved unsuccessful, although very amusing.

> 'At 7 in the morning of the Friday the party of between 70 and 100 people set out from the Sun Inn, Dunsfold. Reporters from several major papers had joined the hunt. The leader of the expedition, Mr Dowse, left the inn, heading out to Winterfold and Cranleigh, where a party of London puma-hunters were waiting. The main party were unable to find Mr Dowse and had to go round the roads, searching for him. Eventually they found him and he gave them all a briefing, announcing - perhaps rather proudly:
>
> "I have already had the bait seen to and most of the meat is gone. This means nothing - anything could have taken it. Now what I propose is that we split up into small groups, each with a torch and a camera. Go up this path, turn left and then right and through a quarry. Up to the top and then come back in a line, ending up back here. Watch out for the puma dung we have put down. If you don't, you won't be able to forget it for a fortnight! Good luck, and try not to get lost."
>
> A long line of puma-hunters marched through Winterfold woods, some of them calling "Here, puss, puss, puss!" And, of course, they didn't see the puma. They were told to meet at six crossroads the next day at 6 a.m. Nobody turned up, apart from the Advertiser reporter and one other reporter. At 6 p.m. he arrived at the Dunsfold Sun Inn and War Memorial. He met Mr Dowse, who explained that the six crossroads meeting was later than expected, as they had not started until 6.45 a.m. It had been a good search, but again with no result. Mr Dowse said: "The biggest thing anybody saw was a squirrel, but everybody enjoyed themselves."

Twenty boys from Charterhouse School planned to join the group, which the next day, Sunday, would be centred on Horsell Common. There had been two sightings here, at different times. The rain was pouring' down as the party gathered at the *Sun Inn*. They arrived at the Common but, owing to the rain, the search was called off.

At the *Hurtwood Inn*, Peaslake, on the final day of the search, the party heard that the puma was currently in the Worplesdon area. Mr Dowse said that several local people had told him they had recently seen the animal. He also continued to point out: *"The response from the public has been very heartening, but I think the weather was such as to make quite impossible any serious expedition. We have visited lots of very pleasant pubs. Has the puma been shot on Lord Chelmsford's estates at Chiddingfold?"* Four local people had told him this was the case. One of them claimed to have seen the body. Mr Dowse planned to write to Lord Cheimsford and ask him if this was the case. The reporter on the *Advertiser* drove straight to Lord Chelmsford and asked him the question: "Has the puma been shot on your estates?" The answer was "No," naturally, and Lord Chelmsford gave the following interview:

"Absolute boloney! My wife and daughter have seen the animal so many times that I have no doubt it exists. I don't know when it was supposed to have been shot, but we certainly have not shot it and don't know of anybody who has."

The next week a large, dead, crossbreed dog was found at the Hog's Back. It was the day after the end of the puma hunt, and the police showed the body to two people who had seen the puma. They said it was not the animal they had seen on the Hog's Back.

Some animal paw-prints were found at Hedge farm, Thursley and they were plastercast by the police, who compared them with the plaster casts of paw-prints found at Mudstead in 1964. The Thursley paw-marks were smaller and clawed, so the Advertiser1 reporter came to the assumption that they had been made by a large dog.

The Ministry of Agriculture, Fisheries and Food came to the conclusion that a large animal was operating in the Chiddingfold-Alford-Kindford-Loxford area. A deer was found dead in October 1966 at Alford village, and a dead sheep had been found at Loxford the week before. The Ministry spokesman would only say that there was 'something biggish in the area'. The Ministry could not find any definite evidence as to what had killed either animal, as they had arrived rather late in the day. They noted that both animals had been torn about by something powerful. I feel that the beast concerned was either a large cat or large dog, or maybe a fox or badger.

Two to three weeks later, Dr Maurice Burton published an article in the November issue of *Wildlife and Countryside* which denied that the 'Surrey Puma' existed. He wrote:

> *'Altogether, in the course of these two years, about 400 people have been reported in the press as having seen it, but have not reported it. This is, perhaps, the most remarkable feature of the whole story - that a large animal, so secretive in its native land, should have shown itself on average at least once a day for two years... Not once has an animal been found killed in typical puma fashion, for this large cat pounces on its prey, breaks its neck and then bites into the throat... What we are up against here, and this is what misled the zoo scientists, is that some breeds of dog can leave tracks that are totally un-doglike. Certainly it is something of which I was formerly ignorant.'*

He also pointed out that the kills were probably caused by dogs, that deep scratches were caused by livestock getting entangled in barbed wire. I know of at least two cases where a horse has panicked near a barbed wire fence and come off with some deep scratches, which could easily look like sharp claw marks. Some of the sheep and deer could have died naturally, and before long foxes, badgers, cats, dogs and other predators could have eaten from them.

The paw-prints, to which Dr Burton refers, are those that were found at Stileman's Racing Stables, Munstfed. They were very large and cat-like - even larger than a normal puma's pads. It would seem that a bloodhound made the prints, and that it was kennelled near-by. Bloodhound's forepaws have their claws clipped off sometimes for dog shows, which would explain why the paw-prints showed no claw-marks.

Dr Burton then comes on to the actual sightings, which he explains away as fleeting glimpses of feral and domestic cats, foxes, dogs, deer, mink, badgers and even otters. He also notes that there is a feral cat around Farnham that was seen in August 1964, and stated that it was a pest control officer who said the sightings were of a puma-like beast. He seemed to think that this was the cause of the puma scare. However, Dr Burton was unaware at this time that there had been some escapees from Chessington Zoo, some years previously. The editor of the magazine *Wildlife and the Countryside*, of which Mr Burton was a founding editor, stated:

> *'There would seem to be little doubt that the London Zoo and the Surrey police who have relied on the Zoo, have been quite wrong in believing that a puma is roaming the heaths around London.'*

In the summer of 1966, at Hurtwood Common, Dr Burton had also found paw-prints which were 5 inches across and sometimes showed claw marks, and sometimes none. He found out later that a local bloodhound made them. Dr Burton was prepared to appear on a BBC Home Service broadcast, at an invitation. Appearing on the same broadcast was Mr Michael Dowse, the leader of the puma safaris. The Ministry of Agriculture, Fisheries and Food were not allowed to give any more opinions on the puma kills they had reported to them. We shall deal shortly with my inquiries at the Ministry. The BBC broadcast was at 4.45 on a Sunday afternoon in November 1966.

On 25th November 1966, the *Advertiser* published an article called 'Dr Burton's Last Word on Pumas'. He wrote a letter to the paper, which it is necessary to quote in full, as it shows what could have caused some of the puma sightings:

> *'The assertion by your reporter in last Saturday's issue, that I am trying to prove that those who claimed to have seen the puma are using vivid imaginations, is quite untrue, and he knows it as well as I do. With a few notable exceptions, their descriptions are clear enough to hazard a reasonable guess at what they saw, the more so once solid information is available as a standard. This information has increased markedly in the last few weeks, so that a clear pattern is now emerging.*
>
> *In the Farnham area, especially to the west of the town, reports indicate the presence of a large feral cat, ginger or sandy in colour, perhaps 3 ft. overall, possibly 15 to 18 inches at the shoulder, and 25 to 30 lbs. weight. Feral cats of these proportions are by no means unknown, and such a cat would, in fact, be little inferior to a small puma. There are indications that this, or one or more feral cats like it range widely over what could be called the 'puma area'.*
>
> *Secondly, to the east of Farnham, in the Hog's Back area, but almost certainly ranging much further afield at times, has been a feral dog, 4 ft. overall and 20 inches at the shoulder; a sandy-coloured greyhound cross with stripes and spots running down the sides of the body and down the legs. An injury to the front left pa had given it a bouncing run. Being completely wild, it had run away readily from people at great speed, with its small head held low. It also has been known to range widely, well away from the Hog's Back.*

Thirdly, another feral dog is known to have been in the Hurtwood area. It is sandy, long in the body, 4 ft overall, 18 to 20 inches at the shoulder, and is a cross (probably) which runs very like a hyena, is shy of people and readily makes off.

In carriage, gait and general behaviour and appearance, domestic cats, and more especially dogs, that have truly reverted to the wild, particularly those born in the wild, will tend to look unlike their wholly congeners, and, as a consequence, can be very deceptive.

Once we have these three animals in mind, it is possible to go back over the sightings of an alleged puma for the past two years, pick out the peculiarities in these three animals, and trace their wanderings with a fair degree of confidence. More important, all three are of much the same size and colour, and all three could be highly deceptive seen at night or at a distance, or even for a few brief moments at close range in daylight. I am assuming in this that the sighting of foxes and the occasional otter, as well as a variety of household cats and dogs seen fleetingly, are being ignored for a moment, leaving these three particular animals as the backbone of the story.

'We also have to eliminate the paw marks from Munatead because, in spite of your reporter's attempt to prove me wrong on this, they bear no resemblance to a puma's paw marks. At Ockham in Surrey, in the fourteenth century, lived a famous scholar, William of Ockham (or Occam). He enunciated a principle which has since become known as Occam's Razor. Expressed simply, this is that of two or more conflicting theories, choose the simpler, as it is the more likely to be right. Our two theories in Surrey of the twentieth century are:

1) that there is a puma in our midst that mysteriously leaves no identifiable traces of its activities

2) that there are a feral cat and two feral dogs, each sandy, and of the general proportions of a small puma. The first is a phantom; the second are all three of solid flesh, and there are photos and a film to prove this.

So if we apply Ockham's Razor, the second theory is by far the more plausible, especially as the use of the word 'puma' was based upon a guess, followed by a misidentification. There have been thousands of feral cats and feral dogs in our countryside from the days of Howel the Good, a thousand years ago, until at least the days of Cobbett in the early nineteenth century. Again and again these have given rise to mystery stories - until shot. Even during the last two years there have been a score of feral dogs and cats that have been mistaken for pumas, lionesses, cheetahs and panthers, in the English countryside - again, until shot, or run over by a car.

Having finally made up my mind on the identity of the 'puma', I propose now to drop the subject - no doubt to the relief of many, until somebody proves me wrong.'

BIG CATS: LOOSE IN BRITAIN

The editor of the *Surrey Advertiser* said that the London Zoo had not withdrawn its original identification of the 1964 Munstead prints.

It was not until the 25th August 1967 that the *Advertiser* produced another story on the puma. This time it was Mrs. G. M. Keys of Wood Street, near Guildford, who observed the puma at a distance of 30 yards. She was in her back garden with her husband, at 7 o'clock one evening. She remarked: *"It moved very slowly and I saw it for about five minutes, and then went in to 'phone the police, while* my husband stayed and watched it."

The beast was a member of the cat family, over 2 feet tall, and was certainly not a dog. Mrs. Keys had seen a puma at London Zoo, and prior to her sighting had thought it did not exist locally. She was now convinced of its existence.

On 8th September 1967 the *Surrey Advertiser* published a second story, headed:

'The puma: three sightings and now a recording.'

Mrs G. Haytor, the landlady of the 'Good Intent' public house, Puttenham, in Surrey, came across a puma which was long and thin, with a long, thin tail, 'tiny, squat ears', a squat face, and a ginger coat which was much darker than a Labrador's coat. The animal was not a fox. She had always believed in the puma, as so many people had seen it, and no doubt she had heard about sightings. She described the encounter to a reporter:

I was out walking with my poodle on Puttenham Common. It was just after 11 a.m. when suddenly an animal I have never seen before slipped across the path, about six feet in front of me, and into the undergrowth. It did not appear to see me. I stood flabbergasted. I was slightly concerned about my little dog and turned round to see where he was. When I turned back the animal had gone. It did not disturb me at all. It was all so peaceful and it all happened so quickly."

Police searched the area with no result, not surprisingly, although this sounds like an authentic puma sighting, and it was confirmed by another sighting. A Mr Mervyn Jones of Guildford told the police that he came upon a strange beast in Woodside road at 1.45 a.m. It was the size of an Alsatian, ginger, with a tail as long as its body. The beast jumped over a fence and disappeared into the wood. A police search found no sign of the animal, which he thought was the puma, beyond a doubt.

However, a short time later there were other reports further away but before looking at these, we must see what else was in the Guildford area at this time.

Mrs E. M. Langford who lived near Guildford, sighted an animal the day prior to Mr Jones's sighting of a puma. She was walking her dogs along Broad Street at about 12.00 on Sunday night (an hour and a quarter before Mr Jones's sighting) when she observed a large animal coming out of the grass, some 8 feet ahead of her. It was moving gracefully, which made her feel it was a member of the cat family, but not a puma. She told an *Advertiser* reporter about the sighting:

'I had just reached the end of the cottages when my dogs seemed to be on the alert. I heard a swishing in the long grass on the other side of the road, as though something was passing through. I stood still and my collie, who can be very aggressive with strange dogs, laid on his stomach and kept very still and quiet. My crossbred dog, who is very friendly with all dogs, was growling and snarling. A few minutes after arriving home I heard a noise outside, like a baby crying, or a cat fighting. It was a different cry from the rather blood-curdling scream of the vixen fox, which we often hear at night. About 18 months previously my daughter and I saw a large black animal under a bush on the common here, and our dogs appeared frightened then. We took them home and went back with a torch, but the animal was gone. We found a large impression in the bracken, and I wonder whether it is the same animal.'

'18 months previously' suggests that the first sighting was in about 1965. The 'black animal' could have been the normal brownish puma, or it could have been the black big cat that was normally seen on the Surrey/Sussex borders during the 1960s. Chris Hall notes sightings of a black puma. More recently, around Camberley, there have been sightings of a black leopard or panther. I doubt whether this is the same animal, however.

Mr Philip Enticknap of Park Barn, observed the puma and heard its cries. He set up a tape recorder, and shortly before Mrs. Longford had her sighting, he recorded an unusual or strange noise. Experts were listening to the tape to see whether it belonged to a puma.

Mrs C. H. Sharp of Albury, stated that her husband was out late at night milking cows. These would normally have been brought in at 9 o'clock, but this time he brought them in at about ten, and his tractor lights were on. Could this have accounted for any strange noises? The other day I heard a cow bellowing through the fog, and what a strange noise it made. Pigs scream as well, which could have also accounted for some of the screams.

August 26th 1967 was the date of another article on the `Surrey Pumas`, in the *Surrey Advertiser.* It was entitled:

> *'Puma is a dead duck'.*
>
> *Col. Marcus Lipton, M.P. for Brixton Division, decided not to ask the Home Secretary if he could organise a capture plan for the puma. He decided this because a recent sighting at Kenley, in Surrey, had turned out to be a large ginger tom-cat. Col. Lipton stated: "This puma business is beginning to look like another Loch Ness Monster. Two witnesses saw it here on Monday. I did not see it, and in view of this Kenley incident I don't propose to take any action unless there is any further evidence to warrant it. As far as I am concerned, for the time being the puma is a dead duck."*

Mr Donald Neal, of Caterham near Kenley, reported seeing an animal the size of an Alsatian one afternoon in late August 1967. He thought it was cat-like, with a long, thin tail and a sandy-coloured coat. The beast went off into an air-raid shelter in a corner of the field where the sighting had taken place. A search was mounted the next day, but the police discovered a large tomcat in the area. They also mounted another search two days after the sighting.

Several days before the *Surrey Advertiser's* article was published, Mr G. Bone, a farm manger of Sunningdale, heard an animal's screams and saw a shiny-black animal, 2 foot high and 4 foot long, moving into some woods at a distance that was described as being 'out of range'. It was in a field on the land Mr Bone managed.

Mr Chilcott of Bognor Regis, was riding his motor-cycle south of Chiddingfold on the night of 17th August 1967. He told Godalming police that a wolf-like animal, 3 feet 6 inches high, was at the grass verge. The beast apparently had 'matted and dirty' long brown hair. A police constable searched the area with no result. This large animal had been seen 25 yards ahead of the speed restriction sign, and it could have been the puma, or a mongrel dog. This was the last sighting that the police ever recorded in their 'puma book'.

The next *Surrey Advertiser* article did not appear until the 8th November 1968, and was suitably called:

'Is the Puma back?'

Early in November 1968, Mr and Mrs. Anthony Kemp of Farnborough had a sighting of the puma. Mr Kemp gave the following description:

'I was walking the dog in the recreation ground opposite to my house when I saw the animal about 50 yards away, near to the main gate of the park. It loped along the edge of the grounds and went out of the gate near to my house. It was travelling at about 10-15 miles an hour, and was about four to five feet long. 'It was sandy-coloured, with a pug face and a long, cat-like tail. It was definitely not a fox or a large cat. I went straight back to my house. As I thought, it had crossed the road nearby.' 'Mrs Kemp also observed the beast, from within the house, and she gave the following description of what happened:

'I was standing by the kitchen window when I was startled to see a large animal run down the path and disappear over the railway line towards Mychett. It was at least four feet long, light brown, with a long tail and pug face. I was a bit frightened, as I knew it was not just a fox or a big cat. Shortly after I had seen it, my husband came in and told me his story, and our descriptions tallied exactly. I was very glad that my baby was inside, or I dread to think what might have happened.'

At one side of their garden path the Kemps found definite pad marks made by a large or heavy animal. They were 2 inches across and 2 inches deep, with each paw print being 2 feet apart (a stride of 2 feet). Each mark was 4 inches away from the other mark. The police from Farnborough searched the area, but nobody else had seen the animal, which had been going from Farnborough Abbey farm to the dense woods of Mychett. The police questioned householders, searched the area and discovered that the park had been empty, apart from Mr Kemp.

That was the last that the *Surrey Advertiser* published on the puma, which may have been shot. In 1968 or 1969 a puma was rumoured to have been killed on farmland by an angry farmer with an unlicensed gun. It was said that he buried the animal and kept silent. Graham J. McEwan noted this at the end of his `Surrey Puma` Section for the 1960s, in his 1986 book *Mystery Animals of Britain and Ireland.*

We will now look at various articles that have come my way, and which give details of sightings, normally without a definite date.

Firstly, I turn to the Ministry of Agriculture, Fisheries and Foods. On 6th January 1988 I was told the following by Mr Malcolm Webb of the Central Publications Units, Publicity Branch, at that Ministry, in Chessington, Surrey:

> *'I don't think the Ministry can do much to help you officially, but I've sent your letter to the editor of our internal staff bulletin in the hope that they may publish it. MAFF staff get out and about all over England and Wales, and are in an ideal position to hear of sightings. You may get some interesting feed-hacks., However, the editor of the bulletin is in a different department of the Ministry, so I'm afraid I can't agree that she'll publish your letter.'*

> Two days later Miss H.M. Hoad of the Press Branch of the MAFF in London, wrote to me. She was probably the lady editor mentioned in the above statement, and she did some research for me, but with no results. Although these two pieces of information are of little use, it does at least show that Government bodies are aware of the cats. I must thank the above two officials for so kindly writing to me regarding my quest.

In his article for the *Unexplained* magazine, Part 2, on the `Surrey Puma`, Mike Goss examined the evidence for this cat. He entitled the article 'Enter the Surrey Puma' and quoted the *London Life* reporter, Mr Michael Vestey:

'Is there really a puma roaming wild and free in the green pastures of Surrey, 30 miles from Piccadilly Circus?'

The answer was of course 'Yes', but as Mike Goss shows, the media played a strong part in keeping the puma saga alive. He notes that of the 362 sightings in the Godalming police book, only 42 could be considered real evidence. A police Chief Inspector, Ronald Noade, was quoted as saying to Michael Vestey:

> *'A lot of ordinary, decent and respectable people have said they saw the puma. Why should they say so, if they didn't? They are mostly the sort of person who wouldn't dream of inventing such a story.'*

He also referred to a sighting mentioned in Dr Maurice Burton's article in the November 1965 issue of *Animals.* On 17th August 1964, at 3.30 a.m. a milkman was driving near Crondall in Hampshire when he ran over a 'strange cat-like animal'. The milkman's minivan bumper was bent, and he observed the cat bound over the hedge. Dr Burton stated that a puma, even a small one, could not get under the 5 inches clearance of a van. He thought a fox or cat could have done this and survived. Some chickens were killed at a nearby henhouse and wrongly blamed on the puma. A fox was shot later, in the act of taking hens from the same henhouse near Crondall. These two events led on to the 1964 'Crondall Cougar' hunt, which resulted in a full-scale search, as previously mentioned. He ended his article in *Animals* magazine by saying: *"There is no doubt in my mind, after sifting all the evidence, that the so-called `Surrey Puma` is no more than a large, feral tomcat."*

Dr Burton also drew upon the *Herts and Bucks Gazette* article of 6th September 1962, which said that the Ernest Jellet sighting near Farnham, was of a large ginger tomcat. As it is, the next article that came my way stated that a large ginger tomcat was shot dead in 1967 at Botley, in Hampshire. This article was in the *Sunday Telegraph* Colour Supplement of 1967, and contains a fair amount of information on the puma. The author was Duff Hart-Davis, who reported on the puma as long ago as 1964, when he wrote an article for the *Daily Telegraph*.

This article was called *'After three years, Surrey is still... hunting the puma'.* The first witness to be interviewed was Mr Harry Walker, of North Chapel near Godalming. He encountered the puma in broad daylight, and said:

> *'I went out of the house about nine o'clock in the morning, like I always do, to make sure the cattle were all right. I looked down across the fields and then I saw this animal coming up the hedge. Ambling along, he was, nice and easy, like a ruddy great cat. A loose kind of walk - no hurry at all. Brown, he was darkish. About 2 feet 6 inches high at the shoulder, with a small head and a long, thick tail. When he got to the corner he went three times round in a circle, like a dog, and lay down in the sun. So I nipped indoors for the gun - I'd been keeping a couple of buckshot cartridges handy on the mantelpiece, and started to stalk him. But when I was about 80 yards off he got up and padded away into the wood - still in no hurry, mind you...'*

The reporter, Mr Duff Hart-Davis, interviewed this farmer and was convinced that this was an authentic sighting. I am inclined to agree with him. The reports were thought to come from an area bordered by Farnham, Petworth, Horsham and Godalming. He contradicted Dr Maurice Burton by saying that the 1964 Munstead paw-prints were very like those of Sabre, the senior puma at London Zoo. Mr Duff Hart-Davis thought it commuted between a large patch of woods near Waigrave in Berkshire and Surrey. He said that a puma was seen there on Easter Monday in 1966 and that in the autumn of 1966 it was seen there again.

The 'huge, reddish-brown tom-cat' shot at Botley in Hampshire in February 1967, was labelled the puma almost at once. The cat could not have made the Munstead prints and was not the same size and weight as the puma. This cat was large, no doubt, and was an estimated three feet long (including the tail, I presume). Mr Duff Hart-Davis gave his view that the puma lived in 4,000 acres of Hurtwood Common, basing itself from Whitefold estate, near Cranleigh. A company of which Prince Carol of Rumania was a director owned the estate.

The estate was wild then, with chestnuts and rhododendron, and would have been an ideal place for a puma to hide. The puma was considered to be between 23 inches high at the shoulders, five foot long and weighing about 120 lbs. Mr Hart-Davis thought it was a female, on account of its size. He thought the puma did not like sheep and was consuming roe-deer and rabbits, as well as other creatures. He was of the opinion that somebody had released it from a private menagerie, or that it had escaped from a wildlife park. He noted that you could buy a puma from a dealer for £120 in 1967, and that you did not need a licence. One policeman who was very tired of puma searches not paying off, said: *"You'd need a flaming army to winkle it out of that lot."*

Anaesthetic guns have a range of only about 35 yards. He believed that the puma would live on well into the 1970s, as the one at London Zoo was 14 years old and still going strong.

Victor Head's article in *The Field* for 8th April 1965, entitled 'Trailing the Surrey Puma', notes eight sightings and also draw upon the police's view of the whole affair. Superintendent Hagley was quoted as saying:

> *'The trouble is that we are often told hours after the animal has gone. To search these vast acres of woodland is worse than seeking a needle in a haystack. Our best chance of cornering the beast lies in prompt reports so we can get on its trail without delay.'*

Superintendent Hagley did not forget the possibility that the puma could be a young lioness, and he mentioned this to Mr Head. A London Zoo spokesman remarked at one point of the saga, in 1965: *"We are 99% certain that the creature is a puma."* Victor Head worked out that a puma would have to kill 84. roe deer a year to survive in Surrey, as in South America pumas lived on mule deer, which weighed 300 lbs. A mule deer is five times as heavy as a roe deer, so a puma would have to kill the equivalent of one mule deer, or five roe deer a week, to survive comfortably. Mr Head notes that farmers were warned to keep as much stock in as possible, because of the puma scare. He quoted Young and Goldman's book *The Puma*, as saying that the puma likes venison so much that it must be controlled.

The authors of this book made it known that this factor:

> *'... makes it essential that this large cat can be given full consideration in any management plans for areas where it occurs on a deer range... Pumas undoubtedly serve as a check on undue increases of deer, which... during the past quarter of a century have resulted in overpopulation, far beyond the available food supply.'*

An introduced puma population for deer control brought with it one problem: Pumas are reputed sometimes to attack man. The puma was never caught alive (as far as we know), and it seems possible that there is now an established puma population in Surrey, as the sightings of the 1970s suggest.

We now turn our attention to Mary Chipperfield's records of escaped animals, and I quote the following passage from her 1972 book *Lion country* with permission of the publishers:

> *'As I mentioned, we keep a book listing 'Incidents', which involve wild animals, and which are reported to us by the police or other authorities, just in case we are blamed for any of them; and here is a random selection from the many the book held, by this time covering a period from two to three years:*

Lioness reported seen several times in Epping Forest, but never found; a cheetah or leopard often observed in south-east London and north Kent, and hunted without success; a 'ferocious' animal with snapping jaws seen but never located in Glouces-ter... a dangerous monkey was caught after trying to savage several people in Biggin Hill... a tiger was hunted by police in Norfolk but never found... wolves in several places were shot and killed.., a puma kept appearing and disappearing in Hampshire, Sussex and Surrey... a tiger was chased by police at Lyndhurst, Hampshire (not one of 'ours', although in our general area), but got away, never to be seen again! Lion tracks were reported and confirmed near Wigan, but the lion that made them was never seen and never found.'

Mrs Chipperfield was one of the many people who spoke about changes in the law, and no doubt her books *Lions on the Lawn* and *Lion Country* led to the 1976 Dangerous Animals act being passed. Now we will look at puma sightings for the 1970s.

- ## Pumas - 1970s Onwards

The first recorded sighting of 1970 occurred in late January. Mrs. Freda Siggers was walking her dog, with a neighbour, on Ash ranges, early in the morning. They observed a strange animal at a distance of 20 yards, and Mrs. Siggers described what happened:

'My dog suddenly stopped and growled, so we turned back. Then we heard a terrify-ing screeching, like a baby screaming. It wasn't a bird; it was such a piercing screech. We turned to make for home. I looked back and saw the puma crossing the path into some bushes only 20 yards away. It turned towards me. It was a brown mottled col-our and was bigger than a Labrador dog, and had a long tail. Its gait was definitely cat-like. It was quite light at the time, and I am quite sure of what I saw. It was not a dog and it was not a fox. I saw the `Surrey Puma`. I have heard of the `Surrey Puma` before but I never believed it existed. Now I know.'

She was so worried about the puma that she banned her nine-year-old daughter Sharon from going on the ranges. Mrs. Siggers's sighting was recorded in the *Aldershot News* of 27th January. Her neighbour, Mrs. White, said:

'I didn't see anything at all. I only heard the noise. It was a howl and a screech com-bined. When I looked round the animal had gone.'

An Aldershot police spokesman told the local paper: *"No special action has been taken following this re-port and there have been no further sightings."*

Mrs Siggers confirmed her sighting for me, in a letter of August 1987, from her home in Ash Vale. She simply quoted the *Aldershot News* article and the above details and quotations came from this article. The *Aldershot News* reported on 10th February 1970, that Mr Bill Richards of the Ash Vale Country Club, had shot a fox which he thought might have been mistaken for the puma. It had been raiding poultry houses around Ash Vale for five years. Mr Richards had opened the door.., and after ten minutes somebody rushed in, saying: *"There's a fox outside!"*

He ran out and saw that his 18 chickens were about to have a close encounter of the vulpine kind. Mr Richards borrowed a shotgun from a neighbour and shot the fox dead. He said later:

> *"It was unusual to see a fox out in broad daylight, especially in a built up area such as we are in. The club is not far from where a woman thought she saw the 'Surrey Puma' recently. I think it could very well have been this fox that she and other people have mistaken for a puma. It's an easy enough mistake for anyone to make, seeing a large animal looming up."*

So was this fox the cause of the puma scare?

No, the puma appeared again, on about the 30th April 1971, and the incident was recorded in the *Camberley News* for 4th May. Mrs. Shirley Winning of camberley in Surrey, was at her job in the Road Research Laboratory, Crowthorne, when she looked out of the window. She observed a large, black, unidentified beast, much larger than the biggest dog. She reported the incident to a reporter:

> *"I was working one evening last week. I looked out of the window and saw this huge animal. It was about 500 yards away, and was standing near some thick woodland. It was just walking along, and walked just like a huge cat. It was massive, and it reminded me of the way a lion or tiger walks. Then I remembered that, a few years ago, there were reports that there was a puma on the loose in the Bagshot or Camberley area. I know I was not imagining things, because two friends were working with me at the time and they saw it too. If it is a puma it could be dangerous."*

A spokesman at the Laboratory carefully noted: *"I haven't heard anything about a wild animal wandering about."* Mrs. Winning thought that it was far too large for a cat, and she questioned: *"Could it be a puma?"* Remember that pumas are not black. Could this beast have been a panther, such as that seen in April 1987, near Sandhurst, Camberley? Maybe this is what it was. We should remember that a black beast, sometimes called the 'Surrey Puma was seen hanging around the Surrey/Sussex border in the 1960s. The above sighting fits in very nicely for later reports, in 1979.

Another definite big cat sighting came later. On 28th May 1971, an article appeared in the *Farnborough News*, entitled: 'That puma's on the prowl again'. Miss Gale Harvey of Farnborough in Hampshire, saw the puma rush past her window. The encounter was described by her in such detail that I can do no better than quote what she said:

> *"I was indoors doing some ironing when I heard a deep roaring noise outside. I looked out of the window and saw the puma, which appeared just to have leapt from a tree. It ran past the house and chased after a white terrier dog, then disappeared in some waste land across the road. When I went outside to look there were great footprints on the garden path. It had dug up a piece of turf where it landed. The footprints are the same size as others my father has been finding at the bottom of the garden for about a month.*

Its face was cat-like and ugly, its body was a brownish-grey colour and it had a big tail. I've never seen a puma before, but this thing was certainly terrifying. I have never seen anything like it before in my life."

The paw-prints were 3 inches wide by 4 inches long. They were made by a very large animal. The police station at Farnborough just said:

"We have been informed and have investigated the incident, but we are unable to say what the animal definitely was."

4th June 1971 saw another published report of the puma, also in the *Farnborough News.* The article was called: *'Enter the `Surrey Puma` - on the R.A.F. airfield.'* Mr John Bonner, a bricklayer of Aldershot, was working in an isolated part of the Royal Aircraft Establishment, Farnborough. The puma came out from behind some empty boxes and crates.

Mrs Bonner told the News about the encounter:

"He was working near a fence and the boxes were on the other side. The puma came out from behind them and chased after a bird. It then went back behind the crates. He told me it looked a grey mottled colour, was the size of an average dog and had a long tail. It may have been living off the rabbits and birds on the quiet outskirts of the airfield."

The paper took the precaution of getting a Windsor Safari Park spokesman to give his view:

'It is possible for a puma to live in our climate. They can live for 15 to 25 years and will eat any warm meat such as rabbits, foxes, birds. I would not think it likely that a puma would attack a human. It is more likely just to stalk or walk away and watch.'

On 11th June the *Farnborough News* published an article called: *'It's here again - that puma... '* Mrs. Heather Barber of Farnborough was cycling home along a wooded footpath half a mile from the Queensmead Shopping Centre, when she encountered the puma. Later, she said:

'It was about the size of an Alsatian dog but it had a long tail - about 3 feet long - and large paws.It just ambled across about three or four feet in front of me. I never believed it existed until I saw it. I went home and looked in an encyclopaedia to find out what it was. I never gave it another thought until Monday, when my husband and I went to see whether it had left any footprints. We could not find any.'

The article also said that the puma had been seen at the Royal Aircraft Establishment, and three times around Canterbury Road, Farnborough. On 25th July 1971 an article was printed in the Aldershot News which said that the puma had been seen on common land, next to a fishing pond, off the A30, at Blackwater in Surrey. Trainee welder Christopher Papworth, of Mytchett, was fishing at the time. He gave a clear description of his brief sighting:

'It was about 4.15 p.m. I had just looked at a picnic table and things on a sort of ridge when something caught my eye. I looked up and saw what looked like a large cat. It was about four feet long and stood about two feet off the ground and had a long tail.'

The beast was *'a dirty mustard colour'* and was definitely not a fox, dog or normal domestic cat. The beast was seen to run for twenty yards and disappear into some undergrowth. A fellow fisherman helped Christopher to search the area, and they found some *'pad-like animal tracks'* in some clay at the base of a clump of saplings.

The youth told his father that he had seen the puma, and his father telephoned the police. They were from Yately police station and they made a search of the area, with a negative result. His workmates at the welding college teased Christopher by saying that he had seen the pink panther!

But 27th August 1971 was when Mr Middlemiss of Fleet, who was later to become a witness, told a Fleet News reporter that the puma had been seen 200 years before. He referred them to the entry in William Cobbett's book *'Rural Rides'*, suggesting it was similar to the modern puma sightings. The headline ran:

'It's ye olde `Surrey Puma`!'

We now move to 1972 and the sighting of Mrs. Edna Hughes, of which I have both a letter and an article in the local paper. She was looking out of her house in Bagshot, Surrey, early one morning, when she saw a strange creature around 100 yards away. She told the *Bagshot News* of 23rd June:

'It walked slowly up and down, staring at me. I wish I knew what it was. It was not a dog, and it was too large to be an ordinary cat, and its face was much too flat. It was white, and about 3 feet high when it sat up.'

The paper commented that the puma stories had been going on for years. I wrote to Mrs. Hughes, who sent me a most interesting letter, from which I quote here. It was dated 12th February 1987:

'It was good to hear that somebody did believe in my sighting. The animal that I saw was large and grey in colour. I couldn't make out what it was. I was told later that it could have been a puma. I was in my kitchen by the window when I saw it, on some waste but private land a few yards away. It was staring at me. After a while, I ran up-stairs to my bedroom to get a better look. It was sitting quite still, and still looking to-ward the house. After a while it stood up, walked to one side of the dismantled shed it was on, turned, walked to the other side and jumped down. It was then lost from my view in the bushes etc. When it walked, it had that "roll" that this kind of animal has.

'It took a while for me to run outside to the phone box, as I was a little scared. I rang the police and asked if an animal had escaped from anywhere. The answer was "No". After my sighting was reported in the Camberley News *I was teased by people who know me. I didn't really mind, as I know what I saw. I was annoyed with myself af-terwards for not taking a photo, as I had a film in my camera, that I kept in my bed-*

room.'

I am sure that this is a true and genuine sighting, although I am puzzled that the beast was described in the paper as being 'white', and in the letter as being 'grey'. Pumas are not white, but in certain lights their coat looks light in colour.

In late 1972 a number of sightings occurred at Fleet. Most of them were around Fleet railway station, On 23rd March 1987 I had a letter from Mr G. Daniels, the Area Manager of British Rail, Salisbury. He told me that on 16th March 1987 he had received a letter from me, adding: *"I regret to say that we have no record of a sighting of the `Surrey Puma` around the station, but I wish you luck with your investigations."*

It seems as though the main source for these sightings will have to be the *Fleet News* of September and October 1972.

This paper published a most curious article titled *'Mystery Animal that ran at 40 m.p.h.'* On 5th September 1972, two coach drivers were answering an emergency call to help a coach in trouble at Hartley Wintney. It was as they returned to their home town of Fleet that they encountered the beast, which ran for 150 yards at 48 miles per hour, and then turned left, leaping over a high bank. This sighting was at Elvetham Hall, on the road. The animal leapt into a field near the Hall. The men watched it leaping the bank and bounding along. The Fleet or Hartley Wintney police said that nothing had gone missing from zoos or private collections. Mr Frank Kendell of Fleet made the following statement to the *Fleet News*:

> *'We were passing a house which stands by itself on the right when this thing came out of the garden and into the road in front of us. We were going about 40 miles per hour, and it ran in the road in front of us. We could see it in the headlights. It was not a fox. It had a long curving tail that bent upwards at the tip. It was about six feet long from head to tail, and about two feet six inches tall, and it had dark stripes running round its body, which was a dark brown colour. It had a cat-like head, and it bounded along. It was far too big for a domestic animal. The bank it leapt was about four feet high.*
>
> *It was an extraordinary thing. We could not see what it was, but I have never seen anything like it before. It was a big animal, and if we had hit it, it would have smashed the front of the car.'*

The other witness was Mr Brian Druett of Fleet, in Hampshire. But returning to the Fleet puma scare of late 1972, on 8th September, the *Fleet News* produced another report about the puma. Mrs. Judith Parvin of Fleet reported that the cat walked past the family's house at around 7 o'clock in the morning. It was about two feet high, and did not seem to be an ordinary dog, cat or fox. The beast moved down the road, where it vanished into a garden. Mrs. Parvin said, of where it had gone: *"It could get through the gardens into the woods behind. You can get through to Fleet Pond that way without going very near any houses."* The beast had a long, downward-curving tail. Mr Parvin, his wife and their little daughter all observed the beast. Mrs. Parvin gave an account of what happened:

> *"It was quite fascinating, watching this creature. We were all gaping at the window*

before someone said, 'Quick! Grab the camera!' but it had gone too far down the street by then. I know it was not a fox, because we see so many of them around here. It was more like a cat than anything, and it was fairly heavily-built and had large, padding feet."

Even though they have a camera with them, most people forget about it while the big cat is in view.

Mrs Parvin stated that the animal was brown, and not brown with stripes, as in the previous sighting by the coach drivers, a week earlier. The animal was identical otherwise, it would seem.

On 15th September 1972, the *Fleet News* carried its third item on the puma-like beast. Six railway travellers observed a feline creature at 5 o'clock on a Monday morning at Fleet station, Mr Dennis Long of Fleet recounted the sighting:

> *"We were at the back of the train, and as the train went out we looked across the lines to the up-platform, and saw it behind the railings. The remarkable thing is that the train did not frighten it. Several of us went over the footbridge with a railway man, and it dodged over a fence and made off'.*

Mr Long reckoned that the beast was lighter in weight and more like a lynx than a puma. Then, after consulting a reference book, he decided it was a puma. He told the press; *"It was very much like a big cat. It had a black head and a brown body, with grey markings.'*

The Stationmaster of Fleet Station, Mr Victor Carr, was also a witness.

> *'It had a black head with pointed ears, a brown body with a touch of grey on the underside, and a very long, thin tail. It was sitting on the grass and I saw it get up and slink away through the long grass. Then I saw it shooting through the copse on the other side of a fence. It looked like a lynx you see at the Zoo. There is a lot of undergrowth.'*

It is interesting to note that the area around Fleet station is overgrown - a wild place where a large cat would have found plenty of food. Another sighting reported in the same article was that by news reporter's wife, Mrs. Joan Deverill.

> *'It went in and out between the cars, carrying a fish in its mouth. It threw back its head and tossed the fish up, made a purring noise and caught it, and went on out of sight.'*

Mrs Deverill stayed in the car, obviously fearful that the beast was still around. Her husband was watching the area where the cat had been seen before, while the sighting took place.

The 22nd September 1972 brought news of the large cat once again. This time, Mr Hopson of Fleet observed a large cat-like beast. He photographed the cat as it ran into some undergrowth one evening when he had his first sighting. Then another evening he photographed the feline. Mr Hopson and a news reporter discussed the photo and came to the conclusion that the cat was a large feral Siamese. However, not everyone agreed with the photographers, even though the *News* reporter's photograph of a Siamese cat compared reasonably with Mr Hopson's photograph. Mr Victor Carr, the railway man who saw the cat twice, changed his view that the cat was a puma, to a lynx, and then to a Siamese cat. He had had a second sighting.

Mr Brian Druett, one of the coach drivers who spotted the feline, gave the following opinion: *"The animal was eight times as big as a Siamese cat".* News reporter's wife, Mrs. Deverill, agreed with Mr Druett, and stated: *"The animal I saw was too big for a domestic cat."*

So it seems there could be two animals. One would have been a large Siamese feral cat, and the other would have been the normal puma. However, pumas are not striped. The big cat that was seen by the coach drivers was obviously not the same animal that Mr Hopon photographed. The animal around Fleet station seemed to keep to a rather localised territory. I have no doubt that the beast observed around Fleet station was not a puma. The colouring suggests a large feral ex-domestic Siamese cat. The big cat observed on the edge of Fleet was one of the pumas.

This was not the end of the Fleet puma scare. The next report came out on 6th October 1972, only a fortnight later, by which time the mystery was on a different level. The paper said that support for the theory that the beast being seen was a large Siamese cat came also from a farmer of over 30 years' experience, Mr William Stoddard, of Minley, near Fleet.

> *"1 think I inadvertently started the puma stories. A friend told me that some cattle at Ewshot or Crondall had been chased by an unknown animal, and when he described it to me, I said: "That sounds like a puma." It was probably a boxer dog. I know that white Persian cats were bred at the farm in 1926, but I have never heard of Siamese cats here.*
>
> *There are all kinds of wild animals about here, although people seldom see them. There are lots of foxes, badgers and deer."*

The farm was once called 'Cat Farm', and Mrs. Needham of Fleet told the *Fleet News* that she also thought that the beast was a large Siamese cat. She said that several years prior to the sighting (around 1970), she had seen a large, totally wild, Siamese cat at Fleet hospital. The cat was adopted by the staff, and she noticed it, while she was a patient there. Mrs. Needham also said:

> *'They used to breed cats at Cat Farm, and some of them got away and went wild. When they have been wild for some years, they grow bigger, because they feed on different things, such as birds, rats and mice. I honestly think that is the answer, and this is a Siamese cat. Some of them don't have an awful lot of black on them. They have a dark, creamy coat.'*

So was it a puma, a boxer dog, or a Siamese cat?

Cyclist Mr Charlie Christopher, of Farnborough, was another witness. He came upon the puma at Frimley

Bridges, while out cycling at 5 o'clock in the morning of a late March day in 1973, on the Farnborough road. A large animal ran across the road in front of him. It was 'the size of a large dog', he said:

> 'I saw that it had a large, flat head like a cat. I saw it clearly, as the road was well-lit, and it certainly did not have the pointed nose and features of a fox. I know what foxes look like, as I have seen several on my early morning rides. This was not a fox or a dog, otherwise I would not have taken notice of it. I did not hang about, I can tell you!... I have always had an open mind on the subject of this animal, and I cannot really imagine anyone making up stories saying they had seen it.
> Now I am a confirmed believer in the puma. The way it whipped across the dual carriageway and then turned round and stared at me really startled me.'

The light was not good enough for Mr Christopher to see the beast's colour. He pedalled past the puma, turned round after stopping, and watched it staring at him.

This sighting was recorded in the *Farnborough News* of 3rd April 1973.

The following 22nd June, thus some time after the previous sighting, at Farnborough also, the puma made another appearance. It was 4.20 a.m., according to the *Farnborough News* of the above date, and two Farnborough policemen were on duty in Queen Elizabeth Park. They observed an unusual animal from 20 yards away. It had pointed ears, a long tail, and appeared to be three times the size of a normal cat, and ran off into the undergrowth as the men approached.

The report also noted that the policemen were sure the beast was a puma, and a spokesman said they were used to making accurate observations. The police and Farnborough county council searched the Park, but the puma had vanished. A week later, on 29th June, the *Farnborough News* published an article which referred to the same sighting. It seemed that the reporter had managed to contact P.C. Anthony Thomas, one of the policemen who had observed the Puma. He had eight years' experience in the Force, and said:

> 'It was in the early hours of the morning, but the light was good. It stood about ten yards away from me. It was three or four times the size of a cat, with a long tail and pointed ears. It definitely was not a dog or a fox. But I'm not saying definitely it was a puma.
>
> There were other officers in the park with me, so I radioed for help. P.C. King came to my assistance, but he came up from behind the animal. As he came through the undergrowth the animal fled, but he did get a look at it. I never believed all the stories about the `Surrey Puma` before, but I certainly believe them now. There is an animal roaming around.'

P.C. Thomas also said the beast was the same size and colour as a puma, so we may presume it was a sandy or brownish colour. A search of the area found no paw-prints, as the ground was hard, firm and dry. The police chief of Farnborough, Chief Inspector Nevill stated:

*'I think we can now safely say that there is an animal around this area. We are satis-
fied it was not a dog or a fox. The important thing from a police point of view is that
it does not appear to be dangerous. It did not attack the two officers but ran away.
This at least suggests that it may not be a danger to the public.'*

The press also said that the puma had been 'seen' as far away as Southampton in 1973...
In July 1973, Mr Robert Rickard, then editor of *The News*, (which became *Fortean Times* in 1976), was preparing a paper for the International Fortean Organisation, on the 'Farnborough Puma'. He was to address
the Forteans at a meeting in America in August 1973. He spoke from his home in Birmingham to a reporter for the *Farnborough News*:

*'I am researching the mystery animal type of report for a paper to the Convention of
the International Fortean Organisation in America. This type of report has been regularly cropping up in the Sussex, Surrey and Hampshire border area for many years.
The animals have variously been described as pumas, lions, large dogs, a "bull seal"
and even in some cases a "large bird". Sometimes only tracks are seen; sometimes
livestock has been attacked. I know of two cases where police were called out to
search, but no animals were found or reported escaped.'*

He referred, particularly, to a case of New Year's Eve, 1971, when residents awoke to find tracks at Har-
bour's Close, Farnborough. He said: *"Residents saw a curious set of animal-like tracks in the snow in their
garden."* The *News* sent photocopies of this and other reports to Mr Rickard, who also wanted evidence of
the puma in the form of *'photos, sketches, measurements or descriptions of tracks'*. The article in the *Farnborough News* was dated 16th July 1973, and concluded with a reference to the sighting by PC Thomas
and PC King of the puma in Queen Elizabeth Park.

The next sighting was to cause a car crash and could have resulted in the deaths of a young couple. Mr
Dave Mason of Heatherside, and his fiancée, Miss Stone of Tottenham, were getting married the week after the incident. If we go by the report in the *Aldershot News* of 4th August 1973, Mr Mason and his fiancée had just got out of their car, in the evening, at Bisley ranges entrance. They were planning to go for a
walk, but were soon back in the car and driving off quickly. Mr Mason said:

*'I had just climbed the gate near the range when I spotted this animal sitting in the
bushes. It was about the size of a full-grown Alsatian dog, but it was sitting there like
a cat. It was dark-coloured and had pointed ears. I panicked. I drove off, not too fast,
but fast enough to get out of the area.'*

Mr Mason had noted that the beast was larger than a normal domestic cat, and he had heard of the
`Surrey Puma` stories. He had shouted to his fiancée to get back into the car. He was driving down Old
Bisley road when the car went into a skid, overturning. He kicked a door open and dragged Miss Stone
out. She was suffering from minor cuts and shock. The car was in a total mess, and the damage was estimated at £400.

*'The smell of petrol was everywhere and the engine was still running. The fire bri-
gade was called and they handled everything and hosed the petrol off the road... If I*

hadn't seen the beast I would not have driven off in such a hurry.'

The next sighting was reported in the *Farnborough News* of 24th October 1973. Mrs. Vera Barnard of Farnborough was walking her two dogs, Jodi and Max, in Queen Elizabeth Park, scene of the policemen's sightings. The dogs ran off, but when she blew her dog-whistle only Jodi reappeared. She became worried about Max, and sent Jodi off to find him. The dog went off into the bushes, and what happened next was recounted by Mrs. Barnard:

> *"I waited patiently for both of them to reappear. Then something slunk out of the bushes. I had a very good view. I think it was a huge ginger cat. It looked at me and appeared to be afraid of me. I got the impression that it had been woken up. It was definitely not a fox. It did not have the cunning of a fox. I have seen plenty of them.*
> *I could not see its tail as it slunk across the path beside me and went towards the Railway line. It was a bit bigger than Max (a Dachshund), not sleek, very rough, but not unkempt in appearance. The dogs did not know. I was curious but not frightened. It was only when the dogs reappeared and we were all back in the car that I began to think about the `Surrey Puma`.*
>
> *But my real concern is quite different. I wish I knew the danger to the dogs. I have been to the park again, but I have stayed at the top end, near the Farnborough road entrance.'*

This was the last pf these sightings from Farnborough itself. However, just after this sighting, on some soft earth and loose gravel at Mr Charles McCash's home in Fleet, a number of unusual animal tracks were found. Plaster casts were made of the prints and sent on to Farnham Museum by Mr McCash. The curator remarked: *'It is the first time anybody has done anything positive about this puma.'* He would not come to any conclusions about the prints, which he sent on to natural history experts, maybe at the Natural History Museum, London.

In his unpublished gazette of newspaper articles, Mr George Frampton, the folklorist of Tonbridge in Kent, records no sightings between October 1972 and August 1975.

On August 1st 1975, the *Farnborough News* published an article that referred not to sighting but to pawprints. The article was headlined: *'Mystery paw-prints found in the mud.'* Mrs. Valerie Thame of Farnborough was walking with her two children along the path next to Cove brook. The path backed onto the Royal Aircraft Establishment land. Mrs. Thaine described the giant paw-prints:

> *'They were far too big to have been made by a large dog. They have four pads, large claws, and are obviously made by a heavy animal because they were quite deep. They were inches apart and were one in front of the other in the same way a cat walks. My children were frightened by the size of these prints, and couldn't get home fast anough. I can only assume that they were made by something like this puma that people say they've seen.'*

All the evidence suggested that a puma lived in the vicinity of the R.A.E. and Queen Elizabeth Park. The paw-prints were measured by Mrs. Thame and her children on the Sunday. They were even photographed with the paw-prints. The mention of 'large claws' suggests that the prints were made by a large dog, such as a Great Dane, but you may recall that only cheetahs walk without retracted claws, unlike the rest of the cat family.

The year 1976 was also pretty good for puma-spotting. The 9th July *Fleet News* and *Aldershot News*, both carried articles entitled *'Night I saw the puma' - by reporter.'* Mrs. Sally Rose, a journalist at the Camberley News office, had a sighting of the puma. She was on her way back to her house in Wintney, Hampshire. She was on the A30 when a large cat-like animal ran across the road. It had large paws, a 3 feet long body and a sandy-beige coat. It had a smallish head, short hair and appeared to be around 2 feet 6 inches high, and a 2 feet 6 inches long tail. The beast was only 3 yards in front of her car and just loped across the road, to disappear into the forest on the other side. Of course, police searched the area, but no paw marks were found on account of the dry ground. She also gave an excellent account of her view as a witness to a fellow reporter:

> *'I'd swear on oath that I saw the puma, or a very large cat-like creature which wasn't like anything I'd ever seen before, and I hadn't been drinking. I was about 50 yards away when my lights picked up what I at first thought was a large dog. It came straight out of the bushes into the road and I stopped. I immediately realised it was no kind of dog, domestic cat or fox. I knew it could only be the `Surrey Puma`. I was sceptical about its existence before, like most people, but now I know the puma is real.'*

An expert at Chessington Zoo in Surrey made his contribution to the article by saying that pumas can live up to 16 years of age. He also remarked:

> *'Let's just say that if it is a puma, it must be getting very close to its maximum life-span, because these reports have been coming in for about 12 years.'*

Was he aware of reports going right back to 1955?

The second sighting referred to in the article involved Mrs. Jane Skillicorn of Yateley, who was driving down the same piece of road, off the A30, at 10.15 p.m. early in July 1976. She was going along the Eversley slip-road near the saw mills, 200 yards from the earlier sighting. A huge 'cat-like' fawn-coloured beast ran across the road in front of her. She remarked:

> *'I was terrified. I saw huge green eyes in my headlights and slammed on my brakes. It was definitely no dog or deer. It was the puma.'*

> *The police investigated both of these sightings and Fleet police Chief Inspector James O'Reilly said:*

> *'If you get two reported sightings one tends to confirm the other. We are paying attention to the area. We have in mind that there has been a recent increase in the number of deer in that area of the forest due to the drought, as they come to water at a*

nearby reservoir.'

This statement was made in the 16th July 1976 edition of the *Fleet News*. The police also wanted reports of sightings to be made at once, so that a search could be conducted quickly. The 30th July 1976 edition of the *Aldershot News* carried an article called 'Jason prowls gingerly after puma scare'. The scare started when a search was made of Odiham, following a report that a black puma had been seen. The Fleet police were still checking upon the sightings at Star Hill, near Hartley Wintney, earlier in July. However, this black puma report came from a young housewife, Mrs. Barnes of Odiham. She was met with scepticism by her next-door neighbours. Mrs. Barnes, who was hanging out washing on the line at the time of the sighting, said she thought at first the animal was just a large cat. She later told a reporter:

> *'But when I looked closer I could see the animal had huge shoulders like a bear. It is not unusual to see squirrels or hedgehogs, but a real live puma in my own English country garden was a shock.'*

The puma watched her for two seconds, as though wondering what to do, and then it jumped over a ten-foot wall, to disappear into woods. She telephoned the police, who flashed a message to Fleet police station. The officer she telephoned at Odiham police station was PC Christopher Jones, who was off-duty. A motorway police patrol arrived at Mrs. Barnes's home, as did officers from Fleet and Odiham.

No black puma was found, but Mrs. Barnes's next-door neighbours, Mr and Mrs. Cruickshank, said they had a large ginger cat 'Jason', which was seen by the police. Mr Cruickshank allowed Jason to be photographed by a reporter and he arranged to speak to a *News* reporter. He gave the following, rather sceptical statement:

> *'The girl next door said she saw the `Surrey Puma`, but we have had this puma scare for years. I think she must have seen Jason. He is like a large golden Labrador. We can only imagine that Mrs. Barnes saw him wandering around after we had fed him. The only Pumas * I have ever seen usually fly overhead on their way to R.A.F. Odiham.'*

Nobody thought of asking Mrs. Barnes whether Jason looked anything like the 'black puma' she had observed. Jason was a large cat, weighing anything up to 20 lbs. The paper stated that the puma had been around for 13 years, since 1964.

The *News* group of papers reported no more sightings until 1978. must mention that Mrs. Barnes came from Norway, so she may have seen a wolverine or a lynx before this sighting of a large 'black puma'.

---

* The 'Aérospatiale Puma' is a medium-sized twin-engined transport/utility helicopter originally manufactured by Aérospatiale of France. It is also known under the designation SA 330. The SA 330 Puma was originally developed by Aérospatiale to meet a requirement of the French Army for a medium-sized all-weather helicopter. The helicopter also had to be capable of operating by day and night as well as in a wide variety of climates.

In 1967, the Puma was also selected by the Royal Air Force (RAF) and given the designation *Puma HC Mk.1*. As a result of this decision, the SA 330 was included in a joint production agreement between Aerospatiale and Westland Helicopters of the UK.

The first of two Puma prototypes flew on 15 April 1965. Six pre-production models were also built, the last of which flew on 30 July 1968. (From Wikipedia, the free encyclopedia.)

In their records both Fleet and Odiham stations noted the sighting and search. The *Fortean Times* (No.25) of Spring 1978, fills a gap in this period - 1976 to 1978. The 'summer ritual of puma spotting' was making some progress, because Mr Douglas Brown John, a nursing home director, saw a puma-like beast from a distance of 40 yards in the nursing home grounds at Fatcham, near Brighton. The animal was 'a large, grey lean animal with a small head and 3 feet tail'. It disappeared into the woods, but I note that a police search proved fruitless. This report reached the *Daily Mail,, Daily Mirror* and *Daily Express* of 19th July. It seems the *Daily Express* said there were two sightings on 18th July 1977. The puma was a long way from its home territory.

The same page of the *Fortean Times* (No.25) notes that on 14th October 1976 the puma was seen by building workers at the building site, near Gatton Point, Reigate, Surrey. According to the *Observer, News of the World,* and *London Evening News* of 16th and 17th October 1977, the puma was seen by at least six of the builders. As it was, one worker, Mr Livingston, had brought his camera to the site. He saw a large cat, Labrador-coloured, with a lioness-like look about it. He photographed it, but unfortunately the mist of mid-October made the print rather vague.

However, the *Fortean Times* editor telephoned Reigate police, who put him onto the Public Relations Department at the Surrey police headquarters. He was told that they examined the photographs, but although they were definitely of a large feline, the officer concluded that it was a 'large house cat'. The editor, Mr Rickard, was told to write to the builder, Mr Livingston at the Reigate site, which he did, but the letter was returned unopened. The only information gained was that Mr Livingston lived at Shere, a village half-way between Guildford and Dorking.

The same *Fortean Times* article also referred to a report in the *Daily Mirror* and *Daily Express* of 22nd October 1977. It seemed that two farm labourers swore they observed the puma at Send village, halfway between Guildford and Woking, and 15 miles from Reigate. The police searched the area, but found no sign of the elusive puma. I think this sighting was in a field.

The next recorded sighting was in May 1978, when Mrs. Rutherford of Blackwater was looking out of her window at 7.30 one morning. The puma was walking along, then sitting on the railway line. She called to her husband, and they both rushed upstairs to get a better look. She said:

> 'At first I thought it was a dog. It was big and black. But then it moved and it was like a big cat. I'm sure it was a puma. I didn't dare go out. Since I saw it, I have been glued to the window. I only wish I had been near enough to take a picture.'

The sighting was reported to the Fleet police station, and the police checked to see whether a puma was missing from anywhere. We must presume that it was not missing. The puma had last been seen at Blackwater in 1971. Did Mrs. Rutherford see the Camberley panther and not the `Surrey Puma`?

In 1978 Mr W. Middlemiss of Fleet encountered the puma, and published the following letter in the *Surrey/Hants Star* of 13th January 1985. Under the headline *'The Day I Saw the Puma'*, he said:

> 'I read with interest your reference to the new sighting of the local puma, and would like to reply to your request for eyewitness information.

It must be about eight years ago since I took my wife to Farnham Hospital, where she was a nurse. On the way home, about 6 a.m., I entered the Forestry at the side of Beacon Hill Road, overlooking the army catchment area, in company with my Jack Russell terrier. I was walking down the firebreak on a real beautiful morning when this animal emerged from the bracken, about 30 yards ahead on my right. It walked cat-like across the break, slowly, and I couldn't have had a better view. It was the size of a big springer spaniel and was very wet, obviously from dew, and looked dark grey in colour. Its condition was unkempt and ragged, and it was un-aggressive. My terrier took off in hot pursuit, barking like mad. I knew it was a cat, because when Mick went after a dog he went silently.

I called him and in his own time he came back rather excited but not injured in any way.'

I wrote to Mr Middlemiss and received back a number of most interesting letters. The first proved to be only a more detailed account of his letter to the *'Star'*. It was dated 17th August 1987:

'I am a senior citizen (67) with a service background (RAF). Now to the "puma". Obviously you have my letter to the Star in your possession... It was in body size about as big as an adult springer spaniel... It looked rather ragged, especially the tail. The colour was dark, being wet, almost black. Its legs were not too lpng and its walk was almost crouching, with the head moving slightly from side to side... It was not a very nice-looking animal.., it had a neglected, lost look about it hard to define...

My neighbour recently took me to see a deer carcass in the woods quite near to my sighting. The deer had been brought down after a struggle, and eaten. All that was left was the head and rib cage. Another little episode?'

The next letter from Mr Middlemiss was shorter and was dated 14th September 1987. Its details convinced me that the animal was a cat:

'I saw the Scottish wildcat and lynx in Kingussie wildlife park in Scotland, and these in no way resembled the animal I saw. Mine was larger and with a long hanging tail. One thing I did forget to mention was the yellow eye which I could see quite plainly against the dark head... '

I think that Mr Middlemiss's sketch of the animal's tail ruled out a lynx, wildcat or any other smallish cats. I think he saw a small, possibly female puma (*Felis concolor*). The cat could have killed the deer, as cases from Exmoor and Surrey in the 1960s have already shown.

In 1988 I obtained another eyewitness's account of a sighting from Mrs. Margaret Bradshaw of Frimley, near Camberley in Surrey. She enclosed a map with her letter, and a photocopied letter from naturalist Di Francis to her. Mrs. Bradshaw said:

'I was interested to read your appeal in the Camberley News this week. I indeed saw

the `Surrey Puma` some 8 years ago when I was walking my dog in the woods near to where I lie. It was a summer morning. I saw what I thought was a black dog running through the undergrowth and I immediately looked for an owner, as I always do, but this animal then went up a large tree, just like a cat climbs.

It had a cat-like face and a long curly tail. I watched it for a while as my dog saw it too, and stood barking at the foot of the tree for some while. I then became frightened and ran away, but it took a while for my dog to retreat, as she does not like "cats". Eventually it came down the tree, again like a cat, and went off the way it had come. I went home and told my husband and he laughed at me and said I had been drinking! He is now my ex-husband!! '

I enclose a copy of a letter I received from Di Francis in Torquay, who appealed for information on the radio in 1983. I enclose also a copy of a map, and it may help you to see where it was. I still walk my dog there and always look for it again.'

The animal that was seen was definitely a large black cat, but was it the puma or was it a different beast? I think it was a black panther, or a British big cat. Mrs. Bradshaw's letter was dated 20th April 1987, while the letter Di Francis sent to her was dated 13th February 1983. Di Francis said that she was puzzled as to why Mrs. Bradshaw said the cat had a 'pig-like' tail. Di Francis compared the 'small worm-like tightly curled tail' with the 'very long thick and rather beautiful tail' of the British big cat. She thought that Mrs. Bradshaw's sighting was not the only one from Frimley, and indeed she noted such sightings in her book. Mrs. Francis suggested that if Mrs. Bradshaw wanted to learn more, she should check on sightings in the local press and take a few walks in places with trees and streams.

Mrs Bradshaw's husband took a sceptical view of her sighting, like many people have done, but we now have enough eyewitness accounts, kills and photographs to convince people that these felines do indeed exist. The sighting was near to an army barracks, which suggests that the beast was an army-connected animal, possibly; it was on Frith Hill, along a public path.

The next major sighting was in July 1980, at 3 o'clock one morning, when cleaning supervisor Mr Patrick Doughty was travelling along the A325 Farnborough road from the Bush Hotel, Farnham to the *Queen's Hotel*, Farnborough. He was a mile from the *Queen's Hotel* when a large, brown-spotted beast ran across the road, very fast. He had to swerve to avoid the phantom felid and he had a good but brief look at the beast. He later gave this account to a reporter on the *Farnborough News*, which published an article called 'Cheetah knocks spots off Puma' on 18th July 1980:

'I thought I must have been dreaming at first, so I put on the headlights full beam, watched as it cut across my path and saw it nip between some railings, before disappearing into bushes. My first reaction was that it was a large dog, and because of the speed I felt it may have been some type of greyhound. But when I looked again it was far too big. Its body was about four feet long and it had a pair of huge, very powerful-looking front legs.

In the beam of the headlights I was able to get a glimpse of its head, which confirmed to me that it was no dog. I could also pick out spots on its body, which was a browny col-our, and I'm pretty certain it was a cheetah. I carried straight on to the hotel, reported the sighting, and thought that might be the end of the story.'

About 11 hours later, night-porter Mr John Bedwell was doing a security round of the *Queen's Hotel*, Farnborough. Since he was outside the hotel, he had a clear view of an unusual, large cat. He gave this account of his sighting to the *Farnborough News:*

'I was making a security check at around 4.15 a.m. and heard a screeching, growling sound. Then this big cat appeared. It was lightly-coloured, with pointed ears, and was bounding, not running, alongside a wall. I must have been about six yards away from it.

It was a really creepy feeling. The animal disappeared into some bushes and I did not see it again - and I don't think I want to.'

This sighting was presumably not of the same animal. I think the animal in the first sighting sounds more like a cheetah, or even a hyena, but the second sighting might have been of a puma. The alarm was raised, and Miss Wildbur, the hotel's assistant night manager, was awakened at 4.30 a.m. The police were called and arrived to search the area, wearing heavy gauntlets for protection. They found nothing but a number of paw marks, which could have been made by a domestic cat. A police spokesman would not say whether the animal was the 'Surrey Puma'. However, Mr Doughty and Mr Bedwell seemed sure of what they had seen.

A Windsor safari park spokesman gave his view that they had lost no animals, but *'whenever we get a report like this we always check thoroughly to make sure that none of the animals has escaped - it is not worth taking any chances.'*

Also in 1980, on 8th August, the *Surrey Advertiser* published an unusual article called 'The Puma lives - or is it only in the mind?' Mrs. Annabelle Ward was hot on the trail of the puma, following two recent sightings. She started off by giving a brief summary of the puma myth or facts, whichever way you take it. She approached Mrs. Vivien Wilkinson of East Horsley, who claimed to have seen the puma at the same place where her husband had seen the animal five years before, in 1975 or 1976. It would seem that at 5 p. m. of the 27th June 1980 Mrs. Wilkinson was looking out of her window, when she saw a large tawny feline beast from a distance of 30 yards. It was at the bottom of her garden.

The puma-like animal was higher than a red-setter dog, with a thick tail, which almost touched the ground. The animal loped across the lawn and went through a gap in the garden fence. She wondered whether the animal was the `Surrey Puma`, no doubt spurred on by the sighting of her husband, Mr John Wilkinson. Neither of them reported their sightings to the police. She either wrote a letter to the *Surrey Advertiser* or went to see them at one of their offices. She mentioned that a deer had been savaged in a neighbour's field a year earlier. Maybe the deer met its end through the medium of a hungry puma.

Mrs Wilkinson also remarked to Mrs. Ward: *I am familiar with countryside animals, and have never seen anything like it before. I am entirely satisfied it was a big cat.'* On 20th July 1980, Mrs. Earle, an associate

lecturer at the University of Surrey, and her husband, from Guildford, were walking at Pockford, near Chiddingfold, where they spotted a 'cat-like animal' lope up a hill and go across a field. It moved from 50 to 100 yards away. The Earles had their dog with them, and the country was wooded. Mrs. Earle wrote an account of her sighting to the *Surrey Advertiser* and said later on to Mrs. Ward, *"I'm country born and bred, but I couldn't recognise it. Obviously Mrs. Wilkinson and I saw the same thing."*
Was it the `Surrey Puma`?

Mrs Ward then approached the police, the Guildford Borough and Waverly councils, as well as the London Zoo. A London Zop spokesman said that it was 'highly unlikely' to be the 'Surrey Puma' of the 1960s, adding the sceptical statement:

> *'Pumas don't live that long - 12 years would be very good. And as there appeared to be only one creature at the time, the the chance of proliferation is almost nil.'*

The Councils issued no licences either, but a Guildford Borough Council spokesman summed up their view by stating: *"If somebody kept one illegally we would probably hear about it on the grape-vine."* Mrs. Ward knew of the 1976 Dangerous Animals Act, as she speculated that a puma could have been hidden away after this Act, and escaped or been loosed.

It is interesting to note that Mrs. Earle said in her letter to the *Surrey Advertiser*:

> *'I am country born and bred and can recognise a fox, deer, and most breeds of dog and cat by their shape, colour and movement, but I could not identify this animal. It was dark honey-coloured, paling to a creamy-white belly, of size and length of leg similar to a red setter. Its movement and tail were feline. Was this the `Surrey Puma`?'*

The dog with them was a Jack Russell which ignored the animal, whereas it would normally have chased any animal. On 25th July 1980, the *Surrey Advertiser* published an article, which briefly said that about five cats had disappeared from Purford Place, near Send, in Surrey. Were they taken by the puma, one wonders? Wildcats maul domestic cats, and there is some evidence of this. big cats have occasionally been seen wandering after domestic cats.

Mrs Mary Alexander of Guildford wrote to the *Surrey Advertiser*, which published her letter on 12th September 1980, to the effect that she was going to Guildford on the A281 at Birtley Green, on 31st August 1980, and that she and three other people in the car saw an unusual dog (or puma). The animal was seen three times in the car headlights, as the people swung around in the car. Mr Chris Hall wrote an article called 'Puma sightings in Surrey', in the *Fortean Times* (No. 34). Mrs. Alexander wrote the following paragraph in her letter to the *Advertiser*:

> *'Its tail and manner of moving were very like those of a big cat. Its head, build and length of leg made it clear that it was not a dog... and one could easily imagine it to be a puma. It appeared to be a crossbreed of some type, with similarities to a Great Dane, but the tail was longer and thicker than any I have seen on a dog. Its eyes glowed green in the lights as it trotted along unconcerned by the traffic. It was on our nearside for two of the views, and all the occupants of the car are convinced that it*

*was a dog, although not a type with which they were familiar. Could this be the
'Surrey Puma'?'*

By September 30th 1980, a 14-year-old schoolboy reported that he had seen a puma from the distance of a few feet while he was cycling to Bramley Youth Club at about 8.30 p.m. The headlights of the cars passing by showed up the puma-like beige beast at the roadside. The puma ran off toward Cranleigh village. Chris Hall said that a strange hum had been heard around there all through the summer of 1980. However, after this sighting was published in the *Surrey Advertiser* of 3rd October, Mr G.S. Elliott of Palmers Cross, Bramley, wrote a letter to that paper. It was published on 10th October:

> *'I am sorry to have to disillusion your readers, but (the puma) is undoubtedly a very
> large lurcher dog, part Irish wolfhound, I suspect, which unfortunately is not kept
> under control by its owner and is allowed to roam the neighbourhood at will. It is of
> such size that I initially mistook it at a distance to be a deer. The risk to sheep stocks
> must be significant, and I am sending a copy of this letter to the Superintendent of
> Police.'*

According to the *Surrey Advertiser* of 27th February 1981, Mrs. Joy Critts observed the puma at Holmbury St Mary in Surrey. On 20th August 1983 the *Camberley News* published an article that awoke many people: *'With four strides, the puma is back!'* The sightings had occurred since 1981, around Crowthorne and Bracknell, both in Berkshire. It would seem that the sightings have already been chronicled by Di Francis, in her 1983 book *Cat Country: the Quest for the British big cat.* Rupert Bray, who accompanied me on an expedition to Exmoor, told me that he interviewed various people around Wellington College, and he was informed that a large wild mongrel dog was shot in the grounds after the sighting. Was this the end of the Crowthorne puma?

Returning to the article of August 1982, the sighting was in woodland. A lady staying with friends in Crowthorne was walking through woods in between Brookers Row and Old Wokingham Road when a very fast animal, three times the size of a domestic cat, black, large and cat-like, crossed the 23 feet wide path ahead of her in only four strides. The newspaper report said that police would be keeping an eye on the woodland area. They also referred to the Chief Inspector of Bracknell police, Alan Davies, who issued a standard police statement:

> *'We are treating this sighting seriously. This woman comes from Gloucester and had
> no idea there had been previous sightings of a cat-like animal in the village.'*

The paper also noted that a large search was carried out in July 1981 after a number of people saw a 'puma-like' animal in Wellington College grounds. It would seem that even Windsor safari park was called in, when a paw-print was found.

In May 1983 the *Surrey Advertiser* published a letter written by Mr Wilfred Blunt of the Watts Gallery, Compton. He said that reports of pumas in the Westcountry and Buckinghamshire were delighting him. He also produced some interesting evidence for the native puma:

> *'I now have some grounds for believing that the puma may once have been a true na-*

tive of this country. A small fragment of bone, dug up in the grounds of the Watts Gallery, Compton, has been identified by an amateur local zoologist as "almost certainly part of the pelvis of an elderly female puma, or cougar (Felis concolor)", but I do not wish to "do a Dacre" on your readers, and many hard years of scientific work lie ahead before certainty is established. It seems likely, however, that perhaps millions of years ago, the puma was hunted to extinction by our brutal ancestors, as was the much-maligned wolf in the seventeenth century.'

He then went on to quote the 'Harmsworth Natural History', and the writings of W.H. Hudson, a famous South merican naturalist. They said that pumas were gentle and harmless creatures. Mr Blunt also noted the 1960s 'Save Our Wolves' campaign, in which several wolves were loosed into Scotland. The public at first thought the campaign had something to do with Wolverhampton football ground! There was an outrage when the public discovered that the campaign would involve real wolves. They claimed that wolves ate children, which was true. The loosed wolves were shot by worried farmers, who thought they would lose their livelihood (sheep). Mr Blunt comically suggested that a 'Save our Puma' Society should be formed at once, to look after the needs of the puma. He said that pumas only need 15 to 20 lambs a day, and a few hundred square miles of hunting ground. He even put forward the idea of charity runs, lectures and coffee mornings in aid of the pumas! People should wear fake puma-skin anoraks, and all development must stop in Devon and Buckinghamshire! He finished by saying: *"We are all guilty. Let us act before it is too late"*

On 15th July 1983, an article called 'Puma Rumour' was published in the *Camberley News*. The article said that Hartley Wintney police had received a report from a woman who lived on Hazeley Heath, near Heckfield. She had seen a 'large black cat about four and a half feet long on the heath' at the weekend. A police spokesman for Hartley Wintney police station said: *'This is becoming quite a regular thing every year. We have not heard of any livestock being attacked, and no investigation is being made at the moment.'*

In the *Surrey/Hampshire Star* of 21st July 1983 appeared an article titled *'Man spots panther on his fence'*. A man living in Farnborough told the police that he had seen a large, black panther-type beast jumping up onto his garden fence at midnight one Sunday. After sitting on the fence the cat jumped down, and the man could see that it was decidedly a cat, but four or five times larger than the domestic variety.

The sighting was being treated seriously by Farnborough police. A week later the *Surrey/Hants Star* published another article:

> *'The beast is seen again.*
>
> *The beast of Farnborough is travelling further afield. After reading the story in the 'Star' of the sighting of a large, cat-like animal in West Heath road, a woman has called Farnborough police with news of another sighting. She would not give her name to the police but said her son had seen a large, black cat-like animal, about three feet tall, on the ranges near Caesar's camp, Aldershot."*

Touchstone, the magazine of the Surrey earth mysteries group, in July 1984, an article was published called 'Out of Place Animals', by Bob Skinner. This referred to an article in the *Banstead Herald* of 19th May 1983, called 'Cheetah on the Loose'. The article was summarised by Mr Skinner as follows:

> *'In May 1983 a motorist saw what he described as a cheetah run across the road at Walton Heath, near Barnstead as he was driving to Dorking. The witness was well aware of what cheetahs looked like, as he had lived in South Africa, and was quite used to seeing wildlife run across roads, especially cheetahs. No reports of any escaped animal from the Zoo at Chessington or private menageries.'*

This case was interesting and surprising, as I think the animal seen must have been the same beast that crossed the road between Farnham and Farnborough, in 1980. It was either a cheetah, a puma or a hyena. There was definitely a hyena on the south side of the Ashdown forest in 1971 and experts from the Natural History Museum confirmed its paw-prints.

The *Guildford Times* of 17th September 1983 carried a sighting report of a large brown cat-like animal, 'with tufts on its ears, big furry legs and a cat-like face' which was seen by a train driver, Mr George Christy, on 10th September. The animal was roaming along the railway track just outside Cobham station. Mr Christy was driving a train towards Guildford at the time and he also said: "I saw it was a puma." big cats are often seen near used and disused railway lines. Some of the reports have come from Scotland, some from Exmoor and some from Surrey.

The *Camberley News* of 10th July 1984 carried an article that questioned: 'Was Mystery animal the `Surrey Puma`?' Mrs. Maureen Delaney, a nurse living near Camberley, was walking on army land in Frimley when she encountered a puma. She described her encounter to a reporter:

> *'I was really frightened when I saw it in front of me. It came out of shrubbery about 70 yards away from where I was walking my dog. It was about three feet high and was a golden-fawn colour. It was much bigger than a normal cat or dog and it moved with a graceful movement like a big cat. I'm sure it was some thing like a puma or a mountain lion. I'm just thankful that it didn't see me or my dog.*
>
> *It just carried on walking away, and I ran off with my dog in the opposite direction. I was quite taken aback.. I'm used to seeing dogs and even deer, but I wasn't expecting this.'*

There was a sighting at Crondall in Hampshire, according to the *Farnham Herald* of 29th August 1984. The witness was not named.

The *Farnham Herald* of 7th December 1984 provided us with another 'Puma spotted' article. In the first week of December Mr Les Hardaway of Grayshott was driving his son to work at Whitley, in the darkness with the headlights on. After turning off the A3 road, 'a big, buff-coloured cat' ran across the road and dashed off into the woods, but only Mr Hardaway saw it. His wife told the *Farnham Herald*:

> *"My husband told my son about spotting a large cat and he started laughing, treating it as a joke. But later, when we told one of the men decorating our house, and who lives at Whitley, he said a puma-like animal had been seen on several occasions*

around his area, and his wife once saw it in the driveway of their house."

So what did they see? I think the only explanation can be a puma, as the sighting would be in keeping with all the other puma sightings.

On 3rd January 1985, the *Surrey/Hants Star* published an article which really confused people, as it was entitled 'Phantom Puma of Camberley raises its grey-whiskered head...' The puma was seen by Mr Bruce Hart. At the time of the sighting, which was in the early hours of 1st January 1985 he was walking his Alsatian and small mongrel dogs along Golf Drive, Camberley. He said to a reporter:

> *"Although it was hard to see in the darkness, the animal appeared beneath a street light. It looked like a large Alsatian, with a small squat head and a tail that stretched half the length of its body. My dogs knew the difference between this and, for example, foxes, which are seen quite often. It was something strange and certainly sent a cold shiver down my spine."*

Mr Hart told Camberley police about the incident and they searched the area without any success. A spokesman said:

'The puma has been sighted on several occasions over the years in Camberley, and as far away as Chobham. We still do not know if it really exists.' This statement was followed by a most interesting footnote from the editor of the *Surrey/Hampshire Star*.

> *'If it still lives, the puma must be one of the world's oldest, as it has been reported around this area for at least 20 years! Local sightings have ranged from inside the R. A.E. airfield to local commons. One year it became known as the phantom first-footer when it walked around a Farnborough house on New Year's morning, leaving strange tracks in the snow and setting animals howling. If any readers know more, or spot it themselves, let us know - especially if you manage to snatch a picture...'*

Mr Middlemiss replied to this appeal, as did Mrs. J.A. Atkinson of Camberley. She had the following letter published in the *Surrey/Hampshire Star* on 24th January 1985:

> *'Puma Sighting:*
>
> *About a fortnight ago, on the first day of the recent snows, my husband and I were walking on the Lightwater Common with our four dogs, when we heard a shrill noise in the near distance. At this, one of our dogs hung back and refused to go any further. On looking in the direction of the noise we saw a large, grey animal moving very fast up the hill. My husband thought it was a large dog, but as we watched it bounded and leapt in a definite cat-like fashion, with its very long tail streaming out behind it. It was gone in no time, moving with extreme grace and speed. We are both convinced that we had a rare glimpse that day of the elusive `Surrey Puma`.'*

In a letter dated 21st April 1987, Mrs. Atkinson gave me permission to quote the above letter. She wrote:

'With reference to your appeal in the Camberley News, I have seen one of the `Surrey Pumas`, and enclose a copy of the letter I wrote to a local newspaper on this subject. The sighting was on a very quiet day, with no one else in the area; the shrill noise that we heard was apparently from some horses in a nearby field. The animal ran alongside this field and must have frightened the horses.'

The next incident came from the *Farnham Herald* of 15th February 1985. There was a drawing of an unusual paw-print in the snow. It did not look like a puma's print, and was certainly not the mark of a normal cat. The prints looked like those perhaps left by a hare or large rabbit. Maybe a wallaby that had escaped left them. The caption under the sketch read:

'Romantics and troublemakers will already be muttering "Surrey puma". One look at this half actual size paw print, and the alarm is raised. Maybe the reader who found this mark in the snow recently and sketched it accurately, had the same thoughts, though how he drew and looked over his shoulder is in itself a puzzle. Perhaps additionally mind-boggling is the fact that the single tracks were some 24 inches apart. Oh dear... '

Maybe a normal animal left the prints, which thawed overnight, producing a strange effect that led to all sorts of theories. A prowling animal such as a kangaroo may have caused the `Devil's Hoofprints` case, from Devon. (See the 'South Devon' section of this book for a summary of that incident.)

The next sighting was recorded in the *Surrey/Hampshire Star* of 20th March 1985. Mr John Headington of Darby Green was going to work in London and was driving along the M3 one morning. The company-director saw a 'cat-like' animal, of 100 lbs. in weight, running along a foot-bridge over the M3. Mr Headington said that the animal had a 3 ft. long body, with a square-shaped head, and a long thin curled-ended tail. He said:

'I am a dog breeder, so I know a dog when I see one. This ran like a cheetah and it was far too big for a cat. I am 100% convinced that this was the puma.'

The next sighting occurred in May 1985, and I heard of it straight from the lady concerned, Mrs. Robson of Crookham village, near Aldershot. She provided me with a very convincing case in a letter of 24th April 1987:

'About ten years ago, big cats seemed to lurk behind every bush in this area of Hampshire, and I admit that at that time I was extremely sceptical, believing that 'sightings' were due to excesses in Gale's Ales, rather than to keen eyesight, though I do know several sober and unimaginative citizens in this village, who swear blind that they have seen a big cat.

However, my views have been drastically revised following my own experience in the summer of 1985, when I was awoken from my slumbers at about three in the morning by an extremely loud caterwauling noise that was obviously being made by a very large animal. I got out of bed, and in the moonlight saw a large dark brown animal, which bounded off into the undergrowth.

The following morning I went into the garden to see if there were any traces of this animal, and found in the grass where the animal had been, a very dead rabbit, which had been mauled. I did not mention this incident to the local press at the time, as the story had gone cold, and there had not been any sightings for such a long time that I thought I would not be believed.

Imagine my surprise, therefore, to read in the Fleet News the following week, a report of a farmer in the next village of Crondall who, while walking through a cornfield with his female cat, had been followed by a 'puma'. I rang the gentleman concerned and we compared notes, and I have no doubts that we had both seen the same animal.

The house I live in is fairly isolated, with a large semi-wild garden of about an acre, and it backs on to unused farmland and woods, so that we are quite used to the presence of foxes, cats, deer etc., and are very well acquainted with their individual sizes, noises, and the manner in which they move. The animal I saw was smaller in height than a deer, and was a different shape, being a far more muscular creature, with a more compact body, and it was certainly much, much larger than a domestic cat, badger or fox, moving in the bounding manner of a very large member of the cat family.'

In my view, this sighting was definitely of a big cat. The farmer whom Mrs. Robson referred to was Mr John Ballantyne, of Travers Farm, Crondall. He was walking near a cornfield when a dark-brown animal ran towards him, crouched out of sight on seeing him look at it, and then it bounded away. Mr Ballantyne gave the following description of the sighting to the *Fleet News* of 12th July 1985:

'It was the size of a big Alsatian and had a large flat face with cat-like ears. It was 40 yards away and clearly visible. I first saw it 15 years ago. As far as I'm concerned it has never left the area. I've found large cat-type paw marks on my land quite regularly when it has been muddy. It would be easy for such an animal to live off wild animals like rabbits and avoid being seen by keeping to the woodland areas.'

Mr Ballantyne's first sighting was in 1970, and was also on his land.

An article from the *Farnham News and Times* of 31st March 1987 stated:

'Name that Animal...

Gayle Masson was amazed to see what looked like a cross between a cat and a weasel near her home in Bordon. She started feeding the animal and made vain attempts to catch it. Eventually she contacted the R.S.P.C.A., and Inspector Martyn Hubbard lent her a trap. When the creature was captured it was discovered to be a small spotted genet, which is usually only found in Africa, Southern France and Spain. Inspector Hubbard believes it must have been someone's exotic pet because it is tame. Vet Giles Spaull is now taking care of the genet, and anybody who knows where it came from is asked to contact the R.S.P.C.A. at Portsmouth.'

Chris Hall, the puma researcher of Fleet, Hampshire, has been researching into that animal since about 1978. He told me that he had joined with writer Graham J. McEwan in 1980. Mr McEwan decided to revise his book on mystery cats with Chris Hall, and they jointly wrote a book about mystery cats all over Britain. However, although they have not yet published this book, Mr Hall says that one day they want to publish it, possibly through private printing. Mr Hall also said:

'The full story of the `Surrey Puma` is on record in Surrey local newspapers and in the memories of local people, and there is nothing to stop you looking it all up as we did, but it will take you weeks!

Incidentally, the Caniberley puma is not always black, though I think you are correct that all the latest reports (c.1982-84) have been of black animals. The most recent report was last autumn at Crondall, the village where the whole saga began 25 years ago.'

This passage comes from a letter dated 25th April 1987. In a later letter of 26th May 1987, Mr Hall said that he thought the theory that 'black pumas' were a new species or sub-species of the native wildcat, was probably true.

I must thank Mr Hall for all his help.

We now move on to what – at the time of writing – was one of the most recent sightings of a black big cat around Camberley. In April 1987 I visited that town and heard about a man who claimed to have seen the puma on the gates at Sandhurst Military Academy. I wrote to him through the Abademy and received a most interesting reply in a letter of 15th April 1987, written from Yately, Caniberley:

'On leaving the staff college at about 5 p.m., the passenger in my V.W. Caravanette suddenly exclaimed: "Look at that! what is it?"

By the time I looked, it was 80-100 yards' distance, and the brightness was fading out of the light. It looked in shape like a black leopard (as I found out when I looked in an encyclopaedia). As there was snow on the ground, I examined the area at about 8 the next morning, to see if I could locate any paw marks. There were several, 4-5 inches long by 2-3 inches wide approximately. I wished I had my camera, or some plaster of Paris to take a cast. I also noticed rabbit footprints in the area, looking as if it had perhaps been pursued. The spoor marks gave me that impression. You could say I was only guessing.'

The man who saw this leopard/puma was Mr Brian Stevens. In a second letter of 13th June he sent me a map of the staff college. The sighting was next to the tennis courts. The big cat was seen running for about 100 yards around one of the tennis courts. Mr Stevens noted:

'Course taken by black leopard. Spoor-mark of paw. Path taken by me in van at time of sighting by my passenger, who drew my attention to witness.'

We have now reached the end of the 'Surrey Puma' chapter. I know that there have probably been other sightings, and I am sure that one day the puma myth shall be proven. I intend to carry out some research in Surrey and Hampshire soon, as I believe there are still a number of big cats in the area. The legend can be read about in all the publications referred to in the Bibliography, and in them the details of other sightings be found.

The puma has survived as a factual beast since 1955 and is now, in 1988, thirty-three years old!

Notes to Chapter Five

1) On 28th January 1988 I heard from Dr Ernest Neal, the famous badger expert who was rewarded an M.B.E. for his work with badgers and conservation. He is a very fine naturalist and mammologist, who has recently moved to Bedford. In a letter to me he observed:

> 'Dr Maurice Burton would be interested in your letters and ideas about big cats. He is very elderly, but I think he is still alive... It is a good idea, collecting all the information you can. Unfortunately the majority of sightings are unreliable and vague, so it is difficult to sift out the good from the useless.

2) The *Ghost Casebook* by Elliot O'Donnel, published by W. Foulsham of Slough in 1969, gives a number of references to mystery cats and werewolves. One such story may be an early reference to the 'Surrey pumas', and dates from the mid-nineteenth century. I shall quote the story direct from the 'Ghosts from My Notebook' chapter, with the publisher's permission:

> 'First, a case from Hampshire. The sister of a well-known author told me there used to be a house called "The Swallows" standing in two acres of land, close to a village near Basingstoke.
>
> In 1840, a Mr Bishop from Tring bought the house, which had long stood empty, and moved into it the following year. But after he had been only a fortnight in occupation, two servants gave notice to leave, swearing that the place was haunted by a large cat and a baboon, which they constantly saw stealing down the staircases and passages. They also testified to hearing noises as of somebody being strangled, coming from an empty attic near where they slept, and hearing the screams and groans of "a number of people being horribly tortured" in the cellars just underneath the dairy. When they went down there to see the cause of the disturbances, nothing was ever visible.
> 'In a matter of days other members of the household began to be harassed by similar manifestations. The news spread quickly through the village, and crowds of people came to the house at night, with lights and sticks, to see if they could witness anything.
>
> One night, about midnight, when several of the watchers were stationed on guard in the empty courtyard, they all saw the forms of a large cat and a baboon rise from the closed grating of the large cellar under the old dairy, rush past them, and disappear in a dark angle of the walls. The same figures were repeatedly seen afterwards by

many other persons.

Early in December 1841, Mr Bishop, hearing fearful screams accompanied by deep and hoarse jibberings, apparently coming from the top of the house, rushed upstairs, but as he reached the landing all was instantly silent, and he could discover nothing. After that he set to get rid of the house, and was fortunate enough to find a purchaser, a retired colonel. But this man was soon scared out of it too, and in 1842 the house was abandoned. It was later pulled down and the ground used for the erection of cottages. But the hauntings then transferred to them, scaring people almost out of their wits. The cottages were speedily vacated, and no-one ever daring to inhabit them, they were eventually demolished and the site turned over for allotments.

There were many theories as to the history of "The Swallows", one being that a highwayman known as Steeplechase Jock, the son of a Scottish chieftain, had once plied his trade there and murdered many people whose bodies were supposed to be buried somewhere on or near the premises. He was said to have met a terrible and decidedly unorthodox end by falling into a vat of boiling tar.'

I must thank the publishers for letting me quote the above story. I think that the menagerie cats may have been the cause of this haunting - a puma screaming at night, and occasionally being seen. Maybe the baboon had lived with the large cat and they both haunted the district. Were they ghosts, or just elusive animals?

3) Arthur C. Clark's *Chronicles of the Strange and Mysterious* (1987) which was mainly written by John Fairley and Simon Welfare, and was published by Collins of London, has a section mentioning the `Surrey Puma`. All the sightings have already been dealt with, except for a recent one:

'As it (the puma) hangs out amongst some of the most expensive real estate in Britain, the `Surrey Puma` has naturally had some distinguished witnesses. Maurice Gibb of the BeeGees pop group saw it at his home in Esher in January 1985. He said: "We were sitting around watching television, when the guard dogs suddenly tensed. I let them out and they were half way across the lawn when they stopped dead, and this huge shape sprang across the driveway and disappeared."

Mr Gibb had the large pug-marks examined by experts from nearby Chessington Zoo. Their verdict was "puma".' Chessington Zoo is prepared to admit that they believe there are pumas roaming in commuter country. Interesting!

- Chapter Seven -
OTHER SOUTH-EASTERN CATS

- KENT

In 1905, a jackal was shot dead in Kent. Where it came from is a mystery, but Charles Fort chronicled it and other mystery animals in his book *Lo!* The report came from *The Times* of 2nd March 1905, and at that time a number of other areas of the country were afflicted with puma-like beasts or wolves/jackals. You can read about all the strange sightings of the period 1904 to 1906, which was full of strange phenomena, in Charles Fort's books, and in another book of phenomena, *Living Wonders* by Bob Rickard and John Michell, published by Thames and Hudson Ltd., London, in 1982.

In 1963 a cheetah was hunted in southeast London, and the search also spread to north Kent. However, I have already referred to this in 'The Surrey Pumas' chapter of my book. In 1971 a number of people were reported to have observed a puma-like beast in the Tilmanstone area, near Folkestone. Mary Chipperfield wrote in her 1972 book *Lion Country*:

> "A cheetah or leopard was often observed in South London and in North Kent; hunted without success."

This was the 'Shooter's Hill cheetah', but I do not think it was the puma that was seen at Tilmanstone in 1971

Let us now examine all the evidence available.

Starting in 1988 I wrote to Mr Fred Arnold of Folkestone, who had a sighting of a puma in 1973 Sadly, Mr Arnold was in hospital at time and he died in May 1987, aged 85. However, Mrs. V. Newring, his cousin, was kind enough to send me two articles from the *Folkestone Herald* of 1970, which were his prized possessions. I can do no better than to quote these two articles verbatim. The first, of 1973, ran:

> 'Was it a puma the driver saw?
>
> *After a spell of two years, has the mysterious puma returned to the Dover area? An animal was seen in the Tilmanstone area two years ago, at various times, by a number of witnesses. Some claimed it was a wild puma. Then it disappeared as suddenly as it arrived. Now another animal, possibly again a puma, has been sighted between Capel and Alkham, by Mr Fred Arnold as he drove along a country lane between the two villages. He claimed that the animal - about seven feet long - leapt from a bank, touched the centre of the road in front of his car, then leapt gracefully over the opposite bank and out of sight.*
>
> *Mr Arnold says the animal was covered in brown hair and was sleek and graceful. "I*

have never seen anything like it before," says Mr Arnold. The R.S.P.C.A. are making enquiries but there are no reports of any sheep being killed by the animal. Mr Arnold returned to the spot with a friend and they found foot-marks about the size of a man's hand.'

This article was dated 10th January 1973, it would seem.

Mr Arnold was obviously qualified to know what a dog would look like, and, anyway, whose dog would leap high banks at such speed as Mr Arnold saw this animal do? Dogs do not measure seven foot in length, but pumas can easily do so. It sounds as though Mr Arnold observed a large puma, and on account of its size, I would say that it was a male. It has also been noted that Peter Cookson of Lympne, in Kent, observed a *'large, cat-like animal'* which was striped, bounding across the Canterbury-Lympne road at 3.30 one morning in June 1972.

This sighting was reported in the *Folkstone Herald*.

The second article was also from the *Folkestone Herald* of 27th January 1973:

> *'That puma is sighted again:*
>
> *A second sighting of what is believed to be a puma running wild has been reported by a Sellindge man. The animal, originally sighted in the Alkham Valley a fortnight ago, was this time seen at Wye by ex-gamekeeper Mr Duncan Taylor of Sellindge. Mr Taylor was driving home from Faversham one night last week when he saw the animal at White Hill, Wye. "It was huge, with a three-foot-long tail. It was very broad," he said.'*

Faversham was the centre for the panther, or puma, scare of 1979. But I must note that all the above sightings took place within easy reach of two travelling menageries, which had only recently closed down, by order of the government. I also believe that another gamekeeper and Tony Jepsom, an R.S.P.C.A. inspector, found puma-like, large paw-prints in the same area of Kent in 1973, probably in January.

Then, some time in the early 1970s, a black panther cub was caught by a fisherman in Kent and taken home by him. This cub appeared to have come from Colchester Zoo, who stated that they had lost such a cub. It had been stolen and was considered valuable. This incident was recorded in an early issue of *The News*.

Howlett's Park, near Canterbury, has been the scene of various escapes since it was founded as a private zoo by gambler Mr John Aspinall in 1956. The zoo specialises in gorillas, tigers and clouded leopards. There are large breeding colonies of Siberian and Asian tigers at the zoo. It is run unusually, in that the keepers try to get to know the animals individually, but this policy has resulted in tragedy, such as the time when two keepers were killed in 1980. However, it also has its rewards.

There was an escape story from the 1960s, when two gorillas escaped on Christmas Day, entered a keeper's cottage and devoured his family's Christmas dinner! They were eventually recaptured.

Wolves have escaped on two occasions from Howlett's Park. The press had a field day over each of these escapees, and on one occasion the lone female escapee was recaptured with the bait of a bone. She was very frightened, according to Mr Aspinall, in his 1976 book *My Animal Friends*, which helped to boost funds for Howlett's Park. In his book, he refers to the case of the diving-tiger, a two-year-old called 'Zemo'. The tiger was grown-up and lived in the Aspinall's house at Howlett's. Zemo's favourite game was jumping on a sack and tearing it to bits. The tiger was sitting down under a bush one day when he spotted a coal-man delivering large bags of coal in a lorry. The poor man was little to know that a tiger would launch itself through the air at him!

Zemo stalked the man, thinking this would be a great game, as he was normally rationed to pouncing on two bags a week. He flew at the man, who was sitting on top of the sacks in the basement, intending to have a rest and a smoke. As he struck a match, he yelled in terror to see a tiger fly past him! Zemo tore the ten sacks apart, frightening the poor coalman out of his wits. The butler of Mr Aspinall's house rushed down to the basement and rescued the man, who was on his knees, blubbing the Lord's Prayer. He was given two large brandies to settle his nervous system, and was driven home in a taxi. The following day another man came and collected the lorry.

Stories such as these can come from any private menagerie, and prior to the 1976 Dangerous Animals Act, people were keeping all sorts of animals.

We will now draw upon the newspaper articles and letters, which I have received regarding the escapees from Howlett's Park. On 2nd March 1987, Mr Robert Southwood, the administration manager at that zoo, wrote to me on the subject of the clouded leopard (*Neofelis nebulosa*), which had escaped in late 1975:

> 'The clouded leopard you refer to escaped from Howlett's some 10 years ago and, despite a large reward being offered for its safe return or for information leading to its safe return, it was shot by a farmer who had caught the cat in one of his traps.'

The cat had lived for eight months in the wild, and was shot by the farmer, who claimed it had been killing his lambs. The cat escaped apparently in September 1975, and was shot in April 1976. This leopard could not be accountable for the earlier sightings of large cats, such as pumas, near Folkestone and Dover in 1972 and 1973

On 13th October 1987, the Superintendent of Canterbury police replied as follows to my letter asking for information on the subject of big cats on the loose:

> 'Unfortunately our records for the period mentioned are no longer available and I am therefore unable to assist. The local paper for this area is the 'Kentish Gazette', St George's Place, Canterbury, and the R.S.P.C.A. have an office in Palace Street, Canterbury.'

The *Kentish Gazette* Group Editor, Mr Alan Bensted, wrote to me on 26th October 1987:

> '... Enclosed please find some cuttings from our newspapers which I hope you will find useful. I shall be publishing part of your letter in this week's 'Gazette'.'

BIG CATS: LOOSE IN BRITAIN

These articles described all the escapees from Howlett's since 1981.

A real break-out came on 18th October 1983. The front page article of the *Kentish Gazette* spelt out all the trouble, with head line saying: *'Tiger terror for villages. Inquiry demand after escape. High risks. Some-one will die unless...* 'Unless Howlett's was more careful, was the general feeling of people.

It would seem that intruders let loose five tigers early in the morning of 18th October 1984 Four of the tigers were recaptured inside the zoo grounds on leaving their cage, and all were put back inside. The lone female tigress was chased and eventually shot half a mile from the park, in a back garden at Bekesbourne. After being loose for two hours, the tiger died in the garden of Mr and Mrs. Paul Taylor.

The Zoo noted that the intruders must have broken in during the night, intent on releasing the tigers. Mr Matthew Mills also of Bekesbourne Lane, said: *"The first I knew anything was happening was when I heard the three shots that killed it."*

Mr Mills was one of the angry villagers who voiced their concern to the police and press. His father, the Taylors' neighbour, said:

> *"It seems incredible that nobody was warned. Anybody could have walked out into the road and come face-to-face with a wild animal. It makes you shudder when you think what could have happened."*

What *actually* happened, was that once the tiger was loose, it headed down Bekesbourne Lane. The Zoo staff had discovered the escapees at 7.40 a.m., but they did not report that any were missing until the tiger was shot at 9.40 a.m., two hours later. It would appear that the Canterbury police were only informed by one of their own policemen, Rural Police Constable Nigel Chandler, who came upon the cat in Bekesbourne Lane. He was several hundred yards from where the tiger was eventually shot. He warned householders to stay inside, while endangering his own life. Mrs. Taylor was walking alone up the road, and she was pulled into the safety of his police car by PC Chandler. She was not angry with the Zoo, but was sad that the tiger was shot dead in her garden. In her opinion the animal was not frightened. She told the *Kentish Gazette*:

> *"The policeman said I should go home. Then he saw the tiger come up the road be-hind me, and told me to get in the car. Almost immediately two keepers arrived in a Landrover. They went into the garden and followed the tiger into the back and shot it. We love the animals and the Zoo. We like the way the animals are kept there. I just think it is very sad they had to kill the tiger. Surely they can use drugs these days. It was just wandering around and then it stood and looked at our goat. She didn't take much notice and just stared back.*
>
> *It was all over in a couple of minutes. Animals have got out before, but never any-thing that we have worried about. Now I just feel angry that they had to kill it."*

Mrs. Taylor's goat, a white Sarnen, was photographed staring at the garden, with all the children's toys on the lawn. She looked somewhat curious but not frightened. The Zoo staff removed the tigress's body in their Landrover and drove off, no doubt wondering what would happen next.

As it was, the *Kentish Gazette* pledged to make sure that an inquiry was held. They thought that the highest possible authority should be informed of the incident, and that security measures must be tightened. The reporter talked to two people who were in local authorities. The first was Cllr. Fenn, a former Police Superintendent, who represented the area on the city council. He said: *"I am surprised and concerned that the Zoo staff did not report the escape to the police straight away. We should be told why."*

The second man, dir. John Ash, vice-chairman of Bekesbourne parish council, said they accepted that the Zoo was on their doorstep, but he was worried about security. He was quoted as stressing to the *Kentish Gazette*:

> *"The incident was a prime example of the extremely high risks run through lack of communication. The morning's activities highlight that security can never be infallible and this has always been the worry. It is of paramount importance that the residents do not live in fear of unknown escapes."*

The parish council demanded a 'definite procedure' for informing the police and villagers of any escapees. The Zoo owner, Mr John Aspinall, gave an explanation to the Press Association that afternoon. The statement was published in the same edition of the *Kentish Gazette* and read:

> 'At 7.40 this morning it was discovered that the main gate of a large Indian tiger enclosure had been unlocked by an intruder in the early hours of this morning. Five tigers had been let loose, including Gelam and Patra, and three of their off-spring - two young females of one year and ten months, and one female of two years and ten months.
>
> The zoo staff managed to get four of these animals back into their enclosure, three by tranquillisation and one by guidance. But the fifth got past the perimeter fence and headed across the fields towards Littlebourne. The animal was free for some minutes and had to be shot to prevent her from entering a built-up area. All the locks on the cages are being changed today, and extra security measures are being taken, while the police have been requested to help identify possible suspects. The Health and Safety Executive has been informed.
>
> We very much regret the loss of this tigress, but it will not halt our breeding programme. Howlett's and Port Lympne have bred over 300 tigers in the last 15 years.'

Having completed the reference in the *Kentish Gazette*, I now refer to two articles from the *Daily Telegraph* of October 1987, at a time when a fierce storm had ripped trees across southeast England and caused widespread loss of life. On 17th October the *Daily Telegraph* published the following article, which I quote with permission:

> 'Leopard at large: Two leopards escaped from Howlett's Zoo Park at Bekesbourne, near Canterbury, when a tree crashed through their cage. One was recaptured, but the second leopard was still at large last night.'

A week later, on 24th October, a second *Daily Telegraph* article appeared, which said:

> *'Leopard spotted. The clouded Leopard, which escaped from Mr John Aspinall's Zoo near Canterbury, Kent, when a tree crushed its cage during last Friday's storms, was still on the loose last night. Officials said there had been two possible sightings, but attempts to lure it into traps had failed.'*

Radio stations also covered the leopard's escape, and I listened to a broadcast in a car on 17th October 1987.

The leopard featured, with Mr Aspinall, in a tabloid newspaper when the animal was recaptured. It was so tame that it was curled around his neck, I believe!

That seems to have been the most recent escapee from Howlett's, which has a long history of escapees. We must give credit to this zoo, and its larger sister zoo, Port Lympne, both of which have contributed widely to saving endangered species of animals. Howlett's is only 50 or so acres in area, so it is really partly a safari park and partly a zoo.

However, Howlett's was not responsible for all the big cat sightings around Faversham in the late 1970s and early 1980s, which I am about to chronicle. May I thank here the staff of Howlett's for helping me in my enquiries. This Zoo is well worth a visit.

The Faversham panther or puma may be a scare involving two cats: a fawn puma and a black panther. I have had to rely on the *Fortean Times*, (Nos. 28 and 30), and a mention in *The Unexplained* magazine. Early in January 1979, a 'large black animal' was seen by a lecturer, Mr Peter Latham, of Faversham in Kent. The sighting was of a 'mysterious' animal and took place near his home. Later, Mr Latham's neighbour had found large paw-prints that crossed her garden, in the snow. Two boys were out ferreting in woods near Faversham when they encountered *'a large black animal'*. This was reported in the *Sunday Mirror* for the 14th January, and quoted in *Fortean Times* number 28. On 31st January 1979 the *London Evening News* reported that a puma hunt was going on at the Earl of Guildford's stately home, Waldershare Park, which is about five miles from Dover. The *Fortean Times* noted the confusion between pumas and pigmented leopards, or black panthers. Mr Chris Flood, who farms near Faversham, had encountered the beast, which he thought might have been a panther. He told the *Daily Star* of 21st February and the *London Evening News* of 24th February: *"At first people round here thought it was just a large domestic cat, but it is far too big for that."*

Nothing had been reported as having escaped from any local zoos or wildlife parks. However, large paw-prints were found on Mr Flood's land, and the police stated that they were baffled. They warned people to beware of a 'dangerous large black cat', and they sent plaster casts to Howlett's Park, who obviously had uncomfortable memories of escaped animals from their establishments, so they said they did not know what made the prints. The casts were then sent to London zoo, who passed them on to a higher authority: the Natural History Museum. The experts gave their view that a large dog had made the paw-prints.

Chief Inspector Carey was in charge of the police search around Faversham, so he said at first:

"Some very sensible people have made reports of seeing it, so we can't dismiss it as nonsense." He passed the paw print plaster casts to London Zoo, telling one reporter: *"They have the best brains in Britain on this kind of thing."* This was in the *London Evening News* of 5th March 1979. Chief Inspector Carey was interviewed by the Kent *Adscene* for the 15th March, and by the *London Evening News* for the 14th March. Although he had earlier told the *London Evening News* the following, he shelved this idea:

'It could be a big dog, but everyone who has seen it says it does not look like one.' He was now to be quoted as suggesting quite flatly: *'At last the residents of Faversham can stop worrying... Two of the country's top experts say the print is not made by anything from the cat family and is almost certainly a dog. The mystery is now over.'*

The *Fortean Times* editors thought that the saga was *not* over, and they asked about the Natural History Museum. (Phenomena investigators and scientists do not go hand-in-hand!) The local villagers and farmers were not content, and they recalled how the country was wooded and lonely in places - ideal for the panther-like beast that had been seen. They knew it existed, because two dead and ravaged sheep were found near Faversham. Mrs. Valery Martin of Kent spoke to a lady from near Boughton, when Howlett's Park was mentioned. Mrs. Martin was quoted as writing:

'I asked her about the animal. She had not seen it, but knew several people, including children, who had. The animal was seen in the main village street during the recent snowy weather in the third week of February. Two sheep were also found dead and mutilated. The villagers were most annoyed at the 'experts'' opinion of it being a dog. They say it was definitely feline in appearance, and not a golden retriever, Labrador or Fox, or - as had also been suggested - a large domestic Tom.'

As regards Howlett's Zoo Park, Mrs. Martin said:

'He kept tigers, lions, cheetahs and black panthers, but I've not heard of any recent escape. Remembering the terrible fuss of many years ago when one of his panthers did escape and was shot, I do not think another such occurrence would pass unnoticed.'

Mrs Martin was obviously recalling the clouded leopard escape of 1975/76. The 'Forteans' would have come up with the suggestion that the beast was a ghost of the shot clouded leopard. The police station at Herne Bay were rather unhelpful, for the same reason. Inspector Gabriel stated to me in a letter dated 15th October of the same year: *'I refer to your letter of 7th October 1987, and regret that I am unable to provide you with any information about any large cats in the Faversham area. The local newspapers are The Faversham Times and the Faversham News'.*

The most recent reference to the Faversham cat comes from a letter in the *Fortean Times* (No. 45). I quote the letter verbatim:

'Big cat encounter on 30th August 1985. At about 9.30 in the evening I decided to put our corgi pup outside. I put on the kitchen and outside lights and looked out of the kitchen door. Standing and staring at me, about 5 feet from the door, was a sandy-

coloured cat-like animal about 2 ft 6 ins tall, lithe, with long legs and a long thin tail held vertical. The eyes were huge, round and bulging. It turned and disappeared up the garden steps. It definitely wasn't a panther, and was nothing like I've seen before.'

Signed: A. Grizzel, Faversham, Kent.

Was the beast a puma? It certainly does not seem to have been the same 'large, black animal' that had been seen earlier. The mystery of the Faversham cat will remain.

An article in the *Sunday Express* of October 1987 stated:

'Big Cats in Life or Death Peril

The future of eleven lions and tigers and two bears hangs in the balance after a council used court action to seize them from a run-down former circus. The animals used to be kept in a field near Maidstone, Kent, but after a court decided they were not part of any circus they were taken to Longleat Wildlife Park. Now Maidstone council has written to forty possible homes for the cats and bears, but an environment officer has warned that if nowhere is found soon they may have to be destroyed. The animals used to be part of Cross Brothers Circus. The owner, Michael Cross, handed everything over to his friend Peter Hill, but stayed on as trainer. Hill was then taken to court by the council after locals voiced fears about the cats escaping. Magistrates decided the menagerie was not a draw, and fined Hill £300 for keeping wild animals without a licence. He dropped plans for an appeal and the council seized the animals. It is appealing for anyone who can give the animals a home to come forward.

The circus had once been owned by the Cross Brothers, who ran into trouble when two tigers mauled a man after escaping.'

And finally the *News of the World* of September 1987 said just this of the poor beasts:

'Lions' Reprieve.

Three Lionesses from a squalid circus have been offered a home by an unknown private benefactor. The three were given a temporary home at Longleat Wildlife Park, Wiltshire, but were due to be destroyed because of their inability to integrate with other lions.'

So the animals were saved!

We shall now travel northwards to the counties of Suffolk and Norfolk, scene of the 1985 Thetford panther scare.

- ## SUFFOLK and NORFOLK

There is one sighting that occurred some forty years ago that is very interesting. It is recorded in Tabour's and Underwood's book '*The Ghosts of Borley*', published in 1973. I quote the relevant passage with the permission of the publishers. I must first stress that Borley Rectory in Suffolk has been described by veteran investigator, Mr Harry Price, as 'the most haunted house in England'.

The house was haunted by a phantom nun, her lover, a monk, a phantom head gardener, a former incumbent (the Rev. Henry Dawson Ellis, 1833-1892), a phantom coachman, and a phantom dog, and at least two ghostly cats.

Various strange and unexplained events have occurred around Borley since 1800 or so. The Rectory had been a ruin since 1939 and was eventually pulled down. The passage reads:

> '*Mr R. James Westworth-Day, the noted author and journalist of Ingatestone, Essex, described to us a night he spent with a friend at Borley, under a full harvest moon. It was some four months after the fire. They explored the roofless dining-room and as much of the ground floor as they could. But when Wentworth-Day suggested they look upstairs, he met an immediate and grim refusal from his young soldier-companion, who seemed convinced that there 'was 'something' at the top of the main stairs, watching them, something 'huge and black, something that squatted, exuding evil'. Wentworth-Day raised the gun he carried, but his friend begged him not to shoot, feeling that a shot might start 'something unpleasant', and would probably bring local people to the spot to see what was afoot.*
>
> *The two men left the ruined building and stood for some time in the bright moonlight under a tree, looking at the black, empty windows of the house. They both felt that something malevolent was watching them. Suddenly something shot between Wentworth-Day's legs; he felt harsh bristles and shaky, undulating muscles.*
>
> *It was a gigantic black cat. It rushed into the house and did not come out again. A year later Wentworth-Day told us that he met a London journalist who said that during a night he had spent at Borley he became convinced there was something very odd about the upper regions of the ruins. As he stood outside, watching the place, a huge black cat shot like a bullet between his legs and hurtled into the house 'like a shot from a gun'. It never appeared again, and when he made enquiries at the nearby farm he was told that they had no black cats, nor had anybody living around there, but that many of the people who spent a night in the garden saw a cat go into the house, always at high speed and never returning.'*

I believe that these sightings were in approximately 1939 and 1940.

The rectory was also haunted by another thin grey cat, which was normally seen around the Rectory Cottage, as the authors of '*The Ghosts of Borley*' mention. They referred to 'Animal Ghosts', published in 1913 and written by Elliot O'Donnell, who also investigated many ghosts in the early twentieth century.

The previous rectors, notably the Bull family, had been *known* to keep up to thirty cats. Three of these found rest in the cats' cemetery, which was dug up in another part of the extensive rectory gardens. Mr and Mrs. John Turner were the residents of the Rectory Cottage from 1947 to 1950, and were the main witnesses of the ragged grey cat. It would seem that the cat could be heard scratching near their bed. In October 1949 a down-to-earth guest, Mr Ronald Blythe, a former librarian and writer from Colchester, once noticed it in their bathroom. The grey ghost-cat chased one of the Turner's two cats and disappeared when it could not physically have done. The cat must have suffered in its lifetime, for it was described as being *'thin and miserable-looking, grey-white in colour, with a scraggy tail'*. The *Fortean Times* (No. 30) reported the following:

> *'In the week beginning 11th June (1979) there was a bear scare in the forest at Thetford, Norfolk. From the descriptions given by motorists travelling the A1066 at Snare Hill, it was supposed to be a small Himalayan or Malaysian bear, escaped - you guessed it - from a travelling circus. I wish I had £1 for every travelling circus that's sneaking along our by-ways, distributing exotic aliens.'*

This information was also contained in the Sussex *Bury Free Press, Sunderland Echo* and national press for 15th June 1979.

The *Daily Mail* for 20th April 1985 reported that a black panther was observed near the king's forest, near Elveden, Suffolk, on April 17th 1985. Some birds were found dead in the area at the same time. The *Sunday Express* for 21st April and the *Bury Free Press* for 20th April also carried this story. A big cat appeared at Honington, near a U.S. Army base on 19th April; it was light brown, with long ears and a four-foot long body. This last sighting was featured in the *Daily Mail* of 26th April, the *Daily Telegraph* of 20th April, and the *Bury Free Press* of 26th April. The *Sunday Mirror* also carried the story on 21st April.

These facts were reported in the *Fortean Times*, (No.44). I wrote to Bury St Edmunds police station to obtain some information on big cats in Sussex. They replied on 28th October 1987: *'Unfortunately, on this occasion I am unable to assist, but suggest contact with the following two local newspapers: Bury St Edmunds Free Press, and Anglian Daily Times. Additional contact with the RSPCA at Cambridge may prove valuable.'*

The *Bury Free Press* sent me the only article they had ever published on the subject of mystery cats. On the 26th April 1985 they had reported that a mystery black animal with flaming red eyes was appearing in the Thetford Forest between Mildenhall and Thetford, on the Norfolk/Suffolk border. A lorry driver first saw the beast when he drove past the Elveden war memorial on the All. He described it as being large, black, with flaming red eyes. This was a week before the article was published.

The second sighting was when a serviceman at RAF Honington told the police that a panther had jumped out in front of his car at Rymer Point, on the A1088. According to the *Fortean Times* (No. 44) these articles referred to the same black animal that was seen over the border, still in the Thetford Forest in Norfolk.

The third sighting involved an engineer, Mr McAllister. An article was published on 21st April 1985, in the *Sunday Mirror*, which tells the story:

'Red-eyed beast hunt stepped up:

A panther was being hunted yesterday in 5,000 acres of forest. The search was being stepped up in the dense king's forest, near Thetford, Norfolk, after three sightings of the black beast in three days. A walker reported seeing 'Two red eyes staring from bushes', and a motorist said the panther sprang in front of his car. Pheasants have been found ripped savagely apart, but no animals are missing from the near-by wildlife park.'

A second article, also from the *Daily Mirror* of a later date, reads:

'Panther Mystery:

A mystery beast thought to be a panther terrorised two dogs and stalked their owner. Engineer Brian McAllister was walking his dogs - one of them a 14-stone mastiff - when they disturbed the beast in woods near his house in Thetford, Norfolk. They ran back scared stiff, he said. "It followed me part of the way home".'

At this point four theories had developed as to what the Thetford forest panther might be.

1) Di Francis told the *Bury Free Press* on 26th April:

    'The type of sightings in your area are certainly in keeping with the sightings all over the country, and I believe could be of what I call the British big cat. Science says this animal does not exist, but this cat does not look like anything we know. It is a flesh-and-blood animal, and a nocturnal hunter which feeds on small creatures, and lives in remote woodlands. It has a puma-type head with pricked-up ears, but is unlike a panther or leopard.

    Of course, almost every county in the country has its own black dog legend, and Suffolk is no exception. According to legend, the animals make all manner of curious noises and have eyes like burning coals - often associated with the Devil. But that's a legend. I believe this is a flesh-and-blood animal.'

2) The second theory was also reported in the same *Bury Free Press* article. Mr and Mrs. Washington of Littlefort, Cambridge, suggested that the beast was their black chow dog, 'Tarka', which was lost in September 1984. The couple had been on a caravanning holiday near Southwold, when Tarka ran off after being stung by a wasp. Mrs. Washington was certain the dog was trying to find its way home to Littleport. She told the *Bury Free Press* that Tarka was a very shy dog, and on previous occasions had been mistaken for a monkey and a bear! She also remarked:

    "Tarka knew the Thetford forest area well because we took him there for walks."

3) The next theory came from a statement sent to me in a letter from Superintendent Wade, of the Norfolk Constabulary Station, Thetford. The letter was dated 26th October 1987, and was in reply to one sent by me:

'Although there were rumours circulating in the Eastern region that a large black animal similar to a panther was loose in the area during or about 1978/79, no positive sightings were made. I am sorry, but enquiries among the officers in the Thetford area have failed to produce any useful information.'

The Superintendent's statement that a black animal had been seen in 1978 and 1979 in the Eastern region seems to suggest that the black chow was not responsible for all sightings, as he only went missing in September 1984, though it might have been responsible for some of the four or five reported sightings in 1985. I was interested in what the officer had to say, and began to write to some local wildlife parks.

4)   Not all the parks replied to my letters. However, two local Norfolk wild-life parks *did* reply. The first came from the director of Banham Zoo, near Thetford. They had obviously been the park which checked their big cats and found none had escaped. Mr Gaymour stated:

'We regret that we are unable to help you in your quest as the only experience we have is with snow leopards and black leopards at our park. We have, for your information, enclosed our zoo fact sheet on snow leopards which you might find of interest.'

This kind gesture was most interesting, as the snow leopard is an unusually rare cat, only found in Northern Asia. The fact sheet declared that this animal could hunt in territories up to 100 square kilometres (38 square miles). A puma is said generally to hunt with a 30 mile radius of one point, although it can travel 100 miles fairly quickly. The sheet also suggested that snow leopards can leap distances of up to 15 metres (50 feet). The Thetford 'panther' must surely be some sort of cat, as it is capable of jumping enormous distances. The puma is noted for its jumping, but it is rarely black. The Zoo has a pair of black panthers and a pair of snow leopards.

Bearing the above in mind, I can only say that there appears to be a panther-type cat loose in the Thetford forest region.

•   OTHER NORFOLK CATS

Norfolk has a long history of mystery cats. One pile of prehistoric fossilised bones was classified '*Panthera peroides'*.

The mystery cat saga seems really to have taken off in about 1964, in which year a puma-like cat was seen at Cromer, Norfolk. Perhaps it came from the now-closed Cromer Zoo, which more recently lost a lioness. In her 1972 book 'Lion Country', animal trainer Mrs. Mary Chipperfield wrote: *'... A tiger was hunted by police in Norfolk but it was never found...'*

The News, No. 9, April 1975, records the case of Mr Bill Crane, a council rat-catcher, who was summoned to a rubbish tip at Langham in Norfolk, after a lorrydriver observed two lion cubs 'romping in the rubble'. This was on 15th January 1975, and was reported in *The Sun* of 16th January. Mr Crane suggested: *'I haven't found any unusual footprints. I think it's a bit of a tall story - the animals were probably foxes.'*

Either the lorry driver really *did* see two lion cubs or, more likely, he observed two foxes playing. Foxes coming into cities are bound to bring in the odd unusual animal sighting.

There were no other sightings in this area to my knowledge.

The *Nottingham Evening Post* of 5th January 1984 reported that a 350 lb. lioness had escaped from the closing Cromer Zoo, Norfolk. The seven-year-old beast, called 'Liza', was to be tranquillised by a vet, Mr David Allison, in the zoo grounds. However, she made off, leaping over the perimeter fence and making off across the fields. Liza had been on her way to a private owner, Mr Garett of St Austell in Cornwall. The owner of Cromer Zoo, Mrs. Olga Kerr, a daughter of Coco the clown, told the police that the lioness had escaped after hitting her head on the top of her travelling crate, in which she was about to be transported. Norfolk police told people in the area to stay indoors, and they eventually managed to corner the lioness, where they killed her with a shot from a rifle.

The police had called in a helicopter and police marksmen. They heard that Mrs. Kerr considered the whole incident a 'tragedy'. An interesting fact was that the zoo was up for sale at the time. The animals had been on the market since August 1983. Although Mrs. Kerr owned a crossbow, she could not bring herself to shoot her valuable animal.

• OXFORDSHIRE

In Oxfordshire there were sightings of a puma-like beast in the 1960s, and the area was termed the 'holiday area' of the `Surrey Puma`. In 1964 there were only two sightings of the animal, one being seen on 20th November at Nettlebed.

However, more recently, on 13th May 1983, a lioness called Aga escaped while her trainer entered her cage at Didcot. The lioness was loose for the rest of the day, until she was finally cornered in a garage. She had terrorised the villages, according to Mr Paul Screeton in his article for the 'Journal of the Northern Earth Mysteries Group', No. 24, for October 1983. We may presume that Mr Screeton's source was a newspaper article, the source of most Forteans' evidence of phenomena.

• THE NEW FOREST

According to the *London Evening Standard* of 4th February 1965, a woman 'phoned them to say that she had seen the 'Surrey Puma' on the lawn at her home in Woodlands, near Southampton. Then, four miles away in the New Forest area of Hampshire, a girl encountered, in a village, a puma-like beast. This was on about the same date as police at Lymington hunted a tiger. The tiger was never caught.
In February 1973 an animal that was larger than an Alsatian and resembled a puma, was observed at Winsor, near Southampton.

In September 1972, three brothers, aged 12, 10 and 6, were walking their Alsatian dog at Woodlands near Southampton, when they observed a large animal crawling through some long grass at the edge of the forest. They were interested to know what it was, so they moved towards it Andrew (aged 10) was closest to the beast, and he told the *Southern Evening Echo.*

'It was larger than an Alsatian dog but looked like a cat. It had a big head with stick-up ears, like cat's ears, and its eyes looked fierce.'

They later identified the beast as a puma, from a wild-life book. The animal was tawny-brown and frightened their dog. When Andrew slapped its lead against his thigh the strange animal bounded away. Later, the boys' mother found cat-type paw-prints in the area; they were in a clay ditch and had definite claw marks upon the toes. The cat seemed to move in great leaps and bounds, which suggests it really could have been a puma. It was known that a farmer in the Southampton area did keep a puma, but that it had not escaped.

Since 1970, a black panther-type big cat has made appearances from time to time in both the New Forest and Hampshire. It seems that this beast was around as long ago as 1965, because Mike Goss states, in the 'Surrey Puma' section of his six-part series of articles for *The Unknown* magazine of 1985:

> *'In February 1965 police warned visitors to the New Forest to look out for the "leopard-like" beast that had dashed in front of a 17-year-old girl cycling near Ashurst.'*

I have no doubt that Marwell Zoological Park was not behind this leopard on the loose. I think that this black panther escaped from a train crash in the Wylye Valley of Wiltshire, when it must have travelled the 25 or so miles to the forest. The black leopard of the New Forest must have died in about 1978, as there have been no recent sightings here. It is true that in 1979 to 1980 there was a black panther-type cat at Favershaxn, in Kent. This same black panther was probably accountable for the black-cat sightings in Sussex. I have developed the theory that since the 1970s a black panther-type cat has been living around the Camberley and Crowthorne areas, in Berkshire and Surrey.

• SUSSEX

There were various reports of a black big cat and a brown-coloured big cat in Sussex, during the 1960s, and to the mid-1970s.

In mid-July 1971 two policemen observed a puma-like cat at Nutley in the Ashdown forest. According to *The Times* of 23rd July, the cat was 'black and tan with streaks of yellow'. The cat attacked a dog at Outback Farm. Although the '*News*' authors wrote to the people at the farm, they never had a reply.

In the same article, other reports are recorded, all of which are associated with the infamous 'Surrey Puma'.

The first sighting came from a male driver, who told the police that, in June 1972, he had seen a big cat jumping a five-foot high fence, on the Folkington to Polegate road in Sussex. In the same *London Evening News* article of 14th June, it was reported that a Polegate taxi driver on the same road had later seen a *'large cat-like animal that can run up to speeds of 35 m.p.h.'* The man told Polegate police: *'It was several times larger than a [domestic] cat."*

On 6th March 1975, two girls were riding their horses at Brooks Green, near Horsham, when they were thrown from their mounts. It was early in the morning and they were hacking through a field. The animal was a large, cat-like creature, which resembled a puma, and it would seem that the horses had shied at the sight of this beast. The manager of a local caravan site had also observed the puma. He informed Horsham police of the incident. Later, in the afternoon of the same day, the police mounted a search of the area. Armed with guns, and with Alsatian police dogs, they combed the area. For once, something definite was found - hairs, and prints which showed *'definite cat-like characteristics suggesting a weight of 90 to 120 lbs.'* This was in the *Sun* of the 7th March 1975.

Only two days later, a woman from Barns Green claimed she had noticed the puma beside the M23 at Pease Pottage, on the other side of Horsham. An anonymous 'phone caller to the *Sussex County Times* stated that the puma was captured by the police at Donkey Bridge, near Brooks Green. The caller also claimed that the RSPCA were involved, although both of these official bodies denied that this was the case.

Two weeks later it was discovered that a man kept a pet puma on his farm at Southwater, Sussex. The ten-months-old puma was blamed for the sighting, although this was never proved. Somebody should have made plaster casts of its paw-prints, and compared them with the paw-prints at the scene of the first sighting involving the two horse-riders. Some ten years prior to these sightings, on 12th October 1964, the 'Surrey Puma' was seen by a dog-walking lady in woods near Robins Garth kennels, in West Sussex. Although she could not see the cat's head, the lady told the *Midhurst and Petworth Observer* the next day that she was in no doubt that it was indeed the puma. She described it as being 6 ft. big, including tail, about 3 ft. high and a fawn colour. Her dogs ran after the puma, which disappeared into the woods, 'spitting and making screeching sounds'. Paw-prints were later observed near a farm. These prints showed clear claw marks.

Bearing in mind all these well-publicised incidents, I sent off letters to as many people and authorities as possible in Sussex. While waiting for some replies, I noted the recent sightin of a black mystery big-cat, which were referred to in Janet and Colin Bord's article 'Big Cats - tall stories?' in *The Unexplained* magazine, No. 114.

The first sighting was when Mr Colin Carter was walking on the South Downs at Belle Tout, near Eastbourne. Late in June 1979 Mr Carter observed a 'black cat-like creature the size of a pony', disappearing into undergrowth. He watched it cross the track in front of him. This sighting was by the coast and only ten miles north-west is a zoo-park, which might possibly explain the cat's origin.

A similar cat was seen in early September 1979, at the Tilgate Forest, near Crawley in Surrey. This sighting was some 25 to 30 miles from the first sighting. At a distance of 75 to 100 yards, Mr and Mrs. Clarke watched a large, cat-like animal, standing quite still in the middle of the Tilgate Forest track. The cat watched them for several seconds, but when Mr Carter whistled, the cat bounded off into the bushes. It was between 2 and 3 ft. high, with a small head, pointed ears, and a long tail. The cat was either dark brown or jet-black in colour. Enquiries revealed that local people saw the beast. The Zoo Park was at Berwick.

I also came across the following article in the *Daily Telegraph* of 16th August 1987, which may explain some of the sightings:

'Tigers snatched: Two tiger cubs were snatched from Gerry Cottle's circus near Eastbourne yesterday.

Animal Rights protestors are suspected.'

This circus is one of the biggest in the country, and went on to Wolverhampton in about September of 1987. Mr Cottle always speaks out against people who say that animal training is cruel. It may be that somebody *did* steal the two cubs. Once the animals are grown-up, will they be released, like so many other big cats have been in past years?

I will now quote the relevant passages from the Sussex letters, which I have received so far. Mrs Marjorie Christopherson of Dorman Park, near East Grinsted, wrote to me on 21st January 1987:

> *'I am afraid I cannot help you much - as I hate all cats – small, big or gigantic! We certainly heard the rumours that a largish animal had been seen in Surrey occasionally, which people thought resembled a puma or something which had escaped probably from private ownership or a zoo. Then no more was heard until we read in our local paper that a blackish animal had been sighted once or twice in our Ashdown Forest here. Then no more - everyone said it must like Surrey better and had gone back! Personally I think it must have been a largish dog or Alsatian staying around, for there are a lot of sheep on the Forest and a lot of sheep-worrying goes on, from time to time.'*

They passed me on to the Ashdown Forest estate agents, to whom I wrote at once, and received a most interesting reply dated 4th November 1987. Mr T. K. Padgham, the principal estates surveyor, wrote:

> *'Unfortunately we have no knowledge in this Department of black panthers, pumas etc. on the Ashdown Forest, although a colleague remembers some reference in the local press. However, I have forwarded a copy of your letter to the Clerk of the Conservators of Ashdown Forest who, together with his rangers, manages and patrols the Forest. Hopefully he will be able to let you have any available information. You may wish to make enquiries of:*
>
> *1) The Editor, Sussex Express, Temple House, School Hills, Lewes East, Sussex.*
>
> *2) The Editor, Kent and Sussex Courier, Tunbridge Wells, Kent.*
>
> *3) The Editor, Evening Argus, Brighton, East Sussex.*
>
> *4) The News Editor, BBC Radio Sussex, Brighton, East Sussex.*
>
> *Also, the person to contact in connection with the Wild-life Reserve on the Ashdown Forest is understood to be Mr D. Pentry, Spring Hill Farm, Forest Row, East Sussex.'*

I wrote off to all these people and at the same time I found a letter, sent to me, from Superintendent T. All and dated 12th October 1987. It contained a flat denial of any information of such cats on the Forest. Mr J. R. Nicholls, the Clerk and Forest Superintendent of the Conservators of the Ashdown Forest, wrote, on

6th November 1987:

> *'Although there were reports in the 1950s of Wallabies on Ashdown Forest, we have never heard of any large cats. We certainly have never seen any evidence to lead us to believe that we have any living in the area. The only large cat we know of locally is a 19 lb. silver tabby belonging to my personal assistant!'*

However, they were interested to know whether I found any *'firm evidence of big cats on the Ashdown Forest'.*

On 30th November 1987, Mr P.G. Bird. Deputy News Editor of the *Evening Argus* in Brighton, wrote again rather disappointingly:

> *'We would be pleased to help your research, but we do not appear to have had any reports of pumas or panthers on the loose in Sussex There were a number of reports from other parts of the country, including, I believe, East Anglia.'*

He had probably read some of the many newspaper reports on the Exmoor Beast and the Thetford panther, on the Norfolk/Suffolk border, with which I dealt earlier in this section. I also observed two comparatively recent reports which were mentioned in the *Fortean Times*, No. 44:

- 1984, October 2nd - Danehill, large wildcat; size - collie; colour dark reddish with tabby stripes, long pointed ears. *Mid-Sussex Times.*

- '1985 February - Ashurst. Many sheep and deer savaged in last 3 months. 2 dogs blamed and sought. *West Sussex Gazette.'*

In the second report, one of the 'dogs' was said to be a collie with a white tip. It was also noted by Di Francis that her big cats sometimes had white tips. I wrote to the Danehill police station, at Danehill. P.C. Peter Bidhead wrote, on 20th November 1987:

> *'Danehill is a small village on the edge of Ashdown Forest. I am the village policeman. Although I have only held this position for 2 years, I have lived in the area for 20 years, but at no time was I aware of a lynx-like cat having been sighted locally. I have made numerous enquiries in the village in an effort to find information about the lynx, but unfortunately nobody seems to have any knowledge of its existence. I have a great love for wildlife myself, and would be interested to know where you read about this lynx.*
>
> *I am sorry not to have been much help to you, but I shall continue to enquire. It has been suggested that the lynx sighting relates to another village of this name on Exmoor. Please let me know how you get on, and don't hesitate to telephone or write if I can be of any further help.'*

I wrote a second letter to P.C. Bidhead, including all the information I had to date on the Sussex cats, in the hope that he might be able to help me further.

To end Sussex mystery cats, I must refer to the early editions of *The News*, that journal which has now become known as the *Fortean Times*. Robert Rickard wrote an article in February 1976, called 'To Round up on Mystery Animals'. He had noted a report in *The Times* of 23rd July 1971, which we looked at in the first paragraph of this section. The paper said that the animal was a puma, but a reporter had got the wrong end of the stick, because Bob Rickard received this letter from Mr Alistair Witley of Outback Farm, Nutley, on the southern side of Ashdown Forest, which says the animal was a hyena:

> *'Our first signs were over-large 'dog' paw-prints on the woodland paths, and portions of half-eaten wild rabbits in the cattle drinking troughs in the fields. Our first clear sighting was when it seized our little pet-dog (a Tibetan spaniel weighing about 10 lbs) at a distance of about 12 feet. I managed to throw a shovel and hit it, causing it to drop the dog and make off.*
>
> *Many subsequent sightings could be condensed thus: very heavy strong dog with fierce eyes and round pricked ears, yellowish in colour splotched with darker marks. It spent much time lying around in whatever field our sheep flock were in, which frightened us, but in fact never attacked them. (Mind you, it was not with us at lambing, in March, or it might have been quite a different story. It didn't arrive until early May.) It appeared to camouflage itself with the sheep to catch rabbits. It urinated in the water-troughs, and was excited by our little dog. We were very lucky in being helped by Dr John Lisgoe, a marine biologist living locally, and a professor at Sussex University, who helped us to collect paw-prints, both in plaster casts and in digging up the actual earth, which he took up to the Curator of the Natural History Museum, South Kensington, who positively identified the beast as an African spotted hyena, from the hairs and prints.*
>
> *We were warned that it was very formidable, which couldn't be doubted if you get it as closely as we had. I had a good shot at it in late October, as it stood by the woodside, but whether I killed it or just terrified it away I cannot say. It crawled into the dense undergrowth and we didn't dare follow it in case it was wounded. Neither our family nor neighbours have seen or heard of it since.'*

Perhaps somebody on the edge of London had driven to the Forest and let it loose, or perhaps it escaped from a zoo. Who can tell? My thanks to Thames and Hudson of London, for letting me quote the above passage from John Michell aand Bob Rickard's book *'Living Wonders: Mysteries and Curiosities of the Animal World'*, 1982.

We shall now travel northwards and westwards to Bedfordshire.

• BEDFORDSHIRE

Luton was home of a so-called 'lion' in 1981. All had details about the mystery animal. Mr Adrian Grier observed a loping, large creature on the Toddington-Tedworth road at 1.30 a.m. on 9th June. The animal was running alongside the road and appeared to be a lioness, although at first Mr Grier thought it was just a Great Dane dog. He went straight to Luton police station, where officers enquired whether it could not just have been a cow, a dog or a deer. Mr Grier was sure that what he had seen run for ten yards was a lioness.

When asked to describe the animal, Mr Grier told the *Luton Herald* of 11th June:

> *"It must have been about six feet long, more than three-and-a-half feet tall, power-fully built and the colour of a Great Dane. It had bloody great feet and was loping along. It didn't look like a cow.'*

Luton police sceptically conducted a blank search of the area on 10th June, and checked local zoos, but no lionesses were missing.

A second incident occurred at 11 p.m. of 11th June, when a man was walking on Marsh Farm estate, near Luton. After an interview with his wife, the *Luton Herald* ran a story about this sighting. She said that he had encountered a very large animal, which made him go as 'white as a sheet'. He said that it was the largest dog he had seen in his life, being the same colour as a Great Dane, but more like an Irish wolf-hound. It had a short coat and appeared to be formidable. He thought the animal was a dog because he could not think what else it might be. *The Luton Herald* was playing on the idea that it might be a danger-ous lioness.

A lady motorist came forward on 28th June, to say that she had observed .a large creature near to Marsh Farm estate. The creature ran across the road in front of her, and disappeared into nearby woods, she said:

"The animal was quite huge, streamlined and very fast."

So was a lioness on the loose?

> *I had a letter from a reporter on the 'Herald' and he said:*
>
> *'We are most interested to learn of your writing, and would very much like to carry a feature on your book in a future edition. We were interested to learn of the Luton lion, and would like to base a story on this, together with details of your book.'*

They did this in November 1987, I believe. I can also add a footnote to the above three incidents. In a letter of 28th April 1987, Mrs. Victoria Handley of the Falconry Centre, Newent, Gloucestershire, told me: *'Have you tried Whipsnade Zoo? I believe they lost a large cat, and also Windsor Safari Park must have plenty of stories.'*

Whipsnade is near Dunstable, in Bedfordshire, and I have corresponded three times with its manager, Mr Manton. The zoo is connected with the Zoological Society of London. London Zoo is a different organisa-tion from the Zoological Society. The cat that Whipsnade lost was a lioness, and I do not know whether she was ever recaptured. Mr Manton knows nothing about it, and he was involved in the `Surrey Puma` hunt of 1964. The 'Luton Lion' could well have been only a stray mongrel dog or a deer.

There have been no more reports from Bedfordshire, although there was the case of the Cuffley lioness in

1983, at Cuffley in Hertfordshire.

- **ESSEX**

Essex is the home of an animal called the 'Essex Puma'. The first suggestion of a mystery cat in this county came from Mr Peter Barclay of Crondall, in Hampshire, whose house was the centre of puma sighting in the 1960s. He said, when I interviewed him, *"I have heard of the Essex puma."*

On 1st August 1987, Mrs. Anthea Turner of Hitchen, Herts., the former editor of *Terrestrial Zodiacs News*, wrote to me:

> *'You could try Andy Collins of Wickford, who gave a talk about three years ago, and came to an Andy-like conclusion that they (the cats) were evoked from another dimension.'*

In a late letter from Mr and Mrs. Saward, who run the Caerdroia project at Benfleet in Essex , and dated 22nd July 1987, I received the reconmiendation to write to Andy Collins, at a given address to which I wrote, but he did not reply. Maybe he had moved house. Mrs. Jenny Randles, the eminent UFO investigator and author of many excellent UFO books, wrote the following passage in a letter dated 11th October, to me:

> *'During my time at ASSAP, quite excellent case reports were filed on big cat investigations in Herefordshire and Essex by Andy Collins and Mike Goss. If you contact ASSAP in High Wycombe, Bucks., it is possible you will be able to get access to these.'*

ASSAP is the Association for the Scientific Study of Anomalous Phenomena.

As far as I know, reports have been filed on the Essex puma, Harrogate panther in Yorkshire, mystery cats in Hertfordshire (just north of London), and also a report on mystery cats on the Isle of Wight. As luck would have it, the Association's secretary, Dr Hugh Pincott, moved to Frome in Somerset in May 1987, where he opened an excellent mystery book-type bookshop. I was able to purchase a number of interesting books through Dr Pincott's shop. I also asked him about getting access to ASSAP files, and he told me they were thinking of providing a service that would allow the public access to these files.

In the meantime, trying to obtain more information on Mr Collins' theory, I found a reference in Cara Trimarco's article 'A Survey of out-of-place cat sighting', in the July 1983 edition of the 'Journal of the Surrey Earth Mysteries Group', quaintly called *Touchstone*. Mrs. Trimarco, as a young girl, had seen a large lion, which she believed was some sort of psychic manifestation. She wrote:

> *'It has been suggested by Andy Collins in Earthquest News 5 that out-of-place cat sightings are linked with man-made areas of water such as reservoirs and water-towers. Following his research into the Fobbing puma and other alien cat sightings in Essex, Andy Collins found that they were often seen near to such structures. He suggests that the man-made interference with the land, in creating large unnaturally sited expanses of water, may have resulted in some disturbance of earth energies, trigger-*

ing off this kind of paranormal manifestation.'

Mr Collins' theory was most interesting, and I at once thought how often the 'Beast of Exmoor' was seen near reservoirs - at least five times. The same applied to the 'Surrey Puma'.

On 27th November 1987, phenomena investigator Mr Mike Goss of Grays Thurrock, in Essex, wrote a fascinating letter to me. He gave me a number of leads, which I followed up. I quote:

> *'I started a book myself a long while ago, but couldn't find a publisher interested in doing it. Some of what I wrote went into the series I wrote for 'The Unknown' last year. However, 'The Unknown' can be read at the following address: Ruth McArthur, Editor, Sovereign Publications, Sovereign House, Brentwood, Essex. They have published a number of articles on 'Phantom Felines', including my articles. I am afraid I don't have Alan Gardiner's address, but maybe you could reach him by sending a letter c/o Fortean Times. I have more or less given up writing on paranormal or mysterious subjects now, and disposed of my old files on mystery animals.*
>
> *I would like to wish you good luck with your book again. I think there is a need for a thorough analysis of the subject, but it's a pity there isn't more in print already. As far as I know, the Bords' book 'Alien Animals' and Graham McEwan's 'Mysterious Animals of Britain and Ireland' are the only two recent ones. And of course Andy Roberts' 'Cat Flaps!' (Published by the Centre for Fortean Zoology).'*

I had written to Mr Alan Gardiner about Sussex mystery cats, and to Mr Goss about the Essex puma. From there, I wrote to *The Unknown* magazine and received a letter and photocopied articles. In Part 1 of his six-part feature for 'The Unknown', Mr Goss refers to the Essex puma. He notes that in April or May 1978, van-drivers at the Lesney matchbox toy factory, near Fobbing, in Essex, reported seeing a 'biscuit-coloured beast, with smooth fur and at least six feet long, from the tip of its tail to the tip of its nose - no way could it just be a large dog.' Mr Goss also notes that these men told the Essex police.

Four years passed, and in August 1982 the hind-quarters of another puma-like beast were seen going into undergrowth near the Essex water company's Fobbing depot. The possible danger caused police and a local zoo manager to be wary. The manager of what might have been Colchester Zoo stated: *'If the description we have been given is correct, then it is almost certainly a puma. It could be dangerous, particularly if it is surprised.'*
The police had not seen the beast themselves, but they were *'taking the situation seriously'.* Residents were asked to watch out for the 'Fobbing puma' or 'Corringham cougar'. A week later the zoo manager and police had changed their views about the animal. The beast's description was 'one of the very large breeds,of dogs'. A police spokesman said: *'If it had been a puma... we would have had another sighting by now.'*

Five days later, a walker reported seeing the puma cross the track in front of him on a footpath near the scene of the first sighting. There was another alert and farmers were warned to keep watch on their livestock. The police thought the puma would be hungry, but it did not re-appear. This short sighting period brought in Andy Roberts, who came to the conclusion that the cats came from another world, as an apparition caused by man's interference with water. The area around Fobbing is flat and marshy - the sort of land used for industry.

In November 1983, at Horndon, about five miles from the 1982 sighting, two women reported watching a 'very alert black panther', in a field. The time was 2 p.m. and, as Mike Goss recounts in the September 1985 edition of *The Unknown*, the beast was observed through powerful binoculars for a fair length of time.

The lady could have been on the alert for strange beasts, thought Mike Goss, as she had read about 'that thing down on Exmoor'. He thought she might have seen a dog, such as a Dobermann, at first. But she told him that two of her dogs - both Dobermanns - were in the house at the time of the panther's sighting. Mike Goss thought that this was a true sighting.

The Corringham police station answered my request for information on 11th December 1987. Inspector A. W. Frazer wrote:

'Your letter has been passed to me as the officer in charge of the police station covering the Fobbing area of Essex, although I don't believe I have been here long enough to recall the incident personally. Some of my longer-serving officers have vague recollections and they believe that there was in fact more than one sighting at Fobbing. I have taken the opportunity of speaking to Mr Terry Smith, editor of our local Thur-rock Gazette *newspaper about your project and he will be only too pleased to appeal to his readers for any information on this subject and to forward this information on to you.'*

As yet I have not heard from the *Thurrock Gazette.* Mr Andy Collins also noted that the sightings were near the White Lion public house, on top of Lion Hill!

• HERTFORDSHIRE

To illustrate the truth behind the Essex puma scare, I must refer to a later case noted in nearby Hertford-shire. The following item comes from the *London Evening Standard* of 10th May 1988:

> *'Lioness hunt in the suburbs by Steve Doughty.*
>
> *Early risers were stunned this morning to see a lioness roaming through a quiet suburban street. The animal was sighted as it foraged through back gardens in Sutherland Way, Cuffley, Hertfordshire. Police who raced to the scene brought up a helicopter to help track the animal.*
> *A police spokesman said:*
>
> *"We haven't found the lion yet, but we have had several sightings from people in the road. We are taking them seriously. One of the sightings is by a policeman."*
> *First to see the big cat was Mr David Messing as he got up to go to work.*
>
> *"I looked out of the window and there was a lioness in the back garden," he said. "First I thought, I can't believe this. And then I thought, No one else is going to be-*

lieve this."

"It was definitely a lioness - it had no mane," Mrs. Vera Duncombe, who lives in Sutherland Way said. "The gardens in this street are very long with lots of trees, and there are woods at the back, so there is plenty of cover. It's all very worrying.' But by mid-morning the great lion hunt was taking on less important tones after animal expert Yvonne Bickers from Bexbourne Zoo thought the animal prints could be those of a big dog. It was true to say that no zoo had reported seeing an escaped lioness'

The two other witnesses were Mrs. Gwen Shipman and a policeman. I think that this big cat sounds more like a large puma than a lioness. It could well be the same cat that has been seen in Essex, and possibly Buckinghamshire, although the so-called 'Chilterns puma' was seen some way from Cuffley.

With further reference to the Essex puma, I have just received a letter from the *Thurrock Gazette* reporter, Mr Harris, dated February 1988. He enclosed an article which was appealing for people to write to me, and tell me about their sightings of the Fobbing puma. The article's only information on the puma was this:

'Several sightings of the big cat were made some years ago. Long-serving policemen in the area can remember the incidents but have been unable to fix an exact date.'

My letter had been passed on to the '*Gazette*' by the Fobbing police. The man who replied was a reporter, Mr Harris, who said: *'We only received one reply after our article on your book. Letter and copy of article attached.'*

The letter was dated 23rd December 1987, and was from Mrs. A. Black of South Ockendon, in Essex. She wrote:

'Re your sightings of 'Puma of Fobbing', my husband and I were returning from my daughter's home in Basildon, when we were startled by a long animal that crossed right in front of our car... It came from the hedge on the hillside, cut across our car and onto the field on the other side. It was a foggy night so it looked rather ghostly. It was about 11.30 at night, and we both said it must be a big cat because of the long body and small head and the strength it used to bound over the hedges, also the action. That was about six years ago. Your advert is the first I have heard of other people seeing it. We thought it had escaped from Billericay, as a man there had quite a few animals about the time it happened.'

Notes on "Other southeastern cats" and "Surrey Pumas" chapters

1)   On pages 173-180 of *This Haunted Isle* by Peter Underwood (Javelin Books, London, 1984, 1986) there is a section on 'The Tower of London'. On page 175, Mr Underwood, a President of the Ghost Club, described this incident, which could refer to an escaped menagerie beast:

'It was near a door in the Martin Tower that a sentry in 1815 encountered the figure of a huge bear - which is not as unlikely as it may seem, as a menagerie of wild beasts was kept at the Tower from a very early date, and the last animals were only removed to zoo-logical gardens in Regent's Park in 1834. Marshalling his courage, the soldier promptly thrust at the enormous form with his bayonet, but the blade went clear through the phantom creature and stuck fast in the door.

As the hairy form began to advance towards him, the soldier collapsed and only lived for two days, repeating over and over again in his lucid moments the awful ordeal he had undergone.'

Was the soldier drunk at the time? Or did he have something wrong with his brain? Or did he actually see a ghost? We can only guess. Incidentally, a detailed account of the London Tower Royal Menagerie and the London Zoo can be found in *'Unnatural History'* by Colin Chair, published by Appleyard-Shuman Ltd., 1967.

2) Elliot O'Donnell's *Casebook of Ghosts*, pp. 240-242, has an account of an interview with a retired keeper of London Zoo, in the summer of 1900. He was approaching retirement twelve years previously, in about 1888, and was one of the keepers who looked after a new East African lion. It was shy of everybody save the old keeper.

One day it caught a chill and became ill. The keeper went home and, after reading the evening paper, he decided to go for a walk. His daughter allowed his granddaughter, Mary, to come with him. The girl asked her grandfather to take her to Regent's Park, which he did. They were walking down Crowndale Road, having come from St Pancras Road, and arrived at Gloucester gate around dusk. As they headed along the side of the zoo at Broad Walk, Regent's Park, a lion approached them. It was the young zoo lion that was ill. It was thought to have escaped, but its eyes showed 'great happiness'. It came right up to the couple, but as the old keeper reached out to touch it, the lion disappeared. Mary had known all along that it was just a ghost, as she said it had a 'curious light' all over its body, which was 'a kind of glow;. It was not a bit natural.' Neither of them were afraid. The next morning, a keeper rushed up and told the old man that the young lion had died at 8 o'clock, which was the same time that they had seen it in the park. The keeper happened to be going round the Zoo twelve years later with the same granddaughter, Mary, when they met Mr O'Donnell, and he commented on their being shut up in cages. The keeper stated that he had seen the animals' ghosts a number of times after they died. Elliot O'Donnell wrote a book called *Animal Ghosts* in 1913, but his *'Casebook of Ghosts'* was not published until he was in his nineties in 1969.

3) The following quote is about deer in the New Forest. It shows that there were feral dogs in the country-side, killing livestock and wildlife back in the reign of Henry VIII (1509-1547). It is from p.198 of *Hamp-*

shire and the Isle of Wight by Brian Vesey Fitzgerald (published by Robert Hale Ltd.)

> *'In the dark room of the Verderers' Court there hangs just below the stags' heads a piece of rusted iron, which is known as Rufus's stirrup', and through which it is said, all dogs had to pass to escape clawing'. The practice of 'clawing' dogs commenced so far as one can make out, in Henry VIII's reign. The great mastiffs kept by the foresters were a continual source of trouble, owing to their depredations among the deer, so expeditation, or clawing, was introduced, the mastiffs having three claws struck off each of their fore-paws and being rendered harmless to the deer. Today you can keep any dog you like in the Forest, and he may keep his full complement of claws. And Rufus's stirrup dates from the sixteenth century. All these laws originally hinged on the deer.'*

This practice could have led to people making mistaken sightings of 'big cats', which were just mastiff dogs, with round heads and no claws. There can be no doubt that a clawless mastiff's paw-print might look quite cat-like. Maybe the name 'catmore' had something to do with this practice. According to p.110 of *'The Buildings of Britain'*, Catmore village is in Berkshire. The book is called *'Berkshire'*, and is one in the *'Buildings of England'* series by Nicholas Pevsner/Penguin Books. The Catmore church is called St Margaret's, and dates from Norman times. The Royal Forest covered most of Hampshire and parts of Kent and Dorset, and extended nearly to Berkshire. The New Forest is what remains of this vast estate, owned by English kings from William the Conqueror. As there was boar in the forests, there would have been plenty of prey for big cats. I think that Catmore might have been named after some local wildcats. The forest was used for hunting and was stocked with deer, both native and imported. Many mediaeval manuscripts describe what went on there. In the reign of King John (1200-1216), one of the hunted animals was the 'wildcat', which presumably was the Scottish wildcat (*Felis sylvestris Grampia*).

4) This cutting appeared in the tabloid paper, *The Sun*, of 26th June 1987:

> *"Park Hunt for a Lion!*
>
> *An escaped lion is reported to be roaming the wilds of suburbia. And baffled bobbies are taking the sighting seriously, especially since lion fur was found in a local park. Police first heard about the mystery lion when a woman in Staines, Middlesex, reported seeing the king of the jungle on her way home from the shops. Police were sceptical until fur found in Laleham Park was identified as genuine lion's fur. "Alert! No lions have been reported missing from zoos, circuses or a nearby safari park. But one bobbie, fresh from deepest Laleham Park, was taking no chances. 'I don't mind admitting I stayed very close to our patrol car just in case we did find something nasty in there,' he said."*

Laleham Park is in Staines, Middlesex, situated to the southwest of central London. It is near to Chertsey and Heathrow airport. It is a good distance across roads to Cuffley, where several people saw a lioness on 28th April 1988. Richard Hanham, the Chief Inspector of the Metropolitan Police Station in Staines, wrote to me:

"The incident referred to was in 1987, when a member of the public believed he had seen a large lion-like animal in Shepperton. Police officers searched the area and subsequently found tufts of hair which were taken to Windsor Safari Park. A lion-keeper compared the hair found with that of a lion. They were clearly not the same, and it was finally decided after enquiry that the hair came from a dog which was regularly groomed in the park by its owner."

Pawprints found at Motcombe in Dorset, in 1994

Pawprint found in Battlesbury Woods, Warminster in 2002

Pawprint found in Battlesbury Woods, Warminster in 2002

Big cat, Farnham, Surrey, 1992, photographed by David Dell, used with his permission.

Big cat, Farnham, Surrey, 1992, photographed by David Dell, used with his permission.

`Durham Puma` photographed by Philip Nixon in 1992,
used with his kind permission.

Nick Morris's iconic pictures of what appears to be a black leopard near Kidderminster in 1992; this is often described as the most conclusive photograph yet of an alien big cat in the British countryside. A video was taken at roughly the same time, which showed a very similar creature walking by a hedge and being mobbed by crows.

The late Mrs. Joan Amos - for many years the doyenne of British Ufology, and a lady with her own unique take on the British big cat phenomenon.

Peter Tavy, on Dartmoor - where Joan Amos lived and worked

The Wildcat (*Felis silvestris*), sometimes Wild Cat or Wild-cat, is a small predator native to Europe, the western part of Asia, and Africa. It is a hunter of small mammals, birds, and other creatures of a similar size. There are several subspecies distributed in different regions. Sometimes included is the ubiquitous domestic cat (*Felis silvestris catus*), which has been introduced to every habitable continent and most of the world's larger islands, and has become feral in many of those environments; more recently the house cat is considered as a full species on its own, *Felis catus*.

From Wikipedia, the free encyclopedia.

The Leopard Cat (*Prionailurus bengalensis*) is a small wild cat of South-east Asia. On average it is as large as a domestic cat, but there are considerable regional differences: in Indonesia the average size is 45 cm, plus 20 cm tail, while it is 60 cm/40 cm in the Amur region. The fur is also quite variable: it is yellow in the southern populations, but silver-grey in the northern ones.

From Wikipedia, the free encyclopedia.

Geoffroy's Cat (*Leopardus geoffroyi*) is probably the most common wild cat in South America. It is about the size of a domestic cat. Its fur has black spots, but the background color varies from region to region; in the north, a brownish yellow coat is most common. Farther south, its coat are grayish. Melanism is quite common both in the wild and in captivity.

From Wikipedia, the free encyclopedia.

The **Jungle Cat** (*Felis chaus*), also called the **Swamp Lynx** (although not closely related to the lynxes), is a small cat with a rather short tail (length 70 cm, plus 30 cm tail). Dependent on the subspecies the colour of the fur is yellowish-grey to reddish-brown. While vertical bars are visible on the fur of kittens, these bars disappear in adult cats. Due to the pointed ears and the long legs this cat resembles a small lynx (hence the name "swamp lynx").

From Wikipedia, the free encyclopedia.

PART THREE

- Chapter 8 -
THE ISLE OF WIGHT MYSTERY CATS

Since 1983 there have been about a hundred sightings of at least two mystery cats on the Isle of Wight. The first I heard about these cats was in a letter of August 1987 from naturalist Mr John Homan, who lives in Freshwater. He has allowed me to quote the following rather long passage from his letter, which summarises the mystery cat sightings:

'As mentioned to Trevor Beer in past correspondence, I have not made any special study of the phenomenon, really only read with interest the numerous reports that have appeared in the County Press over the past few years. I mentioned the matter to Trevor, knowing his own interest and research into the Exmoor animals, including his own sighting - or possible sightings, since it is some time ago when he told me what he had seen.

First, of what I do know, I do not recall any sightings being reported relating to a wolf. I believe some sightings of the cat(s) have used certain types of big dogs as an example of the size of the animals seen when describing them. Further, on the matter of wallabies that you mention, I have never heard of any of these being loose on the Island. As far as I know they don't have any at Robin Hill. I think you are confusing the Island with somewhere else, possibly, because I do remember reading something about free wallabies years ago. Was it the Isle of Man?

You mention feral cats at Freshwater, and there certainly was a letter in the county press by a lady who remembers hearing them howling down there at night in the early 1940s when she was a girl, and commented that no one living nearby could keep a domestic cat. They either disappeared, or were found badly injured. I have been down there many times fishing until dark and have never heard or seen anything larger than a fox! One must assume that whatever lived there moved away or has long since died out.

As to the big cats, there have been so many sightings that it is hard to believe that they do not exist. Possibly a pair, or one each of more than one species. I doubt very much if it/they came from say the Isle of Wight Zoo. I suspect that they may have come to the Island as cubs and illicitly - as so many animals are and so were quietly "set free" one dark night. Even when encountered close to they have shown no belligerence, or threatened to attack. The movement of the animals seems generally to have been more in the East Wight, Ryde area, Rinstead, across to Brading etc., then across to Newport - numerous sightings in 1984, Parkhurst Forest area, then across to Hamstead, Ningwood, Cranmore, Freshwater area, and almost finally Headon Warren, above Totland, near Alum Bay. It is interesting that until the snow of last winter, when footprints were seen back in the East Wight area, recordings gradually dropped away and I think there were at most two reported for 1986. Whether the animals are keeping a lower profile or have gone - died? seems the likely answer. A research team did come over twice, and based themselves in Parkhurst forest, but I do not recall that they collected any concrete evidence.

I would suggest that what you really want, in addition to any help your appeal has brought, would be to go through county press books back to, say, 1980, and make copies of all reports. The county press would allow you to do this. I think most newspapers do - but it will take time. It seems to me that to have a record of all Island sightings - a closed environment - would be useful.'

Armed with this information, I obtained the address of Newport police and the Isle of Wight County Press, through the Isle of Wight Tourist Office, they said:

'We have no information on big cats. The Weekly Post *or the* Isle of Wight County Press *newspaper may be able to help.'*

I, firstly, never had a reply from the *Weekly Press*, but I did receive all the photocopied articles from the *Isle of Wight County Press*, which I will summarise later PC Goddard, of Newport Police Station, photocopied two sheets on the Isle of Wight cats. He also advised me to write to Terry Newton, a member of 'British Big Cat Link', a short-lived research organisation, active for a few years in the 1980s. On the Island sightings he advised me to contact Mr Geoff Ward of Wroxhall, on the Island. Neither of these gentlemen was able to reply to me.

The first of P.C. Goddard's photo-copied sheets showed a paw print of 70 mm length, which had been found in the Parkhurst Forest on 6th October 1984. This cat-like paw mark was near to the Noke Gate entrance, and compared with one found at Tonmawr, Wales, illustrated in Di Francis's book *Cat Country*. This is wider rather than longer, and does look like the pug mark of a big cat, similar to that of a medium-sized puma. (We cannot say yet what species the Island cats are.)

The second sheet was a photocopied letter dated 18th September 1984, addressed to the *Island Weekly Post* or the *Isle of Wight County Press*. Mr R.L. Skerritt of Purley Park, near Reading, Berks., wrote:

'I was very interested in the article in the County Press last week re the Mystery Cat". Although my wife and I saw on the Island what we thought to be very large cat, we forgot the incident until we read the article... I am certain now that what we saw must have been the subject of the article. We had only a few seconds of sighting as the animal bounded to the edge of the cliff undergrowth across the field below the obelisk on the cliff path by the Botanic Garden at Ventnor. Enclosed is this sketch which illustrates what we both saw. Perhaps you could convey this information to the persons who are conducting the investigations early next month.'

The caption under the sketch read:

'Sighted, looking south from cliff path, Botanic Gardens monument, Ventnor, Friday 31st September 1984, at 12.15 p.m. Colour: dark brown or black, short fur, length - 4 feet

(estimate).'

The length was from the nose to the tail of the cat. Mr Skerritt told me, in a letter dated 9th June 1987:

> *1)   I am certain that I saw a large, cat-like animal.*
> *2)   The colour was black or very dark brown.*
> *3)   The animal bounded very fast across the meadow, so you could say that it was*
> *timid. You seem to think that the animal was a puma or a panther. I would suggest*
> *that it was smaller than either of them.'*

Just what type of cat Mr Skerritt observed I cannot say yet. The animal was thin and seemed to have a small head. Its size, colour and shape suggest the appearance of a Kellas cat of Morayshire. However, there is no conceivable way that a Kellas cat could have been on the island, unless some clever Scotsman came up with the idea of trapping one in Morayshire and transporting it southwards, which is highly unlikely. It is possible, of course, that the Kellas cat has a wider range than has been considered. On the other hand, Mr Skerritt could have seen a young black panther-cub, although its build does not suggest this. It does look rather like a monkey, with its long, curving tail, but it clearly was a large cat.

Mr Jack Corney, the owner of the Isle of Wight Zoo, sent me a brochure on his zoo. On the big cats, he would only comment: *'Please make yourself known to me, when you come to the Island.'*

I will now move on to a trip that I made to the Island in April 1987, to interview witnesses and to scout around. The result was most interesting, and I have to thank my mother for accompanying me on this enjoyable trip.

We landed at Yarmouth, having come from Lymington, and made our way to a bus which took us to the Parkhurst Forest. While on the bus the conductor told me that wallabies were living on the Island, having escaped from the Robin Hill Country Park. He may only have been joking, but, contrary to Mr John Homan's letter, the brochure does include wallabies at the Park. Other Islanders had never heard of the story.

While tracking through the forest, I found prints, which were the size of a medium dog, but showed cat-like markings and shape. They had the three-lobed pad and the claw-marks of a large cat. I would not like definitely to say that a cat made them, however.

On leaving the forest, I interviewed Mrs. E. Sutton, whose husband had been a forester in the Parkhurst forest for at least thirty years. He had never seen a big cat in the forest. However, while looking out of the window at her home, eighteen months previously, in 1985, they had seen a big cat in the field over the road. Mrs. Sutton described the animal as *'a big cat, but not like the lions and tigers you see at zoos.'* She said that the animal was dark grey in colour, the size of a dog, with a *'distinct head, which went up and over'*. The couple noticed the animal pouncing around in an almost kittenish manner, suggesting that it might have been a young animal.

The Isle of Wight cats are more than one type, for one animal is jet black, while another is smaller and dark grey, or a golden colour. (See the Isle of Wight sighting summary later in this chapter.)

Our next stop was Osborne House, former home of Queen Victoria and her family. Although there were no signs of mystery cats here, I did note that in the Swiss Cottage museum, I was able to observe at close quarters a stuffed wolf. The she-wolf had been shot by the King of the Belgians late in the nineteenth century and presented to Queen Victoria. It had a grey coat with tinges of brown, and had a massive square head.

From Osborne House we continued on our way back to Newport by bus. Mr John Homan, whom I mentioned earlier, answered my telephone call from the bus station in Newport. Unfortunately he was unable to see me at that time, but his letter seems to give all he knows about the mystery cats.

We then took another bus to Afton Marsh, near Freshwater. The area consisted of about ten acres of reeds and bullrushes. On talking to a retired army officer who had lived on the Island all his life, I found that he knew nothing about the feral cats that lived there in the 1940s. He admitted that he was away from the Island for the whole of World War 2, but he was of the opinion that Islanders saw the cats after too much to drink! In other words, he was somewhat sceptical of their existence.

My mother and I then took the ferry back to Lymington.

The only menageries on the Isle of Wight, we had found, were:

1) Isle of Wight Zoo, near Ventnor. This has a large number of cats, whose species are tigers, leopards, black panthers, pumas and cheetahs. Other animals kept are raccoons, monkeys, snakes, giant spiders and coypus. None of the animals are believed to have escaped. The owner, Mr Jack Colney is famous for surviving snakebites, and also for animal conservation.

2) The Flamingo Park, waterfowl and water-gardens, at Spring Vale, Sea View. The largest birds kept here are flamingoes.

3) Tropical Bird Gardens, Old Park, St. Lawrence. Kept here are storks, eagles, owls and cranes, but no cats.

4) Robin Hill County Park, Downend, Arreton, near Newport. There are several cats here, in addition to monkeys, reptiles and birds.

Having now analysed all the authorities involved in my trip to the Island, and its wildlife, I will now deal with the sightings, using the *Isle of Wight County Press* articles.

I wrote to some sixty people on the Island and made an appeal in the *County Press,* using their articles to fill in any gaps in the wealth of sighting reports received.

Mrs Delin Whitehead of Freshwater told me a very interesting collection of tales about some large cats, which used to live on Aston Marsh in the 1940s. She wrote to me in November 1987:

> *'It is a long time ago that I saw this cat, but there have been many sightings by various people on the Isle of Wight in recent years. The County Press office at Newport has the*

various write-ups on them, and I believe there is a person collecting all the information on them. They may be able to help you. Some people say that the present-day big cats are large and tabby in colour, but most reports are that they are large and black like a puma.

But the information I will give you is only the same as I had in the County Press a couple of years ago. Sorry it's the only information I have.

I am now in my early 50s, but when I was a child I lived on the outskirts of Yarmouth. The area was actually called the Tolgate Thorby Road. I actually lived with my great-uncle, grandmother and aunts. We lived in a bungalow with a long garden and an area at the bottom in which we kept chickens, pigs and a horse. Behind that was a marsh and some woods called Thorley copse. One night after dark we were in the house when the chickens started to make an awful noise. My uncle thought a fox had got into one of the hen-houses, as that had happened before, so he went to investigate and when he returned he told us that instead of a fox he had found an enormous greyish tabby cat, much larger than the domestic cat. In fact it was like a wildcat he had seen years before in Hertfordshire. It ran into the marsh and disappeared.

Over the next three years, my uncle and my father used to keep watch, as there seemed to be about three of the cats. They used to call to each other in the marsh and in the woods. My father thought they were mother, father and baby.

One night I had gone out with my aunt and we came back after dark. As we got to our gate I saw a movement in the garden. There was a small amount of light from one of our windows and you could just see the shape of a large cat. He seemed to have a big head, with rather flat pointed ears. But he soon sensed us there and ran off. Then quite suddenly the visits from the cats stopped and we never saw them again. I don't know for certain exactly how old I was when this happened, but I was around about the 7-8-9 age group.

What was strange was that over three years no one in our area seemed to be able to keep a domestic cat. We last saw one come home torn to bits, and he had to be put to sleep. Another cat across the road was even too afraid to go out at night, but that eventually disappeared, and the people that lived there had seen a large animal thought to have been a cat, in their own garden.'

Mrs Whitehead is probably recording not feral domestic cats but true wildcats. I know that the wildcats did not become extinct in Surrey until the 1920s, although many authors would have you believe that the wilecat was no longer existent in England in the 1880s, yet they were on Exmoor until the early years of this century. There is therefore no reason why a family of *Felis sylvestris* could not have survived on the Isle of Wight until the Second World War.

I took out the photocopy if the letter that Mrs. Whithead had written to the *County Press* and found that the details were much the same as in her letter. She told the *County Press* of 19th April 1984 that the cats made 'an unearthly noise' and that they had lost three domestic cats. She also said: 'After that night, we had several visits, and one night I saw an animal in the garden that seemed to be twice the size of a big tomcat.'

There were no reports until January 1983, and this was written up in the *County Press*. A number of people at St Mary's Hospital, near the Parkhust forest, observed a big cat in January 1983, although I have no details. The sightings switched to Ryde, when in the third reported encounter of the big cats, Mr Leo Cox and Mr Kevin Punch, both of Ryde, observed the beast standing in an entrance to a fence, near Great Preston Farm. The police later searched the area, but no trace of the animal was found. However, later Mr Cox returned to the area and he found large cat-like paw-prints in the locality of the sighting. He told the *County Press* of 11th January 1987:

> 'It was just watching us go along the road. It was definitely cat-like and had large
> pointed ears sticking up and bright eyes. We slowed, looked and then ran. I was
> shaking like a leaf when I got home. We had the fright of our lives.'

At 11 a.m. the two men saw this fearsome beast, which was dark-coloured, the size of an Alsatian and looked like a huge domestic cat. The paper said that this was the third sighting of the cat in a month, which suggests that there could have been one or two sightings in late December 1982.

The next sighting was mentioned in the *Isle of Wight County Press* of 1st March 1983. Mr Dave Willett of Elmfield, near Ryde, was working on a cottage near Upper Ventnor in late February 1983. He said:

> 'It was quite exciting. I saw this animal loping down the hill, through the gorge. It
> was like a half-grown lion, the size of an Alsatian, and a golden-sandy colour.'

The animal went out of sight, and Mr Willett and another work-mate ran to the scene. They found some paw-prints. Using plastering paste, they made a cast of one of the prints. The plaster cast shows a pad 3 inches across, with large extended claws. Mr Willett was waiting for an expert on wildlife to tell him what animal made the paw-prints. I think he observed a puma or a carcal lynx. From a distance the latter could be mistaken for certain reddish-coated varieties of pumas. They do not have very long tails, nor do they have short bobcat tails, but half-tails. The fifth recorded sighting of the Isle of Wight cat was in the *County Press* also. Mr and Mrs. Goodwin of High Wyconibe, Bucks., were holidaying on the Island. Mr Goodwin gave an account of his sighting to the local police and to the *County Press* of 12th August 1983. The couple took a short-cut down a lane at Apse Heath to catch the Fishbourne ferry which carries cars. It seems that they were in quite a rush. Mr Goodwin told a reporter:

> "We were rounding a bend when we saw an animal which I am convinced was a
> young member of the leopard family. It was standing in the lane. It stared at us for
> a short while and then bounded on to the bank and through the hedge. It was about
> three feet in length, two and a half feet tall, with facial features of a cat, a stub nose
> and pointed ears. Its tail was long and curled at the end. The animal was a golden
> sand colour and appeared to be in excellent condition.
>
> At the time we were hurrying to the car ferry, but we did stop near Princelett Farm

to tell a lady who was leaving her cottage."

Mrs. Dorothy Bevis, who was the owner of Princelett Farm, Apse Heath, told the *County Press*:

> *"I was out near the road when the couple came up and said they thought they had seen a leopard. I have not seen anything like that."*

I wrote to Mrs. Bevis and she gave me the address of the *County Press* and the *Isle of Wight Weekly Post*. She also said in her letter of 13th November 1987:

> *'I have never myself seen such an animal. Some people once called at my house and informed me they had seen "something" up the road. I believe there have been some sightings on the Island. Perhaps if you were to contact the two Island papers, they would be able to help, as I expect they have reported on any sightings in the past.'*

The *County Press* article of 12th August 1983 also said that the police would not take any action until more sightings were reported. Mr Jack Corney, owner of the Isle of Wight Zoo, said he did not keep leopards and that he knew of nobody on the Island who kept them. However, he did keep other big cats, but none had been reported as having escaped. The next sighting was recorded on 19th August 1983, in the *County Press*. This time it was Mr Noel Watts of Ryde who saw the cat. He observed a strange animal near the disused Ashley station at 9.20 on a Monday morning. The police searched the area soon after the sighting but could not find any trace of the animal. A police spokesman said that no livestock had been killed, and he also noted: *"We need reports of any sightings at the time they happen."* Mr Watts described his sighting to a reporter:

> *'I was leaning on a gate when I saw a movement in the hedge on the other side of the field about 60 yards away. I saw an animal, which moved like a cat, but it was really big. It was ploughing straight through the grass. It was about three feet six inches long, two to two and a half feet high, with a tail about 22 inches long, held almost straight out. It was a sandy colour and looked like a lynx. It certainly had the head of a cat, but it was as big as a Labrador. I watched it for about five minutes. I have been out there again to convince myself of the distance and size of the animal.'*

This sighting was a week after Mr Goodwin's sighting and only four miles from the second sighting, which was at Apse Heath. The paper's article was entitled *'Leopard is spotted again',*

Yet, Mr Watts described what he saw as 'like a lynx'. Lynxes, at least the normal varieties, are not sandy-coloured. However, I think that Mr Watts observed a puma or carcal lynx, both of which can be a sandy or reddish colour, although carcal lynxes tend to have spots and stripes.

The seventh encounter with a large cat took place at Upper Hyde Place, Shanklin, and involved Mr Danny Hughes of Ryde. He saw an animal that looked like a puma, for between three or four minutes, when he stopped his car. The sighting was reported to the police, who arrived later on, but could find no trace of the puma. This was the first time that the animal had been described as a puma. So far we have heard descriptions of a half-grown lion, a leopard, a lynx and a puma. Panthers and tigers were other species that were later suggested.

This latest sighting was given in an article named *'big cat is seen at Shanklin'*, in the *County Press* for 26th August 1983.

The next appearance of the cat - or rather, cats - was on Mr Roy Cheek's farm at Haylands, near Ashey, not far from Ryde. The national press reported that a calf had been found dead and half-eaten in the middle of a field on Mr Cheek's farm, in September 1983. His land was over-run with sightseers once the report reached the national press.

The last sighting of a 'puma-like big cat' by Mr Hughes was near to Green Lane farm. Mr Cheek had 180 Fresian cows, and he said that the calf was born at night in a field containing thirty-five cows. The calf's mother had calved twice and the other calf was unhurt. It seems that some animal could have eaten the calf after it died of natural causes. Mr Cheek's talk to a reporter on the *County Press* was published on 14th September 1983:

> *'There was talk of leaving the remains in the field, with a marksman keeping watch in case this animal - whatever it is - should return. After a bit I told the police I would have to remove the calf because so many people were tramping around to have a look and breaking down hedges! A zoological expert is coming to have a look, to see if he can get any clue as to what sort of creature attacked it. Maybe the one we found was born dead and became a natural target for anything on the prowl. There were claw marks on the face and it had been completely disembowelled. Perhaps it was the work of foxes. Who knows? I wouldn't simply rule out that some bigcat got at it. As a matter of fact I saw something like a large dog lurking in a hedgerow near here the other day.'*

The Police Chief-Inspector Donald Bracey said they had called in the Ministry of Agriculture and local animal experts such as Mr Jack Corney of the Isle of Wight Zoo. He was well qualified to pass a judgement on the carcass. The Chief Inspector summed up the situation: *'It's a bit of a mystery - largely guesswork.'* Mr Roy Cheek, the owner of the calf, wrote to me on 23rd November 1987:

> *'In answer to your letter, we can't help you much. Yes, we dud nave a dead calf and the carcass was half-eaten. But we had no proof that it was killed by the so-called "big cat". We saw nothing. It could equally have been killed by dogs,and foxes will eat a carcass. A Mr Frogbrook on the I.O.W. lost some lambs and he claimed he made a sighting. Perhaps he could give you more information. - I will enclose his address.'*

I wrote to Mr Frogbrook, hoping to get some more material. At the same time I thought it was worth looking at the later articles for 1983. It was about this time that I received a letter from Mrs. M. Watts of Haylands, near Ryde, dated 2nd December 1987. Her husband had seen the puma, earlier, in August 1983, at Ashey station. She wrote:

> *'Unfortunately my husband passed away just before I got your letter. I know he would have been only too pleased to help you. You may quote his sighting in your*

book. All I can tell you is that he took our son's dog for a country walk and was in Station Road, Ashey, when he stopped. He walked across the field and saw this creature sitting in the sun and as he described it to me; he saw the biggest cat he'll ever have seen. It was the colour of a Labrador, the sandy type. He did remark on the ears. I can't tell you the exact date. I did have some paper cuttings but needless to say I can't find them. If I come across them I'll let you know, to have them.'

I think Mr Watts saw a puma, although we do not know whether it was male or female, young or old. The sightings seem to be of at least two different big cats, as the rest of this evidence shows.

At this point I must note that many of the 1983/1984 sightings were chronicled in the *Portsmouth News*, which was quoted in the following summary of the Isle of Wight 'Lynx' in No. 42 of the *Fortean Times*:

'The Isle of Wight Puma: This mystery animal has been sighted many times since our first note that a holidaying couple, Mr and Mrs. Goodwin spotted a 2 foot 6 inches high, 3 foot 6 inches long, sandy-coloured animal they believed was a leopard, in a country lane near Apse Heath. It was only sixty yards away, and they watched it for about five minutes. After looking in a reference book, Alan Goodwin said: "I think it would have been a young adult puma."

A Similar animal was also seen in a field by the disused Ashey railway station. *'Police searches found nothing.'*

- *Portsmouth News* 25th August 1983. Reference to another five sightings since previous report.

- *Portsmouth New'* 12th September 1983. 'on the 14th a day-old calf was found disembowelled and its back legs stripped to the bone on East Upton Manor Farm, outside Ryde. The killing method and amount eaten was proclaimed *'consistent with puma behaviour.'*

- *Portsmouth News* 15th September 1983: A teenager Colin Rea sees a large grey cat-like creature on Newbarn Road, East Cowes, the second sighting in the area in a fortnight. We also learn that one of the investigating policemen, Sgt. John Pritchard had, four years previously, sighted a lion at Wooton. and the capture of an escaped lion at Havant on the mainland.

- *Portsmouth News* 13th October, I.O.W.

- *Weekly Post* 14th October 1983: A late-night sighting at Newport.

- *Portsmouth News* 20th October 1983: We learn of *'23 sightings since May'*. Colours range between black, grey, sandy, silver and reddish. Firestone copse, near Wooton. As usual, after such publicised hunts, there's a discreet silence.

- *Portsmouth News,* 16th, 18th and 19th November 1983. Then a winter hiatus until a *'mottled tan or sandy'* big cat with *'tufted ears and flat, pug-like face'* surprised two men in a parked car on the Briddlesford Road, near Lynnbottom Tip, Newport *'just after midnight'* (no date):

- *Portsmouth New*s, 15th March 1984.

- Our last note to hand: *Sunday Express* 29th April 1984 gives three sightings but says there have been five in last two weeks. Currently a lynx is favoured.

The photograph from the *Portsmouth News* shows Mr Cheek, who lost the calf, Mr Jack Corney of I.O.W. Zoo, and two policemen, standing over the dead calf. Its hindlegs and hind-quarters were untouched, and only the front part had been eaten away.

The next article to be printed in the *County Press* was entitled *'Puma seen at Osborne: marksmen for hunt?'* Four people had seen a *'puma-like'* animal at Osborne estate, East Cowes. It would seem that thirteen different sightings had been recorded, all of which were given to the police on the same day. Marwell Zoo, near Winchester, Hampshire, contacted the Ministry of Agriculture, offering to provide tranquillisers and trained staff. The puma-hunters were never called in, though their services could have ended the mystery by capturing the cat. Mr Peter Hunt, the Island's animal health inspector, thought that the cat was brought to the Island without going through quarantine.

Mr Jack Corney, owner of the Isle of Wight Zoo, now said that the animal that killed the calf was probably a fox. He had found droppings at the site which contained fruit stones and berries, which were part of a fox's diet, and not of a puma. The carcass was also left where it was, in an open field, and Mr Corney thought a puma would drag its kill to a safe place before feasting upon it. These two factOrs are true. I believe that a fox would only eat the calf after it was dead, or very sick. It would need a large fox to kill a day-old calf, which stands quite high; higher than a sheep probably.

The Health Inspector of Animals, Mr Peter Hunt, started his own investigation into the puma/lynx/leopard saga with the theory that somebody had illegally let their pet big cat loose on the Island.

The fourteenth sighting as reported to the police and recorded in the 14th October 1983 edition of the I.O. W. *County Press*. There had been a sighting two weeks previously on the Osborne Estate by two security guards: Mr Pierce and Mr Lumsden, who was a retired groundsman. Both men saw a 'puma-like' animal. Mr Pierce threw a stick at the big cat when it growled at him. The newspaper gives no more details of the sighting, but summarised the story so far, mentioning the calf carcass, the Island's Animal Health Inspector, Mr Peter Hunt, and the following note:

> *'While experts remain sceptical about the possibility of there being a puma on the loose, there has been a substantial number of sightings in recent weeks.'*

All the sightings had been in the east part of the Isle of Wight. The same article also said that on the previous Tuesday, Mr Colin Rea, who lived near East Cowes, had observed a puma disappearing into the grounds of the royal estate. He was on his way home after a day's work, so the sighting was in the evening. He described the animal as a *'large catlike creature'*. Mr John Pritchard, the investigating police officer, had seen a 'lion' at Wooton on the Island four years earlier, in approximately 1980. He had also helped to capture a lion on the mainland. This sighting was also noted in the *Portsmouth News* of 13th October 1983, and the I.O.W. *Weekly Post* of 14th October 1983.

There was a late-night sighting at Newport's Seaclose area. The following article appeared in the *County Press* of 21st October 1983:

> *'Now Island "puma" seen at Newport.*
>
> *There was another twist in the tale of the mystery Island "puma" this week. Latest report of a sighting came from Mr Michael Iggleden of Freshwater. He was driving along Fairlee Road, Newport, late on Tuesday night when the incident happened. Suddenly a black cat-like animal, about the size of a Great Dane dog, appeared in the headlights. He said it reached the centre 'of the highway in one bound, then the opposite pavement with a second leap, before running off into Seaclose Recreation ground. Mr Iggleden reported the incident to the police. There were no other sightings of the animal in the area.'*

No sightings occurred until a 16th March 1984 report in I.O.W. *County Press* gave more details. The article was called *'Mystery big cat: another sighting'*. Between August and November 1983, said the article, there were twenty sightings, mainly in the Hyde, near Shanklin area, the Smallbrook and Ashey areas, near Ryde, Wooton and Havenstreet villages, and at the Osborne estate. The report then went on to tell how two men had seen the cat in a copse off Briddleford Road; the cat was *'lynx-like'*, with a flat *'pug-like'* face, pointed tufted ears which faced forward. It was a sandy-grey or mottled colour and was only six feet away from the men.

Mr Hilding Eklund and Mr Stephen Matthews had parked their car. They were testing Citizens Band Radio at about midnight on March 14th or 15th 1984. Mr Eklund thought the sandy animal was the size of an Alsatian dog, and described the sighting to reporters:

> *'At first we heard a whining, just as if somebody had left a baby there. I thought it might have been interference with the CB aerial, but I shone my torch in the direction of the nqse and all of a sudden there was the oat. It screamed as the torch beam picked it out and I just froze. The wailing was so eerie, and then the growling - I just seized up. My heart didn't stop pounding for an hour afterwards. As the cat vanished into the trees, Steve said: "We should go after it." But I said "No", because we didn't know what might happen or what it might do. It was quite an experience.'*

The paper went on to say that Mrs. Di Francis was going to the Island on a three-months' expedition, to track the cat. She thought it was one of the British big cats, so it would be good to track it on the Island, because the sea restricted its range.

> *The next article, fifteen days after the sighting, was about the follow-up by Mrs. Francis and her hopes for the future. It was published on 30th March 1983, called 'big cat expedition on Island is Devon naturalist's Hope'.*
>
> *'When Mrs. Francis came to the Island she brought with her the skull of an animal believed to be a big cat cub shot last year in South Devon, and casts of prints made at other locations on the mainland. Mrs. Francis, from Torre, near Torquay, South*

Devon, visited the scene of the sighting, which was at Lynn Bottom, near Newport. She soon discovered paw-prints which might have been made by the cats. She photographed these cat-type paw-prints.

Mrs. Francis also talked to Mr Hilding Ekiund, one of the witnesses, and the Island representatives of the 'British Big Cat Link'. She said that a Swedish publisher might provide funds for her hunt on the Island, which would cost £500, covering the equipment, which included tranquilliser darts with radio-tracking devices. Mrs. Francis dismissed any suggestions that the cats might be psychic phenomena, ghosts or figments of people's imagination. With three years' work behind her, she commented to the reporter:

'On occasions these cats have been shot, knocked down by cars, photographed, and have left prints, even droppings. They have attacked and killed farm animals and people have heard their cries. Could a psychic phemonenon be responsible for all that? In no way.'

She hoped to catch a live big-cat, or examine a dead specimen. The paper said that Mrs. Francis thought this was going to be very hard. The reporter also noted that Mrs. Francis had become interested in the subject after reports of a 'puma' in South Devon, and that as a journalist she had traced stories of these cats all through Britain, over many years. '

We shall now look at another sighting that occurred in the same area. Two leading councilors; Mr Morris Barton, leader of the local Council, and Mr Bernard Pratt, OBE, JP, Vice-Chairman, Isle of Wight County Council - were driving back from a meeting with users of Sandown Sports Hall at about 10.45 p.m., two weeks after the other sighting at Lynn Bottom Refuse Tip. They had only a brief sighting. Mr Barton said that the animal disappeared into the undergrowth when they stopped their car. He gave the following statement to the IoW *County Press* of 30th March 1984:

'We saw an animal which was larger than a domestic cat, the size of a large dog, but with the appearance of a cat. It appeared from the grounds of Robin Hill and ran across the road to the Council's Lynn Bottom tip area. It was a sandy, mottled colour with a longish tail and long hindquarters. I have seen foxes and badgers and everything like that we have around here, but it was none of those. I didn't really believe these stories until now.'

On 18th January 1988, Mr Bernard Pratt wrote this to me:

'I was interested to read your letter and do apologise for the delay in replying. Enclosed is a copy of an article which appeared in the Isle of Wight County Press in March 1984, and the story was featured in the local BBC TV News a few days later'.
That same evening I attended, with Morris Barton, a meeting in Sandown that finished about 10 p.m., and when approaching Downend I mentioned the news feature, remarking that "I don't suppose we shall see it tonight." Within thirty seconds, very

near to the Lynn Bottom tip, an animal jumped out of the hedge and crossed the road about twenty yards ahead. It was very dark and happened so quickly that it was not possible for me to give a positive description, but I can say it was the size of a dog yet its movement more resembled a cat. The local ITV decided also to do a story, and I recall saying I did not link it with the stories from Devon as at no time had we heard of any sheep being mauled.

Incidentally, the Lynnbottom tip is only a short distance from the Robin Hill Country Park, who reported that they knew of no missing animals. The Isle of Wight County Press has about thirty reports in their cuttings file on the "big-cat" and I am sure these could be photocopied if you would like this done. I am often in Devon and so knew of the stories from there, from reading the local newspapers. I thought you would like to have the enclosed cutting from a recent edition of the Mid-Devon News. I trust that the contents of this letter are of interest to you.'

This sighting was unusual, in that both the people involved are distinguished members of the Island community and know all about the cat. The news coverage of this sighting was also good. I cannot help wonder in what the cat was, however. It sounded like a puma.

The next reference to a big-cat, probably involving the same animal, was recorded on 13th April 1984, in a short article called: *'Big-cat: three more sightings'*, in the I.O.W. *County Press*. There were three sightings in one week of *'mysterious cat-like creatures'*. Mr Gary Robinson of Cronmore, near Yarmouth, saw the beast in his back garden, and he was quoted as saying:

'It was only 150 feet away and at first I thought it was either a fox or a big ginger cat. When it came towards me I saw that it was sandy-coloured and the size of a smallish dog.'

The animal sounds like a young puma. Also on 13th April 1984, an article was published, describing the events of forty years before, involving Mrs. D. Whithead, and a colony of wild or feral cats, with whose case we have already dealt.

There were three sightings of a black big-cat at Oranmore near Yarmouth, two weeks after Mr Gary Robinson's sighting of a sandy-coloured cat, according to the 19th April 1984 edition of the I.O.W. *County Press*. Mr Bert Ashwell of Cranmore, came forward to say that his son Kenneth and his daughter-in-law Suzanne had stayed with him for a weekend and they had a sighting of a large black cat the size of an Alsatian in a field. They knew nothing of the Island's mysterious cats, and were driving down Hamstead Lane when the sighting occurred. He told the *County Press*:

'I have not seen this animal myself, but my son and daughter-in-law are certain about what they saw. It was a large dark cat, much larger than a normal household pet. I am keeping a lookout for it now.'

Mrs Margaret Slade of Ringwood, and her brother Mr Ron Hill, saw the black panther-type cat in a field while walking her dog. Mr Adrian Knot of Cranmore, who saw the black big cat run from a field into near-by woods, made a third sighting.

A week later another report appeared in the *County Press* of 27th April 1984. One evening at 6.30, Miss Liz Dowers of Brading, was walking her Alsatian dog, `Sabre`, aged 2, in a field when she spotted a 'mottled stone-grey and short-haired cat' moving towards her. It sat down and watched her as she put the Alsatian back in the car and drove away. On returning later to the site with a friend, she managed to find some tracks that might have been left by the cat. The tracks were in the sand, near to where the cat was moving. Miss Dowers described the beast and sighting to a reporter on the Isle of Wight *County Press.*

> *'I just happened to look' up and I saw a movement on the brow of the hill. I kept on walking because I didn't realise there was anything there, then I saw the animal's head. It was about yards away, and the animal started to walk towards me. It certainly wasn't another dog. It was a little bigger than my Alsatian, with a very broad chest and thick legs. It had a cat's face with little pointed ears."*

I think that the animal was a puma. Could there have been two pumas on the Island? One being a sandy and the other a stone-grey colour? Or was the same puma growing up and being seen in different shades of light? We do not even know whether the cat was a puma.

The next incident involved the 'British Big Cat Link' organisation. The article was called *'Paw-print clue in big-cat Mystery; a farmer's find',* and was published on 11th May 1954. A week previously, Farmer Mr Bob Abbott of Newport caught a glimpse of the 'big-cat'. He found strange cat-like paw-prints, and contacted the Island representative, Mr G. Ward, who took plaster-casts of the paw-prints soon after they were made. This was the first time good prints had been found. Mr Ward considered that the prints were very like those shown in Di Francis's book *Cat Country.* He said that they were 'definitely similar' to the British big cat's Marks. The cat had been seen 40 times in 15 months.

When Di. Francis was contacted by the press, she said that she would be renewing her hunt for the Island cats, following this and two other reports. At the weekend two more sightings occurred. Before looking at those, we must note that the sighting was well-investigated and Mrs. Abbot pointed out where the prints were found, to a reporter on the I.O.W. *County Press.* He photographed her with the paw-prints. Judging by the length of Mrs. Abbot's finger by comparison to the print, I would say that it was made by some animal as large as a Labrador dog.

There was a sighting a few days later, which was recorded in the same article of 11th May 1984. Mrs. Ruth Mason was walking in a field behind her home at Binfield Farm when she saw a large cat-like creature which she described to the reporter on the I.O.W. *County Press.*

Mrs Mason stated that the animal crossed the field 'at a leisurely pace'. For about five minutes she watched it through binoculars and said it was a brownish-black cat-like animal. It had a very large head, short legs and a long curly tail. In my opinion she saw a black panther, rather than a puma, which has a small head.

The next day another sighting occurred. This time it was an unnamed Lady I.O.W. Health Authority employee. She did not want to give her name, but stated that she observed the cat bounding across a field on Wooton Common. She said:

> *'It was definitely a large cat. It was a dark colour, with a long tail, and it was throwing out its hind legs as a cat would do. I would say it was about the size of a Labrador dog.'*

This sighting was also recorded in the I.O.W. *County Press* for 11th May 1984.

On 25th May an article appeared in the *County Press*, called 'Two more Mystery Sightings'. This time it was a young housewife of Northwood, who watched a big-cat for thirty seconds from her bedroom one morning. It walked across a field on the other side of the road, before going out of sight into some undergrowth. The lady, who wished to remain unnamed, stated:

> *'It was very dark brown with lighter markings. I am used to seeing domestic cats in the undergrowth near my house, but this was the size of a large dog.'*

Four days later, according to the same article, a woman living in Wootton Village, reported seeing a puma-like, black fox-sized beast. She lived nearby, but was not named.

There was an article in the *County Press* for 13th June entitled *'Mystery big cat raiding my garden - Resident.'* Mr and Mrs. Wilson of Cowes had been having trouble with a large cat 'about four feet long, grey-brown, with a long tail'. Mrs. Wilson had briefly seen the cat in 1983 She heard it afterwards quite often in her garden. The cat entered the back garden and tried to attack her bantams. The cat took two of them, and the vegetable patch was often flattened, or up-rooted.

Mrs Wilson said that the cat had been coming for six weeks, and her domestic tomcat had been mauled by it. During its raids, the big cat snarled and spat, while her neighbours' dogs barked loudly. She thought the authorities would catch the cat if they were prepared to watch the garden. She told the *County Press*:

'The trouble is, I tell people and they take no notice. The police don't want to know. I've rigged up rows of tin cans on strings so that I can hear the thing moving around. Every night I hear it clattering away. It has left paw-marks nine inches long! If the authorities put a trap down in my garden I think they'd catch it. It comes back night after night...

Her husband said: *'It's made a mess of our garden.'*

The article was published on 13th July, a month after a black big cat was seen twice roaming around the Mall of Newport. It would seem that two different big cats were involved in these three incidents. The Wilsons' cat was nocturnal, as was the Mall cat. The incidents all occurred in June and July 1984.

In the early hours of a Sunday morning, Mrs. Hayes of Newport saw a puma-like cat chasing a domestic cat across the highway and into back gardens on Bedford Row. Mrs. Hayes informed police that refuse bags in the area had been ripped open. Twenty-four hours later, according to the *County Press* article 'A Second Sighting of 'Cat in Mall'', of 15th June 1984, Mrs. Drake of Newport had looked out of her bedroom window at 2.20 a.m. and saw a 'big black cat' bounding up the Mall to disappear into Cavendish Place. Although the area is fairly suburban, it is obvious the cat was out scavenging the dustbins. Mrs. Drake stated:

> *'It was most uncanny. It had a small head and ears, long skinny legs and a longish tail sticking up. I'm sure it wasn't a dog - it didn't move like a dog. It loped along.'*

The next sighting was hardly a week later. The *County Press* of 22nd June said that two ladies had been walking along the Cowes-Newport cycleway for a month. One afternoon, just after mid-June, they had seen a fawn-coloured, black-pawed, long black-tipped tailed animal lying in the path up ahead of them. The two walkers advanced towards the animal, which they were later able to describe quite clearly. Mrs. Howarth and Mrs. Woolacott, both of Cowes, were later sure they had seen a cat. Mrs. Howarth gave the following description to the reporter on the *County Press*:

> *'It was just lying there in the middle of the path and from a distance we could not tell what it was. We got a bit closer and then we realised it was some kind of big cat. It had long legs and a very long sleek body and a shiny coat. Then it spotted us and darted into Shamblers Copse. We ran after it to try and see where it had gone but it just seemed to disappear.'*

The ladies walked along the same route every day, so they would have had a good chance of seeing the big cat again. The fawn coat would suit the description of a puma, though these animals do not really have long legs, but powerful, stocky on about 1 to 2 feet long.

We now go down to Ventnor, where the I.O.W. Zoo is housed, As far as I know, nothing had escaped at the time of this sighting. The Johnsons, a six-strong family from Stockton-on-Tees, were on holiday, and went to the putting green, Ventnor Park. They were strolling along Park Road at noon and one of the children, looking into the putting green, saw a panther-like beast.

Mr Johnson told the press:

> *'My daughter said, "Look at that big pussy-cat over there!" We came closer and it stood up and walked three or four paces and then sat down again by a hedge. It was about the size of a Labrador, with pointed ears and a long slinky tail. No way was it a dog or an ordinary household cat. It was like a panther, and we all saw it. There was no-one else around at the time.'*

This sighting was recorded in the *County Press* of 10th August 1984.

Later, on looking through my file, I discovered that back on 27th July 1984, the *County Press* published an article entitled 'Attack on sheep probe: big cat sighting report Mr Ken Fenbrook, a farmer of Northwood, farms rare Shetland sheep in a number of fields on the edge of the Parkhurst Forest. Mr Frogbrook found one of his ewes dead, with a broken neck, in his field, a month earlier. He thought that the ewes were 'sitting ducks' after they broke out of their field through the stock fence. One evening in June the sheep were on land near the Parkhurst Forest, and they were "in sheer blind panic". Mr Frogbrook spent the whole weekend rounding up the sheep. He could not catch a valuable Moorit ram, which was not re-captured until several days later.

The same weekend, Mr Arthur Attrill, farming on the western edge of the Parkhurst Forest, found one of his lambs savagely killed. It was eaten, apart from the head, legs and fleece. Mr Attrill had found a lamb in similar circumstances a week earlier. The first lamb had been dragged over a quarter of a mile into another field.

Mr and Mrs. Frogbrook drove to their sheep one night, and they saw a black big cat crossing the road. The huge jet-black cat leapt across the track in front of their car." Mr Frogbrook said:

> 'It was 3 feet long in the body, with a long tail almost or about the same length. The cat had a blunt head with a muscular body. The cat was in good condition and looked like a predator.'

This was his second sighting, because a week earlier he had seen the cat crossing the nearby Noke Common road. He had brought his sheep to the island in March 194, following two years' crofting in the Shetland Isles. He told the *County Press* of 27th July 1984:

> 'It jumped the whole width of the track and landed in a belly flop in the undergrowth. I stopped and followed it into a field beyond but lost sight of it. But I may have to give up my tenancy now and sell the flock. There's no way I can risk keeping them in the forest.'

This episode occurred about the same time that a forester and his wife saw a dark grey big cat "pouncing about like a kitten" on the edge of the forest near Newport. Mr Atrill, the farmer whom we mentioned earlier, contacted both the police and R.S.P.C.A. He thought that the killings were not by dogs, because there were no dogs in the area, and the lambs were eaten whole. These two "unusual" factors ruled out dogs and foxes and, presumably, badgers. Said Mr Atrill: *"It was something with a very big appetite. These healthy lambs weighed about 70 lbs. each."* The paper said that there had been five sightings of an Alsatian-sized black big cat. They also said there had been a sighting at Cowes.

One which was actually described was Mr Howard Smith's sighting at a yard in Newport. He was driving a fork-lift truck around the yard when he spotted a panther-like cat, which was not an ordinary domestic cat. Mr Smith thought it was a young panther and not a dog or cat. He told his workmate, who had a good view. Mr Smith stated:

> 'It was only about 20 yards away and I watched it for about two minutes. It looked straight at me and did not seem at all concerned. It had a dead rat dangling from its mouth, and it just loped across the yard and went across the playing fields belonging to the school next door. It was a very sleek, black creature, with a beautiful smooth coat. It had the sort of slow, loping walk which panthers and other big cats have.'

This description is one of the better ones given. The animal described can only be a large cat of some sort - a black serval cat, or a young black leopard, perhaps? Panthers and several cats are kept at the I.O.W. Zoo and at Robin Hill Country Park, although none had escaped.

The article *'Mystery Cat: Trap Death Report could provide Link'* in the *County Press* of 12th September

1984 was interesting. Following the capture of a black Kellas cat in Morayshire, Mrs. Francis from Devon was planning an expedition to the Island. 'British Big Cat Link' members were to be in a team made up of naturalists and one professional wildlife photographer. Twenty-four hours-a-day watches were to be kept for a week, with infrared cameras for night-time surveillance. Mrs. Frances commented on the finding of the 'cub', telling the *County Press* of 12th September that the Kellas cat was a British big cat cub, which was later proved wrong. She remarked:

> *'It is a breakthrough, and represents a possible solution to the long-standing nation-wide mystery of big cat sightings. What we need now is the capture of a live adult specimen. This one from Scotland is a male cub.*
>
> *Ideally, if the chances of sponsorship can now be improved as a result of finding this cub, the attempt for the live adult could be made simultaneously in the Isle of Wight, Speyside and Devon.'*

There had been sixty-five sightings on the Island in the twenty-one months since January 1983. One of the 'British Big Cat Link' members and leader of the expedition, of Cufnel Park, London, said that the 1984 study was aimed at getting confirmed evidence of the cat's habitat. They were also going to track and photograph the animal. *"We want to find out as much information as possible about the creature."*

The big cat investigators, all from London, comprised Mr Terry Newton, the regional 'British Big Cat Link' organiser for the south, Mr G. Ward of the Isle of Wight, Mr Patrick Sparks of Wimbledon, an ex-SAS man and the group's photographer, and various other naturalists. The group was based at Forest Farm, near the edge of the Parkhurst Forest.

A month passed by. The 12th October edition of the *County Press* confirmed my suspicions that the cat was very cunning, for the article was boldly entitled *'Island's "mystery cat" outwits Watchers.'*

They did not find the cat, but they *did* talk to Mr Michael Tipping, a night porter at the I.O.W.'s St Mary's Hospital, Newport, who saw the cat in the Forest area. He described to Mr Newton and his colleague, Mrs. Swansen, what had happened. He was in the grounds of St Mary's Hospital one night when he observed a dark grey cat, 18 ins high at the shoulder, with a 2 ft. long body and an upwards-curved tail, about three quarters or half the length of the body. The cat was by a refuse tip (again!) and it headed off across a road. Mr Tipping was sure that it was a cat, on account of the way it moved. This animal sounds like a small or young puma.

The Newport police received the report and drove Mr Newton and Mrs. Swansen to the scene of the sighting. Mr Newton recounted what happened:

> *'It was quite exciting. We were there within half an hour of the sighting and were able to interview Mr Tipping. We searched for tracks, but the ground was unsuitable. I don't think anybody was desperately disappointed about failing to see the creature during the week. It would have been great if we could have seen it, but we all felt it was a valuable week, in all sorts of ways. To be part of a team taking the matter seriously was good; and we feel we did achieve something to further public*

interest in the animal.

> *The Islanders are wonderful. They were very friendly and talkative, and we found out about a number of previously unreported sightings. We have learned to respect the guile of the beast. It is an animal that can go around, apparently leaving no tracks or evidence whatsoever behind it.'*

Mr Newton said that the six members of the team had enjoyed a successful week, making "lots of very useful contacts" with local people. There had been five more sightings since September, for reports had reached about 70 in 22 months. The high spot of the week was the interview with Mr Tipping. Dawn and dusk watches were kept in the Parkhurst Forest every day. The group also searched Ventnor Park and Botanic Gardens.

Mr Patrick Sparks, the ex-SAS man and photographer, operated some infrared camera equipment at the old railway track, near St Mary's Hospital, Newport, as it was hoped that the cat was still in the area. This was twenty-four hours after Mr Tipping's sighting. According to Mr Newton, there had been three sightings around Ventnor Botanical Gardens, where Mr Skerritt had seen the cat in September 1984.

On the Tuesday the group's leader, Mr Newton, went to Scotland to examine two large cats which were trapped or shot in the Speyside/Morayshire area. He went with Miss Francis. 11th December 1984 saw the publication of a column-article headed 'I.O.W. mystery cat" sighted near Ryde, in the *County Press*. On a Sunday afternoon Mr Peter Lockyer of Ryde and his family were driving towards Brading at 4 p.m., when they were near Beaper's Shute, a large cat-like creature the size of an Alsatian, with a mottled tabby-coloured body, ran across the road after leaping out of a hedge on one side and into some woods opposite. Mr Lockyer had a clear view of the beast, as did his wife and their four children. He told a reporter on the I.O.W. *County Press*:

> *'It was so close that I nearly hit it. At first my wife thought it was a fox but it was too big, and the wrong colour. I have read about it in the paper, but until now have never believed the reports. I certainly won't go walking out there alone.'*

This was on 9th December 1984. Lynxes could be described as being mottled or tabby, but pumas are not this colour; nor does the animal sound like a black panther. Maybe there are two pumas, one lynx and one black panther on the Island.

I see that some fifteen days before this sighting was reported on 20th October, an article was published in the *County Press* an article entitled 'Investigators' new bid to track down the big cat'. There had been more sightings in the last three weeks of October, at Shanklin, Arreton Down, Luccombe Chine, Brading Down and St Helens. The sightings inspired Mr Terry Newton of London to tell the *County Press* that his team would be back on the Island that weekend. He was planning a 'stake-out' of a suitable location in a renewed hope of photographing the cat. He said that Exeter University experts were looking at the body of the black Kellas cat, and at two sets of hair found at the scene of two Island sightings. He also said that a paw-print he photographed in the Noke Gate area of the Parkhurst Forest belonged to an unknown species of big cat. The hair samples were said to be 'unusual'.

One of the incidents described involved Mr Edward Ball who lived in a cottage near Ryde. He was sur-prised to find big paw-prints on his about the size of a half-grown Alsatian, and was a very light sandy colour. It had a round face with pointed ears sticking up. It started walking along the hedgerow and I no-ticed it had quite a long tail which was slightly curled at the end. It looked something like a puma."

Running from the house, Mr Perkins pointed out the animal to three allotment-holders nearby. They saw the creature too, but it disappeared through the hedge before they were able to use Mr Perkins' binocu-lars.

On 9th December, Mr Peter Lockyer and his wife were driving in Brading road when a large mottled cat leapt out in front of their car at Beapers Shute, only a mile from Tuesday's sighting. These latest sightings bring the total number of reported sightings of strange large cats on the Island to about 80 since January 1983.

I wrote to Mr J. Perkins of Ryde; he replied in November 1987, and I reproduce it with his permission:

'My house is at the top of a hill, and my lounge window overlooks the countryside on the south side of Ryde and has a clear view of fields and woods. Surely by chance one morning in December 1984 I looked out of the window and saw this animal loping across the field. Straight away I thought there was something unusual about it. I quickly got my binoculars and dashed back to the window just as it went into the hedge at the top of the field. I went out onto the veranda and kept my eye on the area with my binoculars, and about ten minutes later I spotted it sitting outside the hedge further along the field in the sunlight.

I had a perfectly clear view of him through my binoculars. It was sitting on its hind legs with its front paws in between. It had a sandy-coloured coat, darker on its back and sides and very light underneath which I could see clearly as it was sat upright. It also had pointed ears. Eventually it got up and started walking away. Its tail was long and curled at the ends. It just loped away, in no hurry. I am convinced it was a puma. I must confess that until sighting the cat myself, I didn't believe the sightings that had been reported beforehand. The cat has been sighted on a number of occasions in this area since my sighting, and nearly all in the winter months, possibly because there is less cover for it to hide in. Last winter, after a good fall of snow one night, I went out across the fields and was looking again for signs of the cat in the woods. I came across very large paw-prints. Following the tracks for a while, I came across fairly large droppings which again I am sure belonged to the cat. Eventually I lost the tracks in the dense woodland.'

There have been sightings of a big cat in the area of Parkhurst Forest just outside Newport, which is about ten miles away. People who have seen the cat in that area have all said it's black, but the one I saw was definitely tan-coloured, so are there two? Then, about thirty days after this sighting, on 25th January 1985, an article appeared called "big cat now seen by police sergeant" in the County Press. The officer, Mr Heath, was crime prevention officer, Ryde police station. He was standing by a window at his home in Merstone, at 8.45 one morning, a week before the article's publication. He observed a big cat walking across a field. The animal was three times the size of a domestic cat. The officer drew a comparison in its size to the several cats at Robin Hill Country Park. He also said:

It was very plain against the snow and about 100-120 yards away. You couldn't mistake it for an ordinary cat. It was absolutely black, with a very long tail curling up from the snow, and small ears pricked up. It quite surprised me because I've read many reports about the puma, or whatever it is. I had wondered if it was a figment of people's imaginations, but seeing it there in broad daylight like that really shook me.'

There was another account of the sighting in the *Weekly Post*, in an article called *"P.C. spots big cat"*. The only added details were that the cat was the size of a lynx, and it left paw-prints in the snow.

On 30th December 1987, I received a letter from Mr Arthur W. Heath of Merstone, Ryde. The letter describes his sighting in detail, so let me quote from it.

'For some unknown reason it (my letter) only came into my hands today, through my successor in Newport police station. You see, I retired from the Force 18 months ago. Anyway, I hope this letter will be of some use to you in your project. My wife and I live in a very rural part of the Island, Merstone, which is only a hamlet. Chapel Lane has only a few dwellings and across the back are just fields. It was there that I saw the animal described in the copy newspaper cutting I am enclosing. I can't remember the date exactly, but I believe it was the early months of 1985, January or February.

We had a fairly heavy fall of snow during the night and I was in my kitchen preparing to go to work (then still in the police force). From my kitchen window I have our rear garden, which is about 60 feet, then our open fencing, and beyond that a smallish paddock which eventually ends in a blackthorn hedge and then to a larger field.

It was along the blackthorn hedge that I saw what I would definitely describe as a puma-type animal. Jet black against the virgin snow, long and sleek, with a long tail curling up slightly at the tip and a round cat's head with rounded ears pricked up. The animal looked neither left or right, but walked slowly along the hedgerow, from my left, towards the farm and manor, which would be its direction of travel, whilst I only had it in view for perhaps half a minute. It was a wonderful clear view of black against white. Unfortunately I wasn't dressed to follow its path and we had no camera at hand to capture the sight on film. A little later we found many large paw-prints around our gardens and measured these at about 4 inches across, though that was in fairly deep snow and probably wouldn't have been that size in reality.

A gentleman contacted me about the incident. Apparently he mentions these sight-

*ings and was going to see me, but never did, and I didn't take his details. Eventu-
ally the snow thawed and the matter faded into history. I suppose there have been
many sightings of animals throughout the Island, some of different coloured animals, most sightings being fairly close to the Parkhurst Forest on the mid-Wight,
which is the unspoilt part of the Island, consisting mainly of farmland and National
Trust land.'*

This was a most interesting letter. Mr Heath probably saw a black leopard or a black feral cat. Lynxes are rarely, jet-black, and melanistic pumas are practically unheard of. The black big cat was first seen near Newport in 1983, and I see that I have omitted one Newport black big cat sighting from May 1984, so let us now look at it.

The *County Press* published an article called 'big cat spotted twice at Newport on 8th May 1984. Fifteen-year-old student Gavin Parker of Newport saw a strange beast on land off Wellington road. The sighting was at about noon on a Monday in early May. Gavin stated:

> *'It was a big black cat. It was sitting down and was twitching a long tail. In that po-
> sition its head would have been about as high as a Labrador's back. It had some
> white spots on its face and underbelly. I am sure of what I saw.'*

There was a second sighting soon afterwards, but of a different-coloured cat, at Newport. This sighting was also recorded in the article. Mrs. Karen Lambert was walking up the rear of the Priory Park Estate with some children. She was on the Petticoat Lane and up ahead she saw a Siamese cat-like beast in a field. It was not a normal Siamese cat as it was the size of a Labrador, with a dark head and sandy-coloured body. The animal was surprised and ran out of the field towards the playing fields of Carisbrook High School. The sighting was two weeks after a paw print was found in the mud on a farm.

The second sighting of 1985 took place on 8th February. The *County Press* reported that there was a sighting at Beaper's Farm, on the edge of Ryde. Mr and Mrs. Kershaw were driving along the Tyde-to-Brading road at about 8 o'clock on a Sunday morning. The car sustained a puncture shortly after, and they stopped by the entrance to Beaper's Farm.

A large cat-like creature appeared from a bank, leaping down onto the road, and ran across the road and into Whitefield Wood. Mrs. Kershaw ran after the cat, which headed in the direction of a small council yard. She soon lost sight of the big cat. However, both she and her husband gave good descriptions. That of Mrs. Kershaw ran as follows:

> *'It was brown or black, and I would say four times the size of a normal domestic
> cat. It had a smooth velvety coat, which might have had some sort of pattern on it, a
> round head like a Christmas pudding, and a puggy face. It was definitely a cat.'*

The reference to a 'head like a Christmas pudding' was unusual, but as I suppose Mrs. Kershaw had made various Christmas puddings she knew what they looked like.

Mr Kershaw gave a different description:

> *'It was as big as a medium-sized dog and with a tail almost as long as its body. It was 15 yards away from us at the most.'*

This sighting was at the same time that Mr Terry Newton, the British big cat researcher, came to the Island to make arrangements for another study, in September 1985. They were coming to the Island for a month. Mr Newton stated that there had been 85 sightings since 1983. The next report, one week later, was entitled 'big cat ran in front of boy cyclist', and was published on 15th February 1985. This time, the boy's mother, Mrs. Whillier of Newbridge, told the press that her son had seen the creature twice; once in the Newbridge Mill area and once in Station road, Ningwood. She contacted the *County Press* to report the sightings, saying: *"Robert was quite scared by it all."* Mrs. Whillier said that a Newbridge man had also reported seeing the cat. Robert's second sighting was at close quarters, some days after the first sighting. The thirteen-year-old boy said:

> *'The animal was about four feet in length and quite tall. It appeared to be light brown or tan in colour, and had long ears. It ran right in front of my bicycle. It started to follow me as I made my way home, but when I looked around again it ran off and was gone.'*

It was only a short time until the next possible set of sightings, again at Newbridge. This time it was Mrs. Abbot of Newbridge who informed the *County Press* of her experiences and those of her children and friends. The article was called *'More cries at night add to the Mystery'*, and was published on 8th March. Mrs. Abbot stated that her daughter, aged 15, had gone out to feed their pet cat in the garden at night. They both heard sounds coming from the nearby farm. Two years earlier they had both heard the same sounds in the same area.

Mrs Abbot's description reads*: "It's more like a scream than a call. It goes right through you - a horrible scream. It sounds like a mountain lion, only more piercing."* One of her sons had also heard the screams in the area, while two of her other children, aged 21 and 19, had seen a large cat-like beast at Brightstone Down. The animal was also seen at Calbourne by Mrs. Abbot's brother-in-law. It seems as though the whole family had seen the cat.

I wrote to Mrs. Abbot in late 1987, but before looking at her letter, I think we should consider the case of Stephen Weal, aged 15, of Newbridge, who was walking outside with a group of friends at Wellow. He remarked about the incident to the *County Press* of 8th March 1985:

> *'It was like a tiger, but a howling sound. We heard it a couple of times. And we saw something in the dark, just a shape, but it was a really big thing.'*

Returning to Mrs. Abbot's 'sighting' details her letter was dated 7th December 7th 1987, and the relevant passage ran as follows:

> *'So sorry I have only just got round to answering your letter. I can't tell you much more than you have read in the County Press. All I know is I don't want to hear that awful sound again at night. As for my children, my son Chris is a corporal in the army. He was coming back from a night-club at Brightstone with a couple of*

friends and one of my daughters. As they came from the top of Brightstone Downs to come down into Calbourne, they met what they thought was a fox. As they passed, they could see in their lights it was a cat about the size of a Labrador with a long tail. That night several cars coming from the night-club saw the cat. I can't remember who the others were, as it is a while ago now.

Back a few months ago it was seen at Thurley, early in the morning, walking up the road. I will get the address of the lady that watched it and send it to you.

Since then I haven't heard of any more sightings. I have never seen it, only heard it. Tell me, do you know the Island? I am sending you the map from our bus time-table. I have put a cross for the night-club, Calbourne and Newbridge and Thurley. I know you have written to Mrs. Whillier. She lives five numbers down the road from me, so we think that there are more than one cat on the Island as there have been sightings over on the other sides.'

The letter was most interesting. As yet, I have not heard from Mrs. Whillier, but hope to, in due course. On March 22nd 1985, the *County Press* published an article called *'Sights big cat for second time'*. This time it was Mrs. Carpenter in January 1985 of Gurnard, near Cowes, who observed the big cat in a garden at Cowes.

Then she saw it again at almost the same spot, in March 1985. She thought it was the same creature; it was *'leopard-like, jet-black, with a thick tail, and was the size of a Labrador dog'*.

This sighting was followed by an appeal from the ASSAP (Association for the Scientific Study of Anomalous Phenomena) in the *County Press* of 19th March 1985. The Society is interested in anything from ghosts to UFO sightings, to the Loch Ness monster and 'Hound of the Baskerville' type stories. Two of its members had gone to the Island on a previous expedition, and they had left none the wiser on the mystery cat. Mr Seymour of Peckham, London, was the ASSAP South London regional coordinator, and he wanted to know whether the cats were seen in pre-war days. He .was also going to look into all local legends.

On 21st May 1985, an article appeared in the *County Press* called *'Survey of "big cats" sightings possible'*. The article was again about the ASSAP investigations. This time the group was visiting a number of old places, such as churches, on the Island. They visited those at Longstone, Godshill, Gatcombe and St Lawrence. These churches were connected with pre-Christian objects. The Isle of Wight was inhabited in Celtic times, I believe. The article said that the group spent four days on the Island and they covered everything about local legends. They wanted to know whether eyewitnesses of the big cats had experienced any *'psychic awareness'*. Mr C. Seymour said:

'We are open-minded as to what the phenomenon might actually be. We are not sure whether it is a physical entity or not. But without looking at the statements of witnesses in detail it will be hard to progress. We had thought it might not be possible for such a creature to exist on the Island, but after driving around and getting lost in numerous country lanes, we realised it was plausible.'

BIG CATS: LOOSE IN BRITAIN

The ASSAP planned to circulate a questionnaire asking people about their sightings; they were puzzled about the different sizes and colours of cats, as well as the correspondence between sightings and witnesses' characters. The Island was geographically contained for their investigation, which must have helped them.

The *County Press* of 26th April 1985 contained this reference to a mystery cat, entitled *'Dead Lamb victim of the big cat'*. The article described how farmer Mr Ken Frogbrook of Northwood, near Newport, whose sheep had been troubled by a big cat, had now lost a lamb. Mr Frogbrook had found big cat 'spoor' leading into his field, and he lost the Moorit Shetland lamb a few weeks later. The carcass was picked totally of meat, and even the head was missing. He thought that no dog, human, or fox could have done that killing. As he himself had seen the big cat, he came to the obvious conclusion that the black panther-type cat had eaten the lamb. Mr Frogbrook feared for the safety of his 18 purebred, valuable sheep, and wondered what to do about the killing. He had about 12 lambs, 4 ewes due to lamb in a week, and one ram. The previous July (1984) had seen the start of his troubles, and Mr Frogbrook was worried about the safety of the remaining sheep.

The other incident recounted in the article in the *County Press* of 26th April 1985 involved school pupil Gary Sharman. He was walking through woods at Oakfield, Ryde, with his grandfather, Mr Eastman, when he found a number of large animal paw-prints. Fifteen-year-old Gary estimated them as 4 inches by 5 inches. There were some smaller paw-prints at the side, which suggested that the animal might have had cubs with it. Gary was pictured with one of the paw-prints, which does look like that of a puma or leopard-sized feline. He was quoted as detailing the following to a reporter: *"The prints were much too big for a dog, and they were more cat-like in appearance."*

The suggestion of cubs is interesting, and some might say unlikely. We know that there are at least three cats on the Island - a black big cat, a sandy big cat and a dark grey or brown big cat. This is worth bearing in mind. The favourite haunt of the black big cat is Newport and Parkhurst, while that of the sandy big cat seems to be Ryde. We can really only speculate on what the cats might be until we hear more about them. *'big cat" is sighted at Gurnard'* was the title of the next *County Press* article on the cat, in the 25th July publication. Ten-year-old Craig McShane, of Cowes, was on a school bus one afternoon, and when the bus passed Gurnard primary school, he observed at the entrance an 'angry' sand-coloured cat which was larger than an Alsatian. A lady bus superintendent also saw the cat and thought it was 'really angry'. Craig remarked: "It had sharp teeth, its ears were pointing up and it had a curly tail. It was sniffing around." I think Craig observed a puma, although I cannot be certain. Pumas like to sniff around and investigate objects. There had been two sightings of a similar animal in the locality earlier in 1985. In the same *County Press* article of 25th July 1985 was the story of the lamb belonging to Mr Christopher Clifford of Porchfield, which was found dead. Its side was ripped open from haunch to chest and a number of ribs were missing. A rare Manx Loughton, the sheep was not really a lamb but a young ewe. It had a number of large scratch marks or claw marks on the chest and breastbone. Mr Clifford, who was obviously angry and surprised at the kill, said: *"It was a savage kill. Quite a lot of the meat was eaten. It follows the pattern we would expect if the animal had been savaged by dogs or a fox."*

The same night as the ewe was massacred, a couple of hens were taken from Mr Christopher Brownrigg's farm at Porchfield.

If the sandy-coloured cat was the cause of these incidents in July, maybe the black big cat was behind all the incidents at Brightstone Down, in May and June 1985. On 21st June 1985, an article was published in the *County Press*, stating *'"big cat" may have claimed fresh victim'*. Mr R. Kingswell of Rowborough Farm near Sandown, found a dead lamb at Brightstone Down in May 1985. He found another dead lamb one weekend five weeks later, in June. The 60-lb lamb was partly eaten, and Mr Kingswell knew that his neighbour had seen a large cat-like animal in the first two weeks of June.

He took the lamb along to Mr Jack Corney at the I.0.W. Zoo, Sandown, who said the animal was killed by a large creature, but he did not know what species. Mr Kingswell told the *County Press* reporter:

> *'The lamb was too big for dog, fox or badger to kill, and it was eaten. It must have been something pretty big to kill it. Just the skin was left, and the head.'*

Mr Kingswell also knew that there had been a big cat sighting at Bowcombe and also at Cheverton chalk pit, in 1985. Was the cat to blame, I wonder Mr Kingswell also added: *"I'm concerned about further attacks now these two lambs have gone."* Mr B. Peaker, a gamekeeper at Bowcombe, said that the lamb was not likely to have been killed by foxes, dogs or badgers. He was going to keep dawn and dusk watches on the area. Jack Corney of the I.O.W. Zoo, added the point that the lamb was not bitten at the throat, which one would have expected, but he did think that the lamb *was 'killed by some fairly large animal'*.

The paper also noted Mr Grogwell's sightings, and said that there had been 110 sightings in the past 2 years.

The next article was published in the *County Press* of 2nd August, and was entitled *'big cat is seen in Freshwater and Lake areas'*. The first sighting was at 11.30 one morning, by Mr Dick Ring of the Royal Standard Hotel, Freshwater, the area being the busy town centre of School Green Road. Mr Ring was working inside his bottles store when he heard a loud scratching noise on the asbestos roof, which was obviously able to support the weight of whatever was up there. He told his wife to stay inside while he went out to see what was there. He was momentarily shocked to see a big cat, and watched the animal jump from the bottles store roof into bushes behind the adjoining garage.

Mr Ring stated:

> *"I thought it must be a man who had climbed up there, as the noise was so loud. I went outside to have a look, and this huge cat-like creature stopped in its tracks and stared me right in the face. The creature, which was black with noticeably pointed ears, was more than three feet in length and at least a foot tall. It suddenly leapt up and bounded away at speed, and it was then that I noted it had an unusual, semi-bushy tail."*

This sighting was probably of a young black panther, a lynx or a serval. I am not sure which species it was, though it seems to have the characteristics of quite a few species.

The second sighting described in the 2nd August article in the *County Press* was that by Mr Terry Chard of Lake who, as he walked home down Lake Hill in the early hours of the morning, watched a strange beast. The cat had "a kind of spring in its walk" and came from Lake Mall. It went off towards the Old

People's complex, at Towers. Mr Chard remarked:

> *'I saw something trotting across the road about twenty yards away. It definitely wasn't a dog. It had a cat-like head with pointed ears, a long, skinny body, long legs and a very long rounded tail.'*

This description can only suit a serval cat, which looks like a small cheetah with pointed ears. A week passed before a 'filler' article was published in the *County Press* of 9th August 1985:

> *'Fresh sighting: Another reported sighting of a puma-like animal was made by a Newport resident early on Tuesday. Police searched the grounds of the I.W. College of Arts and Technology where the animal was said to have been spotted, but nothing was found.'*

A month later, on 13th September, *'big cat is sighted by dog walker'* was the title of an article. Mr Mick Ford of Parkhurst, near Newport, was walking his Alsatian bitch in a field opposite his home at ten o'clock one morning, when he heard a "sickening" howling from near by He told the newspaper's reporter:

> *'It made me shiver. It was a blood-chilling, deep-throated howl. I heard the noise again, and there was a rustling in the bushes, and this big cat jumped out. It was the size of a Labrador and had a long tail. As soon as I saw it I ran - and so did Freia. I looked round and the thing had gone."*

There were also other people in the vicinity who heard the screams. One was Mrs. Hayles who was walking home late at night. She heard a *"horrible howling"* which must have unnerved her. She told the *County Press* of 13th September 1985: *"It was a growling, mumbling noise. It certainly wasn't a domestic cat or a dog."*

Sounds are very misleading, and the 'yap' or bark of a vixen fox could easily be confused with the weird jungle cry of a big cat. Pumas scream, lynxes yowl, tigers and lions roar, and other cats howl.

Shortly after this incident, two Southern Water Authority workers, Mr Brooker and Mr Holbrook, were driving near the Heritage Centre, Calbourne one morning. It was eight o'clock and still fairly dark, one presumes. The men noticed a beast *"dark brown and bigger than an Alsatian"*, which *"leapt over a hedge with one jump - something no ordinary cat or dog could do."* Mr Brooker reported the *"puma-like"* beast sighting to the *County Press* of 25th October. He had previously been rather sceptical about the existence of such an animal. Now he had no doubts that there was a big cat on the Island.

The *County Press* article was called *'Yet another reported sighting'* and *'big cat is sighted yet again'.* They also mentioned the press coverage of the Kellas cat. The paper seemed satisfied enough to remark: 'Others have been seen or shot in parts of England'. Have any other cats been shot in England? There are rumours and some evidence to support this fact, which prove beyond all doubt the existence of these creatures. We are reaching a point where the Island sightings became fewer. August 1986 was to produce two sightings, as were a few months in the spring of 1986. First we look at the *County Press* article *'big cat has been sighted'*, of 25th April 1986. Mrs. McGrath of Freshwater, was walking alone at the Warren, Freshwater, when she came upon something *'the size of a lion',* she remarked to the *County Press.*

> *'It was crouching in the bushes just ten feet from where I was standing. Although partly obscured, there was no mistaking that it was no ordinary animal. I was very frightened.'*

Mrs McGrath probably observed one of the cats, although I cannot say which one, as she does not give a description of it.

There were other sightings at Freshwater in the spring of 1986. Two men who saw the cat in August were Mr Whittington and Mr Blackwell, both of Newport. They were driving along Forest Road, Parkhurst at 5.30 one morning when a Labrador-sized, long-tailed, jet-black big cat bounded across the road, heading for a factory site. The men were taken aback by the black panther and stopped their car. Mr Blackwell described what happened next, to the *County Press* of 15th August.

> *'It came across the road like a thunderbolt, giving us quite a start. It couldn't have been anything other than a big cat. Richard climbed up a bus stop there and I shinned up a telegraph pole to try and get a second glimpse of the animal. We could see where it had gone down the bank because the undergrowth was flattened.'*

The sighting was at a road adjoining the Parkhurst Forest. Mr Whittington's mother of Newport wrote me this letter on 11th December 1987, enclosing photocopied articles from the *County Press.*

> *'I hope you don't mind me answering your letter, but if you wait for my son to answer, you'll wait forever. I was so impressed with your letter, I felt I had to answer. A couple of weeks back, I had to attend an A.G.M. meeting. A reporter was present, so I asked for his help. As you can see, he was very helpful. I hope you'll have some fun with the photocopies enclosed.*
>
> *We have a small zoo at Sandown and a country park at Arreton but of course, no one knows if our cat came from one of these places, or some private person just let it loose. Sorry I'm unable to help more.'*

This was a very kind letter and I am most grateful for Mrs. Whittington's help. The article in the *County Press* of 15th August also noted that the 'British Big Cat Link' Group were planning to come back to the Island, according to Mr Newton, their leader. They had had three previous expeditions and had not yet actually seen the cats. Mr Terry Newton was to lead the fourth expedition to the Island.

On 18th November 1986 the following article from the *County Press* published an announcement that some good was coming from the big cat saga: *'Tracker to aid Children's Safari:*

> *'A bid by expert tracker and ex-SAS man Eddie McGee to hunt down the mystery-animal which has been dubbed the 'Island Puma' will aid disabled children on an African safari. The visit next week by the man who helped stalk killer Barry Pru-*

dom has been backed by a syndicate which includes Mr M. Lickens, owner of the Savoy Country Club, Yarmouth, and Mr Nan Curtis, former consultant to the three island authorities. A total of £350 will be paid to a charity supported by Mr McGee which is sending handicapped children to Kenya.'

The results of the hunt were never published in the *County Press*. I do know that Mr McGee, who is very skilled in his job, was also involved in hunting the 'Exmoor Beasts' in the spring of 1983.

The following year, 1987, produced only two reported incidents. The *County Press* published an article and a picture on 25th January. It was called *'Prints spark off big cat theory'*, and involved Mrs. Vowles of Binstead, near Newport. One of Mrs. Vowles's neighbours had discovered strange paw-prints and heard peculiar noises on the Dame Anthony's Common area some weeks before. The neighbour told her about the noises and paw-prints, so Mrs. Vowles was aware of the cat when it, or something like it, left four large paw-prints in her garden. She thought that the big cat had left these prints. She stated:

> *'I looked out of my bedroom window down on to the back garden and saw these prints clearly embedded in the snow. From the way in which they were set out, it appeared that during the night an animal had jumped over the fence, from the copse at the bottom of my garden, continued across and over into next door. There were tracks leading off from there. The size of the prints were far too big to be those of a dog or domestic cat.'*

Mrs Vowles was pictured pondering over the paw prints in the garden of her modern house. Behind her is a wooden fence about 5 feet high - a height that only a member of the cat family could jump.

The second article was called *'big cat report from Arreton'*, on 14th August 1987, also in the *County Press*. Mr R. Osman was going to work at Sandown one morning at 7.40 when a big cat ran across the road in front of his car while on the Arreton Shute to Downend road. He thought the beast was the same height as a medium-sized dog, though in the body it was much longer than a dog. The animal was sandy-coloured, with pointed ears. I think that Mr Osman had observed the 'puma' or 'caracal lynx' or 'serval cat' rather than the 'black panther'.

There is nothing more to say on the I.O.W. cats, except that I have not forgotten the following *Fortean Times* reference, in issue No. 46:

> *'Isle of Wight Builder John Ball and four colleagues watched a large cat-like creature for 15 minutes on farmland off Forest Road, Newport, from the first-floor of the building on which they were working. "It was black, like a panther, about five feet long, with a long tail and pointed ears. It moved like a lioness or panther," said Mr Ball. The animal seemed to be carrying something in its mouth, like a rabbit, "which it dropped as it searched for a way out of the field."'*

Isle of Wight *Weekly Post*, 31st May 1985:

> *'Mr Mick Ford was walking his young Alsatian dog in a field near his home in Parkhurst about 10 p.m. when he heard a "blood-chilling" howl, then a "sickening...*

deep-throated howl" from some bushes. Suddenly "a big cat jumped out. It was the size of a Labrador dog." They all ran off in different directions, frightened. Said to be more than 120 sightings of the Island's mystery cat in the past two and a half years, according to the Portsmouth News, 7th September, Isle of Wight Weekly Post and County Press, 13th September 1986.'

I am making further inquiries about an unusual animal, which was shot at Bembridge. *'It had a head like a large fox, a shaggy mane, body almost hairless, large paws, 1940',* according to Janet and Colin Bond in *'Modern Mysteries of Britain: A 100 Years of Strange events'* (Granada, London, 1987, 1988). It could be a wolf, an unusual dog, a big cat, or even a werewolf. The incident occurred at the same time as Mrs. Delin Whitehead encountered large wildcats at Afton Marsh, Freshwater. (See the "Fortean Times, No. 44, Summer 1985, for a case quoting the *Isle of Wight County Press*, 22nd March 1985, of a theatre critic who saw a 'wolf' at Whitely Bank, on the south-east of the Island.) A local man told me he had seen a very large fox there. I am not aware of any other wolf sightings.

- Chapter 9 -
WELSH MYSTERY CATS

A number of sightings and letters have come from Wales. The sightings date from around 1980.

Janet and Colin Bord wrote an article called '*Strange Creatures in Powys*' for the *Fortean Times*, (No.34). It would seem that on 23rd October 1980, Mr Michael Nash of Pant-y-Drain farm in Powys, was working near his farm barn when he heard a clear snoring sound coming from inside his hay bales. Both Mr Nash and his son had previously heard the sound. An unusual, large paw print was in the yard, and Mr Nash had lost four sheep in the past ten days, though not to a dog, he thought.

So Mr Nash telephoned the police, who arrived at two in the morning, and later called up armed reinforcements. Though Mr Nash suggested that they should fence off one side of the barn, the police reckoned that this was not necessary. It seems they were wrong, for by the time they closed in at noon, the beast had gone. The empty lair was found, and three to four inch long pellets were later identified as owl pellets. Wet straw was found where the creature had urinated. After the police and media pulled out, Mr Nash heard the creature snoring again!

A neighbouring farmer lost two sheep, probably to a dog or fox, he thought. This was the point where the Bords were able to telephone Mr Nash and question him. A man known to keep a wild animal at Newtown was now in prison and the animal was no longer in the yard where it had lived. In addition, a circus had been in the area recently.

Mr Nash put a box over the best paw print, so the Bords were able to photograph it. The print was later said to be that of a dog, by world-expert Dr Bernard Heuvelmens. The Bords also contacted the police, who said that no reports of escaped animals had come in, but that a large dog could be responsible for leaving the paw-print.

Mr Nash knew that a woman had seen a cat-like animal between Churchstoke and Sam, ten miles east of Newtown. The police did not know the witness's name, although they recalled the incident. The Bords were told that the creature could have been a fox. The wild animal (a big cat, we presume) had lived in a shed in the Cardigan area, but the police thought the local council had it put down. It was apparently unlicensed. The Bords concluded their article by noting the fact that a district nurse saw a 'lynx', near Churstoke on the Welsh border on 29th September 1980. The nurse apparently fainted after the encounter. The 'Out of Place' section of the *Fortean Times*, (No.34) continues to give us an insight into the Powys beast. On 25th November 1980, Mr Ernest Lloyd of Coedcae farm, Cwmbelan (which is only six miles from Mr Nash's farm), observed a strange cat-like creature leaping and bounding across his land. It was 300 yards away. Mr Lloyd and his neighbour, Mr Vaughan, discovered twelve paw-prints on the hillside. Each print was the size of a small palm. The police joined the search for a time, and photographed the tracks. Mr M.J. Williams, curator of Dudley Zoo, Wolverhampton, gave his opinion that the paw-prints of Mr Nash and Mr Lloyd belonged to a dog.

The national press of 27th November 1980 made fun of the situation by saying *"The puma that woofs"*.

The press felt that the Llangurig beast was the same one as the creature seen by Mr Lloyd. This may or may not be true, but it is clear that Mr Lloyd reckoned that what he saw was not a dog. He said: *"I insist it was more like a big cat."* These articles were published in the *Shropshire Star* and the *Bristol Evening Post* for 26th and 27th November. Subsequently the *Daily Telegraph* and *Daily Express* published the story. The *South Wales Argus*, the *Guardian*, the *County Express and Times*, and the *Western Mail* all carried articles on this subject.

Half-way through December 1980, about 30 miles south-west, over the mountains, at least three animals ravaged flocks of sheep at Llanpumsaint, Dyfed. The creatures killed ten sheep and left others badly hurt. After a period of two days, on 28th November 1980, the beasts were identified as being dogs. This was reported in the *Western Mail* of 28th November.

Around the 13th December, a beast was observed at a farm quite near Llandiloes. The creature was identified as being a not-too-ferocious dog-like beast, reddish-brown in colour. The beast was seen sniffing round the Bounds' dog at Coèlcohion Mawr, Cwmbelan, by Mrs. Bound and her young daughter. But Farmer Mc Lloyd stated that *'a gray puma-like creature'* was what he had observed. This was given in the *Daily Telegraph* of 20th November, the *Shropshire Star* of 15th December, and the *County Times and Express* of the 20th December 1980.

The beast, now termed the "Welsh Puma", featured in the 'out-of-place' section of the *Fortean Times*, (No.35). In the second week of June 1981, the beast was not seen, but only thought to have killed sheep and lambs at Aberystwyth. Later, on the nights between the 11 and 14th June, seven ewes and five lambs were killed at Ysbyty Ystwyth. The RSPCA were called in and with local Welsh farmers, they found large paw-prints at the scene of the kills. Experts (presumably the RSPCA Inspectors) said a black panther could have made the prints. One farmer did actually see the beast and said it was black. Inspector Trevor Caldwell of the Dyfed-Powys RSPCA, stated that he was 'almost certain that the killer was a black panther', for we hear:

> *'We have had three definite sightings in the last week from very level-headed people. It was described as a long jet-black cat, standing about 2 ft. 6 in. at its head. The countryside is ideal for a big cat, with old mine shafts and quarries.'*

Note here, that the black cat near Dunster, in West Somerset, supposedly lives in some disused quarries. The Inspector went on to say that he and Inspector Blyth of the local police had set wire traps for it and had baited these traps with meat. The two men had found many tracks during a day's search on the 10th June 1981. Mr Blyth and Mr Caldwell were doubtful about the effectiveness of these traps, for the latter concluded: *"But we will only catch it if it is hungry, but that is doubtful, as there is plenty of food available."*

This was, yet again, reported in the *Shropshire Star* of 15th June and the *Daily Star* of the same date, and the Welshpool *County Times and Express* of 16th June. That was the last, at the time of writing in 1990, which the *Fortean Times* reported on Welsh mystery cats.

Later in 1981, Diana Francis was able to take some photographs of three mystery cats at Tonmawr, Glamorgan. These she termed the British big cats. Mrs. Francis, who writes books and was a South Devon naturalist, is now living in Morayshire, Scotland. The photographs she and a resident took show a black panther-type cat, and two gray-fawn puma-like cubs. The experts think that Di Francis's photographs are inconclusive. According to her book, she had just returned from Dartmoor and switched on the Television to find that in *John Craven's News Round*, a report was saying that photographs had been taken of some mystery ocelot cats in Wales. Di Francis taped the report, contacted the BBC in Cardiff and before long she was up in Wales. She stayed with some local people and was able to view the cats for herself. She took three photographs: two showed a black big cat rushing across a hillside, and one showed a grey big cat sitting on a hillside. We also find that Di Francis did not take the most controversial photographs - those showing a cub-like cat rising up on its hind legs to grab some meat. Some people tell me that they think this 'cub' is just a feral domestic cat. Others say that Mrs. Francis played around with the cat's paws and head. Mrs. Francis denies such claims, stating that people think she 'rigged' the photographs. What is clear is that the pictures show three large cats in these Islands, and that they could be of an unidentified species.

In 1985 there was a possible sighting near Flint by Justin Morgan, a 14-year-old boy living in Cardiff. Justin said that he and his amateur naturalist uncle were looking out on a valley from his uncle's bungalow window when they saw a large black cat-like creature rushing across the moonlit hillside. It was definitely described by Justin as being 'long and cat-like'. He was positive it was a big cat. A quick look at the map shows Flint to be within easy range of the Chester area, where lionesses and wolves have been reported; also in North Wales is the Snowdonia National Park where (Scottish) wildcats lived until fairly recently. At the time of writing, I have had no less than 13 letters from various authorities in Wales. I quote these letters and photocopied articles, as follows:

·The Curator of Penscynor wild life park, Cilfrew, near Neath, West Glamorgan, Mr Rob Colley, told me, in a letter dated 18th March 1987:

'The only incident I am aware of concerning Penscynor and possible exotic escapees was a request in 1986 for advice about puma-trapping. The request came, I think, from the Forestry Commission and related to reported evidence/sightings from the Margam Forest (W. Glamorgan). Unfortunately, after the initial request I heard no more details. I would suggest you contact the head forester, via the Forestry Commission, Port Talbot, West Glamorgan.'

·Mr P.M. Hughes, the Forest District Manager, replied to my letter. He wrote on the 8th April 1987:

'Although there have been numerous sightings of a large-cat presence in this area, we have no experience or advice available on puma-trapping. If the situation arose that trapping was possible, I would invite Penscynor wild life park staff to implement any trap/captive policy.'

I wrote to Mr Hughes a second time, to get some more information on the elusive Margam Forest pumas. The third letter came from Mr Nick Jackson, Zoological director of the Zoological Society of Wales, and it was dated 23rd March 1987. He could only say:

> *'I am afraid that we have no information about this, and suggest you write to the Zoology Department of the National Museum of Wales in Cardiff, or perhaps that of the British Museum in London.'*

I wrote to Mrs. Cynthia M. Merrett, the director of the Zoology Department at the National Museum of Wales, Cathays Park, Cardiff. She replied in a letter of 8th April, 1987:

> *'We have no authenticated records of 'big cats' loose in Wales, although there are recurring reports of one supposedly living in the Margain country park in West Glamorgan, where it could live on the herd of fallow deer. There have also been 'sightings' of a lynx-like' creature between Barry and Dinas Powys in South Glamorgan in past years. However, nothing has been caught.'*

Scientists tend to say that if nothing has been caught it cannot exist, but once caught, they willingly classify it as a yet unknown species.

The next letter I had was again from Mr P.M. Hughes, the Forestry District Manager at the Afan Forestry District Office, Pontrhydyfn, Port Talbot, and was dated 15th May 1987. Mr Hughes said:

> *'Local press coverage concerning the 'big cat' sightings appeared in the following papers:*
>
> *1) Glamorgan Gazette, on 4th December 1985 and 12th December 1985. Their reporter was Jayne Issacs.*
>
> *2) The South Wales Evening Post, on 13th September 1985.'*

I wrote to both the local papers. The first reply came from Mr Martin Spinks of the *South Wales Evening Post* in Swansea. He said:

> *'I'd be interested to learn more about your proposed book "big cats Loose in Britain" so as. to write a more substantial article on the subject. I would, therefore, be most grateful if you would give me a ring here at the "Evening Post".'*

Rather than ringing Mr Spinks, I wrote back to him. Mrs. Jayne Issacs, of the *Glamorgan Gazette* was most helpful and she sent me the three articles she had written on the Afan Forest Cats. With her permission, I have used the material from the articles in the next part of this chapter.

The first article was entitled *'Mountain Lions stalk Forest'*, and was dated 12th September 1985. Mr David Parnell, the Forester in charge of recreation and tourism at the Afan district Forestry Commission Office stated:

> *'There is no doubt at all. There have been sightings of large cats in this forest for at*

least ten years. The Forestry Commission now officially admits that they exist. We have 25,000 acres and these cats have been sighted from Neath across to Bryn. The animal came through on two successive nights, and we believe that there were two different ones. We were able to estimate the weight of one at 25 kilos (approx. 5 stone) and the other at 20 kilos. One of the recent sightings was near Neath, when an early morning jogger running alongside the forest saw a large cat shadowing him and running inside the trees. We reckon he ran a bit faster after that.

The forest provides an ideal environment for these cats. It would be similar terrain with hills and trees, and the climate here is less harsh with milder winters than they would have in America. There is ample game and there is no reason why such creatures could not live for many years in the safety of the forest.

I have kept a file on the activities of these animals and all the incidents. As far as we are concerned, we are happy to allow them to remain within the forest. They are doing no harm and we will not permit anyone to come in with guns, looking for them. In any case, they run away from people, and the chances of anyone ever cornering one are totally remote.'

Mr Parnell also said that he had taken plaster-casts of the cats' paw-prints as they came through his garden. It was his belief that the pumas were no threat, and that they were rarely seen, as they were so elusive. A policeman at Port Talbot police station confirmed that although there had been sightings, they had no plans to take any action.

Mrs Issacs then contacted Mrs. Susan Howells of Bryn Awel farm, Penybryn, who was out riding her horse on the Aberbaiden to Penybryn road, when she spotted a puma-like cat near a place known as Hafod Heulog.

The cat was moving in a ploughed field, on the edge of the Hafod Heulog woods. Mrs. Howells then described what the cat was like and what it was doing:

'It was walking along and I called out. It turned and looked at me for a second. It had a large head, a fawn-coloured body and a long tail. It was definitely a cat of some sort and looked like a cougar or mountain lion. It was larger than my Alsatian and just bounded off. My horse was absolutely terrified. He was trembling and I could feel his heart pounding through the saddle.

I have never seen anything run so fast. It gave me quite a turn. We had two ewes killed at Pentitla which we thought at the time were killed by dogs. But it was very strange. They were both killed the same way. They were found lying on their backs and had been dragged around. Their stomachs had been ripped away. It was not like a normal, dog-killing incident.'

Pentitla was Mrs. Howell's parents' farm, and the kills had taken place in the spring of 1984. Mr David Parnell, the Forestry Commission recreation manager, had developed the theory that the cats had been released by somebody who kept them illegally as exotic pets for a while and then freed the cats when they were too difficult to handle. He added: *"No one is ever going to admit having done this, and we also know that one escaped in the area recently."* He might have been talking about the same animal that farmer Mr Nash had heard having possibly escaped from the Cardigan area of Glamorgan.

On 10th October 1985, Jayne Issacs wrote another article for the *Glamorgan Gazette*. It was called *'big cats are sighted inside Country Park.'* This time it appeared that the Forestry Commission employees were coming forward. Mr Dave Duggan, a security officer, gave these details about what he had seen:

> *'It was early one morning and I saw it standing on a road in the park. I was only about 15 yards away from it, and it was definitely a big cat. It was bigger than my Alsatian dog, a browny-beige colour, with a thick long tail. Its hindquarters were very musular and it was in beautiful condition. I could not positively identify which type of cat it was but it looked like a mountain lion. It ran into bushes and disappeared.'*

Mr Duggan's two young sons saw the cat two days earlier, while walking home, in the country park. They saw the cat run across the road in front of them, and therefore ran back to their friends' house as they were frightened by their encounter with the beast.

Mr Duggan had worked in the park for two years and was used to all types of animals.

> *"I often hear animals crashing about in the bushes,"* he continued, *"and I have always assumed it was a deer. Now it makes me jump a bit more."*

Another park ranger, Mr Roger Jones, heard the cat earlier in the summer of 1985. He told Jane Issacs:

> *'We were in one of the valleys leading up towards the Forestry when we heard the unmistakable call of a big cat. It was like listening to a wildlife programme from Africa. The call reverberated and echoed around the valley. It was very startling. understand that mountain lions have weak vocal cords, but the call that I heard just rolled around in the manner of a lion. There have been reports of sightings for some time. There is only a boundary wall between the park and the forest and this would present no obstacle to a big cat. At the moment we do not feel that the animal presents any danger and it is very secretive. We do not want people trying to shoot it. This is an ideal habitat for an animal like' that, and it could well live on a diet of venison.'*

Mr Jones had heard that some people thought the animal was a lioness, rather than a mountain lion. He also thought that people believed there were at least two cats, if not a whole family, up in the forest.

Only a year and one month later, on 4th December 1985, Mrs. Issacs had written another article for the *Glamorgan Gazette*, called *'New Sighting in big cats Riddle'*.
Mr Mal Peregrine of Llangynnyd, Mid-Glamorgan, was walking to Top Llan one evening, when he spotted a strange, large cat-like creature in a gateway. Mr Peregrine described the beast to Jayne Issacs:

> *'I could hear something rattling one of the farm gates as I walked up the hill. This*

particular gate is set back from the road a few feet, with hedges on either side. I thought it might be a fox, but when I drew level I could see it was a big, dark grey cat. It was obviously trying to get through the gate. It must have felt trapped because it spat at me and raised its front paw, just like any normal cat when it's cornered.

I stepped back a few feet and it came right out into the road. It had a long tail and it was a smoky-grey colour. It had a cat's ears and a small head. I was within feet of it for several minutes and then it managed to get over the hedge and raced off through the fields.'

Mr Peregrine said that the cat was nearly as large as an Alsatian and much longer. Mr Roy Rees of Llan-gynnyd was out in the fields at night, when a lamb was found dead.

He said: "The animal had been eaten, and only the head was left. The following night I was out with my gun. I saw the cat come into the field and the sheep became very agitated. But it was pouring with rain and by the time I lined up the gun, it was gone. A Mr Wyn Edwards, who lived at Yr Ysfa, Maesteg, saw the animal twice, as he was returning home late at night. The cat was crossing the main road. He said:

> *'I caught it in my headlights the first time. I stopped the car and it turned to look at me. It was beautiful - a big black cat with bright blue eyes. It walked over the road and disappeared."*

Jayne Issacs thought it was a different cat to the one seen by Mrs. Howells the year previously. This cat sounds more like a black panther, or a black British big cat.

The *Daily Mirror* of January 1987 said:

> *'At Rhymney, Mid-Glamorgan, farmers last week were hunting a 'very large dog' which killed 47 sheep.'*

Was the 'very large dog' none other than one of the Welsh big cats? Di Francis carried a section on Welsh mystery cats in her book *'Cat Country; the Quest for the British big cat',* and the first sighting she describes sounds like a Scottish wildcat sighting in the 1950s. I have heard that the Scottish wildcat still exists in the remoter parts of the Snowdonia National Park, although it seems to be pretty rare, as I have read only one reference to it, in a book of wildlife. Foxes also cause a problem in Wales, as this article from the *Daily Mail* of 14th April 1987 illustrates:

> *"Flocking together, Welsh sheep farmers have formed an action group to protest at Labour plan to ban fox hunting which, they say, could virtually wipe out the sheep industry by letting foxes run wild."*

The Port Talbot Police Chief-Superintendent told me in a letter dated 20th August 1987:

> *"I acknowledge receipt of your letter on the above subject (big cats Loose in Britain) and write to advise you that the Borough Councils of Neath and Port Talbot would be better equipped to give you the help you require.'*

Mr Ceri Hampton-Jones, of the Borough Council, Port Talbot, answered my request on 23rd September 1987. He told me:

> 'There have been some reported sightings of something described as a very big cat, mainly in the Margam Forest area of Port Talbot. The local evening newspaper, the *South Wales Evening Post*, first did a story on it a couple of years ago when there were some strange sounds heard in the woods around Glyn Corrwg Forest. More recently (I would say in the last 12 months) the newspaper reported on the sighting at Margam Forest, and the investigations being carried out by the park rangers.

> I would suggest you contact both the newspaper and the country park for more information.'

He gave me the addresses of the *South Wales Evening Post* (to whom I had written previously), and the Margam Forest Head Ranger. I wrote to the ranger, but to date I have received no reply.

I also had another letter, describing the sighting of a lynx, in Dyfed. Mr D.W. Ward of Holybourne, near Alton in Hampshire, answered my 18th October 1987 sightings request in the *Alton Herald*. He wrote on 15th November 1987:

> 'In about 1975 (I am uncertain of the exact date) my wife, two children and I were driving along a private road in what was formerly the county of Pembrokeshire (now Dyfed). It was about 4 p.m. on a clear and dry day with excellent conditions of visibility. On stopping to open a gate across the road, we saw, to our surprise, a cat-like creature, which we later identified from wildlife books as a lynx. The animal was emerging from the undergrowth onto the road, and spotted us, one front paw raised, and stared at us for at least 20-30 seconds. The feeling of surprise was mutual, but it eventually turned tail and ran off into the bushes.

> Nobody in the area had reported seeing such an animal, and, to my knowledge, it has not been since, and appeared to be an adult.'

There have been other sightings of a lynx in Dyfed. The black dog has a definite home in Dyfed, and as long ago as 1813, the Reverend Edmund Jones of Tranch, Newport wrote a book called '*A Relation of Apparitions of Spirits in the County of Monmouth and the Principality of Wales*', which describes some authenticated black dog encounters. These encounters have been quoted in the books '*Cat Country; the quest for the British big cat*' by Di Francis, by Janet and Colin Bord in '*The Secret Country*' and '*Alien Animals*'. Graham J. McEwan also noted them in '*Mystery Animals of Britain and Ireland.*'

I advise people wishing to see a list of sightings to refer to Janet and Colin Bord's book '*Modern Mysteries of Britain: A Hundred Years of Strange Events*' (Granada, London, 1987, 1988). They include sightings from Brechf a, Dyfed; Ysbyty Ystwyth, Dyfed; Leckwith, South Glamorgan; Margam Forest, West Glamorgan; Ton Mawr, West Glamorgan; Churchstoke, Powys; and Llangurig, Powys, as well as Cwrnbelan and Forden, Powys. These sightings were of ginger, sandy, grey, black and spotted/striped cats.

BIG CATS: LOOSE IN BRITAIN

I am certain that the sightings are all genuine, and I should point out that the cats kill sheep in the remote hill regions of Wales, which means that the farmers have a right to deal with them, somehow.

When I made an appeal in the November issue of the *British Farmer* magazine, I received a letter from Mrs. Louise Cook, who later sent me cuttings from the *Gloucester Citizen* newspaper. She lives near Ross-on-Wye, Herefordshire, and has a knowledge of farming and the countryside. In her letter of 15th October 1988, she describes her encounter with what must have been a Scottish wildcat (*Felis sylvestris*):

> *'The only encounter I have ever had is with the savage wildcat, the real wildcat, believed to be only in Scotland and possibly on the mountains of Wales - not, I might add, a domestic cat gone wild, which is vastly different. I reported the incident to my vet., as I felt someone should know of it for the record, and I also wrote to Mike Tomkins, who lives and studies them in Scotland.*
>
> *Looking back on the experience, I now realise how lucky I was as never before have I felt such fear! I absolutely froze as I came upon it around the corner of a building and in that split second before I realised what it was, I just thought it a large domestic tabby, beautifully marked. I went towards it, to stroke it, saying, "Oh, you are beautiful!" when it went down into the attack position, opened its mouth and snarled.*
>
> *I don't mind telling you, I froze - afraid to move, or turn, as I got the impression that it would spring straight at me. We both stayed there for perhaps ten seconds - then I very slowly moved a foot backwards, and very slowly backed away. The cat stayed where it was for a few moments longer, still open-mouthed and spitting, then slunk around the corner and was gone. I never went to see where it went, as I was so shaken - to this day I can feel the cold fear that I experienced. But looking back, it was an experience that I would not have missed, and it was a beautiful savage animal.'*

In a letter dated 14th November 1988, Mrs. Louise Cook wrote this information :

> *'Regarding my encounter with the wildcat, it was here, at the farm, about 3 p.m. on a lazy warm summer afternoon. Should think it had perhaps strayed out of its normal territory as I have never seen it since. We are a bit remote here. Although only about two miles from Symonds Yat as the crow flies, we are nevertheless in rather a quiet area.*
>
> *We have had deer in the fields that have strayed from Welsh Newton Woods (about two miles away) and we also have buzzards that regularly fly around and nest every year up the very quiet lane that leads up to the woods.*
> *A friend of mine who used to live up near the woods, and who used to ride regularly there, once told my daughter that there were wildcats in Welsh Newton Woods. (She took it that he meant domestic cats gone wild - she would not be interested in the difference!) I myself would think that he meant the real wildcat, as he*

was very interested in wildlife and would know the difference. But before I could check with him, he died -went out in the woods for his usual evening ride; the horse came back without him - he had had a heart attack and practically died in the saddle, as you might say. I'm sure it was the way he would have chosen to go. But I really would have liked to have checked it. I'm sorry to say that I did not make a note of the actual date, but I should think it was about 1982. But I often think of Mr Probyn, and feel sorry that I should not have checked with him. Riding out as he did, alone, in the early morning and sometimes evening, he would be able to observe lots of unusual sights in the woods that no one on foot would ever see.'

The *Sunday Mirror* of 16th October 1988 stated that dozens of sheep have been killed near Rhayader (North Wales), yet no sightings of big cats have occurred nearby. Dogs were ruled out as the killers of the sheep.

- Chapter Ten -
MYSTERY CATS IN THE MIDLANDS AND THE SHIRES

• ## THE BUCKINGHAMSHIRE PUMA

The 1983 scare of a puma in Buckinghamshire was an extremely interesting 'cat flap', which lasted no longer than two or three weeks in the spring and early summer.

The Thames Valley police at Aylesbury, Buckinghamshire, told me:

'The last occasion on which any sighting of an unusual animal was made in this area was way back in the 1960s. These sightings were never confirmed.' It would seem that these sightings were confused with the 'Surrey Pumas'. There were no sightings until 1983, and I have built up the following picture of the Buckinghamshire puma from newspaper articles and a letter.

On 17th April 1983 the *News of the World* reported that a puma was seen prowling near a school at Stocken church, Buckinghamshire. A six-hour search by armed police, with a helicopter, failed to find any trace of the mystery beast. Police called off the search, and they apparently had no plans to resume it.

Another (unnamed) newspaper - possibly the *Daily Star* of 17th April, quoted a police spokesman: *"No one has reported a puma missing, but we are not taking any chances. Anyone seeing the animal should not approach it."*

The *Daily Mirror* was another paper which caught onto the story in early May. It would seem that the whole episode had started about 6th April 1983, when retired businessman Mr Philip Vicars observed a strange animal padding across the netball court at the back of Stokenchurch First School. Mr Vicars said: *"It had a body the size of a big dog, a long tail and a small head."*

This was in a full-page 7 article entitled *"No-one told us, say Mums"*, in the *Buckinghamshire Free Press* for 22nd April. He also told the *Daily Mirror*: *"It had dark brown fur and a long tail, and looked like a puma."*

In a later article in the *Daily Mirror* of 7th May, Mr Vicars gave a more detailed account of his sighting:

> *'At first I thought it was a peculiar-looking dog. I went up the garden to get a closer look and saw it was feline and slender in appearance, with a very long thick tail, small head and short legs. It was about the size of an Alsatian and was coloured deep fawn, with merging black spots. It sits down on its haunches just like a cat. None of us is in any doubt that it was a puma.'*

He observed the cat for half an hour, and noticed that on one occasion it was sunning itself on the school wall. Margaret Brooks, Mr Vicars's neighbour, also saw the beast. She told me in a letter of September 1987:

> 'I have kept all the newspaper articles about my sighting of the "puma" but have not unpacked them as yet, but I will forward copies of them to you when I find them. The animal I saw was about the size of a Great Dane dog, and was a tawny colour. It loped across the field and climbed a fence post and over to the other side. That is all I can tell you for now.'

I managed to find records of what Miss Brooks had said at the time of the incident. Apparently she had told the *Buckinghamshire Free Press* of 22nd April:

> 'It was a large tawny cat-like creature. I saw it walking up the bank in the school play-ing-fields. It was about the size of a Great Dane. It was definitely a cat - slinky, with a long bushy tail. I last saw it walking into the undergrowth at the edge of the school swimming pool.'

Local mothers were furious with the police for not telling them that a puma-hunt was on. Although four people had seen the puma at the same time (Mr Vicars, his wife and his sister, and Miss Brooks) the mothers were not even informed or warned to keep an eye on their children. What they told the *Bucks Free Press* reflects this fact. Mrs. Hodgson, a young mother collecting her children from school, commented:

> 'If there really was a cause for concern, we should have been told. The police should have been at the schools on Monday, or have gone around on Saturday with loud-speakers. My children were out playing normally. If I'd known, they would have been kept in the house.'

Another young mother who lived in Stokenchurch remarked:

'I didn't know anything about it until my sister 'phoned from Chichester. She'd heard about the puma on the radio. All I could think of was David playing in the fields outside.'

A third mother, who had been in America during a similar puma scare, commented somewhat forcefully:

> 'Parents there were warned not to let their children play unsupervised or to let them wait for the bus alone.'

A fourth mother, Mrs. Newell of Stokenchurch, who had two children, asked the ultimate question: "I keep wondering if the puma is still in there." She lived near a wood.

Miss Brooks, who had already seen the creature, had the answer as to why the police did not find the elusive feline:

> 'If it had crossed the motorway, it would have been seen. I think it has probably trav-

elled along the motorway embankment towards Wycombe. It's ideal country for it.'

The motorway in question is the M40. It is interesting to note that Mrs. Marshall, whose husband ran a farm near Stokenchurch, said that none of their livestock was missing. She also commented on the dangerous aspect of the puma, as far as her husband was concerned:

> *'He has to go through the motorway tunnel to get to the farm, and I told him to take a stick with him, as it might be lying under there for cover. I can't understand why it hasn't killed anything.'*

The Primary School teacher, Mrs. Morris, gave the children a lesson about the Puma, like the Surrey school children had, in the 1960s. The Chief Inspector of Wycombe police, Tony Miller, admitted that the police had not used loudspeakers. However, he did suggest that the police had taken the scare very seriously:

> *'A helicopter was called in, as you know. They're expensive, and we noted that some sightings of these animals occurred, but there is no tangible evidence of attacks on livestock or people. Police have never found carcasses of dead animals.'*

He also noted that pumas disappear quickly, often never to be seen again.

On 15th May 1983 the *Bucks Free Press* was to report that a dead fox cub had been found, and that at first the puma was the suspected culprit. A party of scouts found the fox-cub.

The Tinker's Wood Youth Association organiser, Mr Jim Hoos, who was taking the 40 youths on a walk while they were spending a weekend at Green Park, Aston Clinton, said:

> *"The cub appeared to have been attacked by a large animal. There were big prints all around. We staked out the tracks so no one could walk over them, and called the police. They sent for forensic experts and took plaster casts of the prints. Most of the kids thought it was a bit of added excitement, but that evening some of the younger ones moved out of their little tents into the larger adult ones.'*

The Aylesbury police said they were not going to connect the incident with a nearby puma hunt. It would seem that the experts knew what had killed it, for a spokesman said: *"The experts think it was probably a large dog."*

A week earlier, at nearby RAF Halton, Wendover, Buckinghamshire, Mrs. Kim Griffin had spotted the "Chilterns Puma", as it was now termed. She said*: "I saw this big black cat. It was only eight feet away and moved off into the long grass"*. This was reported in the *Daily Star* of 7th May 1983. Detectives took a plaster cast of a 5 inch paw print. Armed police were put on standby, and children were told to be kept indoors. Also the fact that Mrs. Griffin had seen the cat in her back garden made the situation even more exciting.

Many newspapers noted the fact that the "Exmoor Beast" was being hunted at the same time. Headlines such as 'Now Two Pumas are tracked' were made to spur on the public imagination, and the press succeeded in doing just that.

Mike Goss also dealt with the "Chilterns Puma" in his articles for the *Unknown Magazine*, which were published in 1985. He wrote seven articles on mystery cats all over Britain. He had aimed to publish a book, but the publishers unfortunately rejected his offer. Mike Goss is a contributor to, amongst other things, the useful *Fortean Times*, which I can recommend as an up-to-date guide to mystery cat sightings that appear in the newspapers.

• THE MALVERNS PUMA

A puma is known to have escaped in this area, but it was soon recaptured. However, there is another big cat loose in this region, which has been around since 1977. Mrs. Armitage-was driving between Eastnor and Upton-on-Severn when she saw a puma run across the road in front of her car. She has since said to me: *"It was dark in colour, with a small head and a long tail. The sighting was on the Herefordshire/ Worcestershjre border".* Mrs. Armitage noted that the animal was higher at the shoulder than a lioness. She telephoned a local farmer, who confirmed that there was a "rumour" of a puma on Malvern common. The animal, loose for a short time, was shot dead by a farmer.

• THE FOREST OF DEAN PUMA

In Gloucestershire there is a puma in the Forest of Dean, which is quite near to the Welsh border. In the 1890s this forest was the scene for Dennis Potter's famous play *The Two Sides of the Beast*, involving a travelling bear and superstitious villagers. More recently, the forest has played host to a large cat, which is thought to be a puma. In November 1985, a number of people reported having seen a puma-like beast in the area of the forest. On 2nd August 1986 the *Daily Telegraph* carried the following report, which I quote here with permission:

'Motorist meets "Puma":

> *'A Gloucestershire countryman, David Hart, believes that he has had a close encounter of the feline kind - a meeting with a puma-like cat in the Forest of Dean. Mr Hart, a motorcyclist of Stantway village, found it lying in the road. "It was about the size of a large dog but it had a cat's head," he said, "and a long tail." The animal remained in the road for a minute before springing over a hedge, to disappear. Its sighting follows several similar reports from the area last November.'*

(See the *Gloucester Citizen* newspaper for articles on the "Westbury Wildcat", as it was called.)

• THE STAFFORDSHIRE PUMA

Staffordshire is the home of the formidable and now infamous Staffordshire bull terrier, involved in much badger-baiting, badger-digging and dog-fighting, in recent years. However, it was not a dog that we are dealing with, but a puma-like cat.

On 23rd July 1980, the *Wolverhampton Express and Star* reported that a puma, or cheetah, was seen in a wooded area between Compton and Aldersley. The beast was observed a number of times near a canal towpath. In the next few days the police, who were looking for a 30 inches high, orange-and-yellow beast, mounted a search. Mr Michael Williams was called out after an unsuccessful search on 25th July. He wrote a detailed letter to the writers Janet and Colin Bord, which was dated 4th December 1980. Part of this letter was reproduced in the *Fortean Times*, (No. 34).

Mr Williams, a superintendent at Dudley Zoo, was armed with a tranquilizing gun. He stated that a teacher had seen the beast in July, in a field by a disused railway line.

The teacher watched the beast for five minutes and described the "puma" as having a cat-like head, pricked ears, thick legs, heavy tail held low, brown in colour, and the size of a large dog.' The man concerned observed the beast being mobbed by crows and it bounded away down the field for 30 yards. It then turned, sat down, watched the teacher (who must have been dumbfounded) and finally ran off.

The man also met a lady who said she had seen a wild animal. The teacher was said to be a naturalist.

Mr Williams went on to say that on another day he was called out with the zoo's cat-keeper, Alan, who had ten years' experience. While searching the disused railway line, the two men observed a very narrow cat-like creature, at a distance of 300 yards. They were only two miles from where the teacher's sighting had taken place.

Mr Williams considered that the animal was too large to be a fox, and that a dog would have been found by the police. The senior cat-keeper followed the beast for ten minutes, but finally lost sight of it. Meanwhile, Mr Williams contacted the Wolverhampton police, who mounted observation posts on all the bridges. The creature did not reappear.

Thus Mr Williams concludes that it was possible that the beast was an elusive escaped or illegally-kept puma. That was the last that was heard of the beast, although only 30 kilometres away, in Wales, sightings were being made. If it is still alive, the beast must be at least eight years old, as all these events happened in 1980, and it is now the year 1988.

• THE WARWICKSHIRE PUMA

On 23rd November 1980, Mr Cotton of Pebworth, South Warwickshire, was strolling along the road to Long Marston when he confronted a beast that he described as being *"jet black, as big as a fox, with a long bushy tail."* The animal allegedly caught a moorhen on one of the nearby ponds, and then made off. This sighting was reported in the *Gloucestershire Echo* of 4th December, and was quoted in the *Fortean Times*, (No.34).

The second sighting of the "Warwickshire puma" was by Mr Michael Marshall of Long Marston, who saw *"a jet-black animal, about three feet long, with a long tail."* The cat-like creature ran off at some speed. Mr Marshall told *The Sun* and the *Bristol Evening Post*. *"It was definitely not a dog, but more cat-like in appearance."* The location of the sighting was 200 yards from a scrapyard. This sighting was of 3rd December 1980 and was reported in the above two newspapers for the 18th December.

- ## CHESHIRE CATS

I have often wondered whether there could be any truth in the Cheshire Cat character, which used to be on every child's bookshelf, in the form of Lewis Carroll's classic *'Alice in Wonderland'*, published in 1865. A *Countryside* magazine article showed pictures of Danebury village, in Cheshire, where Lewis Carroll was born. Once Lewis Carroll characters had been discovered, it was decided to make them come to life in the form of stained-glass windows depicting scenes from the book, and also in the form of weather vanes. One such vane showed the Cheshire Cat and the Mad Hatter. I now began to wonder whether perhaps Lewis Carroll himself, while young, had seen a mystery cat in the woods near his home. However, I was to be much mistaken. Was the Cheshire Cat real?

The answer to much that I wanted to know is to be found in Michael Greene's excellent book, *Incredible Cats*. One of his tales was called 'The Congleton Ghost Cat'. The story goes that in about 1900, a Mrs. Marlow and a friend visited an old abbey near Congleton. The two ladies watched a large domestic white cat launch itself into the air from a gatepost and disappear in mid-air. The cat did the same trick a few days later, again in front of the two ladies, who were in a horse and trap. They later heard from an old lady who had run a local cafe for fifty years, that a former curator of the abbey had kept such a cat, which always disappeared at the same spot, after it had allegedly been killed by a pack of dogs. As it would happen, Congleton is near to Danebury, and Lewis Carroll became a member of the Society for Psychical Research in 1880, therefore he would probably have been interested in the story of the ghost-cat, which was seen by many people before Mrs. Marlow. Who knows, maybe even Lewis Carroll himself saw the creature.

The owner of the cat, the curator of the abbey was called Mrs. Winge. Carrol's 'Cheshire cat' is able to disappear slowly, and the description that he gives of it - 'a large tabby cat with an enormous grin' - could mean that the original Cheshire cat was a British indigenous lynx. Anyway, we must not jump to too many conclusions at this stage. 'Alice in Wonderland' was fiction, not fact.

In more recent years, mystery cats have been seen around Chester. According to Andy Roberts, in his book, *Cat Flaps!*, we read:

> *'In May 1974 a mystery animal was often seen in the Deiware Forest area, to the north of Chester. It was described as about two feet high, like an Alsatian dog, but with a tail like a fox's brush. The witnesses were sure it was not a fox, though'.*

In the national mystery cat "wave" of 1976, a lioness was seen in the Deva Lane, very near Chester Zoo. Needless to say, all Chester Zoo's big cats were accounted for. The creature was seen twice again near West Chester hospital. Police searched the area but could find nothing.' My thanks to Mr Roberts for allowing me to quote the above passage from his booklet, which I strongly recommend as a guide to Northern Mystery Cats (See the Bibliography for more details.) The first incident could have involved a wolf, because Bob Rickard and Janet and Colin Bord have already reported it as possibly being that type of animal. Bob Rickard records the story in the wolf section of his 1976 book *Living Wonders*, which also has a brief section on mystery cats.

The Bords recorded the two stories in *'Alien Animals'* and their sources were newspaper articles.

Hoping to find out more about the Chester cats, I wrote to the Superintendent, Mr Tamson, of Chester Police Station. In a letter of 24th September 1987, he told me:

> *'I have to inform you that our records have been checked and there are no incidents which would be of interest to you. There were sightings some years ago of a large animal in the Malpas area of Chester, which was found to be a large Great Dane dog. We have also made enquiries with Chester Zoo, but they too have no information to offer.'*

It would therefore seem that the Deva Lane lioness could have been a Great Dane, which is often the same colour as a lioness.

Finally, the most recent mention of a mystery cat in Cheshire comes from the *Stockport Advertiser*, which reported that a number of people had seen a mystery animal around the town of Handworth. The article of 4th September 1980 states that Mr Christopher Shenton, a Handworth farmer, thought the beast was a four-year-old stag until he moved closer to it. The animal was described as being *'a black catlike animal, bigger than a cat, with a much more pointed face'*, and it was also described as a *'large white cat'* and as being *'the size of an Alsatian with pointed ears, a cat-like body and tail'*. These sightings were recorded in the *Northern Earth Mysteries* magazine and the *Fortean Times*, both of October 1980. I was determined to find out more about these mystery animals, so I wrote to the *Stockport Advertiser*, asking for some photocopied articles on this subject. They told me to contact the Stockport Central Library. I received from Mrs. Lynne Hamilton, Local Studies Librarian, a note dated 25th January 1988: *'Thank you for your letter about an article from the Stockport Advertiser about a mystery cat. My colleagues have located the article and I am enclosing a photocopy.'*

The article is dated 4th September 1980, and I quote it here:

> *'Seen Anything Strange Lately?*
>
> *Is Cheadle Hulme to become England's answer to Loch Ness, with thousands of visitors seeking to spot a mystery animal? There have been four sightings of a cat-like animal on a plot of open land between the Stanley Green Industrial Estate and Handforth, the most recent by a woman staying at her daughter's home in Cheadle Hulme - the last house before open country. Mrs. Vera Thomson was looking through the bedroom window, late at night, when she spotted "a black cat-like animal" coming up the drive. "It looked bigger than a cat, and with a more pointed face. It had a long tail and seemed to slink past. There are some geese in the garden which normally make a noise when they see a cat or dog, but this time they kept quiet, as if they were afraid," she told the Advertiser.*
>
> *'Cheadle Hulme police were called on last month by someone claiming to have seen a tiger on the Industrial Estate, and a few days later an anonymous caller described 'a large white cat'. And on 2nd August, Wilmslow police were told about an animal the size of an Alsatian with pointed ears, a cat-like body and tail, moving like a big cat, which was spotted on open ground behind Handforth Hall. Police tried to track*

down the phantom beast but no signs of its existence were found, and a police dog failed to pick up any scent. "Since nothing has been seen by children during the entire summer holiday, it seems unlikely there is a dangerous wild animal at large," said a police spokesman. Perhaps Handforth farmer Mr Christopher Shenton has solved the mystery. He says he saw a strange animal when he was spraying potatoes one evening. "I thought, 'No cow is that colour', and when it raised its head I saw it was a four-year old stag about 5 ft. tall, with great antlers."

That was the last we heard of the beast. I should mention that R. J. M. Rickard and Michael Mitchell in "Living Wonders" have referred to a "Cheshire Wolf". The 'pointed face' might suggest that this was not a cat that was referred to in the *Stockport Advertiser* of 1980, but their wolf-like beast. I wonder whether a wolf was roaming Cheshire from 1974 until 1980? Six years on the run, and even more.

The *Liverpool Echo* of 24th January 1978 recorded that a "mystery beast" was roaming Bickerton Hills, Cheshire in mid-January 1978. The *Fortean Times* (No. 25) says that the beast left large paw-prints that Chester Zoo identified as coming from a large dog.

A Mr Mark Richardson and a Mr David Rowbuck, both youths, were out at ten o'clock one moonlight January night in 1978 when they encountered "a young tiger or cougar... partly hidden... but certainly some kind of big cat, and its front legs appeared shorter than its back." A policeman remarked that there had been no missing animal reports or livestock mutilations in the area.

Notes to the "Midlands and Shires" Chapter

1) In *Lo!* by Charles Fort, mystery sheep-killings are recorded from all over the country. The account about a big scare all through Gloucestershire is worth quoting:

2)

'There was a marauding animal in England towards the end of the year 1905. London Daily Mail, 1st November 1905:

'The sheep-slaying mystery of Badminton'

It is said that in the neighbourhood of Badminton, on the border between Gloucestershire and Wiltshire, sheep had been killed. Sergeant Carter of the Gloucestershire police, is quoted: "I have seen two of the carcasses myself, and can say definitely that it is impossible for it to be the work of a dog. Dogs are not vampires and do not suck the blood of a sheep and leave the flesh almost untouched."

Then there follows, in the same newspaper for 19th December:

'Marauder shot near Hinton.'
So then, if in London any interest had been aroused, this announcement stopped it. We go to newspapers published nearer to the scene of the sheep-slaughtering. The Bristol Mercury, 25th November, says that the killer was a jackal which had escaped from a menagerie in Gloucester. And that stopped mystification and inquiry in the

minds of readers of the Bristol Mercury

Suspecting that there had been no such escape of a jackal, we go to Gloucester news-papers. In the Gloucester Journal, *4th November, in a long account of depredations there is no mention of the escape of any animal in Gloucester or anywhere else. In fol-lowing issues nothing is said of a jackal, or of any other animal. So many reports were sent to the editor of this paper that he doubted whether only one slaughtering animal was abroad. "Some even go so far as to call up the traditions of the werewolf, and su-perstitious people are inclined to believe this theory."*

We learn that the large black dog had been shot on 16th December, but that in its re-gion there had been no reported killings of sheep from about 25th November.

The look of this data entails another scene-shifting. Near Gravesend, an unknown ani-mal had, up to 16th December, killed about 30 sheep (London Daily Mail, *19th De-cember): 'Small armies of men went hunting, but the killing stopped and the animal remained unknown.'*

2) On 15th February 1988 I received this letter from West Midland Police at the Wolverhampton suburb of Wednesfield. It was from the Chief Superintendent:

'I refer to your correspondence of 7th October 1987, concerning your book 'big cats Loose in Britain'. We are unable to provide you with police records, but have ob-tained the attached press cuttings which may be of use to you.'

From *Wolverhampton Express and Star.* on the 25th August 1980 the first of three ar-ticles appeared, stating:

'Puma Hunt resumes after Dog attacked.

Police are again on the trail of an animal believed to be a puma, which has been sighted several times in the last two days. The animal was seen today and police im-mediately resumed their hunt with the help of Mr Mike Williams, Curator of Dudley Zoo. This afternoon they were tracking the animal along the disused railway line run-ning through Castlecroft towards Lower Penn. Police said Mr Williams now had seen the animal himself, but could not positively identify it. He is hoping to stun it with a dart gun. The hunt resumed after the animal today attacked a dog being walked by a girl.'

The second article appeared on 25th August 1980:

'Search for Puma Widens:

A police hunt for an animal thought to be a puma switched from Wolverhampton to Wombourne today. Several sightings of the animal have already been reported. Yes-

terday police with tracker dog spent most of the day combing the canal bank and nearby woods between Compton and Aldersley. "Whatever it was then apparently moved to Dunstall and later to Wombourne," police said. "We have had police out early today but there have been no more sightings." The search was mounted after a man walking his dog reported seeing a cheetah-like animal. Police have warned the public not to approach it if they see it. Dudley Zoo Curator Mr Mike Williams hopes to stun the animal with a dart gun."

The third article was dated 28th August, and merely stated:

'Police call off Hunt for "Puma":

Police have called off their hunt for an animal believed to be a puma on the loose in the Wolverhampton and Wombourne area. But they say they are ready to begin searching again immediately there is another sighting of the animal first spotted nearly a week ago. Dudley Zoo Curator Mr Mike Williams and the Zoo's big cat specialist Mr Alan Margerrison have both seen the animal during the hunt. They say it was cat-like in appearance, the size of a large dog, and moved like a cat.

But Mr Williams says he cannot confirm that it is seen clearly or until he receives information that one is missing. The animal has been sighted three times, always close to the disued railway line that runs between Aldersley and Wombourne. Mr Williams said pumas could be dangerous if cornered, frightened or injured. If anyone spots the puma, they should contact the police immediately. Mr Williams and the police think that someone in the area may have been keeping the puma illegally.
'

3) On 4th May 1975, a puma was loose around Blackley, Manchester, but it was a known escaped pet belonging to Mr Jeff Day. It was only loose for 4 hours and was recaptured by police with Alsatian dogs. This was in the *Bath Evening Chronicle* of 27th October 1976. The case was quoted in the *Fortean Times* No. 20.

4) On 4th August 1975, a female leopard cub walked into Mr Ken Pearce's home in Fallowfield, Manchester. It was later handed over to police. It wore a blue collar and was probably an escaped pet, because of this factor. The cub walked through a door which had been left open because of the heat, while Mr Pearce was watching television. The police were not able to find the owner. This case was in the "Daily Mirror" and the *Scunthorpe Evening Telegraph* of the 5th August 1975, and was quoted in *Fortean Times* No. 20.

- Chapter Eleven -
NORTHERN MYSTERY CATS

- ## LONG AGO

As far as is known, there have always been wildcats in Northern England, and they became extinct only in the early years of the 20th Century.

They were known to be particularly savage, and were credited with the death of at least one man. In a recent book called '*Man and Beast*', Mr H. W. Shepherd-Walwyn said this about the wildcat of Bamborough, Yorkshire.

> *'There exists at Bamborough an ancient record commemorating the ferocity of the wildcat. The story is that Percival Cresacre, a youth of distinguished family, was returning home from a fair in Doncaster when as he was passing through a plantation known as Melton Wood, a wildcat suddenly leapt from the trees and attacked him. This man sought with his gauntleted hands to grapple with his foe, but the latter's sharp teeth were too much for him.*
>
> *Badly mauled, Cresacre endeavoured to escape towards Bamborough but the cat pursued him and compelled him to seek shelter in the church at Bamborough. Even here the creature did not relinquish the fight but inflicted such terrible wounds as to cause the death of young Percival, who, in his last struggle, seems to have crushed the cat with his foot against the wall. In the morning man and cat were found dead in the porch of the church where the weird contest had ended.'*

This occurrence took place in the depths of winter, around 1475. Apparently there seems to be some confusion over the name Bamborough, because Andy Roberts calls the scene of the fighting as St Peter's church, Barnburgh. The Cresacre coat of arms shows the battle between man and beast. People have turned this incident into something of a legend and I have found six sources mentioning it. Cresacre had obviously disturbed a starving wildcat, which leapt upon him and he fell from his horse. We must presume that the animal landed on his back and attempted to kill him by biting his neck. Cresacre put up a fight sufficient to frighten the beast, but its hunger drove it on.

The wildcat was growing rare during the eighteenth and nineteenth centuries, and was extinct in many counties during the early twentieth century. Some wildcats survived in the Lake District until 1922. Controversial articles appeared in natural history journals, claiming that the wildcat was still to be found in some areas. What is now certain is that the wildcat seems to have once again have entered the Northern Counties of England. North Yorkshire may soon be a home to the 'Scottish' wildcat (*Felis sylvestris grampia.*)

Black Annis, a legendary cannibal hag, had a blue face and iron claws, and lived in a cave near Dane Hills in Leicestershire. She was said to devour stray children and lambs. "Black Annis's Bower's Close" was said to have been dug out of rock by her own claws. She was associated with a monstrous cat.

The above information comes from Katherine Briggs's book, '*A Dictionary of Fairies*.' Black Annis was remembered by a drag hunt that involved going from Black Annis's Bower to the mayor of Leicester's house. Her identity has been confused over the years, being variously described as a hag, a Celtic goddess, a monstrous cat, an anchoress and a witch. The drag-hunt, the bait of which was a dead aniseed-soaked cat, was phased out in the late eighteenth century, but she was still around until the last years of the nineteenth century. The legend of Black Annis is the cause of a wildcat, according to Anthony Dent in his 1974 book *Lost Beasts of Britain*. In his excellent 1945 book called *Left Hand, Right Hands*, Sir Osbert Sitwell records the deeds of his famous grandfather, Sir Sitwell Sitwell, who owned an estate called Renishaw, near Sheffield. The following passage, from page 15, illustrates this man's amazing exploits and will interest us:

> '*His hunting exploits, like those of his youngest brother Frank Sitwell of Barmoor Castle, were many and famous. The most fantastic incident at Renishaw - only to be matched, indeed', by the even more exotic episode in the time of his son, which I shall relate shortly - occurred early in November 1798, when a "Royal Bengal Tiger" escaped from a menagerie in Sheffield. On hearing of its jaunt, and that it had killed a child, Sir Sitwell "generously went in person, with a few of his domestics, and with much trouble as well as exposing himself to imminent danger" subdued and killed the animal with his pack of hounds, as it flashed its cruel tropical streaks through the cool mountain foliage of the Eckington woods; those hanging woods and deep valleys that were once part of Sherwood forest, full as they always were at that season of bracken and rowanberries, mingling their gold and scarlet, and of pheasants hurtling through the golden and misty air.*'

Sir Osbert Sitwell's source was an article in the *Sporting Magazine* for November 1798. He also continued with a poem called 'Elegy for Mr Goodbeare', from '*England Reclaimed*' by Sir Osbert Sitwell and published in 1927. One passage reads:

> '*Mr Goodbeare could remember when the escaped and hungering tiger flicked lithe and fierce through Foxton Wood when young Sir Sitwell took his red-tongued clamouring hounds, and hunted it then and there, as a hunted gentleman should.*'

Renishaw was also the scene for a mystery sheep-killer, who turned out to be a tall Negro slave and he was going to be killed by the angry farmers who had found him, consuming a sheep in a cave. Sir George Sitwell let the man be freed. This was in 1846, and is also related in Sir Osbert's *Left Hand, Right Hand.*

Mr Bryon Rogers, who writes a column in the *Sunday Express*, wrote an article called 'Now at last I can believe in the country', on 21st August 1987. Somehow a London and North-Western form telegram dated 10th July 1887, had come into his possession. The telegram was signed by 'Allen, Rugby', and reads:
> '*Tiger escaped from 9.42 p.m. ex Broad Street to Liverpool between Wolverton and Rugby stop When found forward to Liverpool stop If found reply.*'

On the back of the form, a Mr Thomas Coleman had written:

> *'Seen between Blisworth and Wendon. Blisworth said not caught at 6 a.m.'*

Mr Roger had no more details on this telegram, but he wondered whether the 600 lb. tiger was ever caught. All these events occurred in the Midlands and northwards towards Liverpool.

Lions have a long connection with the counties of Northamptonshire and Nottinghamshire. In 1919, the *Weekly Guardian* gave an interview with an old-time showman, one Mr Puggy Wilson, who was talking about the Nottingham Goose Fair. He recalled one event at the Fair:

> *There was the great an' on'y Wombelt's as a lion got out one year, an' nearly fright-ened all the folks of Nottingham to death. There was the militia out looking for it, an' all the coppers an' the folk hid everywhere. An' when they were nearly all scared and tired out, they found it fast asleep in the waggon where the band used to play, close to the show."*

This was reproduced in the *Nottingham Evening Post* of 1976. Another story of an escaped big cat comes from the area of Blackpool and Preston. According to the *North Devon Journal Herald* of 16th June 1983, the story was as follows:

> *'The latest speculation on the identity of the beast comes from the Chairman of Philo-graphic Publications, Barnstaple, Lieut.-Col. Charles Tacey. He has produced a cut-ting from Reynolds News, dated 1929, which described a Preston man's encounter with a seven-foot-long cat he found in his chicken run. It proved to be a Sumatra bin-turong, which had escaped from a Blackpool Wildlife Park.'*

The "Beast" mentioned in the *North Devon Journal Herald* is of course the `Beast of Exmoor`.

We shall now look at more recent mystery cat scares, starting with the Nottingham lion scare of 1975.

THE NOTTINGHAM LION

The majority of this chapter is built up of photocopied articles from the *Nottingham Evening Post.*

On the 27th July 1976, two milkmen spotted a strange animal in the region of Tollerton Lane, near Not-tingham Airport. Mr Crowther and Mr Bentley observed the animal walking down the lane early in the morning. Mr Crowther said:

> *'Dave stopped halfway down the drive and was obviously looking at something. I shouted to him to ask what was the matter and he told me to come and look. He said there was something prowling about and then we both saw together what certainly to us was a lion. It was 50 yards away, had its head down and its long tail had a bushy end. It was walking away from us but only very slowly. If I had been on my own I don't think I would have told anyone, because they wouldn't have believed it. But it was*

there and we both saw it together.'

Mr Bentley said:

> *'It was so near to us that had it turned, we would not have had time to get to our van, When I spoke to the police they hardly believed what I was telling them, but we both would stake our lives on what we saw.'*

Chief Inspector John Smith was put in charge of the lion hunt, which began with armed police walking in lines across the ploughed fields. Later a police helicopter was brought in to track the lion. The police had a number of calls from people saying that their dogs were restless. The police made enquiries at Stapleford Park, near Melton Mowbray, where some lions were kept. The officers also searched woods. A local farmer at Clipstone, near Cotgrave, found strange paw-prints on his farmland. Police also toured the villages in the vicinity, warning people to stay indoors.

On 30th July 1976 the *Nottingham Evening Post* reported that the police were still baffled by the escaped lion scare. One passenger on a bus telephoned to say that he had seen a lion in a garden in the Nottingham-Grantham Road, at Radcliffe-on-Trent. The police visited the house, only to find that a Great Dane dog lived there. It was supposed that the dog had been mistaken for a lion. The bus passenger's sighting must have been a brief one. Police received eighteen telephone calls after the first hunt, thirteen of which were treated seriously.

A lion was reported to have been seen prowling in the Bassingfield area, and the police were checking that sighting. A couple in Norfolk telephoned to say that they had seen a lion in a lay-by at Lowdham the previous week, but did not tell anybody because they did not reckon they would be believed.

A fourth report came from a farm-worker at Edwalton, who reckoned he had seen a lion in a field. No more armed officers were going to be called out, even if the lion were sighted. The police search drew a blank, but the officers still treated the matter seriously. Binoculars were used in an effort to sight the animal.

On 31st July 1979 a lorry driver, George Mills of Nottingham reckoned he could solve the lion mystery. He said:

> *'I saw the dog yesterday on the M1 three miles south of Bramcote. It was easily as big as a lion, with long hair. It came down to the motorway to eat a rabbit which had been run over. I thought then of the coincidence between this dog and the lion.'*

The animal was a very heavy, sandy-coloured dog.

A police spokesman advised people to be wary, as they were still not convinced that a lion was not loose. People were still telephoning in to say that they had seen the animal. One caller informed the police that there was a large animal in Bunny Woods. A second caller thought something was crashing through a copse, next to the church in East Bridgeford.

The police were also checking reports that a lion was observed crossing a bridge over the A52 at Beeston, and that another lion was seen on the M1 access road at Ratcliffe-on-Soar. Chief Inspector John Smith, head of the search, said:

'We are getting calls from all over the place but they are being investigated.'

The Chief Constable of Nottingham, Mr Charles McLachan, was surprised at the massive response from people as far away as Liverpool.

By 1st August 1976 Doctor John Chisholm, the Deputy Coroner for Nottingham and Assistant Deputy of Normanton-on-the-Wolds, was said to have been on land near his home when he heard a noise in the undergrowth by a stream. Dr Chisholm investigated and saw the rear end of an animal resembling a lion passing through some undergrowth. He came back to the house and then he and his wife and son, aged 18 watched the lion from an upstairs window. Mrs. Chisholm told the *Nottingham Evening Post*.

'It was apparently trying to get to the stream. My husband and our son Alistair went back out again, and again I saw the animal moving about. At first when we heard of the lion report, we didn't take much notice and found it hard to believe. But if I had known there was any chance of the lion being real, I would not have gone to that area at all.'

The police received another report from Edwalton, and carried out a search in Grange Park, halfway between Tollerton and Normantonon-the-Wolds. They also searched Nuthall, but drew a blank. The amused press reporter chuckled over the fact that a tortoise was found by the police and RSPCA officer, checking where a lion had been seen. The tortoise was found on the A610 road at Temple Lake, near Kimberley. RSPCA Inspector Sutton wanted the owner, or a volunteer, to come and look after the animal. The police search of the woods found no lion.

On the 2nd August it was reported in the 'late news' column of the *Nottingham Evening Post* that a number of paw-prints were found, at the stream where Dr Chisholm saw the lion. The police were checking the spot. Dr Chisholm said definitely:

"There is no doubt it was a lion that I saw. I know a lion's tail when I see one."

So that should dispel the view that what he saw was a Great Dane dog.

The next day police and dogs searched the Tollerton and Normanton-on-the-Wolds. Mounted police were also called in to help with this search.

A police spokesman said that the police were 98% certain that there was a large lion on the loose. Officers were stretched out in a 'line', 75 yards apart, with binoculars, but no guns. The police again visited Grange Park. An armed squad of officers was split up into four groups. One group stayed in Normanton-on-the-Wolds; another in Keyworth; another in Edwalton and, finally, there was one group in Toilerton, where the lion had first been seen by two milkmen, with only one unconfirmed report involving two women, who saw something in a field at Nicker Hill, Keyworth.

Police were alarmed to find some fifty people, including women and children, searching through the field. The same police spokesman stated: *"We can't stress enough that there could be a real danger."*

On 4th August the *Nottingham Evening Post* carried a large article explaining the Dangerous Animals Act that was to come into force on 22nd October 1976. Anybody keeping a lion after that date would be in serious trouble. If you still kept an unlicensed animal by January 1977, you had to apply to the local authority, and if you did not, you would face fines of £400 for damage done by the animal.

The Act covered many types of creatures: everything from cobras to alligators, and lions to polar bears. Domestic animals were excluded from the Act. During the search for the Nottingham lion, RSPCA officers came upon a number of dangerous animals, of which they knew nothing. The RSPCA kept quiet about who owned these animals, as an inspector commented:

> *"We don't want somebody doing something silly."* Lord Devlin said of the Act: *"If a person wakes up in the middle of the night and finds an escaping tiger on top of his bed and suffers a heart attack, it would be useless to point out that the intentions of the tiger were quite amiable."*

Ex-policeman and milkman Mr Bentley, with his mate Mr Crowther, who first saw the lion, said about the Act and the incident:

> *"They were all talking about it, and the general feeling was that it was a bit of a laugh. We knew we were going to be laughed at when we reported it, but you can't let something like that go. I've got two young children myself.*
>
> *I've never heard any stories of wild animals being kept in that area, although there is a farm on the Radcliffe round where there is a lion and a gorilla.*
>
> *The biggest problem round there is dogs. There's one milkman who reckons a dog came for him and he put his boot out and killed it on the spot. There's another milkman who says an Alsatian jumped on him - he said it went straight over his head and he turned round, grabbed hold of it and bit it. He never had any trouble with it after that. All my life I've been interested in wildlife and I know a lion when I see it.'*

The first implication that the lion was a lioness was when Mrs. Bentley added:

> *'Although it sounds fantastic, if Dave says it's a lioness, it's a lioness and nothing less.'*

On the same day as this article appeared, the front page of the *Nottingham Evening Post* of 4th August reported that 'the big hunt goes on... 'Chief Inspector John Smith said: *"We have quite definite sightings of an animal of some sort and we are almost convinced it is there."*

Motor patrols covered the area of Tollerton and Normanton-on-the-Wolds. A reported sighting came from Ruddington during the night of the 3rd/4th August. The police found no trace of a lion. A man who owned 20 lions, decided to advise the police to take some of his lions, and to use them to lure the lion. Mr William Folley of Cradley Heath criticised the way that police were hunting the lion. He apparently stated:

> "They should leave food out for it. It's probably tame, but it's just getting hungrier and hungrier, which could make it kill."

He had obviously not thought that the lion could catch food for itself. A policeman thanked Mr Folley for his advice, but did comment: "We have taken advice from three safari parks and we are satisfied we can get help from them rather than through troubling anyone else further afield."

Ladbrokes, the bookmakers, put odds of 3-1 against the lion being captured before 12 p.m. on Saturday. The 5th of August saw the search taking another turn.

Two lady golfers reported a large lion at about 50-100 yards away at Stanton-on-the-Wolds golf course, and police were checking out the sighting. A second sighting came from a gentleman living at Netherfield, who saw a big animal in a field near to Nottingham Racecourse. He said it was 'a sandy-coloured animal, like a young lioness.'

The tracks at Normanton-on-the-Wolds, where Dr Chisholm saw the 'cat' on 1st August were judged by Mr John Bellamy, Manager of Stapleford Lion Reserve, near Melton Mowbray, to belong to a large dog. He thought that the lion was probably domesticated and was frightened by the large-scale police search. The *Nottingham Evening Post* of 7th August brought an official end to the Nottingham lion scare. The paper said, "There's no lion - Police theory."

A spokesman at police headquarters said that sixty-five sightings of a lion had been received. All searches of the sighting areas had proved fruitless. The spokesman did say that the police would continue to respond to any sightings of the lion or lioness. He said that on one occasion somebody had just seen a large dog, and on another occasion the 'lion' was a large brown paper bag! (This has been a joke in the *Fortean Times* for a long while, and has been repeated at least three times.)

The police had received no reports of an escaped lion, and there had been no attacks on farm animals. Ladbrokes stopped taking bets on the 3-1 odds against a lion being caught before 12 a.m. on the next Saturday. There had been reports of the lion being seen at two places at once. The sightings of the animal continued, despite what Nottingham police said.

Armed police searched Clipstone Woods near Cotgrave, after sightings of an animal in a field. This was also in the paper for the 7th August. Three more reports came in on 8th August, from Normanton and Plumtree. Investigating officers found no signs of the lion.

On the 5th August, "Ralph", 72 years old, performed his poem called "Has anybody seen our Lion?" The poem was designed to entertain the Thursday sing-along at the Age Concern Leisure Centre in Nottingham. The song was extremely amusing, and as I have an unpublished photocopy of it, you may like to see it.

"Has Anybody Seen our Lion?
(Tune: '*Has Anybody here seen Kelly?*')

Has anybody seen our lion?
Maybe you and I
Could say he's a very shy 'un,
Keeping well away from man!
He leaves us all alonio,
Doesn't want a human bonio
While bread and lard is high on
The menu of the island clan!
Has anybody seen our lion?
Big, fierce L-E-O,
His mate is sobbin' and cryin',
'Cos she hasn't got a clue you know,
Just why he left her on the shelf
And toddled off to enjoy himself,
Where no Peeping Tom can spy on
A love-sick Romeo!

By 6th October 1976 there was one claim as to what had actually caused the hunt. According to a *Nottingham Evening Post* article of that date, two students at the University of East Anglia claimed that they had started the hunt by putting on a lion's skin. The University of East Anglia's Rag Chairman said:

> "Their claim was a hoax. We are contacting Notts police to apologise. I was taken in
> by this hoax. Only after closely questioning them, did I find it wasn't true."

A police spokesman was quoted as saying: *"We didn't take the students' claim seriously from the beginning."*

This was the last we heard of the lion until the death of Miss Mary Guilor, who hunted the lion in 1976. As a vet, Miss Guilor had worked at Ravenhead and Lime Street, Kirby-in-Ashfield, since the mid-1950s. She was found dead in a chair.

Miss Guilor was armed with a specially imported tranquillising pistol, which would not kill any animal, but stun them. The pistol's dart took five minutes to work, at a range of 30 metres. She also dealt with dangerous dogs.

It is interesting to note the origin of the lion involved in the following episode. The incident was recorded in connection with Miss Guilor's death in the *Nottingham Evening Post* of 18th April 1979:

> "On one occasion she was alerted when a picnic party saw a lion up a tree in Sher-
> wood. When she arrived the party had vanished, and she tranquillised the lion with a
> civilian marksman standing by. It was not until later that she learnt that his rifle was

unloaded."

It is just possible that the above lion was also the Nottingham lion. If that is the case, then we can explain that the Nottingham lion did exist and was not some creature transported by a UFO, as has been suggested, or just a large dog, or a paper bag.

It is interesting to note that on the 14th August 1978, the *Nottingham Evening Post* had published an article concerning a lion-cub called Napoleon, who needed a home. Napoleon found himself in a crate, in a pub, where he had been rather cruelly treated. Mr John Caudwell, a contractor, found the cub and offered to buy him. The cub was fed with a bottle by Mrs. Caudwell, who said:

> "He had a sore on his head through banging his head and was very weak. He is now growing fast. My husband intended to give him to a zoo, but several zoos have turned him down, so we are asking the public to see if there is anyone who can find him a permanent home."

The lion-cub was beginning to bite his teeth upon his bottle, so Mrs. Caudwell, a hospital catering supervisor, had to work extra hard to feed him.

On the 15th October 1987, the Nottingham Branch secretary of the RSPCA told me:

> 'I am sorry that I cannot help you with any information regarding the lion scare in Nottingham, as the Inspector who was based here at that time has since moved to Cornwall. I have enquired as to whether the Branch was involved in any way with sightings of the lion, and it would appear not, so I do not think we can help you with your investigations.'

The public relations officer at Nottingham Police Station told me in a letter of 24th September 1987: "Unfortunately, any records on the situation you mention will have been destroyed after eleven years, so I am not able to help you.'

It would seem that each police force has its own way of doing things. The Surrey police photocopied/records, which were more than twenty years old.

• THE PENNINES:

The Pennines are the backbone of England. It is on the other side of these hills that many of the northern mystery cats have been seen.

• The Skegness Cougar

I have obtained considerable information on this cat through appeals in two local papers. I originally read about the sightings in Di Francis's 1983 book, "*Cat Country: the Quest for the British Big Cat*", and "*Alien Animals*" by Janet and Colin Bord.

Initially I wrote to the Skegness Hospital where the sightings had taken place. Mr Firth, the manager of Skegness and Spilsby Hospitals, told me the following in a letter dated '4th December 1987:

> 'The only thing I have been able to find out is that Doctor Jamisson thought he saw a puma from the window of Seely House Convalescent Home some ten years or more ago. I am afraid that Seely House has since been closed and demolished. Doctor Jamieson died only this year. You may be able to obtain information from the local press and the police station."

Mr Firth kindly supplied the addresses. This reply was most helpful, and I wrote to the two local newspapers. On about 10th December I heard from Mr Jim Wright of the *Skegness News* :

> "Have you a close-up photo of yourself that we could borrow? Also, are you on the 'phone? I should like to speak to you about the proposed book."

I waited for some more replies before answering this offer.

As Skegness was a seaside resort, I wondered whether the circus had lost a big cat while it was passing through, in about 1976. This theory could be true, but I have not yet found evidence to back it up.

On 23rd December 1987, the *Skegness News* published this letter from me:

> 'Where is the cougar now?
>
> Sir, I am writing a book called "big cats Loose in Britain", and I understand that Dr Jamieson observed a puma about ten years ago (probably in 1976) from a window of the former Seely House Convalescent Home. There was an article published in the Evening Standard of October 1976 on this subject. If any of your readers have seen the "Skegness Cougar", as it is called, since then, please could you be so kind as to ask them to write to me. I have seen a bob-cat in the Mendip Hills of Somerset and Avon, and a puma on Exmoor. Could any readers remember if the cougar was ever seen again?
>
> Yours etc., Marcus Matthews (aged 14).'

After this letter was published I made a number of contacts in the Skegness area. The Superintendent of Skegness police sent me the following statements on 24th December 1987:

> 'I am afraid I am unable to help you in your enquiries as to the incident in 1975 in Skegness. I cannot find any officer who has any recollection of the incident and we have no written record of it now held at Skegness police station.'

It was not surprising that this statement was not much help, as the Chief Superintendent and the police officer fully involved in the search have, seemingly, since then left the police station and force. I heard from the Chief Superintendent (retired) of Skegness police, Mr Ted Beverley, on 25th December 1987. He now lives in Skegness. His letter runs:

'I read your letter in the Skegness News of 23.12.87 with interest. There were re-ports of a "puma" being seen from the window of Seely House (a convalescent home now extinct) by a local doctor, Alex Jamieson (now deceased). He was attend-ing a meeting and reported the matter to me personally. I was the local police chief superintendent, and I took the matter seriously. I visited personally and arranged for observations to be kept for some time. The matter received local interest in the newspapers and on Yorkshire TV. However, I'm afraid I must disappoint you. I lived nearby and saw the creature several times. It was a very large ginger Tom-cat with an exceptionally long tail that had black and white rings from the body to the tip. It roamed around the sand-hills and fed mainly on rabbits and wild birds. I saw it several times on the golf course. You couldn't get near it, and it was very agile. I am quite satisfied that this was the creature Dr Jamieson had seen and I later told him so. I think he accepted the fact.

I hope this will be of some interest to you. I am a great lover of cats (big and little!).'

I talked to Mr Jim Wright on the telephone and gave him all the information I had then on the "Skegness Cougar". He published the following article on the front page of the *Skegness News* of 13th January 1987:

'Was Mystery Creature an escaped puma?

A 14-year-old boy has raked up the legend of the Skegness 'big cat' which was thought to be at large in the resort in the mid-1970s. At the time there was national media coverage for what was said to be a cougar - a species of yellowish-red puma that lives in the mountainous regions of Brazil. Marcus Matthews, of Warminster in Wiltshire, is gathering information on all sorts of 'big cat' sightings all over the U.K. One theory is that the local beast might have been released in response to new Gov-ernment Restrictions on the keeping of dangerous animals in captivity.

The late Dr Alec Jamieson, a police surgeon, reported seeing the mystery animal in the grounds of Seely House - a convalescent home on Roman Bank, Winthorpe, which has now been demolished. The sighting was taken seriously by the then Chief of local police,

Supt. Ted Beverly, but subsequent inquiries came up with nothing more substantial than one suspiciously large paw print.

Unfortunately for Marcus, Mr Beverly, who lives in Hesketh Crescent, Skegness, thinks the case for a puma is unsubstantiated. He believed the mystery creature was no more than a large ginger tomcat gone wild, which fed on rabbits and birds around the golf course.

However, Marcus is pressing on with his investigations. He would like anyone with reminiscences of the animal to write to him.'

The *Skegness News* letter prompted Mrs. D. McGowan of Skegness to write me a letter dated 28th December 1987 (approximately) She gave me this food for thought, which has proved invaluable:

'I was interested to read your article in last week's Skegness News. At the time I was a nurse at Seely House and I was in the patients' dining room when Dr Jamieson and about four more officials were sitting at a table having coffee. Outside the window was a wide, long stretch of grass, at the far end a high hedge, for privacy from the beach. This animal was stalking along the hedge. Dark-golden brown, massive chest, thick neck, almost the size of a Great Dane, but heavier.

Dr Jamieson said: "My God, a cougar!" The others laughed and said: "It couldn't be, it must be a big dog."

He 'phoned the police, the newspapers made a report about it. But two days after we first saw it I was on afternoon duty and in the same dining room, talking to Mr Evans. He was the senior nursing officer. It was around 5 p.m. He was going off duty. I was to be in charge until night staff came on. We saw the animal again alongside the hedge, going up towards Butlin's Way. Mr Evans said he was going outside to have a look. I was worried, in case this animal was around the side of Seely, and so I begged him to stay inside. But he came back and said there was no sign of it. A lot of people said it would be a dog. But I don't, believe it, it was too powerful. Where did it come from? No one ever heard of it being anywhere else, only 'round about Seely House grounds. I'd love to hear the end of it. Seely House has been knocked down and bought by the Derbyshire miners, and Dr Jamieson died last year. I've been retired five years. But I was always so glad I was one of the few people who did see this beast. If you hear anything else, will you please tell me.'

I wrote back to her, sending more information. I had a second letter from Mrs. McGowan, the sheet she enclosed gave me the address of P.C. Jock Gartshore, who had left the force, but had been the policeman on the case at the time of the sighting; also the addresses of the *Scunthorpe Evening Telegraph* and *Skegness News*. Mrs. McGowan also stated, about the original sightings:

'Mr D. Evans was the senior nursing officer I told you about. He was due off duty. I was on duty until night staff came on at 8.30 a.m. It was 5 p.m. We were in the same dining room when the cougar went by. Mr Evans went outside the building to see if he could see it. I was relieved when he came back and hadn't seen it. '

Following all this advice, I wrote off to both Mr Gartshore and Mr Evans. I obtained the following statement from Mr Gartshore, in a letter dated 18th February 1988:

'In reply to your letter of 13th February 1988 regarding the cat at Seely House, Skegness, I was a police officer at the time of this incident and went to Seely House

on various occasions to obtain reports of sightings of a puma.

I fear that the original witnesses to this incident may have had vivid imaginations of a puma on the loose because in the various visits to the scene, I never saw the animal. I was the officer who first went when Dr Jamieson 'saw' the creature, but on questioning him and the other witnesses I formed the opinion it was a large domestic cat, or similar. I did see paw-prints, however, and could not say, at the time, whether they were cat, dog, or what. Should reports state that I saw the animal, I can assure you they are misleading.

There may be some evidence that rabbits and birds were eaten in an area of gorse bushes and sandhills between the beach and Seely House, but that is all I ever saw. There were no dung droppings or fur that could be found, and what there was in the area was examined by Mr John Yeadon, of Natureland, Skegness, at the time, bringing us to the conclusion that it was a domestic animal of big proportions.

There have been no further reports to my certain knowledge of "the cat" as it was then termed. And nothing was ever found (i.e. skeleton, etc.) The site has now gone. I hope that this will help you in your book. Should you consider coming to Skegness, please get in contact with me. You may like to follow up the story of the lion or lioness which escaped from a circus touring Gainsborough in about 1974/75, in which several police officers sought refuge in a police panda. Lincolnshire police Alert newspaper had an extremely funny story on it.'

Mr T. A. Gartshore was obviously rather sceptical of the puma's existence, but his statement showed that some (very?) large animal was around the area. Was it a feral domestic cat, a stray dog, or a genuine big cat? Mr D. J. Evans, S.R.N., now a member of the Norfolk Residential Care Home Association, owning an old people's home in Sheringham, Norfolk, wrote me the following statement in a letter of 28th February 1987:

'I'm afraid I cannot remember a great deal more to what you have already got regarding the Skegness puma. I was present when Dr Jamieson sighted a very large fawn-coloured cat in the grounds of Seely House. Looking at it from a first-floor lounge window (allowing for some distortion of the glass) the animal was certainly too large for a domestic cat.

The one feature I recall was its rather long tail in proportion to the rest of its body. It walked along by the wire fence in full view for quite a long way before disappearing into the bushes. The second sighting was, I believe, some time later, when Mrs. McDowan and I were standing by the window of a ground-floor room. I think the animal on this occasion walked towards the window before walking off into the bushes. I did, on several occasions after these sightings, explore the area around where we had seen the cat. But I saw nothing to suggest the actual size or feeding habits, or its lair. The several tracks there were made by the very large number of rabbits in the hospital grounds.

I am sorry I cannot be of more help to you on this occasion. Time dims the memory. Certainly, at the time the sightings caused quite a lot of excitement. I think we were all convinced that it was not the "ginger Tom from next door".'

Mr David Evans's letter seemed to confirm the existence of the big cat. I have also heard from an 86-year-old former farmer, Mr Amos White, of Chapel St Leonards, near Skegness. The following extract comes from his letter of 24th January 1988:

'Reading your letter in the Skegness News, I feel I must write to you. I am a retired farmer and I shall be 87, if I live until 24th July 1988, being the third generation on the farm, having to retire on account of bone marrow deficiency and poor circulation owing to blood veins becoming furred up. The farm was very isolated and I was living on my own. I remember very well indeed about the animal you mention. I would have thought it was more like a lion than a puma. It was round my house for several days. The huge paw-marks were on the garden and also on the panels of the front door, when it had stood on its hind legs, leaving dirty paw-marks on the white panels on the door. I took my gun and plenty of cartridges up to my bedroom in case it broke in during the night.

I went to Ashford police station to enquire if I shot it, would I get into trouble. They told me to shoot first and ask questions later. I thought it might be a valuable animal that had escaped. The last I heard about it was in Huttcroft, a little village midway between here and Mablethorpe.

The farm I had was a Quaker colony, with chapel and burial ground, in one of my fields, before my family bought it. The rooms had huge oak beams across the ceilings. It was known as Quaker's Hill Farm. In my young days, the grass and corn was all cut by scythe, and all the other work by hand. The council roads had ruts six inches deep, made by the horses and wagon wheels. I had to walk 2 miles to school in all weathers, down lonely lanes, all alone.'

It would seem that in the mid-1970s a lioness escaped and roamed across Lincolnshire and Nottinghamshire, causing the "Skegness Cougar" and the "Nottingham Lion" scare. It was eventually recaptured in 1978 or 1979 in Sherwood Forest.

I sent Mr Amos all the correspondence I had obtained on the "Skegness Cougar". He wrote me a second letter, in which he gave me more insight into the lion,. The letter was dated 4th February 1988, and contained the following most valuable information:

'It appears that the animal you wrote about, in the paper, was not the one that was round my farm, I was a patient in Carey House, next to Seely House, and saw all the rabbits running about on the lawns outside. I have never seen rabbits with such large ears, in my life, which would make good meals for the large cat that you mentioned. The animal I saw was most certainly a lion. The first time I saw it I was only a few yards from it, and I was in my car, and it jumped over the ditch and crossed the road. For three or four days it spent its time round my house.

In the 1950s it was a difficult time to make a living on the farming. 30 stone fat pigs sold for £5, light week-old for 7/6d each, and down calving heifers £15 each, fat cattle were about the same price.as a man's weekly wages, 30 shillings a week. Eggs 20 for 1 shilling, butter 1 shilling a pound.

I had to carry water for cattle and clean out cowsheds, before walking 2 miles to school down lonely country lanes, all alone in all weather. Living on fat bacon, suet or fruit dumplings, seven days a week. Now they say fat is a killer. Tobacco is a herb and smoking a pipe never hurt anyone. It is these bought cigarettes that are killers. I used to grow my own tobacco. Any daily paper would give me a fortune to hear what I have endured in my lifetime.'

This letter was fascinating, even if not all of it was to do with the "Skegness Cougar". Getting back on the subject of big cats, Lincolnshire probably has more black dog legends than any other county in England. Are these black dogs just black panthers? Di Francis seems to think so and has devoted a chapter of her book "*Cat Country*" to the black dog.

I must now note that the *Scunthorpe Evening Telegraph* published their only article on the "Skegness Cougar" on 21st September 1976. This article was the sole source of information for Janet and Colin Bord, Di Francis and Andy Roberts, in *Cat Flaps*.

'... September (1976) gave us two cases, The Leicester Mercury *reported a large-scale police search in the Bermunda village area of Nuneaton, the day after a puma-like animal was reported to have been seen. Police checked the zoos in the area, but no large cats were missing. A "cougar" was reported on the 20th in the grounds of a seafront convalescent home at Skegness. Police gave the story a high credibility because the witness was the town's police surgeon, Dr Alec Jamieson. He said: "It was a large sandy coloured cat about 5 feet long. Definitely a cougar." He called in P.C. Jock Gartshore, who also saw the beast. Staff at the home said they had seen the thing several times over the previous few weeks and dismissed it as just a large unusual dog! A search in the grounds found paw-marks measuring 2 inches by 3 inches across, and later an R.S.P.C.A, Inspector and a naturalist hid in the grounds with cameras, but again, predictably, nothing materialised. Dr Jamieson remains convinced he saw a cougar, and thinks it may have been the "Nottingham Lion" on a walk-about.'*

That seems to conclude my "Skegness Cougar" chapter, except to say that the same issue of the *Fortean Times* No. 20 (February 1977), reviews the case of a lion at Upton Chester, Cheshire. The police found no trace of the lion, and Chester Zoo had not lost one. The date of the incident was 23rd October 1976, and Chester is on the other side of England, about opposite to Skegness on the East Coast. The foot and car patrols later established that the lion was none other than a Great Dane dog (See my 'Cheshire Cats' section). Chester Zoo denied that the lioness could have been theirs, probably because the scare was only half a mile from them, and that was the last thing they wanted on their doorstep.

At the beginning of 1975, on 21st April, the *Wolverhampton Express and Star* of Staffordshire, reported that a black panther, 3½ ft. long, and 1½ ft. to 2 ft. tall at the shoulder, with "very bright eyes", was seen. Its appearance and sightings by residents spurred on a police search of Willenhall. Nothing had escaped from the local zoo, which leaves us with a 'private owner' explanation. The cat was not caught.

• THE HARROGATE PANTHER

There is supposed to be a mystery cat at Harrogate, a large town in North Yorkshire. Andy Roberts has already covered the panther, in a chapter of his booklet *Cat Flaps*, using ASSAP files and several conversations with local people. I have not undermined his research, but have merely added to it. The local paper, the *Harrogate Advertizer*, is supposed to have published a single article on 1st October 1985, but enquiries with Mrs. Sharon Fahy, the editor's secretary, revealed no such story. However, she put my letter forward for publication. She also sent me an article from the *Harrogate Advertizer* of 27th September 1985, about an entombed cat. The story concerns a domestic cat, which was trapped for 17 days before being rescued. I will not repeat the story here.

Mr Arthur M.G. Kenneas was the Harrogate man who sent me details of the book by Sir Sitwell Sitwell, called "*Left Hand, Right Hand*", which recounted the escaped tiger in Sheffield's Rentshaw Estate, in 1797. I wish to thank him here for telling me about this book, which is referred to in the 'Long Ago' section of this chapter.

Mrs Jean Nettleton wrote to me on 1st September 1987, to say that she had written a book on her own domestic cats. She had submitted it to Michael Joseph Ltd., the London publishers, who could not publish it due to 'paper shortage, as animal books sell a lot.' They gave her the address of Joy Adamson, to whom she sent the book. Mrs. Adamson wished her luck with the book, and said she liked it. Mrs. Nettleton re-read her book after seeing my letter and explained to me that she had six cats, one of which is very heavy:

> '*One, poor soul, weighs 28 lbs. due to glands, but she is a happy soul, but cannot get around much."*

The world record weight for a cat is 33 lbs, which is only about ten pounds under the weight of the smallest fully-grown puma. Feral cats can attain large sizes, and i wondered whether somebody might have mistaken a large feral cat for a panther. Andy Roberts is convinced that the `Harrogate Panther` was the same as the black Kellas cat. I therefore began to make some enquiries, hoping to uncover some evidence that would lead us to the panther.

Mr R. Johnson, Force press officer of North Yorkshire police headquarters at Newby Wiske in North Yorkshire, gave me the following statement on 8th December 1987:

> '*Unfortunately I am not able to send you any police records on the incident, but I can tell you that after reported sightings from members of the public, quite extensive searches were carried out by the police in the fields and woods in the vicinity of Harrogate golf club. Police horses and dogs were used but no signs of it were ever found, and the original sightings were never confirmed, so the mystery remains.'*

According to Paul Screeton's article 'Diary of a Cat-Flap', *Folklore Frontiers*, no. 4, BBC Radio 4 series,

'The Archers' of 28th February 1983, referred to a 'mystery big cat' or 'puma' killing ewes around Ambridge, Yorkshire. The story was fictitious, but might have been based on truth.

Mr Roberts analyses three sightings in the Harrogate area in *Cat Flaps*. All the sightings were in Autumn 1985, so the golf course search must have been around that date. I received a letter from Mr Brian Cooper of Starbeck, Harrogate, who sent me the second edition of *Cat Flaps*. He wished me all the best with the project and asked me to return the booklet when I had finished with it, which I did. His letter was dated 12th January 1987. He is one of the three witnesses referred to in Mr Roberts's book.

I also received a letter from Mrs. Limee, the Mayor of Harrogate's secretary. She wrote the following from the Mayor's Parlour in Harrogate Council Offices on 22nd December 1987:

> *'I am afraid that all I can find for you are some vague memories of the incident you describe, and you were right in assuming that the cat had escaped from Knaresborough Zoo. The Zoo is now closed but the local RSPCA at the Area Communications Centre in York may be able to help. I have pleasure in enclosing a copy of the Dangerous Wild Animals Act 1976.'*

The photocopies are from a volume of Laws and there are eight pages of Laws on the keeping of wild animals. It is designed as "an Act to regulate the keeping of certain kinds of dangerous wild animals" and was passed through Parliament on the 22nd July 1976. The Act may well have brought about the closure of zoos like the one at Knaresborough.

• THE DERBYSHIRE PUMA AND FRIENDS

Perhaps the best place to start with this 1986/1987 cat 'flap' is with a letter from the man most involved in it: P.C. Eddie Bell, a policeman and a naturalist, of Stanley, County Durham. In a letter of October 1987, P. C. Bell wrote out the whole 'flap' in the form of a rather lengthy diary, which I quote here.

17.9.86: Sunday. 1st sighting - Thinford Inn roundabout, near Springfield. Lorry driver used his CB radio to contact a woman to tell her that he was trapped in his lorry cab by a large cat - Described as larger than an Alsatian, cat-like, black in colour with white markings on its chest. Seen at 8.00 p.m. and sat for several minutes. On arrival of the police it had gone and the area was searched - no trace. The police who spoke to the lorry driver confirmed that he was very nervous and frightened by the incident. Next day a search was made by the police and dogs, but no signs of the cat.

19.9.86: Tuesday. I visited the area but found no signs or marks.

On checking locals in the area, three incidents came to light, previous to the above sighting:

1) A local farmer had chased a 'large lurcher-type dog', black in colour, from a lamb kill days before at Croxdall. The lamb was described as 'half eaten out'.
2) Locals said that their horses had been terrified and when they went out the horses were dancing around very terrified. (They were used to dogs.)
3) Two reports of suspicious and unknown deer deaths in the Croxdall area. Croxdall is a large estate of farm and woodland about 2 miles from Durham city and midway between Thinford Inn

roundabout and Durham.

30.9.86. Second sighting - seen at Fishburn Coke Works by a worker there, described as a mountain lion with small face, long tail, big chest, sandy coloured with white chest markings. 2 feet tall, and he saw it run in front of his lorry at night and then climb up a pile of coke, which was about 10 feet tall and very steep.

22.9.86. I went to Fishburn Coke Works, which is a large barren area of coke heaps and waste, with no cover or vegetation, but a rabbit population and resting seabirds.

There was an underground passage about 3 ft by 4 ft in size and it ran 80 feet underground. It carried piping for the coke-works. In the soft coke dust in the bottom there were footprints (See photographs enclosed). In addition, when the animal was seen to run up the side of the coke heaps, there were indentations some 3 inches across, and whatever ran up the heaps was athletic and fast. I could not walk up the surface of coke. In addition there was a dead and eaten seagull (only wings were left) - presumably caught by something.

23.9.86. Large black cat sighting at Ferryhill; seen by five local children and a man.

26.9.86. Spotted at 7.30 p.m., off Al, near Bowburn interchange. Very large black cat about 4 ft long and 2 ft high. It was carrying a rabbit in a field next to the motorway, this sighting being about 1 mile from the previous sightings.

2.10.86. Spotted at Durham Road, Springfield. Large cat, brown and black striped, 18 inches at the shoulder. A dog was seen to run from it, petrified.

5.10.86. Visited Fishburn Coke Works. No new tracks at the coke works.

10.10.86. Sighting at Al Motorway underpass, at Westernform Quarry (still in the immediate vicinity). It was described as large and black. The area was checked but there were no signs.

25.10.86. First sighting outside original area. It was seen at Castleside, near Casett - a vast area of woodland and countryside. Large black cat. No other details.

26.10.86. Dead sheep found at a farm at Bowburn, near to the original sightings. Sheep is dead in the field with 3 other dead sheep nearby. Carcass almost cleared out and meat and blood actually licked from the skin. About 24 lbs. of meat taken and carcass not torn again, so feeding 2 or more animals. Killed apparently by bite to back of the neck - no markings on the legs. No bite marks on bones, and meat apparently rasped from the bone - there were small pieces of meat or sinew etc. Just like wood raspings on the carcass. 3 other sheep appeared to have died of fright some way from the kill. However, no signs of prolonged chasing - the kill had been made by an animal that had stalked the sheep along a fence, attacked and landed on this specific sheep. The farmer had never seen any kill like it, and when the knacker-man took the remains away, he had not seen any dog or fox damage comparable with this kill. In addition, when the skin was removed, the signs on the shoulders beneath the fleece and the large bruise with scratches through it showed where the paw of an animal had struck it.

BIG CATS: LOOSE IN BRITAIN

On the night, apparently, the farmer's wife had tried to let the dog out and it would not go. The knacker-man (with 40 years' experience), had also found a bruise and scratches on the shoulder of one of the other sheep, the kill being made in the corner of the field, where the sheep would shelter from the gale force winds and rain of previous nights. Puncture wounds in the flesh were, to him, not dog teeth marks.

29.10.86. Large cat spotted making towards Wingate Quarry nature reserve - described as being larger than an Alsatian, dark brown, ears on top of the head. The lady who spotted it had seen none of the previous publicity.

5.11.86. Farmer's son had spotted a large cat in a field off the A68 at Sarley (near to Coke Works sighting) - large black cat sitting in a field, looking around. He saw it for 5 minutes and said it was definitely a cat. 1.00 p.m. Report of a cat seen at Wingate, going towards Peterhill and Castle Eden Drive (a nature reserve). The cat was larger than Alsatian, narrow, deep-chested. Long tailed, black and definitely a cat. It ran in a loping fashion and the person who sighted it had two Alsatians which would not go near it. Footprints found. Cat seen in a stream valley and ran uphill over open country.

5.11.86. Seen near metal bridge 2.15 a.m. Moving in the headlights of a bus. The witness was driving. It was described as being large, bigger than an Alsatian, black with a long tail. It was a good sighting.

8.11.86. Bowburn Farm. A dead calf was found. The calf was newly-born and was very healthy (born at 11 a.m.). Calf halved - head, front legs and its ribs left, the rest of the body was missing. Lips eaten and the ears were chewed. No lick marks and area of tearing. Ears also were missing. The backbone was severed by a bite and the lower parts of the body were missing.

12.11.86. Ferryhill section/Bedbury interchange road - Report from the previous night of a black cat seen in a field there. On driving there, I saw in the field a small black dog, with a small face, drooped ears and a curly tail (obviously it was the 'cat' in the above sighting).

On approaching the dog to catch it, it bit my left hand and I received hospital treatment. The dog ran off! I was featured on TV and the dog owner rang. He said it was missing for 7 days, and apologised for it biting me.

20.11.86. sighted at Springfield - large black cat. No other details.

30.11.86. Motorcyclist and girl friend saw a large black cat in the headlights at the side of the road; large dark-coloured cat, 2 ft. tall and had leapt over a fence into a field. The rider looked really surprised when he was seen, by me.

5.12.86. Seen near Bumopfield - large cat, tortoiseshell markings, lynx-like with pointed ears, heavily built, stumpy tail, greyish belly.

9.12.86. Castle Eden Drive. A man walking his Jack Russell dog in woods saw 2 black shaggy animals in the woods, after which his dog was frightened by them, and he was so frightened he ran off.

<u>11.12.86</u>. A farmer, at 10 p.m., at Bishop Middleton, reported seeing a large brown cat pass within a few yards of his farmhouse. It had a longish tail. The cat moved off, but 2 days earlier he had had a sheep killed identically to the one at Bowburn - large part eaten away and not a dog kill. The carcass had gone. In addition many had sheep elsewhere and they had two sheep which had suffered deep scratches on their sides, as if scratched by a large animal.

<u>7.1.87</u>. 1st sighting of the New Year at Steeply Quarry, in the snow. A large cat, Rottweiler size, black with a short tail. On checking the footprints, I found them almost certainly, to be those of a Rottweiller dog. It was a terrible day and I was called from my sickbed (I was off with 'flu).

No sightings until 1.9.87. A coach-driver reported seeing a large black cat, the size of a puma, prowling on a road between Butterwith and Trinden. Actually, there was a sighting on the 20.8.87 - A large cat was seen at Beamish, near Stanky (a wooded area). It was described as being like a bob-cat, with a sleek coat, quite unlike that of a domestic cat. It was larger than a Scottish wildcat and was smaller than a puma. It was seen by a man who is a graduate in Biology.

Then finally on 12.10.1987: A black cat was sighted off the A167 road of the North Roundabout (near the original sighting) by a man going to work. It was described as 2 ft high, 3 ft long, black and grey, with a thin tail. Apparently looking like a *'small cheetah.'*

This brings us up to date. The sightings also included ones from a wider area than described, in fact in the space of two days, I had sightings at Wide Open (3 miles north of Newcastle) and just outside of Middlesbrough (about 50 miles apart). However, the major sightings occupy three distinct areas:

1) Bowburn/Croxdall/Springfield areas. Always a large black cat; areas of 'kills' and footprints, I found.
2) Castle Eden Drive, Ferryhill, Peterhill area: One set of foot-prints from the area, and some of the better sightings.
3) Stanley/Beamish/Bumopfield areas. Few sightings (the area is heavily wooded in part). All sightings of a 'Lynx-like' cat. The areas in which the sightings occur are all farmland and wooded areas, with villages and towns nearby, and a reasonable population. After the initial sightings, these have now settled down to being sporadic

Many thanks must go to P.C. Bell for all the work he has done so far, and I wish him the best of luck in his researches.

The rest of this section is made up of newspaper articles being quoted, and from some letters from witnesses. I believe there could be two black panther-like cats, also one puma-like, and one lynx-like, all loose in a very wide area of Co. Durham.

The *Hartlepool Mail* of 4th August 1986 reported that a couple of young people observed a Labrador-sized cheetah-faced cat at Bowburn. They said that the animal was a big black cat, with a 3 ft. long tail. A spokesman for Durham city police said the animal may have been a wildcat, which was very large and was beccitting more common in parts of Britain. The man reckoned the cat was the sort of animal that couid be dangerous.

The couple observed the cat near to their home, in the early hours of the morning. Stewart Wilson, who saw the cat, said that it was black in colour, with white paws. He also stated: *"I know some people must think me mad, but my wife and I both saw the animal quite clearly. At first I was convinced it was a dog, but it padded along like one of the giant cats."*

This was reported in the *Northern Echo* of 2nd August 1986.

On 23rd September 1986, Brian Rothery observed a large cat near Faraday Street, Ferryhill, where he lived. He was walking his dog on old colliery land and saw that the cat was stalking some youngsters who were playing there. He told the *Hartlepool Mail* of the following day's date:

> *"I saw this big black thing and at first I thought it was a small horse. Then I realised it was too long to be a horse. It was standing with its head down towards the grass. It could have been stalking the kids, judging by the way it was standing."*

He told the *Daily Express* and the *Sun* of 28th September that *"it was two or three times the size of my Doberman."*

Mr Rothery told me the true version of the sighting in a letter dated 18th August 1987:

> *"First of all it was not a puma. It was the newspaper who called it a puma. My sighting was in a field near where I live. I had just walked across the same field five minutes before, also with my dog. As I came back towards the same field I saw a dark shape standing still. I had no idea what it was, so I walked closer and saw what looked like a large cat. It was fifty yards from where I was standing. There were some boys at the top about 150 yards from it. They also saw it. I was not going to get any closer, as it was a quarter to eight and getting dark. The cat was about the same size as my Doberman dog. It was just standing still and sniffing the around, so I turned and ran off the other way, and that's the last I saw of it.*
>
> *The cat has been seen a few times around County Durham. The first, a mile away in a lay-by. The man who saw it was sitting in the cab of his lorry as it walked past. It then jumped up at the cab and ran off. There was a story in the local paper of four sheep that had been killed. One was ripped apart, and the others' hearts had stopped. The local R.S.P.C.A. reported they had tracked it to where it was living. They would not say where, just to stop people shooting it."*

It would seem that Mr Rothery had read the local papers like most people, and had learnt a lot from their articles.

Before Mr Rothery's sighting, on 15th September, 1986, the *Hartlepool Mail* reported that a motorist had seen a large black cat, bigger than a police dog, run into a field, with a smaller cat, behind the Thinford Bridge Inn, on the A167. The cats were said to be black pumas, and Durham police were hunting for them. The *Thinford Inn* is on a roundabout south of Durham city.

On 26th September 1986, Mr Charles Charlton, an ex-Windsor wildlife park warden of four years' experience, said that the creature was unlikely to be a puma. He reckoned it was just a dog or a wildcat. On 4th October, P.C. Eddie Bell and Dr Nigel Dunston of Durham University Zoology Department, said they planned to track the puma. They had six sightings and also a set of plaster casts, 3 inches across.

On 8th October, the *Sunday Express* published an article on five cat sightings so far. One of the sightings was that of the lorry driver, Mr Dave Dawkins, who saw his cat about 24th September. The RSPCA Inspector, Mr Bill Crisp, said the cat's lair was known and that they were watching it through infra-red binoculars.

The next reported sighting was by Mrs. Florence Watson, an old-age pensioner of Deaf Hill at 11.45 a.m. on 29th October 1986. She told the *Hartlepool Mail* the next day:

> *"I couldn't believe it. I just looked from round the house towards the bottom of the garden and there it was, just staring straight at me. I didn't run away or anything, not because I wasn't frightened but because I couldn't believe what I was seeing. It was quite a bit bigger than an Alsatian, with a cat-like appearance, and was dark brown with a straight neck and pointed ears. After a few seconds, it just turned tail and ran off over the fields."*

Mrs Watson was hanging out washing at the time, and was only 30 yards away from the cat. Peterlee police said:

> *"We didn't find any trace of it, but the ground was hard and it wouldn't have left any tracks."*

P.C. Eddie Bell said:

> *"I have an open mind on what Mrs. Watson saw, and whether it is the same animal that has already been sighted in the Bowburn and Fishburn areas in recent weeks. Certainly it was a large, unusual-looking animal and it may or may not have been a cat."*

Andy Roberts, who wrote a brief chapter in his booklet *Cat Flaps*, reckoned that Mrs. Watson had probably seen a Doberman dog. However, Mrs. Watson confirmed her sighting to me, in a letter dated 3rd September 1987, and sent me a copy of the above newspaper article, and one other article, also mentioning her sighting. She thought she had seen a 'mystery cat'.

Paul Screeton notes in his article on the Durham puma, for his magazine *Folklore Frontiers*, No.4, that the big cat was seen near where two or three weeks previously, a journalist colleague (unnamed) had seen a strange beast cross the road. He stopped the car to look around and after several minutes realised that just before him, in the ditch, was 'the most evil-looking dog' he had ever seen. The man drove off, leaving the dog alone. The *Northern Echo* of 31st October (two days after Mrs. Watson's sighting) carried a story entitled 'Puma-like beast spotted near station'. The animal - or, rather, animals - were held responsible for sightings in an area of 60 square miles, south of Durham, taking in Bow burn, Newton Aycliffe, Spennyineer and Ferryhills.

PC Bell was said to be taking ten days' holiday to track the mystery beast, with Durham R.S.P.C.A. Inspector Bill Crisp. P.C. Bell stated:

> "A lot depends on the weather. I'm not going to see anything in gale force winds and torrential rain. I am fairly certain it is not a puma we are looking for, but sightings suggest there is some kind of large cat out there. As a keen naturalist, I am fascinated by all this, but I'm keeping an open mind until I find some definite evidence about its identity. But I am convinced that it is something out of the ordinary."

Mr Crisp was quoted as rather worriedly stating:

> "I want to get to the bottom of this mystery before some trigger-happy character injures this creature."

On 25th September, the *Northern Echo* had published a story, not on Brian Rothery's sighting, but on the previous ones. Mel Mason, their reporter, was sent along to P.C. Bell and Dr Nigel Dunston of Durham University zoology Department, to see what could be gathered on the continuing saga.

P.C. Bell at first said it could turn out to be just an abnormally large tomcat. On the other hand it could be something much more exciting. He continued:

> "We are going to see what the countryside is like, where it is likely to lie up and live, and where it would kill. We hope we may be able to get a look at it, to see what it is, and look at the possibility of trapping it in the future."

He also contacted *Cat-Country* authoress and naturalist Di Francis, who was ready to give her opinion that it was one of the British big cats. He agreed with her, and also was of the opinion:

> "From the sightings in Durham it seems possible the type of cat she has been studying is the type we have here: a cat about the size of a Labrador - three feet long, with a fairly long tail, ears on the top of its head, and dark grey or brown."

By 8th November the *Northern Echo* headline was *'Where's My Puma?'* Eddie Bell was staying near his phone, hoping to hear from anybody who had seen the puma around. A week had passed since the last sighting, and even the BBC Natural History Unit had approached PC Bell. The animal had been seen twelve times.

By 7th November, things were looking up because PC Bell had talked to two new witnesses. The *Northern Echo* covered the story with the headline *'big cat seen twice'*. The first sighting was by a man walking his dog, at Wingate, and the second was early on the morning of 5th November. The second witness was a coach-driver, who observed the cat at Metal Bridge, near Ferryhills. Mr Raymond Richardson of Bowburn spied a large black cat run from a disused cemetery at 2 a.m. at Metal Bridge. In the first sighting, the dog-walker spotted a large black cat, bigger than an Alsatian dog, near a stream. When it was disturbed, the cat bounded off towards the coast.

The next piece of news came from North Yorkshire, where on the same day as the Wingate sighting (6th November 1986), police stated that a lady motorist had seen a 'black panther' at Croft. She observed the cat at 8 p.m. It jumped into the road and walked slowly past her car.

Inspector Ronald Johnson, of North Yorkshire constabulary, commented:

> *"The woman was quite sure it was not a black dog, and said she had a good look at it. We are keeping observations. No searches are being set up, but we would like to hear from anybody else who thinks they may have seen it, or if there are any incidents of sheep-worrying in that area."*

PC Bell considered that there were at least two cats, for he said:

> *"... I honestly and truthfully can't see it would be the same cat; it is at least 16 miles from the last sighting. It is more likely that if it is a cat, it would be a different one, but I would be very interested to hear about any other reported sightings in that area."*

This was in the *Northern Evening Echo* of 8th November. Croft is near the Middleton Tyas road. It would seem that back on 6th November there had been a sighting at the back of Wingate auction salerooms, by naturalist Mr Arthur Hardy and Mr Stephen Dodsworth. Mr Hardy stated:

> *"It was bigger than an Alsatian, jet black in colour with pointed ears on the top of its head, and a very long tail."*

The cat was curled up in short grass, behind the salesrooms.

On 18th November, a man from Shildon, Mr Kenneth Robinson, said he had spotted a black big cat from a train in April 1986. He reported the sighting to PC Eddie Bell, who told the *Northern Echo* of 15th November:

> *"I have to give credence to this sighting. Mr Robinson has been very accurate, whereas other witnesses have been vague. He says he has seen a puma before, and that, he claims, is what he saw."*

PC Bell was thinking of camping out for a few days, and he also thought that the puma could not be too dangerous.

Back on 13th November, the *Northern Evening Echo* carried another report of a mystery cat. This time P.C. Bell was called to a field at Gipsy Lane, halfway between Bradbury and Ferry Hill station. One night somebody had observed a black, Labrador-sized, long curly-tailed beast in this field. When P.C.Bell investigated, he confronted a black mongrel dog, which bit him. He received a tetanus jab at the hospital, and decided that the beast was responsible for the sighting.

At Shincliffe, near Durham, a young calf was also found half-eaten, but it was thought to have died from natural causes and been eaten by foxes. However, despite these two incidents, Supt. Barry Purdy, Commander of Durham Sub-division, commented:

> "We'd like to hear from people who regularly go out walking - or even poaching - to report anything they may come across which may indicate where this animal has its lair. We have been checking out quarries and old railway lines."

He did not want people to go tracking the beast themselves, because he thought the animal might be dangerous.

On 18th November there was a possible sighting of a cat running behind the police station at Newton Hall. P.C Bell was called to comment on the latest incidents, and he warned people to be sure that they were not just seeing a large dog. He also insisted that the Newton Hall cat sighting meant that the puma would have to have crossed Durham city, and he reckoned that somebody would surely have seen it. However, we now believe there are two black big cats, one lynx (a bob-cat?) and probably one puma-type cat of a sandy colour.

On 23rd November Mrs. P. Screeton - wife of journalist Paul Screeton - reckoned she observed a big cat from a distance of 100 yards, near their home at Seaton Carew. She said that the cat was the size of a Labrador, black, with sleek hair, and that it moved in a feline way. Being a Sunday, she was surprised that motorists did not notice it.

On 26th November, Mr Screeton saw an old black Labrador frisking about, and he wondered whether this was what his wife had seen, or whether it was something different. Mr Screeton sent me a copy of "Folklore Frontiers", No.4, and using this magazine and photo-copied newspaper articles from the *Northern Evening Echo* and the *Hartlepool Mail*, I have managed to piece together the continuing saga of the Durham cats. The sightings are continuing, and no doubt will do so for many years to come.
Paul Screeton told me, in a letter dated 15th July 1987:

> "In 'Folklore Frontiers', No. 5, I noted that the Northern Echo *of 8th January 1987 reported the police officer investigating sightings was called the previous day to West Cornforth. A process worker... Malcolm Conolly, saw what he believed was a big cat, which left tracks in the snow. However, PC Eddie Bell thought they were left by a dog, possibly a Rottweiler.'*

The Durham cats are probably breeding, as the sighting at the *Thinford Inn* roundabout of a larger and a smaller cat suggests, so PC Bell will probably be kept busy for many years with these reports. Are we really dealing with an indigenous cat? Photographs prove that the cats are there, but what is needed is a cat, alive or dead, so that cryptozoologists can carry out tests to determine what the cat may be. The Kellas cat is one type of mystery feline, but there is a larger type - or types - loose in the British Isles.

- ·THE NORTHUMBERLAND PANTHER

According to the Sun of 15th December 1977, there was a puma loose in Northumberland. The article, which was a brief sentence, read:

'Puma Hunt:

Armed police and farmers in Bettyhill, North Sunderland, Northumberland, were hunting yesterday for a sheep killer believed to be a puma.'

In the October 1983, No.24 edition of the *Northern Earth Mysteries News*, Paul Screeton wrote an article called *'Wild in the Countryside (Northumberland deliverance)'* He was writing about his own sighting of a mystery cat on 8th May 1983:

'The wildlife of the Northumberland countryside is diverse and affords glimpses in daylight of deer and foxes for the observant. However, driver John Watson and I were unprepared for the huge cat which crossed the car's path, driving between the Hurl Stone and another megalith in Alnwick's Hulne Park. The date was 8th May. My impression was that a large all-black cat of panther form crossed the road 100 or so yards ahead of us, from right to left, and disappeared into the undergrowth. To me it was as tall as an adult Doberman pinscher, twice the length and low-slung, moving with a powerful, quick feline gait. Afterwards, John felt it moved slower and was greyish. Why I blurted out after the sighting: "Was that a deer?" is a mystery also, as it in no way resembled such an animal.

Despite the high strangeness, John neither braked nor stopped. I had a loaded camera in my pocket and it never crossed my mind to attempt to take a photograph. In fact, our whole lack of coordination and inability to have a common perception of the event strike me as odd.'

Mr Screeton noted there had been many mystery cat sightings in the May of 1983 - the Exmoor Beasts hunt, the Buckinghamshire Puma hunt and various others. Mr Screeton was investigating megalithic stones in Northumbria, which are connected with earth mysteries. (All the *Mystery Magazine* staff and writers are loosely connected with each other, and thus Forteans may also run their own Mystery Magazines.) In the *Folklore Frontiers*, No.4, Mr Screeton adds to what he had already said about his sighting:

"Yet it suddenly vanished. It did appear from a spot where there was a gateway. For some this has paranormal significance. It occurred at grid reference NU 084 204 on the map, below Harehope Hill (hares often being associated with lycanthropy). Lay hunters may find some significance in the location."

Later, Mr Screeton found out that Hulne Park was 20 miles from the region of Bettyhill, North Sunderland, where men hunted a puma in December 1977. Mr Screeton also had dreams of savage big cats, instead of savage dogs, of which he had previously dreamt. He saw what appeared to be a lioness at Greatham railway station. Enquiries revealed that the lioness was just a docile old Alsatian. The sighting was quite near Rosden and it was a foggy, damp day. It does seem likely that Mr Screeton did see a black panther, as he stresses that he means a black leopard (panthera pardis). He also recorded his sighting in the *Sharman* Magazine, No.10, in 1985, where he called the article *"A Personal Black Panther sighting in Northumberland"*.

When Janni Hawker, author of '*The Nature of the Beast*' wrote to me, she also enclosed a cutting from the *Westmorland Gazette* of 31st July 1987. The article was entitled '*Mystery Beast Savages Hens*'. Mr and Mrs. Shuttleworth of Brathway, near Ambleside, Westmorland, had lost 15 hens to a mystery predator. They had kept hens for the past eight years and were mystified when six young hens were found ripped apart. They had been placed away from the older hens, which, four nights previously, had been pecking them. There were claw marks everywhere, and a panel had been broken and six hens savaged; one was missing and the other five were ripped apart. Mrs. Shuttleworth had the panel of the old shed replaced, with 24 nails, and a new quarter-inch window put in the frame. The Shuttleworths had found blood outside the shed, which suggests that the predator made off with the missing hen. The window was protected by wire mesh.

On a Wednesday morning, of the week the *Westmorland Gazette* published the story, the window was found smashed, the glass was broken, and the wire mesh had been ripped open by something powerful. Three hens were dead, and the rest were alive.. the predator must have been choosy. The nest-box hay was strewn around the old shed.

Mrs Shuttleworth blamed a badger, as she did not believe that a red fox could climb through her window. She understood that foxes only took hens to feed their young, yet some hens were left behind, some having their backs torn away. Mrs. Shuttleworth reckoned that the badger was trying to get at the eggs inside the hens. A neighbour had lost five hens two years before, and a badger was seen at the scene. A badger was also seen at Brathay meadow, near the Shuttleworths' home, only the night after they lost their first hens—six; in the second raid, six hens, and the third resulted in the deaths of three more hens. The couple were at their wits' end after three weeks of raids, and were planning to sell the hens.

However, Miss Joy Ketchen, conservator with the Cumbria Trust for Nature Conservation, thought it was 'very unlikely' that a badger would leave claw-marks everywhere. She said: "*It very, very rarely happens. It is much more likely to be a fox or a dog, and almost certainly it is going to be a fox.*" It was not a badger, because they were very lazy, and their main foods of earthworms and beetles made them unlikely to be The first raid had resulted had resulted in the deaths of the culprits. She reckoned that foxes and dogs were more aggressive, and if they had tasted blood before, they would often attack hens. The Trust's badger expert, Mrs. Jane Ratcliffe, was planning to visit the Shuttleworths, to see whether she could give them any advice.

I thought dogs and foxes would not leave claw-marks, and the forcing of a window was uncharacteristic of both of those animals. To my mind, the most likely culprit was a cat - either a domestic cat or a feral cat; or maybe even a large big cat. To my knowledge, there have been no sightings of mystery cats in Cumbria. However, I must point out that these northern moors are very bleak and sparsely populated, so sightings would be few and far between.

I wrote to Mr and Mrs. Shuttleworth, to find out whether they knew of any mystery cats in their region. They replied:

> "*We have been very upset about losing our hens to a badger. In three attempts it killed 15 hens (took none) and just tore their bottoms out, obviously looking for eggs... Many people rang us to tell us that it happened just the same to them. So it*

was very consoling. Had it been a fox it would have taken them and gone for their heads.

In just one field from my hen-house we found roughly nine badger setts. But they never bothered our hens before. Lots of people say there is always a rogue badger. Anyway, that was dealt with in our own way, as it is against the law to harm any [badgers]."

Mrs Shuttleworth, who was writing to me on 24th November, passed on the address of the *Westmorland Gazette*. I then wrote to this paper, appealing for information on mystery cats. (big cats in Scotland will be dealt with in a separate publication.)

Notes to the "Northern Big Cats" chapter

1) For local and area newspapers in the northern part of England, with references to the 'Durham pumas', see the *Hartlepool Mail* and the *Northern Evening Echo*, both of 1986. See also the *Aberdeen Press and Journal* and the *Midlands Evening Gazette* of the same year.

2) *"Watch, the Trust for Environmental Education Ltd.,"* the Green, Nettlehain, Lincolnshire, told me this in a letter of 23rd September 1987. The writer was Sandra Skipworth, who works under Mr Wayne Talbot, Watch education Officer:

> *'big cats in the U.K. I'm afraid that we do not have any relevant information... Your local library may also be able to supply you with back inssues of the B.B.C. Wildlife Magazine, and advise you on how to find books on a particular subject. I am sorry we have no information about this topic, but the advice may be of some use.'*

3) I have reason to believe that Andy Roberts's reference to a big cat in the Ilkeston area of Derbyshire in 'Cat-Flaps' may be incorrect. He quotes an article in the *Derbyshire Evening Telegraph* of 8th February 1983, which states that Mr Vincent Mizuro observed a large black puma-like cat, stalking two of his ducks. He said it was much larger than the stuffed Scottish wildcats in museums, and it was on a mound. He observed the animal at 100 yards and was not sure whether it was one cat or several. He said that he was inspired to tell of his sighting after reading 'Cat Country' by Di Francis.

The sighting was one on its own, and obviously not too clear. The animal may have been a dog, actually, stalking the two ducks.

The Chief Inspector of Ilkeston Police Station is Mr B. Dudley and he wrote the following in a letter dated 23rd September 1987:

> *"Unfortunately I am unable to help you, as we have no information which would assist with your project."*

I think that the Scottish wildcats and the Kellas cats are the cause of some northern cat sightings, because it is now known that they are pushing south of the Great Glen. Northern England has plenty of places named after Scottish wildcats and wolves, as any map will show you. The Pennines may hold mystery cats, and the Yorkshire moors are ideal big cat territory. The 'Harrogate panther' was indeed an escapee from Knaresborough Zoo, according to a man whom I met from Harrogate. He stated that a disillusioned zoo-keeper had loosed the panther undetected, and later let out lions and wolves. He was sacked from his job. The *Daily Telegraph* of 5th February 1987 contained a short news item of relevance:

> *'Puma Drowns:*
>
> *A puma which escaped from the Jay Miller circus at Melton Mowbray, Leics., drowned as it tried to swim a river."*

The report surprised me, as I thought circuses did not keep pumas because they cannot be taught to do tricks.

4) I received the following note from Mr Paul Screeton, the journalist who showed an interest in the Durham cats, on 24th March 1988:

> *"I'll be running an article by Eddie Bell on the Durham big cats. in the next issue of* Folklore Frontiers. *It will be the full version of his piece in a nature magazine (part adapted in the enclosed cutting for you to keep.) It will carry additional material to that in the mail piece I've written."*

Folklore Frontiers, No.7, April 1988, can be obtained from Mr Screeton at the address given in the 'Reference' section of this book.

The enclosed cutting was from the *Hartlepool Mail* of 17th March 1988, and was an article in Mr Screeton's new monthly feature "Countryside Concerns". It was based upon a telephone conversation between Mr Screeton, and big cat Investigator Eddie Bell, and also on Bell's article "The Durham Cat - the Story So Far", in the *Durham Monthly Conservation Bulletin* of January 1988. I wrote off for a copy of this Bulletin. Mr Screeton summarised this article in the *Hartlepool Mail*, and he also noted other points about the saga. I was fascinated to find that the Hancock Museum, County Durham, recognise the fact that there is a hybrid cross-bred wildcat/domestic cat, in their area. They thought there were a number of them, and that they were larger than both feral or wildcats. So they do believe in wildcats in County Durham!

5) This cutting was in the *Middlesborough Evening Gazette* of 16th June, 1987, and it stated:

"Monster Moggie back on the Prowl

> *The elusive giant cat of County Durham has made another appearance after lying low for six months. This time the mystery moggie has been spotted just outside Sedgefield village by land-drainage contractor Gordon Mason and his son Jonathan as they headed for their depot at West Layton farm. The pair chased the brown creature with white-tipped tail, but only got to within 300 yards of it before it escaped into fields. Said Gordon:*

> *'It definitely had a cat-like head, but it was much larger than the average cat. A foot-print we found was about twice the size of a cat's.'*

> *"The latest appearance has intrigued Durham police wildlife expert, constable Eddie Bell, who has been keeping a record of the beast. During the past two years he has chased up numerous leads."*

6) Following an appeal for information in the *British Farmer* of November 1988, I received three letters. One came from the Lancaster area, on the Western side of the Pennines, describing a black panther-type cat. Mrs. Sylvia Woodhouse of Roeburndale West, 14 miles from Hornby, Laneaster, wrote this on lst November:

> *"My brother Malcolm and I were seeing to sheep, early April, and we were riding a farm bike, and we saw a big black cat, much larger than a domestic cat. Big round face, long whiskers, large black tail, about the size of a fox. It was approximately 25 yards off us, eyeing a wild duck up for its dinner. It saw us and scooted off down into the wood. It had been seen in the east side of Roeburndale (we are west). The "Lancaster Guardian" reported one had been sighted. (I think in the Clampham area, Ingleton, Yorkshire).*

7) There is obviously one black panther-type cat on the Pennines, but the sightings have been as far apart as Northumberland and Lancaster, so we can presume that there are about twenty black panther-type cats in the Pennines area alone, as it is large enough to support them. I advise all people to read Janni Hawker's 1987 novel *'The Nature of the Beast'*, which was made into a BBC television film, and was shown on television in April 1988. (See Bibliography.)

• ## The "Highland Hellcats" - Scottish Mystery Cats Borderlands:

The following article was published in the *Sunday Times* of 6th March 1988:

> *'Scots Leopard Shot:*

> *The trail of dead pheasants led Willie Thomas to the rarest predator to have stalked the Scottish Borders since the last bear,'* writes Mark Porter, Head Gamekeeper at Minto Estates near Jedburgh. *Mr Thomas had been baffled as to how his birds had been slaughtered in their pen, with its 12 foot fence. They had been mangled in the jaws of a rare Bengal leopard-cat, found in southeast Asia.*

> *"I saw this creature - it looked like a cross between a leopard and a wildcat - running from a pen with a dead bird in its mouth," said Mr Thomas. "I automatically raised my gun and shot it, and then fired again to make sure. I instantly thought, 'What have I done?', but the cat had killed seven of my birds, biting straight through their bones."*

> *But it was not until last Tuesday that it was found to be a Bengal leopard-cat. Mr*

Jerry Herman, of the Royal Scottish Museum in Edinburgh, had to identify the cat (Felis bengalensis) which is spotted and relatively small, measuring just over 3 feet from head to tail and weighing up to about 11 lbs. The cat shot in Scotland belonged to a private collector in Cumbria, whose premises had been burgled last autumn when the cat escaped. It is now in a deep-freeze, awaiting the taxidermist.'

The article also had a drawing of a leopard-cat from southeast Asia, which would include tropical forest-covered islands such as Java. *

I wrote to the man concerned and to Mr Jerry Herman of the Department of Natural History at the Royal Museum of Scotland on 18th March 1988. I had this statement in a letter from Mr Herman:

'Concerning the cat which was shot recently in the Borders, it was a young male leopard-cat, (Felis bengalensis), from south-east Asia, and weighed 3.5 kg or about the same as a local domestic cat. It had formerly been kept as an exotic pet by someone in Cumbria, but had been lost or stolen last last year. Although I identified the cat from the borders, I am not generally in a position to help you on the subject of big cats etc. in Britain. I suggest that you contact Di Francis, who has a special interest in such matters."

Mr Herman gave me her address in Banffshire, Scotland.

I heard from the gamekeeper concerned, Mr William Thomas, in March 1988. He was writing from Minto, near Hawick, and told me these facts, which cover the story very well:

'I shot the cat in a pheasant laying-pen at 2 o'clock on Saturday afternoon, 20th February 1988. The cat had climbed a 10-foot high netting fence to get in. It killed 7 birds - 3 cocks and 4 hens - out of a total number of 700. These pheasants are adult breeding stock. Some are caught in the wild. Some were over-wintered in a 100 x 50 yards wire netting open-topped pen. I was really very lucky to catch the cat when I did. I was putting some birds into the pen when I saw some pheasants lying dead. When I examined the first bird I saw that a fair bit of it had been eaten. The bones had been eaten through along with flesh, indicating that what had done the damage was quite large. I walked along part of the pen and found another 5 birds. Some had their neck broken, others had been bitten on the head. The pen being on slightly undulating ground and having some fir branches in as cover and shelter, it was not possible to see all the pen area from our position. The pheasants were in a highly agitated state, so whatever had killed the 7 birds was either still in the pen or in the immediate vicinity, so I rushed back to the house for a gun and came back, and went to the part of the pen where the pheasants were making the most noise.

FOOTNOTE: Some years ago the Bengal leopard cat and three other southeast Asian small cats were moved into the genus: Prionailurus

That was when I saw the cat. It was against the bottom of the netting so it could not get a run at the wire to get up and out. It started to run parallel to me when I shot it from a distance of about 10 yards.

I contacted the local S.S.P.C.A. inspector Mr Bruce from Lillieshaf. He came over on Monday morning and took it into the vets, to see if he could identify the cat. They could not help, but suggested I contact the Edinburgh Museum, which I did. I spoke to the Assistant Curator, Mr Jerry Herman, who came down on Tuesday morning and took it back to the museum for positive identification. He 'phoned me later in the day and told me that it was a leopard-cat, possibly sold to a woman in Cumbria from Edinburgh Zoo.

The local radio and press got hold of the story and through this I received a telephone call from a Mrs. Mosscrop in Cumbria. She told me that the cat had been hers. She had bought it from Edinburgh Zoo in December 1985 when it was 6 months old. Her place was broken into the following June 1987 and the cat was stolen or let loose.

So the cat had been lost for 8 months before it turned up here. The cat was male, weighed 7 lbs, measured 30 inches head to tail and was 11 inches at the shoulder. Mrs. Mosscrop told me that when she lost the cat it weighed 6 lbs, so wherever it had been it did all right.

There were two other sightings of the cat that weekend. The first was a Mrs. Anne Pyrmont from Minto, who saw it at 10 o'clock on Friday night near the little village of Bowden, which is about 6 miles north of here. The second sighting was by Mrs. June Bruce on Saturday afternoon at 4 o'clock, about 2 miles north-west of here. Mrs. Pyrmont positively identified the cat after seeing my photographs, and Mrs. Bruce, when her husband took the dead cat to the house'

This letter was very interesting, and I must thank Mr Thomas for allowing me to use it.

- CONCLUSION -

I would like to say that I personally believe that there is sufficient evidence to maintain that the big cats *do* exist in the British countryside. I intend to continue my investigations into all the sightings and when eventually, as I plan to do, I establish the numbers and distribution of these elusive animals, I shall be able to present another book on the subject, which should prove their existence. At this point I would like to state that at least 10,000 people have been involved in either seeing or hunting the big cats, and that there are at least 20 people who are worthy of the title "Researcher into big cats Loose in Britain". Some of the theories have definitely been proved, and others have certainly been disproved.

One thing is certain: the cats are sufficiently established to continue to breed, and sightings/incidents will continue in the future. We must remember that these cats need protection, and I hope that one day an Act of Parliament will help legally to conserve them.

Another positive conclusion is that more than one species of large feline lives in this country. I am also convinced that there have been many unreported sightings, and each time I go to Exmoor I meet local people who say that they have seen one of the beasts, but that they do not report it for fear of ridicule. Many people only report their sightings after a bolder person informs the police or the local paper that he has seen a big cat. I believe that people are now becoming more aware of these animals, and I can name more than one instance where the witness has declared that he, or she, contacted a local person, say a farmer, who seemed very unconcerned, just taking the sighting for granted. The reason for this was that the local person had heard or seen so much of the cat that its existence was accepted.

One question is always being raised: "Are these cats dangerous?"

From what I know, I can say that very few people have suffered. However, if a cat is cornered, the person involved should beat a hasty retreat. Failing that, a stone should be thrown at the cat, as this will probably deter it from coming closer. Animals generally only attack humans when cornered. If leopards, lions and tigers are loose in this country, as I suspect, then we may eventually have a man-eating problem on our hands.

Finally, I wish the big cats all the best in the future.

- EPILOGUE -

"Beast of Exmoor clue as Wildcat is found Dead" was the headline of Emma Lee Potter's article in the *Sunday Express*, 19th February 1989, page 17.

A farmer, Mr Norman Evans, had come upon a large wildcat in remote woodland near his home in Richards Castle, Ludlow, Shropshire. The cat was a dead sandy-coloured male jungle cat, 3 feet long including tail, with black-tipped ears and 1-inch long teeth. The jungle cat weighed 17 lbs. It could have died from starvation because it had a back injury, possibly caused by a car. The cat was thought to have lived in the wild for up to five years, and it lived on "lambs, rabbits, pheasants and chickens". Jungle cats (*Felis chaus*) came from Egypt and South-east Asia. Scientists thought it extremely unlikely that the animal was the one that prowled Exmoor in Devon. They stated that it did prove that large cats can and do survive in the wild for long periods in Britain. They thought there were other cats loose.

Mr Evans photographed the cat on the bonnet of his truck before taking the cat to the South Shropshire Countryside Project – who in turn took the cat to Ludlow Museum. The cat was identified as a jungle cat, or swamp cat (*Felis chaus*?), found in Egypt and Southeast Asia. The cat was a pale, sandy brown colour, with dark stripes down the inside of its long, thin legs and it had vicious looking one inch long teeth! The cat weighed seventeen (17) pounds and was a male jungle cat aged about five years old. Ludlow Museum curator Mr John Norton. Mr Norton stated: *"People often talked about seeing big cats in the wild in this area, but we never believed them before."*

Evans also showed it to Ludlow vet Mr Gareth Thomas who stated:

> *"Due to its injury it might not have been able to hunt and possibly died of starvation. It's quite likely that there are a number of these things in various parts of the country. They might have escaped from private collections, or have been illegally imported as kittens In the past the idea of this kind of animal living in the wild seemed pure fantasy. It just shows they can exist round here in wild. I would imagine it might have been living in the open for its entire life, perhaps five years, because it showed signs of domestication."*

The cat had minor back injuries, suggesting it was struck by a car and its thin, emaciated condition also suggested it was inhibited from hunting prey successfully and thus had starved. The origins of the cat were unknown, although it was presumed to have escaped from a private menagerie or wildlife collection. The cat appeared to have been loose for some time as several people had had sightings of a large cat-like beast on the English/Welsh border near Ludlow. Mr David Watkins, a farmer near Leintwardine told the *South Shropshire Journal* of Friday 17 February 1989 that he had several sightings of a cat-like beast between March and October 1998 on his farm.

> *"It was a small sheepdog size with piercing eyes resembling a cats. I never got the chance to get very near to it because it was very wary. I only saw it by torchlight so I am not sure of its colour. But I do know that my sheep were being killed at that time and they are not being killed anymore!"*

Mr Barry Jasper, a farmer from Seifton, reported a sighting to the Ludlow Museum of a strange sandy col-oured animal which appeared to be hunting near his farm, while he was fencing. He described the cat as follows:

> *"It was the size of a Labrador dog and appeared to have longer legs than most animals. When I tried to approach it, it noticed me and ran off incredibly quickly. It was like nothing I have ever seen before."*

Mr John Norton, the Curator of the Ludlow Museum, kept the cat in a deep freeze until local taxidermist Mr David Bytherway stuffed the cat for Mr Evans. Mr Norton commented on the jungle cat to the news-papers:

> *"People often talked about seeing big cats in this area but we never believed them be-fore. It is a big, but handsome animal, certainly capable of catching sheep or deer and killing them for food. Its discovery is one of the most exciting things we have had at the museum. We were all thrilled to get the chance to see something like this."*

Mr Thomas wrote a letter to me dated 12 March 1989 in which he stated:

> *"I have no further details of the cat - Felis chaus – regarding its origin in this country. We have not had an unexplained spate of killings here recently even when the cat was alive. There is a strain of domestic cat in this area with a speckled coat, which turns up on farms and has a few tabby stripes on legs and face and is larger than a domestic cat, but with a normal long tail, unlike the chaus cat. I wonder whether this Felis chaus may have interbred with a Queen Felis catis to produce a cross bred? It may not be biologically possible. But where they do turn up they are given nicknames of 'The Wild Cat' or the 'Lynx' and usually are tameable."*

It is therefore possible that we are dealing with hybrid (cross-bred) cats. Certainly the jungle cat had many similarities to one of its supposed hybrid grandsons, who I observed and photographed in May 1989 at Mr Thomas' Ludlow surgery. The supposed hybrid grandson appeared to be a young male do-mestic cat quite larger, smoky grey in colour, with a black stripe down the base of his back-like a jungle cat with black stripes on his legs. Like a jungle cat, the cat had a strip of black fur under each leg. How-ever, it was tame, having been brought up in a farmhouse kitchen whereas the rest of the litter on the Leinwardine farm were brought up as feral farm cats and not house-cats. The only way you could conclu-sively prove that the jungle cat and the domestic cats were related would be by analysing the chromo-somes. The jungle cat is obviously stuffed, so this method might prove quite difficult!

I do not know how long it will be before everyone accepts the cats as a reality, but nobody can doubt that they *do* exist.

Marcus and his Mum, CFZ, March 2007.

- APPENDIX -
OTHER MYSTERY ANIMALS
OF BRITAIN

BIRDS

Every time there is a storm, numerous migrant birds appear in places such as the Scilly Isles, whereupon twitchers' – bird-watchers - arrive from all over Britain to watch them.

Quite often, exotic birds fly off from their bird-gardens, as do flamingoes. Sometimes parrots, canaries and budgerigars escape from their cages and survive in the wild. There is an established colony of parakeets in this country, although I do not know its exact whereabouts.

I remember glimpsing an escaped red and green parrot on the Wiltshire/Dorset border, in about 1981. It transpired that the bird had escaped from its home at Tollard Royal, on the same county boundary. All I remember was the sight of a long-tailed parrot-like bird flying off towards some trees. Two friends with me also observed it.

INTRODUCED SPECIES

Among the introduced species of this country are mink, coypu, rabbits (which were introduced by the Normans); also the sika deer. Perhaps we should look at the unidentified alien or introduced animals that have established themselves in this country.

1)   Apes and Monkeys

On the night of 8th July 1974, 80 baboons disappeared from the West Midland Safari Park, in the Wyre Forest on the Worcestershire/Shropshire border. Mr Tom Mann, who was the general manager at the time, commented to the *Birmingham Evening News* of the 13th July 1974:

> *"When they got out, they were reasonably harmless, but after four days on the run in strange surroundings, being frightened by gunfire and possibly hungry, they could be a different proposition. We have reluctantly issued orders to our hunters to shoot to kill, if necessary."*

By the following Saturday, the baboons - with the exception of four or five, which were still loose - were recaptured. Three were dead. According to the *Sunday Mercury* of 18th August 1974, the baboons had still not been recaptured. They were not dangerous, according to Mr Paolo Sepe, the general manager. However, the local official committee of authorities were told by Mr Brian William, the managing director of a Birmingham zoological firm, that his firm had purchased 38 baboons from the Park and that all of them were fierce and strong, and that the larger baboons could kill an adult man. The committee was horrified, but although official statements were made, nothing more happened for some time.

Then in September and October, the four escaped baboons were seen at Oldington Woods, Foley Park, near Kidderminster in Worcestershire. On the Stourington road a driver saw a baboon cross the road. It saw him, then dashed back into the woods. Adjacent to them the timid baboon discovered a British Sugar Corporation factory, and experts believed that the sweet smell was attracting the animals to the area. Nobody at the factory had seen them. This information was obtained from the *Birmingham Evening Mail* of 28th October, and the *Sunday Mercury* of 27th October.

In the same reference, I read that, according to the *Sun* of the 13th and 14th August 1987, a number of baboons had escaped from Lambton Safari Park, Chester-le-Street in County Durham. The baboons numbered 57 at the zoo, and officials were trying to establish how many had actually escaped.

The following day, two returned to the zoo, presumably through hunger. The newspaper stated that on the 12th August thirty Chester-le-Street residents had telephoned the police to say that they had seen baboons swinging through the trees, so the police took the sightings seriously. In September, seven crafty baboon ring-leaders were seen clinging under coaches, thus escaping by evading security checks at the Lambton Safari Park. The manager, an expert, Mr Dick Howard, told the *Daily Mirror.*

"From observations we have identified the leaders behind the escape plot, and seven are now being dispersed to other zoos and parks."

One may presume that these three escape incidents have possibly resulted in two breeding baboon colonies. Gorillas are known to have escaped from wildlife parks, but they are normally captured fairly quickly.

The beast, or beasts of Brassknocker Hill, near Bath, have been described as being baboons, chimpanzees and even a lemur, called an aye-aye. There can be no doubt that the beast exists, as there have been about ten sightings since 1977. It is perhaps significant to note that several baboons escaped from Longleat in 1977... However, a Bath policeman thought the beast was a chimp. (See 'Other Westcountry Cats' chapter, earlier in this book.)

The *Daily Telegraph* of August 1986 reported that a green monkey had been seen winging through the trees near Chippenham, in Wiltshire. Later, I discovered from a resident in the area, that the monkey belonged to people 'up the road' at Ford village, near Chippenham. The monkey was later recaptured.
I remember seeing three pet monkeys at a farm on the outskirts of Warminster, in about 1980. They were dark brown, with sharp teeth, and they lived in a cage in their owner's garden. One of them was a savage female, but the other female and the male were quite friendly.

They were only about a foot high, and I do not remember their exact species. They were later taken away when the people moved house. This illustrates the fact that many people keep exotic pets; you can probably buy all sorts of unusual, but not dangerous animals, at the local pet-shop.
Maybe some of you watched the *Bergerac* detective series set on the Island of Jersey, in the Channel Islands, and will perhaps recall the episode when a number of grey monkeys were released by the animal

rights campaigners from a scientific laboratory. Although the animals were eventually cornered in a garage and shot, as they were injected with Marmot's disease, they were able to kill an unsuspecting holiday-maker. Imagine what would happen if this really did occur! Well, I can say that a recent *Daily Telegraph* article stated, perhaps rather bluntly.

> *"Monkey escapes. Police are warning people to watch out for a white monkey which escaped from a car at the Newport Pagnell service area on the M1 yesterday. They say no one should approach it."*

This took place on 3rd October 1987, and as far as is known, the animal has not been re-captured.

One question always cropping up is: "How do these exotic creatures survive the winter?" As far as I know, black panthers, indigenous to Asia and Africa, are capable of surviving the winter on, say, Exmoor, as they originate from the mountainous regions of Northern Asia.

The monkeys may or may not survive the winter. On the other hand, some animals are extremely tough and are able to resist most kinds of climate. Consider for instance the migrant birds, which travel from one hot region to another, often passing through differing climates.

2)   Wallabies: Sussex and southeast England

Since the 1950s, wallabies have been seen on the Ashdown Forest in Sussex. According to the "News" of June 1975, No.10, and *The Sun* of 10th July 1974, there were reports that a wallaby was captured in the High Street of Kinson, in Hampshire, after causing damage. In May 1967 there were sightings of wallabies in Sussex, while in August 1973 there were sightings in Kent.

The fact was that in late August 1973, two wallabies escaped from Heathfield safari park in Sussex. All this information came from newspaper articles, which had been mentioned in *The News* by editor Mr Bob Rickard. In the same "Spring's in the Air" article, Mr Rickard notes that on 5th November 1974, a kangaroo scared folk on the Hampshire/Berkshire border. The police thought the whole thing was a joke, until Mr Donald Rayfield, the owner of a small private menagerie at Bawghurst, near Basingstoke, admitted that his 5-year-old kangaroo, Prufrock, had disappeared over a wall. He told *The Sun*:

> *"He will feed on branches and graze, so he'll be all right until we catch up with him."*

A local paper later said that Prufrock was re-captured.

The wallabys generally come from small private zoos, which find that these animals are remarkably good at escaping. I remember seeing an item on the local southwest news that said a lone wallaby had escaped from a wildlife park on the Isle of Purbeck, on the south coast. This was in 1986, but I do not know whether it was ever re-captured. Wallabies breed remarkably fast, and are said to be extremely quick hoppers. In the intervening years since this book was first written, wallabies have been reported from across the UK, and their numbers are increasing.

3)   The Peak District Wallaby Colony

In about 1940, two red-necked wallabies escaped from a private zoo in the Peak district area of Stafford-shire and Derbyshire. They bred so rapidly that their numbers were about 40 in 1970. However, a few cold winters and other problems reduced their numbers to 12. Recent evidence suggests that they are on the increase once again. Some local wildlife books even show pictures of these animals, which have almost been added to the British List of Mammals. People regard them with affec tion, and apparently in 1971 an intensive study of them was carried out by two leading zoologists. It is a pity that not all the introduced wildlife of our islands could stimulate the same interest and enthusiasm that these wallabies have re-ceived.

4)   Some Known Introduced-animal Stories

There are two stories that are worth mentioning, as they show how much trouble can be caused by an in-troduced species, or an escapee.

Firstly, about 800 hedgehogs now live on the Isle of North Ronaldsay, the most northern of the Orkney Islands. There was a mass round-up of the hedgehogs by the 80 inhabitants, because these animals ate the rare birds' eggs. All were descended from the two pet hedgehogs of the island's postman, which had es-caped some ten years earlier! Many visitors came to the island because of the hedgehogs, and letters ar-rived from all over the world, appealing for live hedgehogs. This information was contained in the *Daily Telegraph* of August 1987.

The second story, from the *News of the World* of August 1987, showed how much havoc a pet ferret caused when it escaped and started to bite people in the "Pennine Rambler" pub, near Bramsholme, in Hull. It escaped down a drainpipe, even though a policewoman managed to corner it.

5)   Porcupines

According to the '*Guinness Book of British Mammals*' and other sources, two colonies of porcupines are loose in this country. Hodgeson's porcupine (hystrix hodgeoni) is native to the central and eastern regions of the Himalayas, China and Malaysia. The crested porcupine is found in Africa, although introduced populations are found in Yugoslavia.

Its scientific name is *Hystrix cristata*. It is known that in 1909 a number of porcupines escaped from the Pine Valley wildlife park, on the edge of Dartmoor, in South Devon. In 1973 the porcupines were doing much damage to the local forestry plantations. According to the Head Forester of Luxborough Forestry Station, near Minehead, in West Somerset, one of the porcupines was shot dead near the River Torridge. The same porcupine had also killed a terrier dog, as the Head Forester informed me in an interview of Oc-tober 1987.

A pair of crested porcupines disappeared from Alton Towers Botanic Gardens in Staffordshire, in 1972, and these also have established a colony. Porcupines look something like a two and a half ft. long hedge-hog, with prickly spines all over them. The spines of a porcupine are said to shoot out, when the animal is attacked. This is, however, now known to be a myth. The quills pull out quite easily apparently, and thus the attacker is deterred from devouring the porcupine.

6)   Raccoons and Bears

There was a sighting, early in February 1975, of a young bear, by milkman David Bowlby, on Skipwirth Common, near Riccall, in Yorkshire. Mr Bowlby had stopped his car to write up his salesbook after his daily 35-mile milk round, when out of the woods ambled a bear! He watched it from 50 yards, on the side of the Thorganby-to-Skipwith Road. Jumping out, he chased the bear and managed to get within 20 yards of it. He also saw it a few minutes later. He recalled:

> "Im sure it was a bear, not fully grown. It was brown with black foot-pads, standing by a tree. It was about as big as an Alsatian dog on all fours; on its hind legs it was about as tall as a 10-year-old child."

Mr Bowlby also knew there had been five previous sightings, and he had heard stories of a bear that escaped from a travelling circus at Malton. However, the shortest route from the Skipwith Common to Malton, or vice versa, was 22 miles' distance, over a number of major roads.

Also on the same day of the sighting, 12th February 1975, a farm-worker, Mr Geoffrey Houseman, walked his dog there. It began to behave very strangely. Mr Houseman apparently remarked very clearly:

> "I couldn't understand it. The dog was barking for a full hour. He wouldn't normally bark like that if it was a rabbit. He's never done that before."

It was assumed that the circus would have reported the loss of an expensive bear. The above information was taken from the 13th/17th February issues of the *Yorkshire Evening Press*. One of the last two articles provided a possible solution to the sighting. The North Yorkshire police checked all the circuses and zoos in the county, and no bears had escaped. However, a raccoon had escaped from Flamingo Park Zoo, near Pickering. Inspector Wilf Scott, from Selby police, did not think a bear could be mistaken for a raccoon, taking into account Mr Bowlby's detailed sighting. He suggested to the press:

> "The difference between a bear and a raccoon ... I'm keeping an open mind about this. There is obviously something running about. It may be a bear and it may be a raccoon. He's no idiot and if he's talking about an animal 5 ft. 10 ins, high, I'm not looking for a raccoon."

The *London Evening Standard* of 19th February 1975 quoted Mr Bowlby:

> "... It sounds so stupid, but when I approached further - gosh - it was a bear. It stood about 4 ft. 6 inches, had brown eyes, a darker brown skin and big black pads."

Flamingo Park Zoo admitted that three raccoons had escaped from the Park, but two were re-captured. However, the spokesman for Flamingo Park Zoo seemed to forget that the raccoon had come from his Zoo, because he stressed:

> "It is incredible to think of anyone mistaking a raccoon for a bear - they are only about the size of a fox - a little shorter and fatter though."

This was also in the *London Evening Standard* of the 19th February 1975. So far I have been reproducing facts taken from *The News*, No. 9, of April 1975.

On the subject of small exotic carnivores, I noted the sighting, first hand, near Devizes in Wiltshire, of what was possibly a genet. Dr Karl Shuker of the West Midlands, commented in a letter to me dated 22nd November 1987:

> *'I was very interested to read in your most recent letter of 7th November 1987 that a genet has been sighted in Wiltshire. Do you have any further news regarding this? I have often read in the past of various small 'exotic' carnivores appearing in the most unexpected places - most recently, a raccoon was found wandering around Wolverhampton, and is presently cared for at Dudley Zoo. Presumably it must be an escaped pet, for it appeared to be in very good health and well-groomed. I've also read of out-of-place mongooses and skunks, but this is the first time that I have read of a genet in the wilds of Britain. You note that a friend of yours from school has actually seen this animal. Was he positive that it was indeed a genet? There are few genets in captivity, and few kept as pets, hence its appear anc here is particularly interesting and unexpected. I'd be very interested to hear of any new developments that may have occurred regarding this animal."*

My thanks to Dr Shuker for allowing me to quote this letter. I am sure that it was a genet which Duncan Robinson observed (see the sighting report in the "Other West-country Cats" section). The only other instance I have seen of a genet is recorded in a local `Surrey Puma` Country newspaper (see the last part of the "Surrey Pumas" section, and "Other Westcountry Cats").

I understand that in 1986, two raccoons were found in an abandoned van in Somerset, and that the animals were being cared for by the R.S.P.C.A., while the police tried to trace the owner.

- BIBLIOGRAPHY -

(in alphabetical order)

Allen, Noel V. *Exmoor's Wildlife*. Quest (Western) Publications, South Molton, North Devon. 1979.

Alexander, Matthew. *Tales of Old Surrey*. Countryside Books, 3 Catherine Road, Newbury, Berks. 1985.

Aspinahl, John. *My Animal Friends*. Howletts Park and Port Lympne Zoos. Jonathan Cape Ltd., London. 1977.

Beer, Trevor. *The Beast of Exmoor*. Countryside Books, 'Tawside', 30 Park Avenue, Barnstaple, North Devon EX31 2ES. 1984.

Bellamy, David. *Mammals at the Zoo*. 'I Spy' Books, 12 Star Road, Partridge Green, Horsham, Sussex, RH13 8RA. 1982.

Benchley, Belle J, *My Animal Babies*. Faber & Faber, 24 Russel Square, London. The author was a director of San Diego Zoo from 1925-1944.

Bord, Janet and Colin., *Alien Animals*. Paul Elek, London. 1980. - hardback, Panther Books, Granada Publishing, 8 Graf ton Street, London, W1X 3LA. 1985, Paperback; printed also in the U.S.A.

Bord, Janet and Colin. *The Secret Country*. Paladin Ltd., London. 1976. Printed in later editions by Paladin, and in the U.S.A.

Bord, Janet and Colin. *Alien Cats in Britain*. 'The Unexplained' Magazine, No. 114. 1982. Write to: Orbis Publishing Ltd., Orbis House, 20/22 Bedfordbury, London WC21

Bourne, Mrs. Hope L. *Living on Exmoor*. 1963. See this for an account of Scottish wildcats on Exmoor early this century.

Bowen, Charles *Mystery Animals*. Flying Saucer Review, November/December 1964. Write to FSR Publications Ltd., Snodland, Kent, MF6 5HJ.

Briggs, Katherine. *A Dictionary of Fairies*. Allen Lane, London, 1976.

Brown, Theo. *The Black Dog*. Folklore, vol.69, p.200. 1958.

Brown, Theo. *Tales of a Dartmoor Village*. Toucan Press, Devon. 1973.

Brodu, Jean-Louis and Meurger, Michael: *Les Fhins Mystre*. Pogonie, B.P., 75665, Paris. Cedex 14, France. 1984. Booklet, 38 pp.
512.

Burnford, Sheila. *The Incredible Journey*. Hodder & Stoughton, London. 1960. Paperbacks, a Division of General Publishing Co. Ltd., Don-Mills, Ontario, Canada, 1963, 1973.

Burton, Dr Maurice. *Is This the Surrey Puma?* 'Nature and Wildlife' Magazine, No.260, November 1966.

Byrne, Patrick F. *Irish Ghost Stories*. - The Mercier Press, 4 Bridge Street, Cork, County Cork, Eire. 1961, 1973, 1975.

Canning, Victor. *The Run'qays*. Puffin Books, William Heinemann Ltd., London.1971, 1978, 1979, 1980, 1981, 1983, 1985.

This is a novel well worth reading.

Cawley, Roger. *The Lions of Longleat*. 1987. Jarold Publications, Norwich. A guide to the famous Longleat Safari Park, which was established in 1965.

Chard, Judy. *Devon Mysteries*. Bossiney Books, St Teath, Bodmin, Cornwall. 1979.

Clair, Colin *Unnatural History*. Abelard-Schuman. London. 1967.

Clark, Jerome and Coleman, Loren. *Creatures of the Outer Edge*. Warner Books, New York, U.S.A. 1978. Was available via 'Fate' magazine.

Clark, Arthur C. *Chronicles of the Strange and Mysterious*. also by Simon Welfare and John Fairley Collins, St James Place, London. 1987.

Clark, Arthur C. *Arthur C. Clarke's Mysterious World*. also by Simon Welfare and John Fairley. Collins, St James Place, London. 1980, 1981, 1982.

Cobbett, William *Rural Rides*. 1830. Reprinted many times. See the section 'Chilworth to Winchester', dated 1825.

Collins, Andy. *The Brentford Griffin: The Truth behind the Tales*.

Earthquest Books, 19 St David's Way, Wickford, Essex, SS11 8EX. 1985.

Dent, Anthony *Lost Beasts of Britain*. Harrap, London. 1974. See the sections on 'The Last of the Wolf' and 'The Catamount'.

Douglas, Atholm. *Tigers in Western Australia, New Scientist*. 24th April 1985. See the last April/May issues of the 'New Scientist' for more comments on the supposed 'Tasmanian Tiger' photographs. 513.

Dunne John J. *Haunted Ireland*. Appletree Press, Dublin. 1977. See the sections on 'The Black Dog of Cabra', 'The Cat of Kilkaie' and 'The Black Dog of Pussie's Leap'.

Doyle, Sir Arthur Conan. *The Hound of the Baskervilles*. 'Strand Magazine' 1889; George Newnes, London, 1902; Penguin Books, London, 1981-2-3-4-5, and many other publishers.

Ekert, Allan *The Crossbreed*. The Reader's Digest Inc.& Ltd., 25 Berkeley Court, London W1X 6AB. 1968, 1969. 'Story of a Bob-cat/Domestic Hybrid\

Encyclopedia *The Children's Encyclopedia of Knowledge - a Book of Wildlife*. Collins, London, 1965, 1968.

Eveayn, Doreen *Our Neighbouring Ghosts*. Illustrations by Sarah Jonas, Ex Libris Press, 1 The Shambles, Bradford-on-Avon, Wiltshire. 1987.

Faversham, Countess of *Strange Stories of the Chase, Fox-hunting and the Supernatural*. Geoffrey Bles, 59 Brompton Road, London, SW3 lOS. 1972. See pp. 81-87, 105-109 and other stories.

Feral Cats and Suggestions for Control. A U.F.A.W. Technical publication; The Universities Federation for Animal Welfare, 8 Hamilton Close, South Mimms, Potters Bar, Herts. EN6 3QD. 1982, 1984, 1985.

Francis, Diana *Cat Country: The Quest for the British big cat*. David and Charles, Newton Abbot, South Devon. 1983.

Fort, Charles *The Complete Books of Charles Fort*. Tower Publications, New York, U.S.A. See especially his 1931 book Lo!

Gandor-Dower, Kenneth *The Spotted Lion*. Little, Brown and Co., Boston, U.S.A., 1937.

Greene, Michael *Incredible Cats: The Secret Power of Your Pets*. Methuen, London Ltd., 11 New Fetter Lane, London. 1984

Gregory, Lady Augusta *Visions and Beliefs in the West of Ireland*. Patham and Sons, London, 1920, 1972.

Hall, Christopher *Stalking the Surrey Puma*. 'The Unexplained Magazine', No.29, 1982. Write for copy to Orbis Publishinq Ltd., Orbis House, 20/22 Bedfordbury, London W2N 2HJ.

Harman, John *Glorious Devon*. Reader's Digest, May 1982, pp.40-45.

Hart-Davis, Duff *After Three Years, Surrey is still... Hunting the Puma*. 'Telegraph'Colour Supplement for Sunday, 1957.

Hasker, Ann *The Night of the Lioness*. (with Patrick Pacheo). pp.35-40 of May 1982 edition of The Reader's Digest.

Hawker, Jannj. *The Nature of the Beast* (Novel): Julia Macrae Books, London, 1985

Head, Victor. *Trailing the Surrey Puma*. 'The Field', 8th April 1965.

Heuvelmans, Dr *On the Track of Unknown Animals*. Rupert Hart-Davis, 36 Soho Bernard Square, London Wi, 1958. French edition: *Sur les Pistes des bétes ignores*. Librarie Plon, 1955. There have been later editions.

Hudson, W.H. *A Shepherd's Life*. Futura Publications, Maxwell House, 74 Worship Street, London EC2A 2EN. 1910, 1979, 1981, 1983.

Jackson, Dr *Feral Cats in the United Kingdom*. Report of the Working Oliphant Ph.D. MRCVS Party on Feral Cats. R.S.P.C.A., Causeway, Horsham, Sussex, RH12 1HG. 1977-1981.

Keel, John *Strange Creatures of Time and Space*. Neville Spearman Ltd., 112 Whitfield Street, London W1P 6DP. 1970, 1975.

Knudtson, Peter *Redesigning Life: Biotechnologists Transform Animals and Create Novel New Life Forms*. (Available from Equinox Magazine, Telemedia Publishing, 37 Queen Victoria Road, Camden East, Ontario, KOK 1JO, Canada. No.27, Vol.VIf)

Jones, Revd. *A Relation of Apparitions or Spirits in the County of Edmund. Monmouth and the Principality of Wales: 1813.*

Lang, Andrew *The Animal Story Book*. Longmans, Green and Co., 36 Rowfoster, London, 1896, 1908 (Editor).

Lawrence, R.D. *Wildlife in North America - Mammals*. Thomas Nelson and Sons Ltd., Ontario, Canada, etc.

Leigh-Pemberton, *Lions and Tigers*. Ladybird Publishers, Loughborough. 1974. John

MacDanus, Darmot *Ghosts of Britain*. See Ch.4, 'Animal Ghosts',

MacDanus, Darmot *The Middle Kingdom of the Fairie World of Ireland*. Colin Smythe, London. 1972.

Maggs Brothers Catalogue No. 89 *Dictionaries and Grammars* (500 Books Ltd.,London. on Linguistics and the Diversity of Tongues) See p. 57 to 58 for a picture of a 1500s Italian wildcat.

Manley, Victor *The Folklore of Warminster*. Coates and Parker, High Strode Street, Warminster, Wilts. 1924, 1987.

Map. *Ordnance Survey Tourist Map of Exmoor*, No.5. 1982. Available on Exmoor in the tourist shops and centres of information. I used this map to work out where various sightings had taken place.

Midgley, John. *Man and Beast*. Methuen, London. 1987. 'Roots of Human Nature'.

Moffat, C.B. *The Mammals of Ireland*: Hodges, Figgis and Co., Dublin. (Proceedings of the Royal Irish Academy, Vol.XLIV)

Matthews, Harri- *British Mammals*: Collins, London. Several editions. son L.

Morris, Desmond *Cat-watching: the Essential Guide to Cat Behaviour*.- Jonathan Cape Ltd., 32 Bedfordbury Square, London WC1B 3EL. 1986.

Morton H.V. *In Scotland Again*: Methuen and Co.Ltd., 36 Essex Street, London WC. Several editions.

Newton Peck, *Wild Cat*: drawings by Hal Frenck. Camelot Books, pub- Robert lished by Avon Books, 959 Eighth Avenue, New York 10019, U.S.A. 1977.

O'Donnell, Elliot *Casebook of Ghosts*: Foulsham and Co.Ltd., Yeovil Road, Slough, Bucks. 1969.

Powell, Jillian Westcountry *Mysteries*: Chapter on 'The Beast of Exmoor'. Edited by Colin Wilson. Bossiney Books, Bodmin, Cornwall. 1985.

Randles, Jenny *The Pennine U.F.O. Mystery*: Granada Publishing, Frog- more, St Albans, Herts. A12 2NF. 1983.

Rickard, Robert *Phenomena: A Book of Wonders*: Thames and Hudson, J.M. and London. 1977.

Mitchell, John do. *Living Wonders*: Thames and Hudson, London. 1982.

Rudkin, Ethel H. *The Black Dog*: Folklore, Volume 49. 1938.

Screeton, Paul *Wild in the Country*: 'Northern Earth Mysteries', October 1983, No.24.

do. *The Durham Puma*: 'Folklore Frontiers October 1986, No.4.

Sinclair, Andrew *The Surrey Cat*: A novel, referred to in 'The News' (*Fortean Times*) 1976.

Snell, F.J. *The Blackmore Country*: Adam and Charles, Ltd., London. 1906.

Stranger, Joyce *Chia the Wildcat*: Corgi Books, Transworld Publishers Ltd., Century House, 61-63 Uxbridge Road, Ealing, London W5 5SA, 1968

Tabouri, Paul *The Ghosts of Borley*: David and Charles, Newton Abbot, and Underwood, Devon. 1973

Guy Talhouet-Roy, *Toute l'Alsace dchir6e par le Meutre d'Elisa*: 'Le Hervede , Figaro Magazine, 21st November 1987. Write (in French) to 'Le Figaro', 37 Rue du Louvre, 75081 Paris, Cedex 02, France, asking for a photocopy of this article.

Thorton, Revd. *Reminiscences of an Old West-country Clergyman.* 1870s. H.W. Cited in *Murder and Mystery on Exmoor* by Jack Hurley, Exmoor Free Press, Dulverton, Somerset, 1973. Still available at the local bookshops.

Underwood, Peter *This Haunted Isle.* ('The Ghosts and Legends of Britain's Historic Buildings'), Javelin Books, Link House, West Street, Poole Dorset, BH15 iLL. 1984, 1985.

Whitelock, Ralph *Mythologic Traditions.* J.lO, Vol.1: Animal Spirits'. Williams, *Superstition and Folklore.* Bossiney Books Ltd., S1ci-h, Michael Bodmin, Cornwall. 1982.

Williams, Michael, Linch, Rosemary and Wreford, Hilary, *Secret Westcountry.* See Ch.4, pp.26-28. Bossiney Books Ltd., Bodmin, Cornwall. 1986.

Young, Stanley P. *The Puma: Mysterious American Cat.* Dover Publications, and Goldman, New York, U.S.A. 1964. Edward A.

Manning-Saunders, *Animal Stories.* Oxford Children's Library, Oxford University Press, Ely House, London W.1. 1961,1967.
iv.

ABOUT THE AUTHOR

Born in 1973, Marcus John Gage Matthews has lived on a small farm near Warminster, in Wiltshire, all his life. He was educated at Sandroyd and Dauntseys schools, and went on to gain a BTec First Diploma in Agriculture at Sparshot College, Hampshire.

He has many other qualifications under his belt, including a Farming Certificate at the Royal Agricultural College in Cirencester. Marcus has also worked as a freelance journalist for several magazines, after gaining an HND in Journalism (Media) at Barnsley - his articles mainly dealing with local and countryside matters.

It was during 1987, at the age of 14, when Marcus embarked upon writing *Big Cats: Loose in Britain* - an in-depth record of big cat sightings. He became fascinated with the prospect that such unknown, powerful, predatory animals were in the countryside, and inspired by Trevor Beer's book *Beast of Exmoor* (Countryside Productions, Barnstaple, Dec 1986), Nigel Brierly and Di Francis, Marcus began searching for information by writing to local newspapers, the police, and councils etc., about the subject. Over the ensuing years, he received replies from around 1,000 people, of which some 250 wrote to him documenting their own evidence. It was a huge task and took him until the age of 18, in 1990, to complete.

Over the years, Marcus has, himself, experienced sightings of big cats, including a bobcat in the Mendips in 1986, a puma on Exmoor in 1987, and another cat in Wales in 2003. In 2002, there was also a sheep killed on his farm - the wounds being a classic example of those caused by a big cat. Marcus is intending to follow up *Big Cats: Loose in Britain* from where he left off in 1990, and it is hoped that this will be ready for publication in 2009. In the meantime, he is currently working on a booklet documenting evidence of big cats in Wiltshire. As well as giving lectures at the annual Big Cat Conference for the last two years, Marcus has also given lectures to the British UFO Association, and various Natural History Societies amongst others. He has also appeared on the *Big Breakfast Show* in 1992, BBC's *Out of this World* programme in 1995, the Richard Hammond Show for ITV in 2006 and *Heart of the Country* in 2006.

Marcus has written many articles on natural history in general, and has enjoyed working with horses, working as a tour guide at Longleat House and currently works at a local Tourist Information Centre.

Other books available from
CFZ PRESS

CFZ PRESS

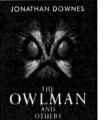

THE OWLMAN AND OTHERS - 30th Anniversary Edition
Jonathan Downes - ISBN 978-1-905723-02-7

£14.99

EASTER 1976 - Two young girls playing in the churchyard of Mawnan Old Church in southern Cornwall were frightened by what they described as a "nasty bird-man". A series of sightings that has continued to the present day. These grotesque and frightening episodes have fascinated researchers for three decades now, and one man has spent years collecting all the available evidence into a book. To mark the 30th anniversary of these sightings, Jonathan Downes, has published a special edition of his book.

DRAGONS - More than a myth?
Richard Freeman - ISBN 0-9512872-9-X

£14.99

First scientific look at dragons since 1884. It looks at dragon legends worldwide, and examines modern sightings of dragon-like creatures, as well as some of the more esoteric theories surrounding dragonkind. Dragons are discussed from a folkloric, historical and cryptozoological perspective, and Richard Freeman concludes that: "When your parents told you that dragons don't exist - they lied!"

MONSTER HUNTER
Jonathan Downes - ISBN 0-9512872-7-3

£14.99

Jonathan Downes' long-awaited autobiography, *Monster Hunter*... Written with refreshing candour, it is the extraordinary story of an extraordinary life, in which the author crosses paths with wizards, rock stars, terrorists, and a bewildering array of mythical and not so mythical monsters, and still just about manages to emerge with his sanity intact.......

MONSTER OF THE MERE
Jonathan Downes - ISBN 0-9512872-2-2

£12.50

It all starts on Valentine's Day 2002 when a Lancashire newspaper announces that "Something" has been attacking swans at a nature reserve in Lancashire. Eyewitnesses have reported that a giant unknown creature has been dragging fully grown swans beneath the water at Martin Mere. An intrepid team from the Exeter based Centre for Fortean Zoology, led by the author, make two trips – each of a week – to the lake and its surrounding marshlands. During their investigations they uncover a thrilling and complex web of historical fact and fancy, quasi Fortean occurrences, strange animals and even human sacrifice.

CFZ PRESS, MYRTLE COTTAGE, WOOLFARDISWORTHY BIDEFORD, NORTH DEVON, EX39 5QR
www.cfz.org.uk

Other books available from
CFZ PRESS

ONLY FOOLS AND GOATSUCKERS
Jonathan Downes - ISBN 0-9512872-3-0

£12.50

In January and February 1998 Jonathan Downes and Graham Inglis of the Centre for Fortean Zoology spent three and a half weeks in Puerto Rico, Mexico and Florida, accompanied by a film crew from UK Channel 4 TV. Their aim was to make a documentary about the terrifying chupacabra - a vampiric creature that exists somewhere in the grey area between folklore and reality. This remarkable book tells the gripping, sometimes scary, and often hilariously funny story of how the boys from the CFZ did their best to subvert the medium of contemporary TV documentary making and actually do their job.

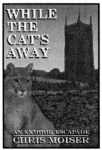

WHILE THE CAT'S AWAY
Chris Moiser - ISBN: 0-9512872-1-4

£7.99

Over the past thirty years or so there have been numerous sightings of large exotic cats, including black leopards, pumas and lynx, in the South West of England. Former Rhodesian soldier Sam McCall moved to North Devon and became a farmer and pub owner when Rhodesia became Zimbabwe in 1980. Over the years despite many of his pub regulars having seen the "Beast of Exmoor" Sam wasn't at all sure that it existed. Then a series of happenings made him change his mind. Chris Moiser—a zoologist—is well known for his research into the mystery cats of the westcountry. This is his first novel.

CFZ EXPEDITION REPORT 2006 - GAMBIA
ISBN 1905723032

£12.50

In July 2006, The J.T.Downes memorial Gambia Expedition - a six-person team - Chris Moiser, Richard Freeman, Chris Clarke, Oll Lewis, Lisa Dowley and Suzi Marsh went to the Gambia, West Africa. They went in search of a dragon-like creature, known to the natives as `Ninki Nanka`, which has terrorized the tiny African state for generations, and has reportedly killed people as recently as the 1990s. They also went to dig up part of a beach where an amateur naturalist claims to have buried the carcass of a mysterious fifteen foot sea monster named 'Gambo', and they sought to find the Armitage's Skink (Chalcides armitagei) - a tiny lizard first described in 1922 and only rediscovered in 1989. Here, for the first time, is their story.... With an forward by Dr. Karl Shuker and introduction by Jonathan Downes.

BIG CATS IN BRITAIN YEARBOOK 2006
Edited by Mark Fraser - ISBN 978-1905723-01-0

£10.00

Big cats are said to roam the British Isles and Ireland even now as you are sitting and reading this. People from all walks of life encounter these mysterious felines on a daily basis in every nook and cranny of these two countries. Most are jet-black, some are white, some are brown, in fact big cats of every description and colour are seen by some unsuspecting person while on his or her daily business. 'Big Cats in Britain' are the largest and most active group in the British Isles and Ireland This is their first book. It contains a run-down of every known big cat sighting in the UK during 2005, together with essays by various luminaries of the British big cat research community which place the phenomenon into scientific, cultural, and historical perspective.

CFZ PRESS, MYRTLE COTTAGE,
WOOLFARDISWORTHY BIDEFORD,
NORTH DEVON, EX39 5QR
w w w . c f z . o r g . u k

Other books available from
CFZ PRESS

CFZ PRESS

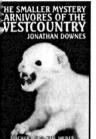

THE SMALLER MYSTERY CARNIVORES
OF THE WESTCOUNTRY
Jonathan Downes - ISBN 978-1-905723-05-8

Although much has been written in recent years about the mystery big cats which have been reported stalking West-country moorlands, little has been written on the subject of the smaller British mystery carnivores. This unique book redresses the balance and examines the current status in the Westcountry of three species thought to be extinct: the Wildcat, the Pine Marten and the Polecat, finding that the truth is far more exciting than the currently held scientific dogma. This book also uncovers evidence suggesting that even more exotic species of small mammal may lurk hitherto unsuspected in the countryside of Devon, Cornwall, Somerset and Dorset.

THE BLACKDOWN MYSTERY
Jonathan Downes - ISBN 978-1-905723-00-3

Intrepid members of the CFZ are up to the challenge, and manage to entangle themselves thor-oughly in the bizarre trappings of this case. This is the soft underbelly of ufology, rife with unsavory characters, plenty of drugs and booze." That sums it up quite well, we think. A new edition of the classic 1999 book by legendary fortean author Jonathan Downes. In this remarkable book, Jon weaves a complex tale of conspiracy, anti-conspiracy, quasi-conspiracy and downright lies surrounding an air-crash and alleged UFO incident in Somerset during 1996. However the story is much stranger than that. This excellent and amusing book lifts the lid off much of contemporary forteana and explains far more than it initially promises.

GRANFER'S BIBLE STORIES
John Downes - ISBN 0-9512872-8-1

Bible stories in the Devonshire vernacular, each story being told by an old Devon Grandfather - 'Granfer'. These stories are now collected together in a remarkable book presenting selected parts of the Bible as one more-or-less continuous tale in short 'bite sized' stories intended for dipping into or even for bed-time reading. `Granfer` treats the biblical characters as if they were simple country folk living in the next village. Many of the stories are treated with a degree of bucolic humour and kindly irreverence, which not only gives the reader an opportunity to re-evaluate familiar tales in a new light, but do so in both an entertaining and a spiritually uplifting manner.

FRAGRANT HARBOURS DISTANT RIVERS
John Downes - ISBN 0-9512872-5-7

Many excellent books have been written about Africa during the second half of the 19th Century, but this one is unique in that it presents the stories of a dozen different people, whose interlinked lives and achievements have as many nuances as any contemporary soap opera. It explains how the events in China and Hong Kong which sur-rounded the Opium Wars, intimately effected the events in Africa which take up the majority of this book. The author served in the Colonial Service in Nigeria and Hong Kong, during which he found himself following in the footsteps of one of the main characters in this book; Frederick Lugard – the architect of modern Nigeria.

**CFZ PRESS, MYRTLE COTTAGE,
WOOLFARDISWORTHY BIDEFORD,
NORTH DEVON, EX39 5QR
www.cfz.org.uk**

Other books available from
CFZ PRESS

CFZ PRESS

ANIMALS & MEN - Issues 1 - 5 - In the Beginning
Edited by Jonathan Downes - ISBN 0-9512872-6-5

£12.50

At the beginning of the 21st Century monsters still roam the remote, and sometimes not so remote, corners of our planet. It is our job to search for them. The Centre for Fortean Zoology [CFZ] is the only professional, scientific and full-time organisation in the world dedicated to cryptozoology - the study of unknown animals. Since 1992 the CFZ has carried out an unparalleled programme of research and investigation all over the world. We have carried out expeditions to Sumatra (2003 and 2004), Mongolia (2005), Puerto Rico (1998 and 2004), Mexico (1998), Thailand (2000), Florida (1998), Nevada (1999 and 2003), Texas (2003 and 2004), and Illinois (2004). An introductory essay by Jonathan Downes, notes putting each issue into a historical perspective, and a history of the CFZ.

ANIMALS & MEN - Issues 6 - 10 - The Number of the Beast
Edited by Jonathan Downes - ISBN 978-1-905723-06-5

£12.50

At the beginning of the 21st Century monsters still roam the remote, and sometimes not so remote, corners of our planet. It is our job to search for them. The Centre for Fortean Zoology [CFZ] is the only professional, scientific and full-time organisation in the world dedicated to cryptozoology - the study of unknown animals. Since 1992 the CFZ has carried out an unparalleled programme of research and investigation all over the world. We have carried out expeditions to Sumatra (2003 and 2004), Mongolia (2005), Puerto Rico (1998 and 2004), Mexico (1998), Thailand (2000), Florida (1998), Nevada (1999 and 2003), Texas (2003 and 2004), and Illinois (2004). Preface by Mark North and an introductory essay by Jonathan Downes, notes putting each issue into a historical perspective, and a history of the CFZ.

BIG BIRD! Modern Sightings of Flying Monsters

Ken Gerhard - ISBN 978-1-905723-08-9

£7.99

Today, from all over the dusty U.S. / Mexican border come hair-raising stories of modern day encounters with winged monsters of immense size and terrifying appearance. Further field sightings of similar creatures are recorded from all around the globe. The Kongamato of Africa, the Ropen of New Guinea and many others. What lies behind these weird tales? Ken Gerhard is in pole position to find out. A native Texan, he lives in the homeland of the monster some call 'Big Bird'. Cryptozoologist, author, adventurer, and gothic musician Ken is a larger than life character as amazing as the Big Bird itself. Ken's scholarly work is the first of its kind. The research and fieldwork involved are indeed impressive. On the track of the monster, Ken uncovers cases of animal mutilations, attacks on humans and mounting evidence of a stunning zoological discovery ignored by mainstream science. Something incredible awaits us on the broad desert horizon. Keep watching the skies!

STRENGTH THROUGH KOI
They saved Hitler's Koi and other stories

£7.99

Jonathan Downes - ISBN 978-1-905723-04-1

Strength through Koi is a book of short stories - some of them true, some of them less so - by noted cryptozoologist and raconteur Jonathan Downes. Very funny in parts, this book is highly recommended for anyone with even a passing interest in aquaculture.

CFZ PRESS, MYRTLE COTTAGE,
WOOLFARDISWORTHY BIDEFORD,
NORTH DEVON, EX39 5QR
w w w . c f z . o r g . u k

Other books available from
CFZ PRESS

CFZ PRESS

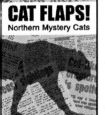

CAT FLAPS! NORTHERN MYSTERY CATS
Andy Roberts - ISBN 978-1905723-1-19

£7.99

Of all Britain`s mystery beasts, the alien big cats are the most renowned. In recent years the notoriety of these uncatchable, out-of-place predators have eclipsed even the Loch Ness Monster. They slink from the shadows to terrorise a community, and then, as often as not, vanish like ghosts. But now film, photographs, livestock kills, and paw prints show that we can no longer deny the existence of these once-legendary beasts. Here then is a case-study, a true lost classic of Fortean research by one of the country's most respected researchers; Andy Roberts. 'Cat Flaps!' is the product of many years of research and field work in the 1970s and 80s, an odyssey through the phantom felids of the North East of England. Follow Andy on his flat cap safari as he trails such creatures as the 'Whitby lynx', the 'Harrogate panther', and the 'Durham puma'.

BIG CATS IN BRITAIN YEARBOOK 2007
Edited by Mark Fraser - ISBN 978-1905723-09-6

£12.50

Big cats are said to roam the British Isles and Ireland even now as you are sitting and reading this. People from all walks of life encounter these mysterious felines on a daily basis in every nook and cranny of these two countries. Most are jet-black, some are white, some are brown, in fact big cats of every description and colour are seen by some unsuspecting person while on his or her daily business. 'Big Cats in Britain' are the largest and most active group in the British Isles and Ireland This is their first book. It contains a run-down of every known big cat sighting in the UK during 2006, together with essays by various luminaries of the British big cat research community which place the phenomenon into scientific, cultural, and historical perspective.

THE CENTRE FOR FORTEAN ZOOLOGY 2004 YEARBOOK
Edited by Jonathan Downes and Richard Freeman
ISBN 978-1905723140

£12.50

The Centre For Fortean Zoology Yearbook is a collection of papers and essays too long and detailed for publication in the CFZ Journal Animals & Men. With contributions from both well-known researchers, and relative newcomers to the field, the Yearbook provides a forum where new theories can be expounded, and work on little-known cryptids discussed.

THE CENTRE FOR FORTEAN ZOOLOGY 2007 YEARBOOK
Edited by Jonathan Downes
ISBN 978-1905723-13-3

£12.50

The Centre For Fortean Zoology Yearbook is a collection of papers and essays too long and detailed for publication in the CFZ Journal Animals & Men. With contributions from both well-known researchers, and relative newcomers to the field, the Yearbook provides a forum where new theories can be expounded, and work on little-known cryptids discussed.

CFZ PRESS, MYRTLE COTTAGE,
WOOLFARDISWORTHY BIDEFORD,
NORTH DEVON, EX39 5QR
w w w . c f z . o r g . u k

Other books available from
CFZ PRESS

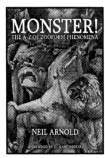

MONSTER! THE A-Z OF ZOOFORM PHENOMENA
Neil Arnold
ISBN 978-1-905723-10-2

£14.99

Zooform Phenomena are the most elusive, and least understood, mystery `animals`. Indeed, they are not animals at all, and are not even animate in the accepted terms of the word, but entities or apparitions which adopt, or seem to have (quasi) animal form.

These arcane and contentious entities have plagued cryptozoology - the study of unknown animals - since its inception, and tend to be dismissed by mainstream science as thoroughly unworthy of consideration. But they continue to be seen, and Jonathan Downes - the Director of the Centre for Fortean Zoology - who first coined the term in 1990, maintains that many zooforms result from a synergy of complex psychosocial and sociological issues, and suggests that to classify all such phenomena as "paranormal" in origin is counter-productive, and for researchers to dismiss them out of hand is thoroughly unscientific.

Author and researcher Neil Arnold is to be commended for a groundbreaking piece of work, and has provided the world's first alpha-betical listing of zooforms from around the world.

CFZ PRESS, MYRTLE COTTAGE, WOOLFARDISWORTHY BIDEFORD, NORTH DEVON, EX39 5QR
www.cfz.org.uk

THE CENTRE FOR FORTEAN ZOOLOGY

So, what is the Centre for Fortean Zoology?

We are a non profit-making organisation founded in 1992 with the aim of being a clearing house for information and coordinating research into mystery animals around the world. We also study out of place animals, rare and aberrant animal behaviour, and Zooform Phenomena; little-understood "things" that appear to be animals, but which are in fact nothing of the sort, and not even alive (at least in the way we understand the term).

Why should I join the Centre for Fortean Zoology?

Not only are we the biggest organisation of our type in the world but - or so we like to think - we are the best. We are certainly the only truly global Cryptozoological research organisation, and we carry out our investigations using a strictly scientific set of guidelines. We are expanding all the time and looking to recruit new members to help us in our research into mysterious animals and strange creatures across the globe. Why should you join us? Because, if you are genuinely interested in trying to solve the last great mysteries of Mother Nature, there is nobody better than us with whom to do it.

What do I get if I join the Centre for Fortean Zoology?

For £12 a year, you get a four-issue subscription to our journal *Animals & Men*. Each issue contains 60 pages packed with news, articles, letters, research papers, field reports, and even a gossip column! The magazine is A5 in format with a full colour cover. You also have access to one of the world's largest collections of resource material dealing with cryptozoology and allied disciplines, and people from the CFZ membership regularly take part in field-work and expeditions around the world.

How is the Centre for Fortean Zoology organized?

The CFZ is managed by a three-man board of trustees, with a non-profit making trust registered with HM Government Stamp Office. The board of trustees is supported by a Permanent Directorate of full and part-time staff, and advised by a Consultancy Board of specialists - many of whom who are world-renowned experts in their particular field. We have regional representatives across the UK, the USA, and many other parts of the world, and are affiliated with other organisations whose aims and protocols mirror our own.

I am new to the subject, and although I am interested I have little practical knowledge. I don't want to feel out of my depth. What should I do?

Don't worry. We were *all* beginners once. You'll find that the people at the CFZ are friendly and approachable. We have a thriving forum on the website which is the hub of an ever-growing electronic community. You will soon find your feet. Many members of the CFZ Permanent Directorate started off as ordinary members, and now work full time chasing monsters around the world.

I have an idea for a project which isn't on your website. What do I do?

Write to us, e-mail us, or telephone us. The list of future projects on the website is not exhaustive. If you have a good idea for an investigation, please tell us. We may well be able to help.

How do I go on an expedition?

We are always looking for volunteers to join us. If you see a project that interests you, do not hesitate to get in touch with us. Under certain circumstances we can help provide funding for your trip. If you look on the future projects section of the website, you can see some of the projects that we have pencilled in for the next few years.

In 2003 and 2004 we sent three-man expeditions to Sumatra looking for Orang-Pendek - a semi-legendary bipedal ape. The same three went to Mongolia in 2005. All three members started off merely subscribers to the CFZ magazine.

Next time it could be you!

Project Kerinci, Sumatra - 2003
In search of the bipedal ape Orang Pendek

How is the Centre for Fortean Zoology funded?

We have no magic sources of income. All our funds come from donations, membership fees, works that we do for TV, radio or magazines, and sales of our publications and merchandise. We are always looking for corporate sponsorship, and other sources of revenue. If you have any ideas for fund-raising please let us know. However, unlike other cryptozoological organisations in the past, we do not live in an intellectual ivory tower. We are not afraid to get our hands dirty, and furthermore we are not one of those organisations where the membership have to raise money so that a privileged few can go on expensive foreign trips. Our research teams both in the UK and abroad, consist of a mixture of experienced and inexperienced personnel. We are truly a community, and work on the premise that the benefits of CFZ membership are open to all.

What do you do with the data you gather from your investigations and expeditions?

Reports of our investigations are published on our website as soon as they are available. Preliminary reports are posted within days of the project finishing.

Each year we publish a 200 page yearbook containing research papers and expedition reports too long to be printed in the journal. We freely circulate our information to anybody who asks for it.

No. Each year since 2000 we have held our annual convention - the *Weird Weekend* - in Exeter. It is three days of lectures, workshops, and excursions. But most importantly it is a chance for members of the CFZ to meet each other, and to talk with the members of the permanent directorate in a relaxed and informal setting and preferably with a pint of beer in one hand. The *Weird Weekend* is now bigger and better than ever, and held in the idyllic rural location of Woolsery in North Devon.

We are hoping to start up some regional groups in both the UK and the US which will have regular meetings, work together on research projects, and maybe have a mini convention of their own.

Since relocating to North Devon in 2005 we have become ever more closely involved with other community organisations, and we hope that this trend will continue. We also work closely with Police Forces across the UK as consultants for animal mutilation cases, and we intend to forge closer links with the coastguard and other community services. We want to work closely with those who regularly travel into the Bristol Channel, so that if the recent trend of exotic animal visitors to our coastal waters continues, we can be out there as soon as possible.

Plans are also afoot to found a Visitor's Centre in rural North Devon. This will not be open to the general public, but will provide a museum, a library and an educational resource for our members (currently over 400) across the globe. We are also planning a youth organisation which will involve children and young people in our activities.

CFZ Field Operatives at Martin Mere in July 2002

Apart from having been the only Fortean Zoological organisation in the world to have consistently published material on all aspects of the subject for over a decade, we have achieved the following concrete results:

- *Disproved the myth relating to the headless so-called sea-serpent carcass of Durgan beach in Cornwall 1975*

- *Disproved the story of the 1988 puma skull of Lustleigh Cleave*

- *Carried out the only in-depth research ever done into mythos of the Cornish Owlman*

- *Made the first records of a tropical species of lamprey*

- *Made the first records of a luminous cave gnat larva in Thailand.*

- *Discovered a possible new species of British mammal - The Beech Marten.*

- *In 1994-6 carried out the first archival fortean zoological survey of Hong Kong.*

In the year 2000, CFZ theories where confirmed when an entirely new species of lizard was found resident in Britain.

EXPEDITIONS & INVESTIGATIONS TO DATE INCLUDE

- 1998 Puerto Rico, Florida, Mexico *(Chupacabras)*
- 1999 Nevada *(Bigfoot)*
- 2000 Thailand *(Giant Snakes called Nagas)*
- 2002 Martin Mere *(Giant catfish)*
- 2002 Cleveland *(Wallaby mutilation)*
- 2003 Bolam Lake *(BHM Reports)*
- 2003 Sumatra *(Orang Pendek)*
- 2003 Texas *(Bigfoot; Giant Snapping Turtles)*
- 2004 Sumatra *(Orang Pendek; Cigau, a Sabre-toothed cat)*
- 2004 Illinois *(Black Panthers; Cicada Swarm)*
- 2004 Texas *(Mystery Blue Dog)*
- 2004 Puerto Rico *(Chupacabras; carnivorous cave snails)*
- 2005 Belize *(Affiliate expedition for hairy dwarfs)*
- 2005 Mongolia *(Allghoi Khorkhoi aka Death Worm)*
- 2006 Gambia *(Gambo - Gambian sea monster, Ninki Nanka and the Armitage skink*
- 2006 Llangorse Lake *(Giant Pike, Giant Eels)*

Richard Freeman searches for the legendary Naga in Thailand

As the Discovery Channel looks on, Jonathan Downes, the Director of the CFZ, examines the skull of the Blue Dog of San Antonio...

Richard Freeman, Chris Clark, David Churchill, Jon Hare with eyewitnesses of the Mongolia Death Worm in 2005

To apply for a <u>FREE</u> information pack about the organisation and details of how to join, plus information on current and future projects, expeditions and events.

Send a stamp addressed envelope to:

**THE CENTRE FOR FORTEAN ZOOLOGY
MYRTLE COTTAGE, WOOLSERY,
BIDEFORD, NORTH DEVON
EX39 5QR.**

or alternatively visit our website at:
w w w . c f z . o r g . u k

Lightning Source UK Ltd.
Milton Keynes UK
178317UK00002B/120/A